Lugosi stars as Dracula in a 1947 summer stock production. (Photograph Taken by Samuel Kravitt; Courtesy of Mrs. Samuel Kravitt)

THE LOST YEARS OF BELA LUGOSI

NO TRAVELER RETURNS

GARY D. RHODES

BILL KAFFENBERGER

FOREWORD BY
GERALD SCHNITZER

AFTERWORD BY
BELA G. LUGOSI

Featuring photographs from the collections of Buddy Barnett, Bob Burns, Bill Chase, George Chastain, Kristin Dewey, Jack Dowler, Lee Harris, Bela G. Lugosi, Dennis Phelps, and David Wentink.

Copyright © 2012 by Gary D. Rhodes and William M. Kaffenberger, Jr.

All Rights Reserved.

This book may not be reproduced, in whole or in part, in any form (beyond that copying permitted by Section 107 and 108 of the U.S. Copyright Law and except by reviewers for the public press), without written permission from the publisher.

Designed by Michael Kronenberg

Printed in the United States

Published by BearManor Media
P. O. Box 71426
Albany, GA 31708
bearmanormedia.com

Unless otherwise noted, all photographs come from the collections of Gary D. Rhodes and Bill Kaffenberger.

Library of Congress Cataloguing-in-Publication Data
Rhodes, Gary D. and Bill Kaffenberger
No Traveler Returns: The Lost Years of Bela Lugosi / Gary D. Rhodes and Bill Kaffenberger
p. cm.
Includes bibliographical references and index
ISBN 1-59393-285-5
1. Lugosi, Bela, 1882-1956. 2. Motion Picture Actors and Actresses–United States–Biography.
I. Rhodes, Gary D.   II. Kaffenberger, Bill.   III. Title.
PN2859.H86L836

Authors' Notes: Some images chosen for this book are of an imperfect quality, but they are reproduced herein due to their rarity and their importance to the narrative.

Also, for the sake of internal consistency, "theatre" has been used as the spelling of choice in this book, even in those cases when the original spelling was "theater."

For my Mom, Dad, and brother Dave, all gone now, who with kindness and encouragement always supported my interest in all things Lugosi during my growing-up years. – *Bill Kaffenberger*

and

For my close friends Kristin Dewey and Jack Dowler, two of all the all-time great Lugosi fans. – *Gary D. Rhodes*

Foreword

by Gerald Schnitzer

"**J**eerriee," Mr. Lugosi monotoned, in his profound baritone voice, "don't *look* at me when I am reading my lines. It makes me *nearvoos!*" I might have just as well been seated in the front seat of a movie house in 1931 and quaked as he expanded his cape, hovered over me, and intoned his classic entrance: "I am Dracula!"

So why was a fresh kid like me, in 1942, from Brooklyn, having a tête-à-tête with film icon Bela Lugosi? Believe it or not, old buddies, Bela and I were going over his dialogue from my screenplay, *Bowery at Midnight*, which at that moment was in production at Monogram Pictures in Hollywood, a life raft for independent producers with meager budgets.

I had met Mr. Lugosi earlier during the production of *Spooks Run Wild* (1941), written by Carl Foreman and Charles Marion. In those beginning years, I was a 1st assistant director, chauffeur, dialogue clerk, "gofer" and mimeographer. I was also responsible for getting Mr. Lugosi camera ready. The most nerve-wracking part of the job was pulling myself together and control my teeth from chattering before knocking on his dressing room, and announcing, "We're ready for you, Mr. Lugosi, sir – 'Camera ready'," I added without stuttering. But then, once he appeared, he put me at ease and said, "Thanks, Jerry. How are you doing?" That was not the pulse beating Dracula. That was a gentleman who took time to connect, to be concerned, to be a *mensch*. And when I delivered shooting scripts to his home in the San Fernando Valley, he and his wife were most gracious, anxious to learn more about my plans for the future.

Dr. Gary D. Rhodes and I were drawn together by chance when he came across a copy of my recently published novelized memoir, *My Floating Grandmother*. Until then he had been trying to locate me, a writer with screen credits for the Bowery Boys and Bela Lugosi films.

A dedicated film historian, Gary sensed that I could add fresh insights into the planetary story of the movie business and fill in "the gaps." When he invited me to write a foreword to this biography, I hesitated, feeling I hadn't spent enough time with this huge personality. Could I possibly send an accurate message to the reader that we're dealing here with a highly sensitive artist and human being, something that might have gotten lost under his own cape?

Unquestionably, Gary Rhodes has opened and widened that cape beautifully. He has peered into Bela Lugosi's complex and fascinating world of time and space with the clarity of today's powerful diagnostic tool, the MRI.

Rich in detail, Rhodes and his co-author Bill Kaffenberger reveal Mr. Lugosi's fascinating plunge into the world of post-war America. And it meant lots of traveling, sleep deprivation, at times receiving untidy small compensations.

And then it came, the tsunami of TV, and an array of stars who, when finding their shows wanting, added comedy horror sketches. And who could create them better than Dracula, who found himself competing with the likes of Milton Berle? And Lugosi's greatest competitor was his growing reliance on drugs. But despite their insidious pull, Lugosi lost none of his skills at performing until the curtain fell and was too heavy to lift.

Gary Rhodes and Bill Kaffenberger's book is bigger than the revelation of Bela Lugosi and his role in our show business phenomenon. It is a mirror reflecting man's desire to leave his footprints and also, as Bobby Burns wrote, "O would some power the gift give us, to see ourselves as others see us!"

Born in Brooklyn in 1917, Gerald "Jerry" Schnitzer became entranced by the cinema at an early age. He gained his initial grounding in the movie business from his father and, later, from the famed non-fiction filmmaker John Grierson, the man credited for coining the term "documentary film."

By 1941, Schnitzer moved to Los Angeles and forged a career at Monogram, the greatest of all the poverty-row studios. Schnitzer's tenure at Monogram found him working on four of Bela Lugosi's most memorable B-movies: Spooks Run Wild *(1941),* Black Dragons *(1942),* The Corpse Vanishes *(1942), and* Bowery at Midnight *(1942).*

But in 1941, he embarked on what would become an even longer professional relationship with Huntz Hall and Leo Gorcey, working on two East Side Kids films before signing up to fight in World War II, and then – after returning to civilian life – six Bowery Boys movies in 1948 and 1949.

After parting ways with Monogram, Schnitzer wrote and directed various documentary films and television programs, including episodes of Lassie *and* National Velvet. *But his greatest fame probably came as a result of his entry into the world of TV advertising.*

Of all the "Mad Men" of the fifties and sixties, Schnitzer was perhaps the most influential. In 1958, working with Kensinger Jones, Creative Director for the ad agency Campbell Ewald, he invented the modern TV commercial by humanizing the ads with real narratives as opposed to actors simply holding up and touting products.

Far more than words or dialogue, images drove Schnitzer's landmark TV commercials, which were essentially short, beautifully crafted human interest films that sold dreams to the masses in the space of thirty seconds or less. As a result, historians credit him with creating the "Kodak Moment."

Lugosi as Dr. Mirakle in Robert Florey's film *The Murders in the Rue Morgue* (1932).

Introduction

Bela Lugosi starred in a large number of classic Hollywood horror films, most famously the 1931 version of *Dracula*. He gave one of his greatest performances in *Murders in the Rue Morgue* (1932), portraying Dr. Mirakle, a mad scientist who supports himself financially by running a carnival sideshow on the subject of evolution. When conversing with the film's young male lead, Dupin (Leon Waycoff), Mirakle explains his situation. He is a man of science, but one faced with the reality of making a living on the road. "This tent is my home!" he declares.

That line of dialogue speaks very much to the situation in which Lugosi found himself when World War II came to a close. Largely exiled by the Hollywood studio system, he had to seek other kinds of acting jobs. Appearing in the 1945 stage play *No Traveler Returns*, Lugosi dreamed of a return to the bright lights of Broadway, but that was not to be.

Instead, Lugosi had to search for other outlets for his talent. Occasionally it seemed as if yet another of his plays might reach New York, such as *Three Indelicate Ladies* in 1947 or *The Devil Also Dreams* in 1950, but none of them did. And Lugosi's role in the film *Abbott and Costello Meet Frankenstein* (1948) likely gave him the false impression that his Hollywood career could be resurrected. Instead he had to hit the road in search of work across the United States.

A few of the early Lugosi biographies wrongly gave the impression that his lack of film roles in the late forties meant that he worked very little between 1945 and the spring of 1951, when he left America to embark on a stage tour of *Dracula* in Great Britain and Northern Ireland.

But that version of events is quite false. Indeed, what we hope to do in this book is to rewrite the history of Lugosi's "lost years" by documenting just how much he did work in the post-war era. Week after week, month after month, and year after year, Lugosi made a living in summer stock plays, vaudeville sketches, nightclub acts, personal appearances, radio shows, and television programs.

To be sure, Robert Cremer's monumental biography *Lugosi: The Man Behind the Cape* (Henry Regnery, 1976) was quite aware that Lugosi found work in the late forties, with its opening pages discussing his summer stock appearance in Norwich, Connecticut in 1948. Then, Gary D. Rhodes' *Lugosi* (McFarland, 1997) chronicled a large number of his forgotten roles from the years 1945 to 1951, so much so that it became the very template for how subsequent biographies like Arthur Lennig's *The Immortal Count: The Life and Films of Bela Lugosi* (University of Kentucky Press, 2003) treat the same period.

Rather than simply repeat what has been said before, however, we have opted to carry out an exhaustive study of all relevant primary sources that could be located. Our methodology features a combination of approaches, some old and some new. For example, the increasing number of digitized US newspapers has proven quite important to our research. At the same time, we have necessarily relied on research trips to a number of brick-and-mortar archives, carefully undertaking page-by-page examinations of old publications on microfilms. We also have dusted off many forgotten files of yellowing paperwork. In addition, we have had the good fortune to interview a number of persons who met and worked with Lugosi in the late forties. Many of them, still alive and well in 2012, have never spoken to previous Lugosi researchers.

Collectively, these primary sources have led us to a clear and rather unavoidable conclusion about Bela Lugosi's career. Our argument is that he was extremely busy between 1945 and 1951, far more so than has ever been understood. Though Lugosi yearned for many projects that did not materialize, his career was hardly over or even stalled. In fact, while his days as a film star were largely behind him, Lugosi was *never* busier during his entire life in America than during the years 1945 to 1951.

True, the work was generally less glamorous than Broadway or Hollywood, but — as our re-evaluation of his spook show appearances reveals — most of it was quite dignified. He was still a celebrity, feted in town after town and city after city. He signed autographs, gave interviews, and kept his career very much alive.

If anything, the key issue for Lugosi was not the caliber of the productions in which he appeared, but rather the relentlessness of life on the road. With each passing mile, he became a little older and a little more tired. Lugosi was roughly 63 to 68 years of age during the period covered in this book, an era in which the average male in America lived only 65.6 years.

And so, Lugosi traveled an important but arduous journey between 1945 and 1951. In short, a tent was his home.

We are confident that more discoveries about these years will be made in the future, as Lugosi likely did even more work in this period than we have uncovered. We look forward to such discoveries, as we think they will go even further towards proving our argument about his career.

As for the present, we believe that our inquiry into Bela Lugosi adds an important new dimension to discussions of one of the greatest cinema icons of the twentieth century. Hopefully, those lost years have now been reclaimed.

Gary D. Rhodes
Belfast, Northern Ireland

Bill Kaffenberger
Hanover, Virginia

**THE LOST YEARS OF
BELA LUGOSI**

NO TRAVELER RETURNS

Lugosi's Dracula meets Frances Dade's Lucy in the 1931 version of *Dracula*. (Courtesy of Bill Chase)

Prologue

On October 18, 1930, a journalist at the *Exhibitors Herald-World* described his recent visit to Universal Studios and his luncheon with actor Bela Lugosi.

During their meal, Lugosi quickly recounted the basics of his biography. He was born in Hungary, where he starred in stage productions and films before moving on to Germany and, finally, the United States, where he worked in the New York theatre. Most famously, he had assumed the title role in a 1927 Broadway version of *Dracula–The Vampire Play*.

"I decided that I would try and hit the ball out here [in Hollywood] for two years," Lugosi told the journalist. "That was in 1928. If I made good, I planned to stay out here. If I flopped, I was going back to New York."

The journalist reported that Lugosi was "not melancholy or doleful when not acting. He has an amazing sense of humor. He can laugh heartily. But when you see him in *Dracula*, you'll decide that he wouldn't smile at even Laurel and Hardy in one of their most riotous scenes."

In this case, the journalist was referring to the film version of *Dracula*, which was currently in production. He added:

> Universal wants to do the thing right, and the best thing it has done so far is to give the leading role to Lugosi, who has a pair of eyes which look through and beyond you, and who makes weirdness a part of his daily life – even carries it into his home.

Despite his aforementioned references to Lugosi's sense of humor, the journalist painted Lugosi as unusual, as strange, as someone who might be mistaken for a vampire.

The journalist not only met Lugosi, but also watched him act. In his article, he told readers about the film shoot he witnessed:

> I arrived on the Universal stage one day in time to see him walk up the dingy stairs of his deserted castle, and down again, holding a candle.
>
> His black mane sweeps back above his forehead. His black cloak droops about him. His black eyes turn at a given moment to show the clear white beyond the rim of the pupils. The candle flickers eerily as the camera cranks. The dull tread of his feet echoes through the silent stage.
>
> Few men can walk up and down a flight of stairs and tell a story while doing it — but he has accomplished it.

The journalist was convinced that Lugosi was "better fitted for the role ... than any one in Hollywood or any other place."

During that scene on the staircase, Lugosi uttered the line of dialogue: "I am Dracula."

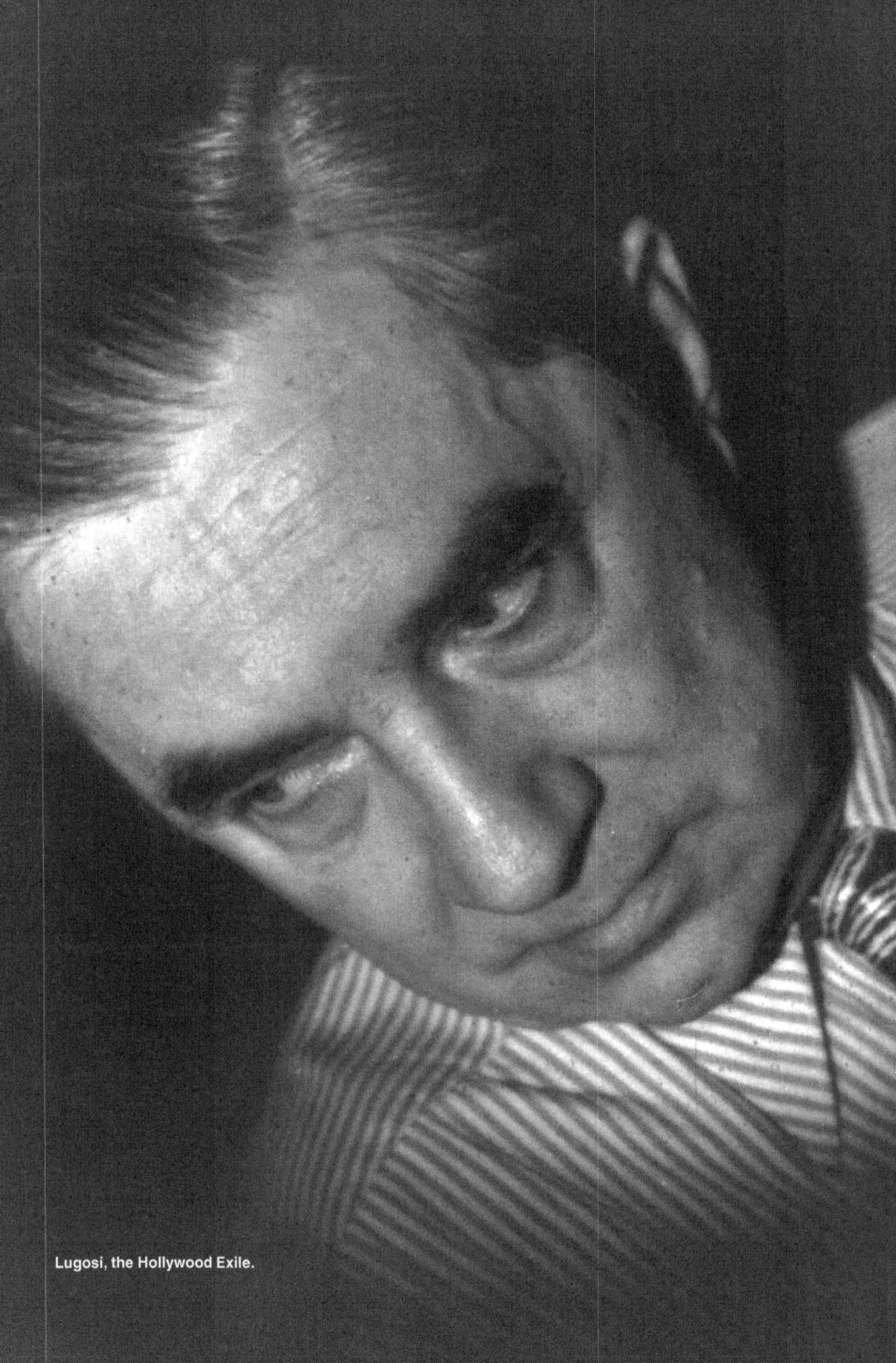
Lugosi, the Hollywood Exile.

Chapter 1

"I know how men in exile feed on dreams."
– **Aeschylus**

Much of the world moved in 1945. Migration, evacuation, and expulsion during World War II resulted in more than forty million refugees. As the war neared its end, hundreds of thousands of Allied troops fought their way to Berlin. Approximately five million German civilians left their homes during the final months of the war; at roughly the same time, millions of Russians were repatriated to the Soviet Union.

In 1945, Ilona Szmik's Hungarian apartment overlooked the Danube. An exterior wall was damaged so badly during the siege of Budapest that a large hole opened it to the outside world. One could easily survey the city without needing to look through a window. Nevertheless, Szmik continued to live in Budapest; she had little choice. Imre Francsek, her second husband, spent the rest of his life in a Russian *gulag* after disappearing in Iran.

Szmik's first husband was actor Bela Lugosi, who had seen combat in the First World War and actively tried to help Allies during the Second World War. He scrutinized the war news each day. He participated in selling war bonds and raising funds for Hungarian causes. He celebrated on V-E and V-J Day. And, like millions of Americans, he looked to a brighter future in post-war America.

Even after victory was declared, troop movements occurred on a vast scale in a world governed by change of so many kinds and to so many people. Change came to Bela Lugosi as well, although in a manner different than he anticipated. And the key transformation occurred to his career, which had been locked in the horror genre since 1931.

Many horror films played theatres in 1945, before and after troops began returning home: *The Frozen Ghost*, *Strange Confession*, *Pillow of Death*, *The Jungle Captive*, *Isle of the Dead*, and *Fog Island*. Lugosi appeared in none of those movies. Nor did he act in *The Vampire's Ghost*, much to the surprise of the *Los Angeles Times*, whose critic spoke more about Lugosi in his review than he did of John Abbott, the film's star.[1]

No, Lugosi appeared in only two horror films in 1945. In fact, he appeared in only two films at all that year, horror or otherwise. RKO filmed both of them. The classic Val Lewton-produced horror movie *The Body Snatcher* (1945) was the first to be released. It starred famed horror film actor Boris Karloff in the title role, which was notably spelled in the grammatical singular. Lugosi's character was not his partner or even a fellow grave robber.

Shortly after *The Body Snatcher* was released, Val Lewton told the press, "We had a hell of a time making the picture. It was great fun."[2] But Lugosi could hardly have shared that belief. Years later, director Robert Wise remembered that Lugosi had been ill during the shoot.[3] And the actor

16 NO TRAVELER RETURNS | The Lost Years of Bela Lugosi

had only been hired for the marquee value of his name, not because the story actually relied upon his presence.

Portraying a janitor named Joseph, Lugosi received approximately seven-and-a-half minutes of screen time in the 77-minute film. Nearly six of those minutes came in a single scene that he shares with Karloff, whose character carefully makes Joseph feel at ease before murdering him. Karloff dominates the scene, but it remains one of the most effective that the two actors ever shared.

Trade publication reviews were strong, so much so that RKO plugged quotations from nine of them into a large, two-page advertisement in *Motion Picture Herald*.[4] Not surprisingly, *The Body Snatcher* drew varying responses across America, as surviving theatre manager reports reveal:

> "I stood in the lobby all evening and watched the patrons walking past the theatre. ... No more horror pictures for me. Enough is enough."
> – Rankin Theatre, Rankin, Illinois[5]

> "Routine horror show which failed to draw any extra business."
> – Paramount Theatre, Dewey, Oklahoma[6]

> "Right good 'boogie man' picture. Doubled with a Western to average business."
> – Ozark Theatre, Ozark, Missouri[7]

Despite poor responses in certain theatres, *The Body Snatcher* was a box office hit, grossing more money than any other Val Lewton horror film. Viewers in 1945 could scarcely have known that it would be the last film that would pair Karloff and Lugosi, whose joint appearance might well have been the reason for its financial success.

On the one hand, Lugosi received second billing onscreen and in most publicity materials. On the other hand, most theatre ballyhoo efforts concentrated on Karloff. The manager of the Hamilton Theatre in Lancaster, Pennsylvania built a miniature stage in his lobby, its scene depicting Karloff carrying away the body of a girl.[8] Lugosi's image was noticeably absent from the publicity stunt.

Lugosi as Joseph in
***The Body Snatcher* (1945).**

Gary D. Rhodes | Bill Kaffenberger   17

The Missouri Theatre in St. Louis constructed a mechanical lobby set featuring a Karloff mannequin robbing a grave. Local radio advertisements featured a "special Karloff recording," and two "decrepit horses" pulled an antique hearse through the city streets. Given that he screened the film near Valentine's Day, the Missouri's manager devised yet another unique publicity scheme. He printed and distributed 25,000 "novel valentine heralds ... illustrating a bleeding heart with Karloff strangling Lugosi and the former holding a valentine with [the] caption, 'Please give me a piece of your heart.'"[9]

In October of 1945, while *The Body Snatcher* was still in general release, Karloff and Lugosi were

Ballyhoo for *The Body Snatcher* at the Missouri Theatre in St. Louis.

Lobby setpiece for *The Body Snatcher* at the Missouri Theatre in St. Louis.

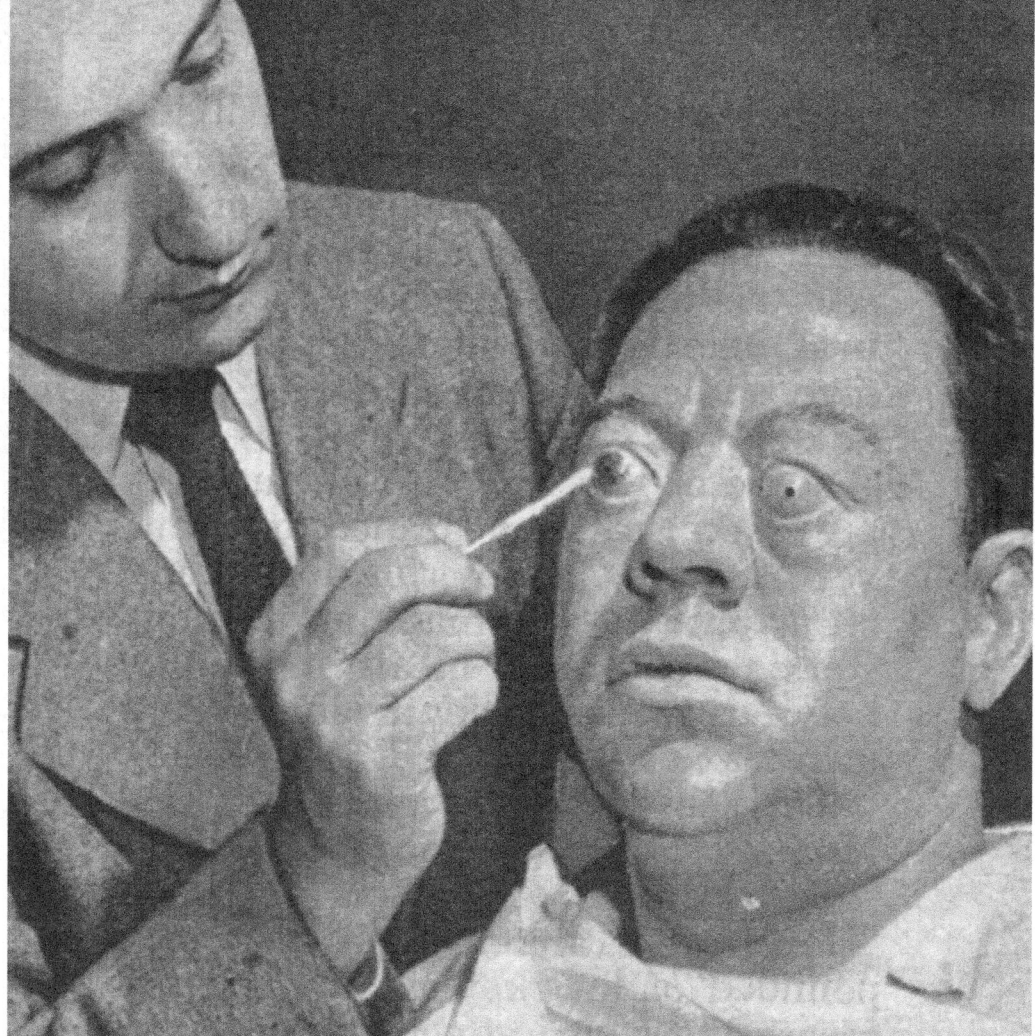

Maurice Seiderman applies zombie makeup to Alan Carney for the 1945 RKO film *Zombies on Broadway*.
(Courtesy of George Chastain)

spotted at the famous Romanoff's Restaurant in Los Angeles sharing a meal and a beer together.[10] The reported scene conjures an image of two friends spending time with one another, but in reality they were never close. If anything, Lugosi was at times quietly resentful of Karloff's success and how it unfolded.

Fourteen years earlier, Karloff had to purchase small advertisements to promote himself in the pages of *Variety*, the same publication that was publishing large ads for *Dracula* (1931), the film that turned Lugosi into a household name. But after portraying the Monster in *Frankenstein* (1931), Karloff no longer needed to buy his own publicity. He not only became a star, but he also quickly became the bigger star of the two.

Lugosi's other film release in 1945 had also been shot the prior year. RKO had purchased Robert Faber and Charles Newman's 1941 story *Zombi* [singular, with no "e"] *on Broadway* from MGM in June 1944, intending it to be a vehicle for the comedy team of Wally Brown and Alan Carney.[11] The original treatment featured zombie expert Dr. Paul Renault as a "lonesome" man who was a "brilliant conversationalist." He ends up traveling from Haiti to New York with the two lead characters, as they are desperate to find a zombie to be the featured attraction at a nightclub. Thanks to Renault, six gangsters who are silent partners in the club become the needed zombies.[12]

The first rewrite at RKO (dated July 22, 1944 and titled *Broadway Zombie*) made some notable changes to the Dr. Paul Renault character. According to screenwriter Jack Jevne, "Years of intensive

Gary D. Rhodes | Bill Kaffenberger

Lugosi as Dr. Renault in the 1945 RKO film *Zombies on Broadway*. (Courtesy of Buddy Barnett)

study have weakened his eyes so that now he wears thick lenses. His manner is eternally preoccupied." The tale continued to morph in the hands of Lawrence Kimble, whose script dated September 8, 1944 became the final version.[13]

Examining the story, Joseph I. Breen, head of the Production Code Administration (PCA) declared that it "seem[ed] to meet" the requirements of the Motion Picture Production Code, but he warned RKO that "great care must be used with the costuming of the native dancing girls, especially as to their breasts, so that there is no unnecessary exposure," adding that their dance moves should contain "no forward bump or unacceptable motion of the body."[14]

Breen also instructed the studio to make certain that, when Dr. Renault uses a hypodermic needle, no shots depicted it "touching the skin." He also made clear that Renault should not "groan" when his body is being buried at the end of the film, as such a sound would suggest that he is being buried alive.[15]

Shooting began in September 1944. By October 27 of that year, RKO decided on *Zombies on Broadway* as the final title. The key production information in the press revolved around the film's zombie "masks."[16] The *Hollywood Reporter* noted that it took Maurice Seiderman twenty days of "intensive work" to prepare five masks for the film, each having the ability to create the illusion that the actor "never moves, blinks, or shuts his eyes."[17]

Hitting theatres on May 1, 1945, *Zombies on Broadway* (1945) became Lugosi's second film release of the year. Some thirteen years earlier, Lugosi had starred in *White Zombie* (1932), the movie that introduced zombies to the moviegoing public for the very first time. Along with becoming one of the most successful independent films of the thirties, *White Zombie* popularized the very term "zombie" to the extent that it was quickly saluted in a 1932 song and, shortly thereafter, a cocktail.[18]

But rather than echo *White Zombie*, *Zombies on Broadway* exemplifies the horror film tradition at RKO, a tradition in which Lugosi had scarcely played a part. Its opening credits feature a dark, hulking cartoon character towering over the New York skyline, immediately calling to mind the studio's most successful horror film, *King Kong* (1933). As portrayed by Darby Jones, the film's zombie Kalaga immediately brings to mind not *White Zombie*, but instead the Val Lewton-produced *I Walked with a Zombie* (1943), in which Jones had memorably appeared. Likewise, calypso singer Sir Lancelot was cast in *I Walked with a Zombie* and *Zombies on Broadway*, again drawing a link between the two.

Despite portraying the important character of Dr. Paul Renault, Lugosi received less than ten minutes of screen time in *Zombies on Broadway*, an approximately 69-minute film. And Lugosi's fight scene featured a stand-in who was noticeably shorter. At the age of 62, Lugosi was getting too old for onscreen brawls. He may also have been somewhat weak or unwell during the shoot.

Unlike the zombie master he played in *White Zombie*, Lugosi's Dr. Paul Renault is essentially a character of the type that he had portrayed on so many occasions since the release of *Frankenstein* (1931), a film in which he had famously *not* appeared: the mad scientist. Renault's underground laboratory features the requisite secret panels and bubbling test tubes, one of which effectively obscures his face at the start of his first scene, thus building a bit of suspense for his visual introduction. Not surprisingly,

Renault's lackey understands that the doctor's experiments – like Dr. Frankenstein's – are "of the devil, not of science."

For *Zombies on Broadway*, actors Wally Brown and Alan Carney starred as Jerry Miles and Mike Strager, the same characters that they portrayed in five other films.[19] Their brand of humor stemmed from a combination of one-liners, physical comedy, and frightened reactions to the horrific sights that they see. Unlike the previous comedians with whom Lugosi had worked – such as the Ritz Brothers in *The Gorilla* (1939) and Jack Haley in *One Body Too Many* (1944) – Brown and Carney were not particularly distinctive or memorable.

Critical reviews of *Zombies on Broadway* were generally acceptable, but reaction from American viewers varied, as can be seen in a sampling of theatre manager reports:

> "Had good business on this comedy-horror picture. It pleased."
> – Paramount Theatre, Dewey, Oklahoma[20]

> "An extremely wacky feature that could have been dispensed with."
> – Winema Theatre, Scotia, California[21]

> "Fun and action. Common folks just can't get enough of it."
> – Gem Theatre, Cornell, Wisconsin[22]

Despite positive feedback at some theatres, *Zombies on Broadway* lost $6,000, and hardly became a distinguished entry in Lugosi's filmography. When asked about the movie decades later, *Zombies on Broadway* director Gordon Douglas did not even recall it.[23]

And that was that. Lugosi's film releases for 1945 amounted to two movies, both of which had been shot the prior year. For reasons that were probably hard for him to understand, his Hollywood career came to a screeching halt. Like so many other persons displaced in 1945, Lugosi moved. He went on the road. He left Hollywood, dreaming perhaps of the day when he would star in more films, but also of a return to the Broadway stage.

On February 5, 1945, *Daily Variety* announced that Bela Lugosi and Ian Keith would head the cast of author Richard Goddard's play *No Traveler Returns*. Ralph Kutsch and Leslie Thomas produced the "Ware-Hazelton Attraction," hiring Rafael Noel as director. The cast included George Pembroke, who had co-starred with Lugosi in the Monogram films *Invisible Ghost* (1941) and *Black Dragons* (1942). Rehearsals began in early February at the Mayan Theater (a 1,491-seat Mayan Revival-style venue in downtown Los Angeles) and continued throughout the month.

Set in Northern India before the war, *No Traveler Returns* attempted to paint a "colorful picture of the effect of Oriental intrigue and mystery upon a group of Europeans."[24] In it, an army doctor (Ian Keith) is engaged to an English woman named Audrey (Karen Venge), but he becomes increasingly interested in a Hindu servant girl (Ann Ainslee). He also grows obsessed with "Indian mysteries" to the extent that his health suffers and he turns to morphine for relief.

Then one of the doctor's patients is mysteriously murdered. An English inspector investigates the crime and quickly falls in love with Audrey. At the same time, a "crooked Native servant" named Bharat Singh (Lugosi) plays on the doctor's superstitious fears. And like the doctor, Singh is fascinated with the Hindu servant girl.

The doctor marries Audrey, but problems mount when a second murder occurs. The trail leads directly to the doctor, but the inspector decides to drop the case, as he is too much in love with Audrey to arrest her husband. But Audrey is no fool. She suspects her husband as well and begs the inspector to run away with her.

By the end of the play, drug abuse and jealous rage grip the doctor, who decides that he must kill Bharat Singh. According to a plot summary in a theatre program, his decision "leads to complications

Bharat Singh (Lugosi) woos Bhemia (Ann Ainslee), a "Hindu girl." (Courtesy of Dennis Phelps)

which bring the play to a dramatic and unusual ending."[25] That ending features the deaths of both Bharat Singh and the doctor.

At the time, Lugosi described Bharat Singh as "really educated, although he camouflages it. He is a very reprehensible character, very foreboding, very ominous."[26] In terms of his costume, Singh recalled several earlier Lugosi projects, ranging from the 1925 Broadway play *Arabesque* (in which he portrayed the Sheik of Hamman) to such films as *Renegades* (1930, in which he took the role of Sheik Muhammed, the Marabout) and *Night of Terror* (1933, in which he played Degar, a mysterious Hindu who, like Bharat Singh, wears a turban).

Murder and intrigue in pre-war India also recalled the plotline of *The Thirteenth Chair*, a 1929 film directed by Tod Browning. That movie predated the screen version of *Dracula*, and so in it Lugosi was able to assume the role of an Indian detective, one of the "good guys." By 1945, however, it would have been difficult for him to portray any character in *No Traveler Returns* other than the villain.

After rehearsals, the play had a break-in run at Santa Barbara's 680-seat Lobero Theatre. The company gave two performances on February 24, 1945, one matinee and one evening. A large advertisement in the *Santa Barbara News Press* promoted the play with a tagline that would be reused in other cities: "The Story of a Strange Obsession."[27]

(Courtesy of the Department of Special Collections, Davidson Library, University of California, Santa Barbara)

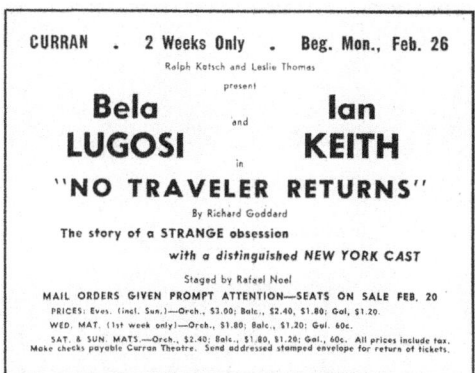

From a Curran Theatre program dated February 5, 1945. (Courtesy of Buddy Barnett)

Published in the March 9, 1945 issue of the *San Francisco Examiner*. (Courtesy of Buddy Barnett)

An article in the same newspaper described Lugosi's Bharat Singh as "a sinister and evil genius whose powers cast strange spells over his helpless victims."[28] A subsequent press account presented similar details: "Lugosi is again cast in his most popular type of role, portraying Bharat Singh, an evil servant, and his diabolical schemes give the plot its mysterious events and unsolved murders."[29] Such publicity drew parallels to Lugosi's horror film credentials.

But the key review of opening night was hardly kind. Litti Paulding of the *Santa Barbara News-Press* joked that "*No Traveler Returns* – And Perhaps 'Tis Just As Well."[30] She proceeded to say:

...what goes on in a bungalow at Ranipur ... is talky-walky-sit-down melodrama. The play, which had its world premiere in the Lobero theater Saturday matinee, includes in its ingredients disembodied spirits going amok, stigmata and schizophrenia as confusing as the dramaturgic story it has been given Ivan [sic] Keith, Bela Lugosi and others to enact. ... there is no mystery, nor is there much dramatic merit. Sorry to say, but *No Traveler Returns* should stay in ... limbo.

Bela Lugosi and Ian Keith have taken a holiday from legitimate drama for an excursion into farce, spattered with Indian proverbs, blond amahs, caricatures of English officers' wives, and salaaming Indian servants, plus drugs and whisky sodas and stolen 'jools.'[31]

Paulding concluded her critique by telling readers that the play was "as cumbersome as an ox cart."

Audiences at the two Lobero performances may well have agreed. The theatre sold only 109 tickets for the matinee.[32] The evening show fared better with 380 tickets sold, but that still represented only about 57% of the available seating capacity.[33] The producers realized sales of $150.50 on the matinee and $765.50 on the evening performance, making a box office total of $916.00, not counting the required ticket tax.[34] The Lobero Theater charged the producers $175 for theater rental, and made a total profit of only $98.82.[35] As a result, the play's premiere performances could hardly be called successful.

From Santa Barbara, the company moved to San Francisco's 1,776-

Published in the *San Francisco Examiner* of March 25, 1945. (Courtesy of Buddy Barnett)

Lugosi appeared in San Francisco on various occasions prior to the production of *No Traveler Returns*. Pictured here in the 1930s, he accepts the key to the city with wife Lillian at his side. (Courtesy of the Bancroft Library, University of California, Berkeley)

From the *Seattle Times* of March 13, 1945.

seat Curran Theatre, as did Lugosi. After opening night in San Francisco, the *San Francisco Chronicle* declared that *No Traveler Returns* was "possibly the longest, dullest play of the season."[36] The *San Francisco Examiner* also used the damning adjective "dull," adding that the play was reminiscent of a "Hindu B picture horror yarn."[37] And the *San Francisco Call-Bulletin* quipped that *No Traveler Returns* should have "emptied the house" as promptly as a theatre fire, but noted that "an audience given to yawns and intermittent spells of coughing tarried on, perhaps with vain imaginings that finally something would happen onstage."[38]

Two reviews of the first San Francisco performance also appeared in Oakland newspapers, where the response was equally negative. The *Post-Enquirer* quipped that the "most frightening thing is that the second act is even cornier than the opening one."[39] Wood Soanes of the *Oakland Tribune* was even more harsh, claiming that Lugosi and Keith overacted, and that it wouldn't even be "worth the effort" to give readers a plot synopsis. He concluded by describing how "stunned audiences groped for the exits" as soon as the play ended.[40]

Bad word-of-mouth and negative reviews had a real impact on ticket sales. *No Traveler Returns* grossed a "very poor $6,000" in its first week at the Curran; its second week was even worse at $5,800.[41] And so the San Francisco run came to an unhappy end on March 9, 1945. For Lugosi and the others, however, there was still a bit of hope: Seattle, Washington.

The producers likely tried to make some adjustments to the play before opening on March 13, 1945. They may have cut some scenes and perhaps rewritten others, all in an effort to correct the problems that critics had pinpointed, but that is mere speculation. What is certain is the fact that, by the time Lugosi and his wife Lillian checked into a room at Seattle's Olympic Hotel, they knew that *No Traveler Returns* was in trouble.

Just before lunch on opening day, a reporter from the *Seattle Times* arrived at Lugosi's room to interview him. After sitting down, he immediately noticed the gold bat pin attached to Lillian's shoulder. She explained that she had purchased it at a local jewelry store. The clerk had given her an odd stare, but that hardly mattered. The store simply didn't know who her husband was.

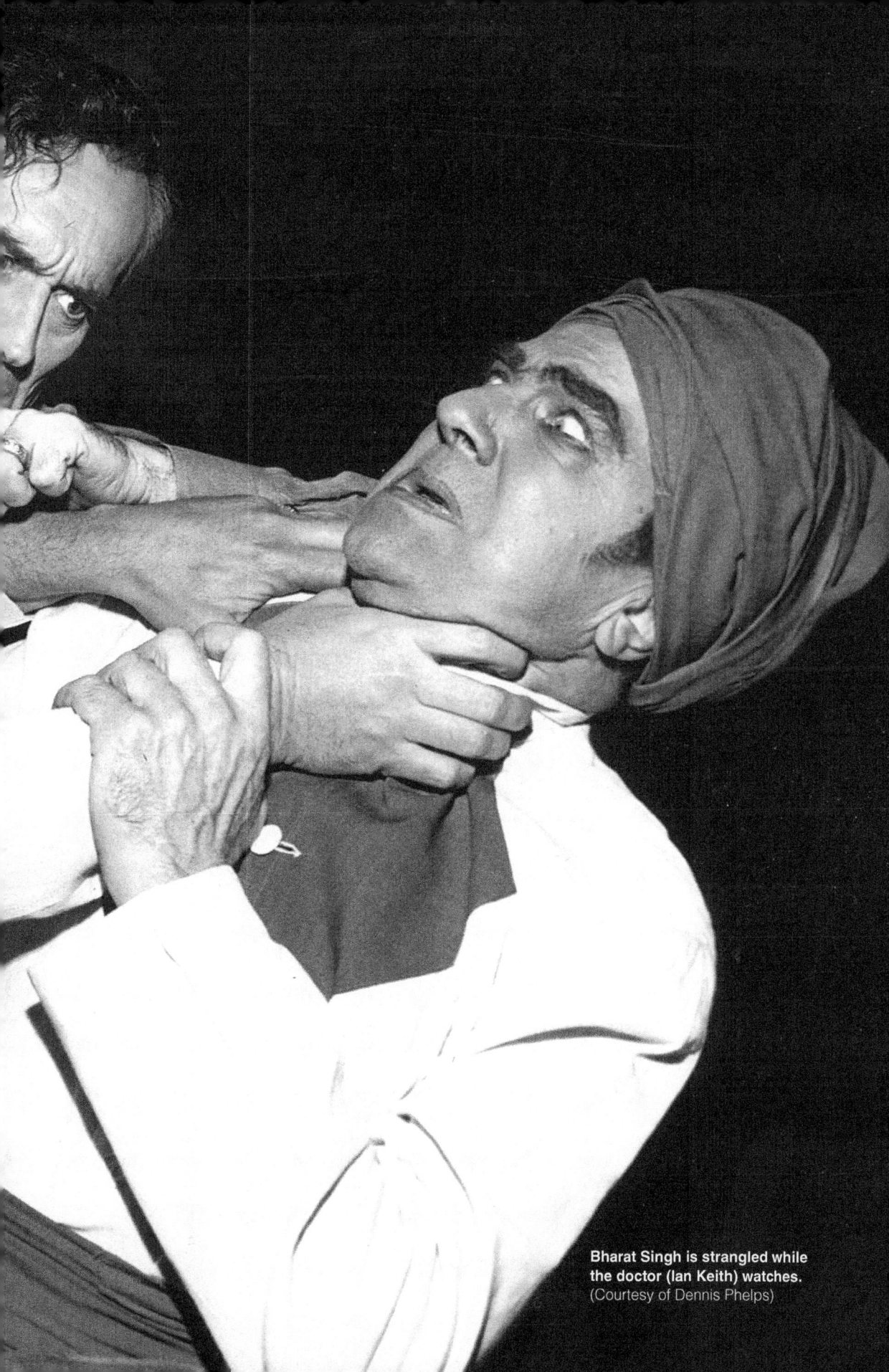

Bharat Singh is strangled while the doctor (Ian Keith) watches.
(Courtesy of Dennis Phelps)

Bharat Singh (Lugosi) with Audrey Chatteris (Karin Venge).

Was and continued to be. Only months earlier, in the autumn of 1944, Lugosi and Lillian had experienced major troubles. The two had married in 1933. In 1938, she bore Lugosi his only child, Bela G. Lugosi, whom the press would often refer to as Bela Jr. Together the couple had seen the actor's film career near its peak, as well as at its lowest ebb in 1937 and 1938. By late 1944, she filed for divorce, then the two reconciled, and then she left him again. But lasting reconciliation came quickly, and, by the time that *No Traveler Returns* played Seattle, the Lugosis seemed to be the picture of domestic tranquillity.

Lillian had insisted that Lugosi curb his drinking and that he smoke his cigars outside of the house, but that was likely a small price for Lugosi to pay. Talking about the reconciliation in October 1944, he admitted, "I have courted her with flowers and candy ever since she walked out. ... I've been shaving regularly. That was one of our troubles. I was a careless husband; as a European I expected things too much my own way in the home. American girls don't like that. They want things more 50-50."[42]

As the *Seattle Times* interview progressed, more of the questions were directed at Lillian rather than at Lugosi.[43] Filling a tobacco pipe for her husband, Lillian admitted, "He is a constant smoker. When he is outside the house, he smokes cigars. The moment he comes in, he lays down the cigar, and I have to have a pipe ready for him. He consumes so much tobacco that we use the denicotinized variety." Lugosi interjected, "She is the best pipe-stuffer west of the Mississippi!" Lillian responded by saying, "You've always said the pipe tasted sweeter when I did it," adding, "Drawing on the pipe is the only way you can tell if its packed properly. I like doing it, but I've never been tempted to smoke a whole pipe. I don't enjoy just that much."[44]

The reporter was surprised to hear that Lugosi chose all of the clothes in Lillian's wardrobe. "I sneak out now and then and get something," she said, "but it's always a flop. When I come back with it, he gives me a Dracula look. All I do is go into the room in the shop, and he picks out things. What he picks out is always swell."[45]

But Lillian quickly explained that shoes were exclusively her responsibility. "Bela has tried to pick them out, but he doesn't have the feel for shoes. Shoes are my private preserve. We agree on everything of course, and Bela agrees on the shoes after I get them. That's the sweet side of him coming out."[46]

When the reporter asked Lugosi if he thought playing villains altered his personality, the actor responded in the negative. Lugosi added, "Dracula was just another part for me. Playing it didn't alter me fundamentally. It's fun to play parts like that. There is one thing about it, however. When you

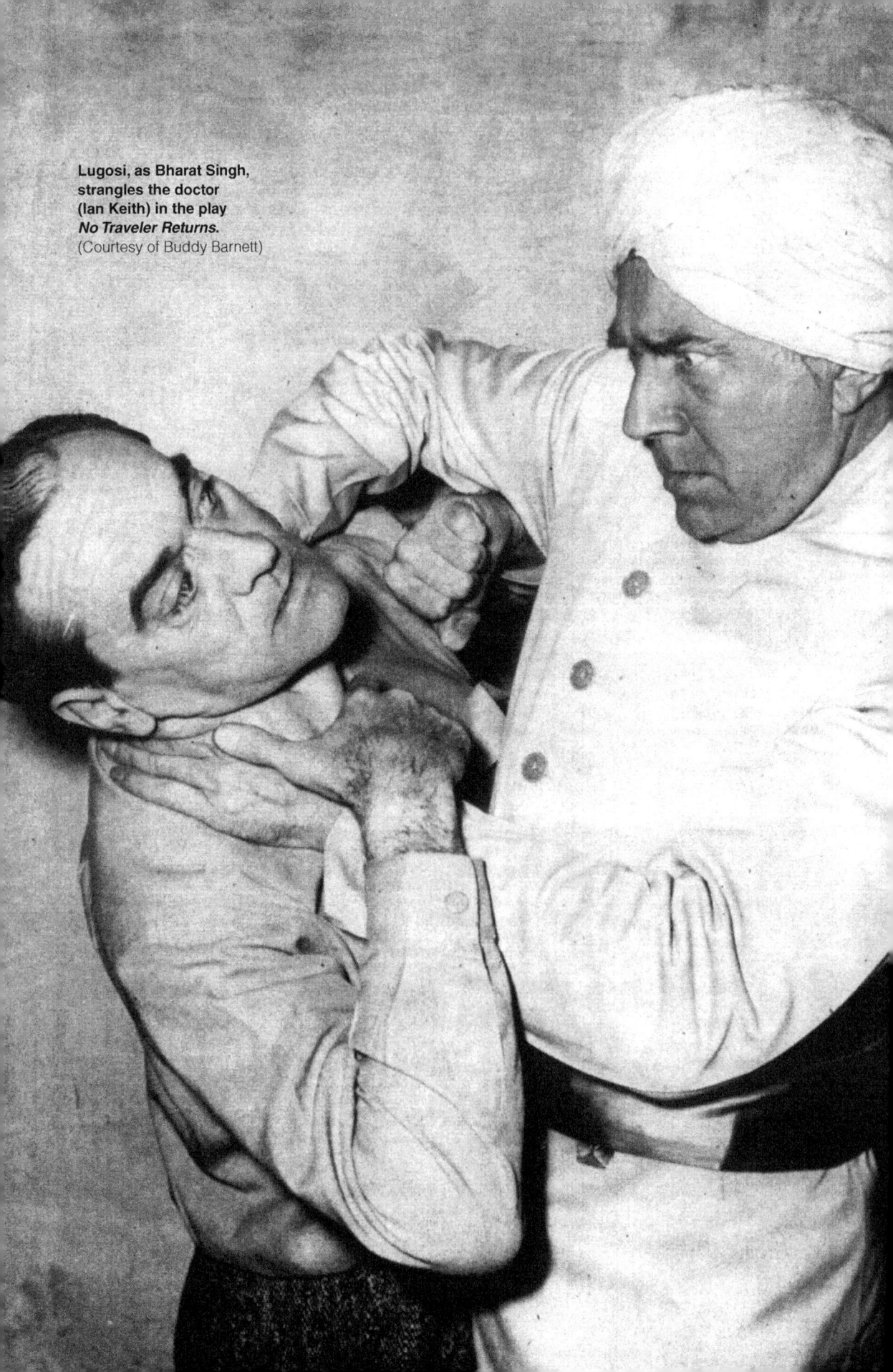

Lugosi, as Bharat Singh, strangles the doctor (Ian Keith) in the play *No Traveler Returns*. (Courtesy of Buddy Barnett)

From the *Seattle Times* of March 18, 1945.

play straight parts you have hundreds of actors competing with you. In this line of work the field of competition is limited. And as a specialty, of course, it has been very fine economically."[47]

Lillian agreed, claiming "He's sweet! Playing those roles doesn't change him in the least. We've been married twelve years and he'd already played *Dracula* on Broadway in 1927 when I met him. I went to see him in a horror role before I married him, of course, to see if I could stand it."[48]

Presumably Lillian watched her husband play Bharat Singh as well. Within hours after the *Seattle Times* interview, he assumed the role yet again, this time at a new venue. *No Traveler Returns* played Seattle's 1,500-seat Metropolitan Theatre, which doubled as a movie theatre. Newspaper publicity heralded the play, promising that it "holds audiences in a grip of tense excitement throughout its three acts and reaches an electrifying climax."[49]

Other publicity touted Lugosi's connection to vampires. One article claimed, "Bela Lugosi, known to millions of screen fans as 'Dracula,' will again portray one of his famous sinister roles which strikes death and terror to those crossing his path."[50] Later, columnist Mollie Sapera jokingly told readers, "Bela Lugosi, of Dracula fame, turned up in town and revealed himself to be a gentleman and a scholar. Contrary to what might have been expected, he brought along no vampires as personal attendants."[51]

Lugosi also brought along no sympathetic critics. Whatever changes had or had not been made to the play, the reviews were not kind. The *Seattle Times* wrote:

> ...neither the mystic manner of Lugosi nor the acting skills of Keith do enough to save the day for the play. ...the author ... apparently had a psychological mystery in mind, but after considerable time spent in only vaguely establishing his premise in the first act, he takes a shortcut to forthright murder melodrama, with drugs and native cupidity as the best materials at hand. In Act 2, the plot clears, but remains too thin to stimulate more than a touch of suspense, although the stars work hard to give it realism...."[52]

The *Seattle Post-Intelligencer* felt much the same, claiming that the play's "capable, experienced actors [are] vastly superior to the material they have to work with here."[53]

Poor box office receipts meant that *No Traveler Return*'s evening performance on March 18, 1945 would be its last.[54] The play was "yanked" six days early, having grossed "only" $6,000.[55] The *No Traveler Returns* company disbanded immediately after the last Seattle show. As a result, a two-night stand at Spokane's Post Theatre was cancelled, as was a planned route to Chicago via Montana.[56] Hopes for an East Coast tour were also shelved.[57]

The cast and crew of *No Traveler Returns* quickly moved on with their lives, some of them hitting the road in other productions. For example, actor Jack Dale – who only had a small role in the play – joined a touring company of *Janie*. When it played Augusta, Georgia in November 1945, a newspaper noted that Dale had recently been "seen on tour with Belga Lugosi."[58] Belga: one of the numerous misspellings of Lugosi's name that newspapers made on a somewhat regular basis.

Without a play, Lugosi needed a new film. Some press accounts announced that Lugosi would play Dracula in the Universal Studios' *House of Dracula* (1945) following his role as Bharat Singh.[59] Edwin Schallert at the *Los Angeles Times* went so far as to write that *House of Dracula* would not be "complete" without him.[60]

But it was. Universal Studios had known for ten years that, even if Lugosi's career depended on Dracula, Dracula did not depend on Lugosi, and certainly not after the 1931 film. The studio had produced the original sequel *Dracula's Daughter* (1936) without Lugosi. Later, the studio cast Lon Chaney, Jr. (in *Son of Dracula* in 1943) and John Carradine (in *House of Frankenstein* in 1944) as the vampire count. In 1945, it would be Carradine, not Lugosi, who made *House of Dracula* "complete."

Bela Lugosi Enlisted for 'House of Dracula'

BY EDWIN SCHALLERT

There's a new thrill for the horror picture followers in the offing. "House of Dracula" is announced by Universal, and necessarily that won't be complete without Bela Lugosi.

The new picture was inspired by "House of Frankenstein," recent release, which has been howling them over in New York, Hollywood and elsewhere. Cult for mystery pictures is, of course, so strong in the eastern metropolis that they had to close the box office for a time, because the crowds couldn't be accommodated.

The Dracula pictures have survived on the screen for nearly 15 years.

From the *Los Angeles Times* of February 17, 1945.

And so Lugosi's hopes for a stage success in 1945 were dashed, and his film career was in limbo. Lugosi may well have believed that many more films were on the horizon, even if they were to be horror movies at studios other than Universal. He could not have known that simply heading back to Hollywood did not mean he was heading back to a vibrant film career. He could scarcely have realized that no traveler returns.

(Endnotes)

1. "Twin Shockers at Hawaii." *Los Angeles Times* 14 Apr. 1945.
2. Wechsberg, Joseph. "Horrors!" *Liberty* 24 Aug. 1946.
3. Rhodes, Gary D. Interview with Robert Wise. 1996.
4. Advertisement. *Motion Picture Herald* 14 Apr. 1945.
5. "What the Picture Did For Me." *Motion Picture Herald* 18 May 1946.
6. "What the Picture Did For Me." *Motion Picture Herald* 17 Nov. 1945.
7. *Ibid*.
8. "Shock and Shudder Angle Sells *Body Snatcher* in Lancaster." *Motion Picture Herald* 6 Oct. 1945.
9. "The Body Snatcher." *Motion Picture Herald* 24 Feb. 1945.
10. *Port Arthur News* (Port Arthur, TX) 14 Oct. 1945.
11. "RKO's Gotham *Zombie*." *Variety* 21 June 1944.
12. Robert Faber and Charles Newman's treatment entitled *Zombi on Broadway* exists in the RKO Studio Records (Collection 3), S-1083 at the UCLA Library Special Collections.
13. The Jevne and Kimble scripts exist in S-1083 at the UCLA Library Special Collections.
14. Breen, Joseph I. Letter to William Gordon, RKO Radio Pictures, Inc. 5 Sept. 1944. The original exists in the RKO Studio Records (Collection 3), P-145 at the UCLA Library Special Collections.
15. *Ibid*.
16. See, for example: "Making Up the Monsters." *Popular Mechanics* May 1945.
17. "20 Days Spent on *Zombie* Masks." *Hollywood Reporter* 19 Sept. 1944.
18. See Gary D. Rhodes' book *White Zombie: Anatomy of a Horror Film* (Jefferson, NC: McFarland, 2001) for more information.
19. The other five films featuring Alan Carney as Mike Strager and Wally Brown as Jerry Miles are: *The Adventures of a Rookie* (1943), *Rookies in Burma* (1943), *Girl Rush* (1944), *Radio Stars on Parade* (1944), and *Genius at Work* (1946).
20. "What the Picture Did For Me." *Motion Picture Herald* 20 Oct. 1945.
21. "What the Picture Did For Me." *Motion Picture Herald* 19 Jan. 1946.
22. "What the Picture Did For Me." *Motion Picture Herald* 6 Apr. 1946.
23. Rhodes, Gary D. Interview with Gordon Douglas. 1989.
24. *No Traveler Returns* souvenir program. 1945.
25. *Ibid*.

26 "Bela Lugosi 'Sweet,' Despite Horror Roles, Wife Insists." *Seattle Times* 13 Mar. 1945.
27 *Santa Barbara News-Press* 15 Feb. 1945. [Lobero Theatre Archives, University of California, Santa Barbara, California Library, Special Collections. Box 3, Folder 18, Production Number 160.]
28 *Ibid.*
29 *Ibid.*
30 *Ibid.*
31 *Ibid.*
32 *Ibid.*
33 *Ibid.*
34 *Ibid.*
35 *Ibid.*
36 Bruce, Hazel. "It's Got Everything – With One Exception." *San Francisco Chronicle* 28 Feb. 1945.
37 Fried, Alexander. "*No Traveler Returns* Proves Dull Fare on Curran Stage." *San Francisco Examiner* 28 Feb. 1945.
38 Johnson, Fred. "But Playwright Was Survivor!" *San Francisco Call-Bulletin* 27 Feb. 1945.
39 First Nighter. "Lugosi, Keith Mixed Up in India Mystery." *Oakland Post-Enquirer* 27 Feb. 1945.
40 Soanes, Wood. "Lots of Ham But No Points." *Oakland Tribune* 27 Feb. 1945.
41 *Variety* 14 Mar. 1945; "Othello Big $24,200, Frisco; Lugosi's $5,800." *Variety* 21 Mar. 1945.
42 *Hutchinson News-Herald* (Hutchinson, Kansas) 29 Oct. 1944.
43 "Bela Lugosi 'Sweet,' Despite Horror Roles, Wife Insists."
44 *Ibid.*
45 *Ibid.*
46 *Ibid.*
47 *Ibid.*
48 *Ibid.*
49 *Seattle Times* 4 Mar. 1945.
50 *Seattle Times* 13 Mar.1945.
51 *Seattle Times* 18 Mar. 1945.
52 *Seattle Times* 14 Mar.1945.
53 Sayre, J. Willis. "Film Veterans in Met. Drama." *Seattle Post-Intelligencer* 15 Mar. 1945.
54 *Seattle Times* 18 Mar. 1945.
55 "Lugosi-Keith Troupe Quits in Seattle, Biz NG." *Variety* 21 Mar. 1945.
56 "Book Road Show at Post Street." *Spokane Spokesman-Review* 8 Mar. 1945; "Lugosi-Keith Troupe Quits in Seattle, Biz NG."
57 *Daily Variety* 5 Feb. 1945.
58 "Rita Mann Given Lead Role in *Janie*, Stage Comedy." *Augusta Chronicle* 25 Nov. 1945.
59 "What's Doing on Stage on Screen." *Oakland Tribune* 26 Feb. 1945.
60 Schallert, Edwin. "Bela Lugosi Enlisted for *House of Dracula*." *Los Angeles Times* 17 Feb. 1945.

Lugosi with his son in the mid-1940s.

Chapter 2

ACCENT ON HORROR

In the months following the end of World War II, the American film industry achieved great economic success. As film historian Thomas Schatz has written, "Hollywood enjoyed its best year ever" in 1946.[1] The industry looked towards greater and greater profits, and why not? Troops returning home could only mean a significant increase for ticket sales.

For the fiscal year ending on November 2, 1946, Universal Studios reported the biggest profits in its lengthy history.[2] Monogram's profits also increased to record levels.[3] And by the end of the year, PRC — a company known for its poverty-row output — had grown confident enough in its role in the marketplace to drop low-budget films from its program.[4]

What did that mean for the horror movie? In 1945, the situation appeared tenuous. On the one hand, studios released numerous horror films that year. On the other hand, in September 1945, *Variety* predicted that "balanced films" would replace "cycles."[5] That was in addition to Universal using "psychological goose pimples" as the basis for a few of their new "chillers," rather than relying on the old "monsters."[6]

But in 1945, perhaps the key question was the very meaning of the word "horror." Years earlier, by the end of 1932, "horror" concretized as the film genre's name, much as other genres had one-word monikers like "musical" or "gangster." And it had served Hollywood quite well, representing a clear narrative tradition in the space of six letters.

In the spring of 1945, however, a new kind of "horror" film complicated the meaning of that word. The Allied liberation of German death camps resulted in many things, not least of which were terrifying non-fiction images. Public screenings of such film footage resulted in part due to General Eisenhower; he believed that Americans needed to see "what the enemy had done." As *Motion Picture Herald* wrote, audiences who viewed the Nazi films "have seen all the Four Horseman of the Apocalypse riding at last over the brink of a fetid hell."[7]

Much of the American press labelled footage of the Nazi atrocities as "Horror Films." A Gallup poll revealed that 60 percent of the American public believed the Nazi "horror films" should be shown in theatres.[8] In St. Louis, for example, 81,500 persons attended 44 screenings of the footage, which had originally been scheduled for only twelve performances.[9] And increased theatre attendance occurred in numerous parts of the country when these "horror films" were screened.[10]

Continued reports of similar "horror films" appeared in the press in 1946, including details of footage shot by the Nazis. In late February of that year, for example, the *Los Angeles Times* described films screened at Nuremberg that showed:

...German soldiers laughing while one of them swung an axe to behead helpless Yugoslavs, of S.S. men swinging corpses after hangings, and of ferocious dogs and starving hogs devouring other victims were shown today on [a] motion picture screen to the international military tribunal.[11]

After mentioning such films as *The Cabinet of Dr. Caligari* (1919) and *Dracula* (1931), another journalist noted that, "In all the grim record of man's inhumanity to man there is little to match the wholesale crimes of which the last batch of Nuremberg defendants now stand convicted."[12]

While the Nazi atrocities onscreen placed pressure on the meaning of the term "horror film," they did not halt Hollywood's production of fictional horror movies, some of which were quite similar to those of earlier years. For example, during the year 1946, audiences saw: Monogram's *The Face of Marble* (released in January), PRC's *Strangler of the Swamp* (January), PRC's *The Flying Serpent* (February), PRC's *The Mask of Diijon* (March), Universal's *House of Horrors* and *The Spider Woman Strikes Back* (both March), PRC's *Devil Bat's Daughter* (April), Republic's *The Catman of Paris* (April), Universal's *She-Wolf of London* and *The Cat Creeps* (May), Republic's *Valley of the Zombies* (May), and PRC's *The Brute Man* (October). And as the year came to a close, industry trade publications reviewed Warner Brothers' new film *The Beast with Five Fingers*.[13]

Such movies were in addition to 1946 comedies like Monogram's feature *Spook Busters* with the Bowery Boys (released in August) and Columbia's short subject *A Bird in the Head* (released in April), as well as a number of horror films that had been released the prior year, but which still remained in general distribution, including Universal's *House of Dracula* (1945).

In April of 1946, *Hollywood Reporter* announced that "horror pix" were gaining "heavier adult patronage," adding that they were "winning universal appeal" thanks to bigger budgets and higher standards.[14] Here the discussion centered not on films like *The Flying Serpent* or *Valley of the Zombies*, but on motion pictures of a different type, those that were more psychological or suspenseful. *Hollywood Reporter* specifically cited such 1946 releases as RKO's *The Spiral Staircase* and *Bedlam*, the latter produced by Val Lewton and starring Boris Karloff. They also drew attention to Columbia's *The Walls Came Tumbling Down* (1946). Horror – in another expanded use of the term – for more discriminating tastes.

Such an elastic understanding of "horror" could well have allowed the *Hollywood Reporter* to name other movies in general release during 1946, including Hitchcock's *Spellbound* (which had premiered during the final days of 1945), as well as a few foreign films that appeared on American screens, including the Swedish-made *The Girl and the Devil* and the British-made *Dead of Night* and *Frenzy*.[15]

Bela Lugosi was well aware of all of these issues, speaking about them to a reporter as early as the spring of 1945, when he said, "scarcely any horror film you can name [of the *Dracula* and *Frankenstein* variety] isn't drawing crowds." After mentioning "those shockers with an ingredient of psychology" in them, the reporter proceeded to ask Lugosi about the "horrors of war" onscreen. The actor promptly responded that audiences liked fictional horror, as they preferred the "unreality" of them to any real atrocities in movies.[16]

Others working in the film industry also understood this expanded meaning of the word "horror." In 1946, for example, Curt Siodmak — the screenwriter of such films as *The Wolf Man* (1941) – wrote that, "Almost every melodrama contains scenes of horror, though the A-Plus producer would never accept that term for his million-dollar creation. When horror enters the gilded gate of top production, it is glorified as a 'psychological thriller.' But a rose by any other name...."[17]

Even if some of those producers eschewed the word "horror," others did not. An article in a 1946 issue of *Liberty* magazine took pains to detail the different kinds of screen horror that existed, going so far as to say: "Horror can be a great many things, from the psychological thriller to the strictly monster tale. The witch scene in Disney's *Snow White* [1937] and the whale in *Pinocchio* [1940] were nothing but horror."[18]

Alan Carney, Lionel Atwill, Bela Lugosi, and Wally Brown in the 1946 RKO film *Genius at Work*. (Courtesy of Buddy Barnett)

Perhaps the larger umbrella of horror as it was being perceived in 1946 could also include RKO's film *Genius at Work*, which paired Lugosi with Lionel Atwill. Why the studio did not pair Lugosi with Karloff in another Val Lewton horror film – as they had in *The Body Snatcher* (1945) — is unknown, as it would have been easy for them to cast Lugosi in either *Isle of the Dead* (1945) or *Bedlam* (1946). But that did not happen, which may suggest that Lewton was simply uninterested in working with him again.

By the autumn of 1945, the Lugosis moved to Lake Elsinore to be closer to their seven-year old son, who was then attending military school.[19] Years later, Bela Lugosi Jr. recalled:

> The military academy held a parade every Sunday afternoon for the parents, and Dad would always put on a show. He and my mother would arrive in a large, black limousine or, later, a sporty blue roadster. Everyone would know that Dad arrived: Bela Lugosi and family were the center of attention.[20]

Lugosi Jr. also remembered that his father loved Lake Elsinore and the nearby Glen Ivy Hot Spring baths.

Another move came in the form of a change of representation. Perhaps Lugosi believed that switching from the Kline-Howard Agency to Harry E. Edington's management in mid-1945 would improve his film career. In addition to working as a manager, Edington had a good deal of experience as a film producer.

Nevertheless, Lugosi's only work on a film set in 1945 was *Genius at Work*. A remake of the 1937 film *Super-Sleuth* starring Jack Oakie, *Genius at Work* was originally titled *Master Minds*. While it was being filmed, the press claimed that Lugosi had leased a two-room apartment in Hollywood, presum-

NO TRAVELER RETURNS | The Lost Years of Bela Lugosi

ably to be nearer to the film set each day.[21]

RKO studio files offer conflicting information regarding Lugosi's salary, which may have been as little as $1,250 a week or as high as $2,500 a week. If the latter was true, Lugosi made twice as much as any of his major co-stars, Lionel Atwill or Wally Brown and Alan Carney, the comedy team from *Zombies on Broadway*.[22] In either event, Lugosi made a higher salary than the $3,500 he received for *The Body Snatcher*. And his contract stipulated that, while his name could come after Atwill's and actress Anne Jeffreys', it had to appear in the same size type.[23]

Production on the film began on August 11, 1945, shortly before the Japanese surrendered to the Allied forces. Lugosi's first day on the set was August 18. He then worked steadily from August 20 to August 25, and then again from August 27 to September 1. He remained on call during the early days of September, and then finished his part of the filming at 10:30PM on September 8.[24]

The whole shoot took 23 days, but then RKO called Lugosi and several others back for a day of filming on November 30, over two and a half months after the production had originally wrapped.[25] That same month, the *Hollywood Reporter* announced that the title was changing to *Genius, Inc.*, but by early December RKO shelved that idea.[26] On December 18, 1945 the studio decided on *Genius at Work* as the final title.[27]

In terms of the film, *Genius at Work* features Wally Brown and Alan Carney as the same characters — or at least with the same character names — as they had played in *Zombies on Broadway* (1945). This time, they are detectives working on a radio show written by Ellen Brent (Anne Jeffreys). Getting mixed up with criminologist Latimer Marsh (Lionel Atwill) means that all three of them get all-too-close to his alter ego, a criminal mastermind known as the Cobra, as well as to his murderous assistant, Stone (Lugosi). But in the end, Brown and Carney's antics – with a good deal of help from the police – bring an end to the Cobra's murderous ways.

Though Lugosi received fifth billing onscreen (under Brown, Carney, Jeffreys, and Atwill) and was rel-

Lionel Atwill and Bela Lugosi pictured near the conclusion of *Genius at Work* (1946). (Courtesy of Buddy Barnett)

Pictured at Latimer Marsh's (Lionel Atwill's) collection of torture devices, Stone (Lugosi) attempts to murder Jerry Miles (Wally Brown) in *Genius at Work*. (Courtesy of Buddy Barnett)

egated to the role of the Cobra's lackey, *Genius at Work* is definitely superior to *Zombies on Broadway*. Lugosi has several memorable moments in the film, from throwing a dagger at Brown and Carney in a nightclub to failing to hit Brown with an axe. He also gets more screen time than in *Zombies on Broadway* (or *The Body Snatcher*, for that matter), appearing in approximately 14 minutes of footage. And curiously enough, Lugosi's character Stone outlives the Cobra, scaling to the top of a skyscraper before being shot down by the police and falling – with a dubbed scream that certainly does not sound like Lugosi – to his death.

The film's pacing and energy also surpass *Zombies on Broadway*. Alan Carney actually provides some laughs, not least of which come from the fact that it is his character — the dumbest in the film — who deduces that Latimer Marsh is the Cobra. That is all in addition to a wonderful opening in which the Cobra kidnaps a wealthy victim from a mansion, a scene that calls to mind such old dark house films as *The Bat* (1926) and *The Bat Whispers* (1930).

All that said, *Film Daily* called *Genius at Work* "uninspired and ordinary," quipping that, "It's evident there was no genius at work here."[28] *Hollywood Reporter* believed the film was "ordinary," claiming it was little more than a typical RKO "program" picture.[29] *Daily Variety* felt much the same, telling readers it was "run of the mill" with "dull moments far outnumbering the laughs." The trade added that, "Atwill and Lugosi provide suitable menace, but are made too much on [the] buffoon side."[30]

Despite poor notices, audience response at some theatres was favorable. *Motion Picture Herald* noted that a Los Angeles preview at the Hillside Theatre "got quite a few laughs."[31] The same publication also published numerous other exhibitor reports:

'The audience got a swell bang out of this one.'
— Auditorium Theatre, Malden, Massachusetts[32]

'Good program mystery thriller with some laughs that should please that type of patron who likes funny mysteries.'
—New Theatre, England, Arkansas[33]

'Used on my double bill program and I thought my house would shake down from all the laughter. I thought it was one of the most pleasing pictures I have ever played on a double bill program.'
— Gray Theatre, Gray, Georgia[34]

As with the critical reviews, these audience responses came long after the film was produced. *Genius at Work* did not appear on movie screens until October 20, 1946. That same day was Lugosi's 64th birthday. By that time, Lionel Atwill had already been dead nearly six months.

But Lugosi trudged forward, having worked on horror film sets for seventeen years. In April of 1946,

This publicity still for *Genius at Work* depicts Alan Carney, Wally Brown, Anne Jeffreys, Lionel Atwill, and Lugosi in a scene that is not included in the film. (Courtesy of Jack Dowler)

Gary D. Rhodes | Bill Kaffenberger

Lugosi in a publicity portrait for *Scared to Death* (1947).

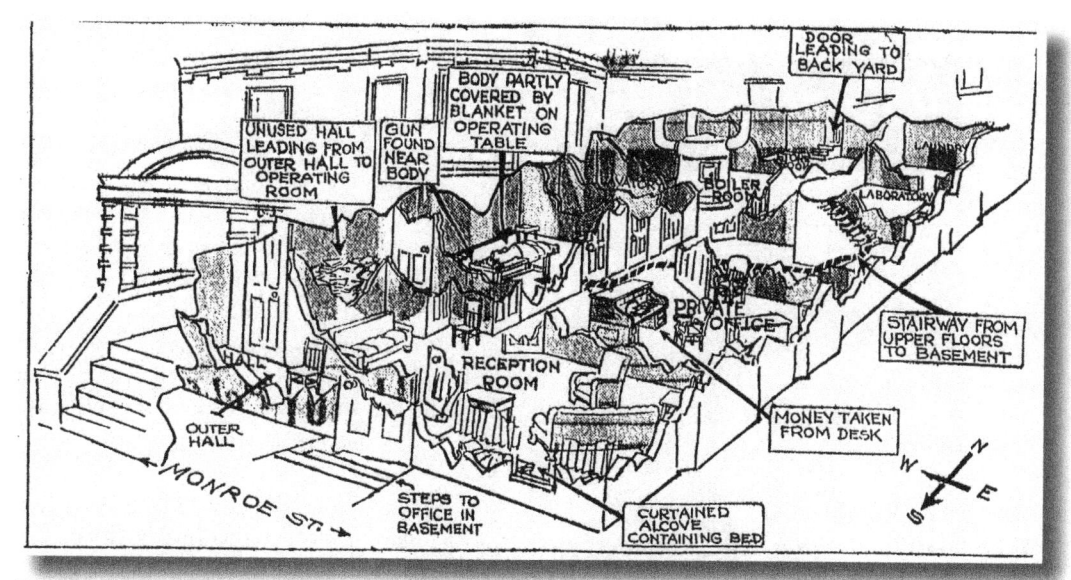

The Wynekoop home – complete with operating table – as depicted by a 1933 newspaper artist.

Jimmy Fidler's newspaper column discussed the careers of Lugosi and Karloff, noting their complaints at being typecast as horror stars. Offering a sympathetic ear, Fidler told readers, "both are fine actors that deserve Grade-A roles. Maybe Hollywood should relent and give them the chances they are pleading for."[35]

Over the years, a number of producers and studios did give Karloff the chance to work in other genres. For example, in 1946, Karloff was the cast in the film version of *The Secret Life of Walter Mitty* (1947).[36] He also appeared in a stage production of *On Borrowed Time* in November of 1946.[37] Though known primarily as a horror film star, Karloff was able to work in non-horror productions, at least from time to time.

As for Lugosi, well, that had been less true since he appeared onscreen as Dracula in 1931. With Harry E. Edington's management, Lugosi nabbed only one new film role during the whole of 1946, Hollywood's "best year ever." Only one film. And, not surprisingly perhaps, it was in a low-budget horror movie.

Golden Gate Pictures produced the film, which was originally titled *Accent on Horror*, as well as – according to one trade publication article – *The Autopsy*.[38] Golden Gate was part of a loose conglomeration of low budget film producers that included Action Pictures. Various persons associated with the organization had worked with Lugosi in the past, including production manager Barney Sarecky, screenwriter Harvey Gates (who worked on one of Golden Gate's westerns), and director Ford Beebe (who directed Golden Gate's 1946 film *My Dog Shep*).[39]

Accent on Horror's storyline had deep roots, dating to a 1933 Chicago murder case. Near the end of that year, police charged the well-known Dr. Alice Wynekoop with the murder of her daughter-in-law Rheta, whose corpse was found on an operating table at the Wynekoop mansion. Wynekoop's defense was that Rheta died while being treated with chloroform.[40] To preserve her reputation as a doctor, Wynekoop fired a bullet into the corpse so that she could claim a burglar killed Rheta.[41] But many believed Wynekoop intentionally took her daughter-in-law's life. There was little doubt that Wynekoop's son no longer had an interest in Rheta, and that he had affairs with numerous other women.[42] Police also discovered that Dr. Wynekoop had taken out a $100,000 insurance policy on Rheta's life.[43]

Frank Orsino, a director at the Academy Guild Theatre in Cleveland, Ohio, read about the case with great interest, and rapidly adapted the tale into a three-act stage play called *Murder on the Operating Table*. He changed numerous details, which helped fend off legal threats from the Wynekoop family.[44]

True Chronicles of an Unknown Playwright—II.

Christy Cabanne, three decades before he directed *Scared to Death* (1947).

But to the *Cleveland Plain Dealer*, it was obvious that *Murder on the Operating Table* was about Wynekoop; the newspaper also noted that the play would open on the very same day as the start of Wynekoop's trial.[45]

Orsino was not only a writer, but also a clever promoter; for example, he sometimes directed Broadway plays at the Academy Guild under different titles in order to avoid paying royalties.[46] And he wrote *Murder on the Operating Table* under the pseudonym Bill Heedle, thus creating a degree of local interest in who the mysterious author really was.[47] A review published after opening night told readers:

> As a play, it seems rather luridly fantastic, talky and too slow in the first act, Mr. Heedle ["whose identity is still a mystery"] has a knack of injecting high-voltage situations that are exciting enough to arouse delighted shrieks from the audience. His dialog could have been written more expertly, for it makes the performances appear somewhat stagey.
>
> ... There are four murders and another attempted killing during the ultra-melodramatic activities, spilling so much blood that the actors almost get their feet wet. Two profane detectives, who are cousins to Mr. Mulligan and Mr. Garrity of *Gorilla* fame, have a grand time brow-beating suspects when the much-hated girl is found shot and stabbed to death on an operating table.
>
> Her doctor-mother-in-law, a strange and jealous woman, and her husband are the first to come under the finger of suspicion. Then a half a dozen other characters are suspected of the sex crime, but the number is cut down by a mysterious killer who glides through secret doors like a shadow.[48]

Orsino's tale resonated with Clevelanders, having a much longer life than Wynekoop's trial or her presence in the media. On June 9, 1935, *Murder on the Operating Table* celebrated its 100th performance in in the city.[49]

It's difficult to determine the extent to which the play was staged in other cities. Gwen Wagner attempted to produce a version in Elyria, Ohio in Februrary 1934, but city officials "raised horrified eyebrows" to the extent that the show was cancelled.[50] Then, at a given point, presumably in the 1940s, Orsino adapted his own story into a screenplay, changing certain key plot elements. The Wynnekoop character became a man, perhaps to allow the opportunity for a noted horror film actor to assume the role. Orsino also limited the number of murders to one, with the victim being literally "scared to death," rather than being shot or stabbed. The play's two detectives transformed into a stupid house detective present for comedy relief, and a confident and fast-talking newspaper reporter.

Professor Leonide (Lugosi) and Indigo (Angelo Rossitto) arrive at the Van Ee home in *Scared to Death* (1947). (Courtesy of Buddy Barnett)

Dr. Van Ee (George Zucco) and Professor Leonide (Lugosi) in *Scared to Death* (1947). (Courtesy of Buddy Barnett)

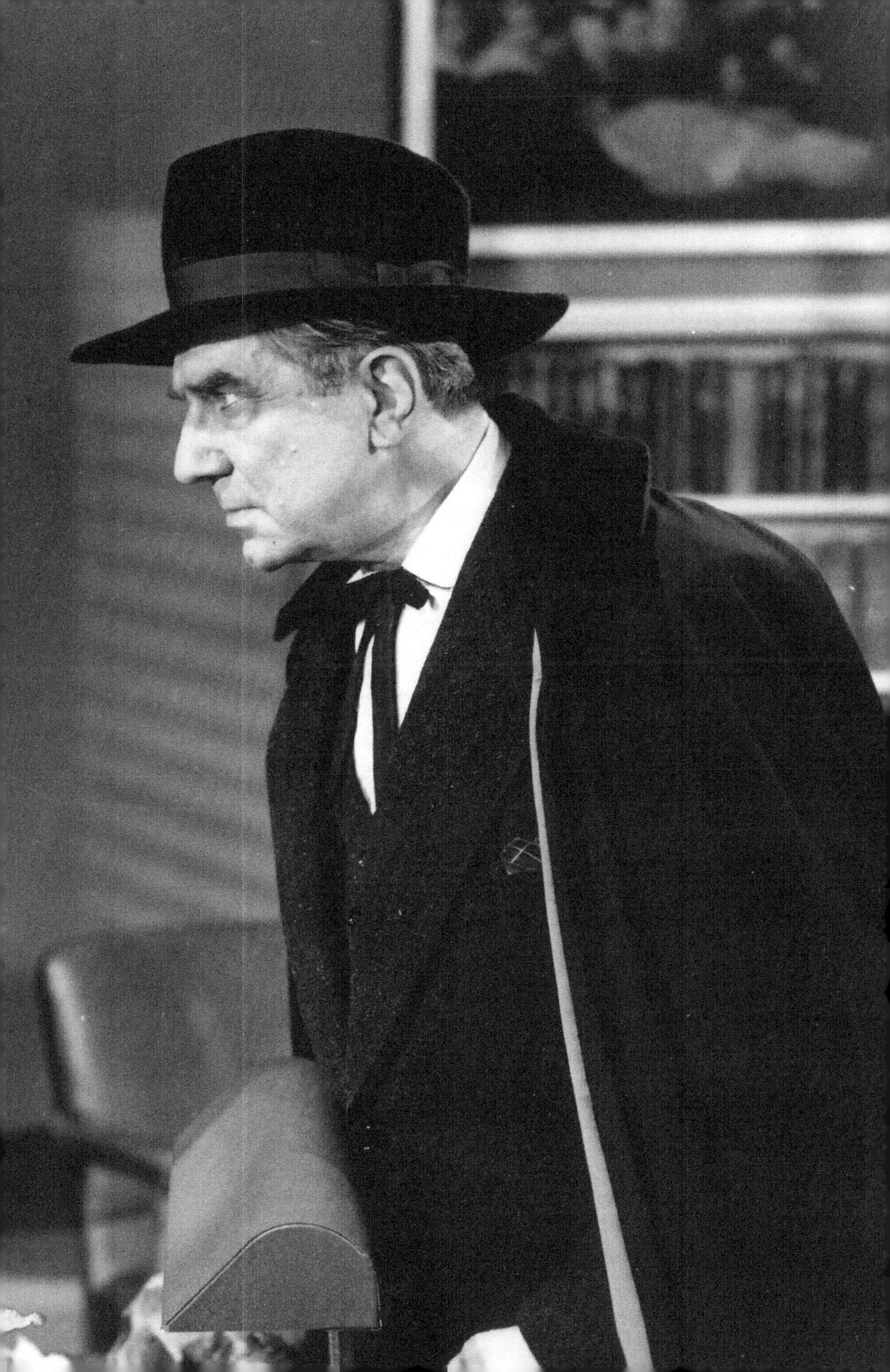

Striking a humorous pose not seen in the actual film, this publicity still features Terry Lee (Douglas Fowley), Professor Leonide (Lugosi), Lilybeth (Gladys Blake), and Bill Raymond (Nat Pendleton).

Orsino's film script – which he sold under yet another pseudonym, "William Abbott" – clearly drew upon the original Wynekoop case. Both the real story and the script featured a home with a "maze of rooms" – as the press once referred to the Wynekoop mansion – that doubled as a location where a doctor treats patients.[51] And both featured a parent who tries to free a son from marriage to an unwanted wife.

In fact, Orsino also seems to have incorporated elements of the Gilbert Wynekoop case, a different event involving Dr. Wynekoop's brother-in-law. While Dr. Wynekoop was awaiting trial, Gilbert went before a jury on a separate matter. They sentenced him to an insane asylum after he was "arrested several times for annoying women."[52] He tried to rape at least one of them. In his defense, Gilbert suggested that he was framed by a doctor who was "trying to 'railroad' him to an asylum" in order to get him out of the way.[53] That element of his case smacks similar to the lead female character in *Accent on Horror*, who believes that a doctor is trying to do the same to her.

The *Cleveland Plain Dealer* proudly announced Orsino's sale of his film script in 1946.[54] For *Accent on Horror*, William B. David acted as producer. The venerable Christy Cabanne directed. He was a prolific filmmaker, having started his career at least as early as 1910.[55] Among his large array of movies was *The Mummy's Hand* (1940) at Universal. Over the years, Christy descended into lower and lower budget movies, such as *Sensation Hunters*, which he directed in 1945.

With Lugosi starring as the mysterious Professor Leonide, *Accent on Horror*'s cast also featured longtime horror film actor George Zucco as Dr. Joseph Van Ee, the South African-born actress Molly Lamont as Laura Van Ee/Laurette La Valle, and Nat Pendleton (who had long played a variety of policemen and other character parts in Hollywood) as house detective Bill Raymond.

To shoot *Accent on Horror*, Golden Gate leased the Gordon Street Studios and announced a start date of Monday, March 25, 1946.[56] On March 28, 1946, *Variety* reported that the company had also "inked" actors Joyce Compton, Douglas Fowley, Roland Varno, and Angelo Rossito (who had appeared with Lugosi in such films as *Spooks Run Wild* in 1941 and *The Corpse Vanishes* in 1942).[57] That article calls into question the announced filming start date of March 25, 1946, unless the first few days of filming concentrated on actors who were already cast.[58]

Perhaps the most unique aspect of the film's production was its use of color film stock. Buoyed by successful box-office returns in 1945 and early 1946, color film seemed to be on the verge of making enormous strides. In March 1946, producer Arnold Pressburger predicted that 50 percent of all films made over the following year would be shot in color.[59] In May of that year, Technicolor announced plans to build new facilities in an effort to double their output.[60] That company's net profits in 1946 would reach $436, 168.[61] But other color film stocks also seemed increasingly well-positioned. A study of Nazi-developed AGFA color film found it achieved "good results."[62] And trade reports claimed that the Thomascolor process would be ready for use in Hollywood film productions by the autumn of 1946.[63]

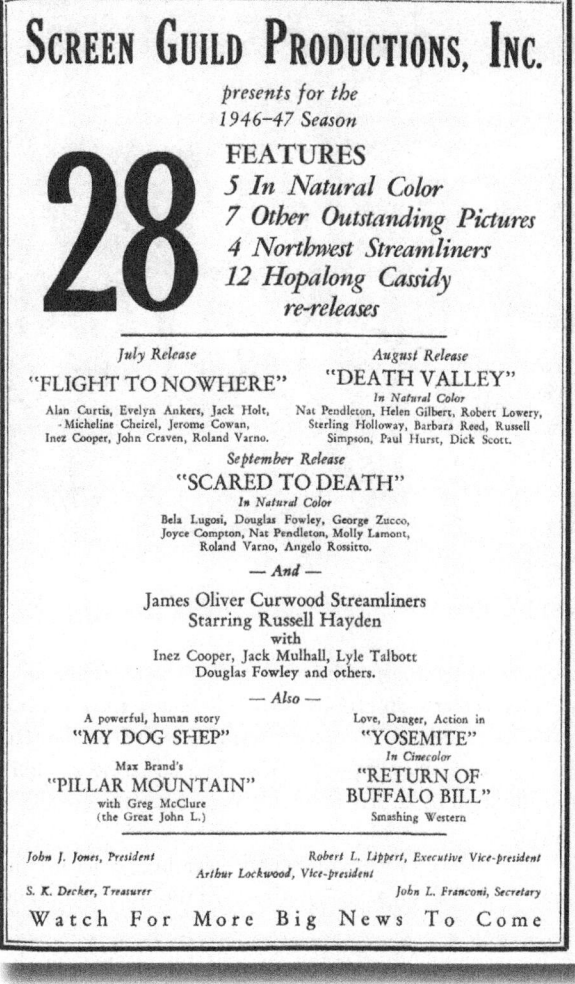

Advertisement published in the *1946-47 International Motion Picture Almanac* (New York: Quigley Publications).

For *Accent on Horror*, however, Golden Gate opted to work with yet another company, Cinecolor, whose stock featured a two-color process (as opposed to the three-color process that Technicolor was then using). William Crespinel founded the company after having worked on various color film stocks since 1907, when he joined Charles Urban's Kinemacolor company. Crespinel had also been the principal photographer for *The Glorious Adventure* (1922), the first feature film shot in color.[64]

Having started Cinecolor in 1932, Crespinel gained much traction in the forties due to the several advantages that his system offered. Filmmakers could shoot Cinecolor stock in standard black-and-white cameras, and it cost only 20 to 25 percent more than shooting black-and-white. The Cinecolor lab could process and deliver color rushes within a day.[65] And Crespinel and his associates even visited sets to help provide advice and assistance. In fact, that is likely how Crespinel's son – under the stage name Lee Bennett – received the small, but pivotal role of Rene in *Accent on Horror*.

Though its reputation was largely tied to B-movies, Cinecolor was definitely experiencing a boom shortly before, during, and after the *Accent on Horror* shoot. By April 1946, the company had obtained a half million dollars in new capital needed for its expansion.[66] Within the space of a month, *Hollywood Reporter* touted seven different features filmed in Cinecolor, their studios ranging from Universal and Hal Roach to PRC and Monogram.[67] In fact, between March and May 1946, the company doubled its output.[68]

As for *Accent on Horror*, its production time at the Gordon Street Studios was brief. During the week of April 2, 1946, set construction was already underway at Consolidated Studios.[69] The production moved there effective April 8 due to prior commitments at Gordon Street.[70] And, though it is difficult to determine precisely when it happened, at some point by early May, Golden Gate rechristened the film with the title *Scared to Death*.[71]

During the shoot, Hollywood journalist Gene Handsaker interviewed Lugosi on the set. When asked about the secret of scaring someone to death, Lugosi responded that sincerity was the key: having a deep conviction about the awful deed you were about to do.[72] "Of course, [you] don't do it" he told Handsaker, "but you must believe you are going to; the minute you play it with tongue in cheek, the effect is dead."[73]

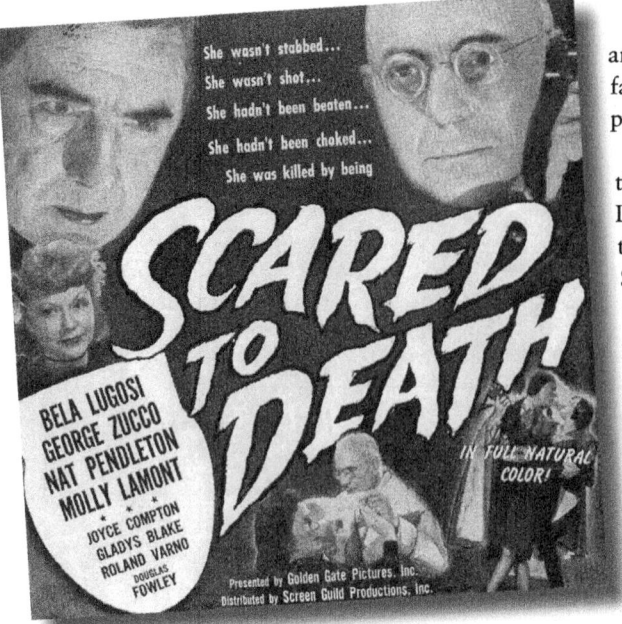

Artwork published in the film's pressbook.

Handsaker then proceeded to ask Lugosi the most bizarre form of death he had visited upon one of his screen victims. He couldn't respond with *Scared to Death*, as he murders no one in that film. Though he was sometimes prone to forget individual horror films and their release titles, Lugosi responded to the question by clearly remembering *The Black Cat* (1934), "where I skinned Boris Karloff alive. Cute, isn't it!"[74]

Few memories from the set survive, though actor Douglas Fowley told his wife an ancedote regarding Angelo Rossitto. She later relayed the story to film historian Jack Gourlay:

> Doug … told the story of the little guy playing this character that disappears into a secret passage of an old house. One day on the set, Angelo disappears into the secret passage, got stuck in there, and couldn't get out. Filming was brought to a halt while they rescued Angelo. As they broke open the secret passage door, they all shouted out, 'Okay, Inyougo [sounds like Indigo], out-you-go.'[75]

After watching *Scared to Death* many years later, Fowley's wife realized that the "Inyougo, out-you-go" line did not appear in the film.

Other surviving accounts of *Scared to Death*'s production appear in the film's pressbook, though these might stem as much from a publicist's imagination as from anything else. One of them purports to describe an on-set incident involving Lillian Lugosi:

> Mrs. Bela Lugosi … was shocked to hear two women visitors discussing her husband in highly unflattering terms. 'I'll bet he's a nasty person at home, too,' one of the women remarked to her companion. That was too much for Mrs. Lugosi. She turned on the visitor and asserted: 'Really, it's only his acting. You see, I know. I'm his wife.' This sent the visitor and her companion scurrying in embarrassment from the set, probably to return to their native habitat, in the Middle West to regale their neighboring gossips with stories about 'sinful Hollywood'[76]

The pressbook also claimed that Lugosi actually knew hypnotism and used it on fellow actors. "You can't successfully fake a murder scene," Lugosi said. "You've got to make yourself believe that you really are going to kill. And the illusion is furthered if your 'victim' believes it, too."[77]

By April 19, 1946, principle photography on *Scared to Death* came to an end.[78] Editing was underway during the first half of May.[79] Contractually, Golden Gate produced all of their films exclusively for release through Screen Guild Productions, including *Scared to Death*. For 1946 and 1947, Screen Guild intended to release twelve or more features per year.[80] That plan extended to such Golden Gate productions as *Rolling Home* (1946) and *My Dog Shep* (1946).[81]

Screen Guild was apparently doing well in 1946. In February of that year, trades announced that the company had arranged a national "set-up" for its releases in all territories of the US except Milwaukee, "where a deal [was] in negotiation."[82] By May, *Hollywood Reporter* announced that the company would release a total of 28 films in 1946, five of which would be in Cinecolor. Twelve others would be reissues of Hopalong Cassidy films.[83]

Exactly how *Scared to Death* fit into Screen Guild's evolving plans is difficult to determine. *Film Daily* reported that a print of the movie would be screened in Chicago at the company's first annual sales meeting during the second week of May 1946.[84] If that happened, the company employees likely viewed a work print with no musial score.

On July 19, 1946, *Hollywood Reporter* noted that Golden Gate's William B. David – not someone from Screen Guild – had made an agreement with Lugosi to do a personal appearance tour with *Scared to Death*, which was set to open in San Francisco "in two weeks," meaning sometime in August.[85] A trade advertisement claimed that *Scared to Death* would be released in September, and then half-page advertisements published in *Motion Picture Herald* and *Daily Variety* announced *Scared to Death* would be an "October Release."[86]

Leonide (Lugosi), Ward Van Ee (Roland Varno), and Terry Lee (Douglas Fowley) in *Scared to Death* (1947).
(Courtesy of Jack Dowler)

Gary D. Rhodes | Bill Kaffenberger

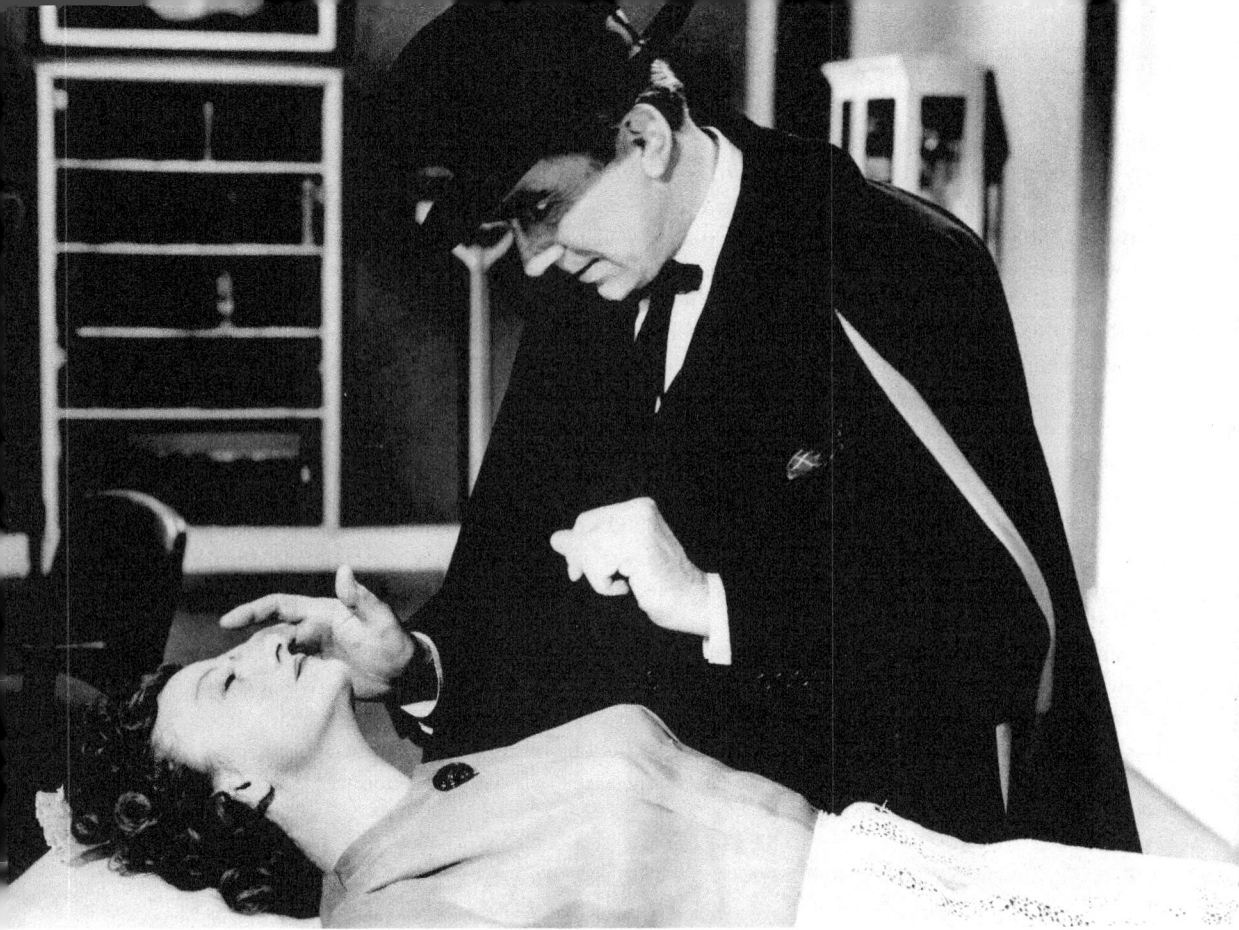

Lugosi and Gladys Blake in a publicity still for *Scared to Death* **(1947).** (Courtesy of Jack Dowler)

But in late July, Screen Guild's vice president in charge of distribution revised the release date to November 1.[87] On August 15, *Scared to Death* received its copyright at roughly the same time that *Daily Variety* told readers that Lou Adrian was scoring the film.[88] Just over a month later, a *Scared to Death* synopsis appeared in *Film Daily*, yet another sign of its imminent release.[89]

However, for reasons that are hard to determine, Carl Hoefle replaced Lou Adrian as the film's composer.[90] Delays meant that the music was not recorded until early October.[91] Then, on November 14, Screen Guild announced that release copies of *Scared to Death* were in the "printing" stage.[92] Curiously, *Hollywood Reporter* announced that the company was in fact ahead of schedule on eight films, one of which was *Scared to Death*.[93]

Why the prolonged post-production phase? Perhaps some of it resulted from Screen Guild requiring Golden Gate to make changes to the film, including what may have been an unsatisfactory musical score. Or perhaps the delay resulted from other kinds of factors. Screen Guild continued to grow in 1946, making distribution deals with Banner, Screen Art Pictures, and the Fortune Films Company.[94] But in September, *Film Daily* referred to the company's "general franchise problems."[95] Internal issues may also have contributed to *Scared to Death*'s delay.

At any rate, *Scared to Death*'s official release date became May 3, 1947, over a year after it was filmed. But that hardly ended its long road to theatre screens. While it did play some theatres that month, it did not debut in New York City until June and played most American theatres from July onward.[96] Indeed, it was still playing some theatres in December 1947 when Dr. Alice Wynekoop was finally released from prison.[97]

Offering advice to exhibitors, the film's pressbook presented a number of possible exploitation strategies to entice ticket-buyers:

STREET BALLYHOO: Hire a man and dress him in the weirdest kind of costume you can get your hands on. A combination Dracula-Apeman-Frankenstein outfit would be perfect. Have him walk through the busiest thoroughfares in your town jumping at people shouting 'Boo,' sneaking around corners frightening pedestrians, and generally making an eerie nuisance of himself. Have a sign painted for his back which might read: If you become 'scared to death' looking at me – Don't forget to see *Scared to Death* in full natural color at the Rialto Theater starting Wednesday. This is the eeriest, weirdest, chilling-est film ever shown on the screen.[98]

BLINDFOLD STUNT: The heroine, Molly Lamont of the thrilling mystery film, *Scared to Death*, is morbidly afraid of having her eyes blindfolded, and this phobia of hers plays a prominent part in the film story. Set up a 'blindfold' booth in your lobby with an usher or usherette in charge. Have your man – or woman – draw the attention of a small crowd of people, and, when they are assembled, explain your stunt to them. Ask for a woman volunteer from the audience, and proceed to blindfold her with a green scarf – in keeping with the film story. Then subject her to a number of frightening sensations. You might rub something slimy along her arm, suggesting it to be a snake. You might drop some red paint on her hand, telling her it's blood, which, of course she won't believe while blindfolded – but just watch her reaction when the blindfold is removed! You might toss a small cat or kitten into her arms telling her it's some sort of small, wild animal. Any number of variations on this theme can be thought of. Request that the audience watching the woman be quiet while these things are happening, or else the effect will be lost – and then just watch the fun your patrons will have![99]

Other suggested ballyhoo efforts included having a journalist follow patrons selected from the audience

Along with playing a red herring role in *Scared to Death*, Lugosi serves in much the same capacity for this publicity still with Molly Lamont. His character is never this physically aggressive in the film's running time. (Courtesy of Jack Dowler)

while they are subjected to being alone in a graveyard at midnight or wandering through a "haunted house."[100]

Such exploitation campaigns may have had an effect on a few viewers, but they certainly didn't sway the film trades. *Film Daily* ignored the movie, as did *Harrison's Reports*, even though both publications reviewed most American film releases. While believing that *Scared to Death* had a "certain attraction through the use of Cinecolor," *Motion Picture Herald* argued that the audience would "likely shrug the whole thing off."[101] *Variety* was harsher, calling the film "a dull, poorly put together melodrama that fails to generate [the] goosepimples expected by a Bela Lugosi vehicle." The same critic believed the film's art direction was its "best" attribute, but knocked Cabanne's "uneven" direction and George McGuire's "bad editing."[102]

Perhaps the only endorsement in the national press came not in the form of a review, but instead as a single sentence in Walter Winchell's syndicated column: "*Scared to Death* throws a few scares in you, with Lugosi pitching the shudders."[103] Winchell may have not even seen the film when he wrote those words, which were likely read by more potential ticket-buyers than any trade review. Like Jimmie Fidler, Winchell had long been a Lugosi supporter.

The occasional city newspaper reviews were not particularly kind. Noting that the film's screenwriter was from Cleveland, the *Plain Dealer* said that:

> [Frank Orsino] rewrote his favorite melodrama to serve as a vehicle for Bela Lugosi. Despite all the revamping, it is still a preposterous and overplayed shocker which will make you shudder only once or twice. ... Lugosi, of course, tries his most hypnotic, lurid tricks on the girl. ... the tale's corny action too often aroused the audience's snickers yesterday.[104]

The newspaper did praise Cinecolor, claiming it helped to create "a fairly eerie atmosphere." Similarly, an exhibitor in Georgia reported, "This chill-thrilling picture was helped greatly by being in color."[105]

Aside from snickering viewers in Cleveland and perhaps a few ticket-buyers wowed by the color in Georgia, it is difficult to determine what audiences thought of the film in 1947. Its most successful screening probably came at the Million Dollar Theatre in Los Angeles, where it generated $25,000 during a one-week run. However, many of those dollars might have resulted as much or more from the popular Mills Brothers, who appeared live onstage with the film that same week.[106]

Overall, it seems that the key person who really benefited from *Scared to Death* was Frank Orsino. After selling his script to Golden Gate, Orsino made a deal with Paramount for his movie scenario on Tchaikovsky. The studio planned for him to collaborate with Ayn Rand on the finished screenplay.[107] Orsino – still using the pen name of Walter Abbott – went on to write other scenarios, as well as to form a production company in California.[108]

Viewing the film today reveals its many strengths, including the use of color. By October 1946, William Crespinel of Cinecolor had adopted a policy that imposed a budget minimum on producers who wanted to use his system. He told the industry press:

> We find that it is financially impossible for the producer of a low-budget feature to provide the proper lighting, makeup, and color harmony, with the result that Cinecolor has often been shown to disadvantage.[109]

But Crespinel's complaints would surely have had no roots in *Scared to Death*, which not only employed Cinecolor's suggested makeup styles, but also featured art direction that clearly planned for the use of color.

Green lampshades and bedspreads, blue and red dresses, and a red robe create a wonderful visual interplay with walls that in some rooms were painted red or blue and walls in others that featured patterned paper. Indeed, Harry Reif's art direction becomes one of the film's greatest joys, and not just due to the colorful props. Rooms like the parlor are far more elaborately dressed than sets in most low-budget horror films of the forties.

Some modern critics complain that the film's narrative is incoherent, but that is hardly the case. Overall, *Scared to Death* operates like an old dark house film, with the additional feature that the home — which is replete with secret panels, and which was once used as an insane asylum — doubles as a physician's office. And Laura Van Ee's life (as portrayed by Molly Lamont) is under constant threat until she is literally scared to death.

Within the old house are a number of persons who might be responsible for her death, including her husband Ward Van Ee (whom she refuses to divorce), his

Here again a publicity still for *Scared to Death* attempts to pose Lugosi as more menacing than he is in the completed film. In this case, the frightened woman is character Jane Cornell (Joyce Compton). (Courtesy of Buddy Barnett)

father, Dr. Van Ee (played by George Zucco), the magician and hypnotist Professor Leonide (played by Lugosi, who wears a vampire cape), and Leonide's faithful dwarf Indigo (Angelo Rossitto).

The bulk of the onscreen action takes place over the course of a few days, with the narrative set entirely at the Van Ee home, save for opening and closing sequences (and a few brief other shots) that take place at a morgue. As a result, the viewer – much like the characters in *Scared to Death*, as well as in films like *The Cat and the Canary* (1927) and *The Old Dark House* (1932) – is trapped inside the old home. The only difference is that Cabanne does not produce high contrast lighting and dark shadows, presumably due to the film's use of color. The house is not "dark," but rather deceptively bright, much like the Overlook Hotel in Kubrick's *The Shining* (1980).

Scared to Death offers a degree of comic relief in the form of house detective Bill Raymond (Nat Pendleton), who is madly in love with the domestic servant Lilybeth (Gladys Blake). Their interplay harkens back to the dawn of cinema, in which some of the earliest fictional films depicted brief, humorous romances between cops and maids. And it provides the kind of comic relief on which horror films of the thirties and forties often relied.

Lugosi's role of Leonide clearly invokes Dracula, given that he wears a cape, but the character also serves a purpose similar to a number of Lugosi's other film characters, including Tarneverro in *The Black Camel* (1931), Degar in *Night of Terror* (1933), and Peters in *The Gorilla* (1939): Leonide is a red herring, meant to keep the audience from guessing the identity of the real culprit.

And yet, Lugosi treats the role with great respect. He seems to relish many of his lines, offering an appropriately theatrical performance in the best sense of that description. After all, Leonide even turns to the camera at one point to offer a poetic soliloquy: "Laurette. Laurette. I'll make a bet. The man in green will get you yet!"

All of these strange goings-on take place during what is in fact a flashback, something that we learn

This publicity still attempts to depict the conclusion of *Scared to Death*, in which the audience learns the bizarre past of Laura Van Ee/Laurette La Valle (Molly Lamont). (Courtesy of Buddy Barnett)

in the opening scene. Laura Van Ee rests on the slab in the morgue, her voice narrating the story from beyond the grave, a device that Billy Wilder used to great effect a few years later in *Sunset Blvd.* (1950, aka *Sunset Boulevard*). And she is a particularly unreliable narrator, conveying information through the film's scenes that lead us down false paths in our effort to learn who caused her death.

Periodically we see her on the slab and hear her voice taking us into yet another film sequence, into yet another of her memories. Punctuated by Carl Hoefle's memorable score, these shots remind us that the lead female character is dead, and – thanks to an *in media res* structure – was dead even before the film started. Here again *Scared to Death* seems ahead of its time, as the death of a lead female character in a horror movie was something quite unusual in the 1940s, but it would later become a plot device explored in films like Hitchcock's *Psycho* (1960) and Moxey's *The City of the Dead* (1960, aka *Horror Hotel*).

At *Scared to Death*'s conclusion, we finally learn who scared Laura Van Ee to death, as we learn that she is in fact Laurette La Valle, a French dancer who at some point immigrated to America. While in occupied France, she denounced the character Rene – her dance partner and lover – to the Nazis. They sent him to a concentration camp where, coincidentally, Professor Leonide was also imprisoned.

The cruel Laurette admits that she denounced Rene simply because she hated him. Here is a key link from Orsino's film script to his earlier play *Murder on the Operating Table*, in which the woman who dies is a much-hated character. In *Scared to Death*, the police must apprehend Rene because he has committed murder. Despite the somewhat peculiar fact that he is disguised as a woman, the police easily catch him. But we need feel no sympathy for the woman dead on the slab. None at all. Unlike the typical female character in horror films of the era, Laurette deserved to die. In addition to her cruelty to Rene, she has in fact collaborated with the enemy during wartime.

Perhaps what is most curious about *Scared to Death*'s conclusion is that it is not only brief, but also somewhat vague. Laurette tells the Nazis what they want to hear, that Rene is a spy, but we learn little else. In some prints, even that information is missing, which serves to obscure matters further. We don't know why the Nazis developed an interest in Rene, any more than we know why Leonide ended up in a concentration camp. Those facts remain an unsettling mystery inside a film that explicitly references the very death camps seen in the "Nazi horror films" projected at American theatres in 1945.

A larger puzzle was the horror film itself during the period of *Scared to Death*'s production and post-production phase. The horror film and its audience were undergoing changes that were increasingly noticeable as 1946 progressed. It wasn't just that some parents complained about them, as a number of women did in Columbus, Ohio during late 1946 and early 1947.[110] No, the horror film had withstood those kinds of attacks for years.

Theatre manager reports published in *Motion Picture Herald* from 1946 suggest something else was at work. For example:

> *House of Dracula*: We say this is definitely our last horror film. There seems to be nothing gained by frightening the children away.
> – Winema Theatre, Scotia, California, May 4, 1946

> *House of Dracula*: Used this for a Saturday midnight show and this is where it belongs. Wouldn't recommend it for any other time.
> – Sparks Theatre, Cooper, Texas, May 25, 1946

> *House of Dracula*: About a year ago or so, a chiller-diller like this would be very good for our theatre, but today it is strictly [a] one-day showing and not any too good even for one day. The producers are making entirely too many chillers. Again we say when our patrons who like action, thrill, and westerns don't buy chillers it's time for a considerable curtailment of this type of picture.
> – Fountain Theatre, Terre Haute, Indiana, September 28, 1946

Such accounts suggest that the old-style of horror film featuring monsters and mad scientists were losing ground.

Even an expanded definition of horror would not serve the genre well in 1947. Surveying the upcoming season of releases in late December 1946, *Film Daily* told readers that there would definitely be "fewer psychological mysteries" on the screen the following year.[111] In short, horror film production – however one defined the word "horror" – was on the wane.

The dramatic decrease in the number of horror films produced in 1947 was only part of the story, however. By the end of 1946, the American film industry began to undergo serious changes. Trade publications noted decreased movie attendance in early 1947, a trend that continued into the summer. Lower ticket sales meant lower box-office receipts, even as ticket prices were rising. All of this came at a time of increased operational and production costs at the studios.[112] If 1946 became one of Hollywood's most successful years financially, 1947 would prove to be one of its worst.

And so Bela Lugosi was an exile from a film genre in retreat and an industry that was itself under siege.

(Endnotes)

1. Schatz, Thomas. *Boom or Bust: American Cinema in the 1940s* (Berkeley: University of California Press, 1997).
2. "Universal Profit in Year Record High $4, 565, 219." *Motion Picture Herald* 1 Feb. 1947.

3   "Mono. 44 Weeks Net Doubles to $318, 824." *Film Daily* 12 June 1946; "Monogram Had $216, 999 Profit for 26 Weeks." *Motion Picture Herald* 22 Feb. 1947.
4   "Drop Low Budget Pix from PRC's Program." *Film Daily* 26 November 1946.
5   "Balanced Films Replace 'Cycles.'" *Variety* 5 Sept. 1945.
6   "U's Madness Vice Monsters." *Variety* 11 Apr. 1945.
7   "Horror and Newsreels." *Motion Picture Herald* 12 May 1945.
8   Gallup, George. "Public Says U.S. and Germans Should See Nazi Horror Films." *Washington Post* 20 May 1945.
9   "St. Loo Blueprints Nazi Atrocity Pix for All U.S." *Variety* 13 June 1945.
10 "Horror Pictures Shock Patrons, But None Protests." *Motion Picture Herald* 12 May 1945.
11 "Tribunal Shown Nazi Horror Film." *Los Angeles Times* 27 Feb. 1946.
12 "From the Nazi Nightmare." *Dallas Morning News* 23 Aug. 1947.
13 See, for example: "*Five Fingers* All Thumbs; *Mr. D.A.* Pre-Sold by Radio." *Hollywood Reporter* 20 Dec. 1946.
14 "Horror Pix Win Heavier Adult Patronage at BO." *Hollywood Reporter* 4 Apr. 1946.
15 "*The Girl and the Devil*." *Motion Picture Herald* 26 Oct. 1946; "*Dead O' Night* Brit Sleeper; Queen Royal Burleycutie." *Motion Picture Herald* 28 June 1946; "*Frenzy*." *Film Daily* 4 Aug. 1946.
16 Johnson, Fred. "Dracula Sees Film 'Fear' as Escapism." *San Francisco Call-Bulletin* 10 Mar. 1945.
17 Siodmak, Curt. "In Defense of the Ghouls." *The Screen Writer* (Feb 1946).
18 Wechsberg, Joseph. "Horrors!" *Liberty* 24 Aug.1946.
19 "Actors Move Far." *New Orleans Times-Picayune* 22 Sept. 1946.
20 Lugosi, Bela G. "Biography." Available at http://www.lugosi.com/biography.html. Accessed 21 Dec. 2011.
21 "Actors Move Far."
22 The production file in the RKO Studio Records at the UCLA Library Special Collections supports the $2,500 a week figure, with Lugosi paid for three weeks at a total of $7,500. The same is true of a contract in the RKO legal papers, contained in a separate file not housed at UCLA. However, a budget sheet for the film at UCLA suggests Lugosi was paid a total of $4,781.25, which supports a $1,250 per week salary, with 27.5% overhead. Figures courtesy of Gregory William Mank.
23 RKO legal file for *Genius at Work*. Information courtesy of Gregory William Mank.
24 RKO production file for *Genius at Work*. Information courtesy of Gregory William Mank.
25 *Ibid*.
26 "Title Changes." *Hollywood Reporter*15 Nov. 1945.
27 RKO production file for *Genius at Work*. Information courtesy of Gregory William Mank.
28 "*Genius at Work*." *Film Daily* 5 Aug. 1946.
29 "*Black Angel* Arresting; *Genius at Work* Ordinary." *Hollywood Reporter* 1 Aug. 1946.
30 "*Genius at Work*." *Daily Variety* 1 Aug. 1946.
31 "*Genius at Work*." *Motion Picture Herald* 10 Aug. 1946.
32 "What the Picture Did for Me." *Motion Picture Herald* 8 Feb. 1947.
33 "What the Picture Did for Me." *Motion Picture Herald* 12 Apr. 1947.
34 "What the Picture Did for Me." *Motion Picture Herald* 26 Apr. 1947.
35 *Joplin Globe* (Joplin, MO) 18 Apr. 1946.
36 "Karloff Adds Scenes." *Hollywood Reporter* 16 Aug. 1946.
37 "Karloff Scores in *On Borrowed Time*." *Hollywood Reporter* 6 Nov. 1946.
38 *Hollywood Reporter* 25 Mar. 1946.
39 *Daily Variety* 23 May 1946; *Daily Variety* 7 May 1945; *Daily Variety* 10 July 1946.
40 "Confession of Dr. Alice Wynekoop Tells How Her Daughter-in-Law Rheta Met Death." *Chicago Tribune* 25 Nov. 1933.
41 "Dr. Wynekoop to Plead Not Guilty Today." *Chicago Tribune* 4 Dec. 1933.
42 "Tell of Earle's Notebook Full of Girls' Names." *Chicago Tribune* 24 Nov. 1933.
43 "Money is Motive for the Slaying, Police Theorize." *Chicago Tribune* 26 Nov. 1933.
44 Pullen, Glenn C. "Footlights and Bright Lights." *Cleveland Plain Dealer* 17 Jan. 1934.
45 "Bright Lights." *Cleveland Plain Dealer* 15 Dec. 1933.
46 Reesing, Bert J. "Star Dust Can Blind Young Hopefuls to Acting Needs." *Cleveland Plain Dealer* 31 Mar. 1958.
47 Pullen, Glenn C. "Footlights and Bright Lights." *Cleveland Plain Dealer* 26 Mar. 1934; Pullen, Glenn C. "Footlights and Bright Lights." *Cleveland Plain Dealer* 20 Jan. 1934.
48 McDermott, William F. "Guild Premieres Play." *Cleveland Plain Dealer* 26 Jan. 1934.
49 "Among Cleveland Players." *Cleveland Plain Dealer* 9 June 1935.
50 Pullen, Glenn C. "Footlights and Bright Lights." *Cleveland Plain Dealer* 21 Feb. 1934.
51 "Wynekoop Home a Maze of Rooms." *Chicago Tribune* 23 Nov. 1933.
52 "Dr. G. Wynekoop Is Committed to Insane Asylum." *Chicago Tribune* 14 Dec. 1933.
53 "Jury Disagrees on Insanity of Wynekoop Kin." *Chicago Tribune* 8 Dec. 1933.
54 Pullen, Glenn C. "Frank Orsino's Old Shocker Bought for Boris Karloff." *Cleveland Plain Dealer* 5 May 1946. This article refers to Lugosi starring in the film, and so it seems the mention of Karloff's name in the title is merely a typographical error.
55 "Christy Cabanne." *Film Daily* 19 Sept. 1946.
56 *Daily Variety* 26 Mar. 1946.
57 *Daily Variety* 28 Mar. 1946.
58 It is also possible that Golden Gate was simply a little late in announcing these contracts, or that *Variety* was late in publishing news of them.
59 "50% of Pix in Color Seen by Pressburger." *Film Daily* 29 Mar. 1946.
60 "Technicolor Will Build to Double Plant Output." *Film Daily* 3 May 1946.

61 "Technicolor Net $436,168 in 1946; Footage Gains." *Motion Picture Herald* 10 May 1947.
62 "Good Results Seen with Nazi Agfa Color." *Film Daily* 10 Apr. 1946.
63 "Thomascolor Process for Actual Work in Fall." *Film Daily* 10 July 1946; "Thomascolor Will Grant Free Licenses for Tele." *Film Daily* 12 Aug. 1946.
64 Belton, John. "Cinecolor." *Film History* Vol. 12, No. 4 (2000).
65 *Ibid.*
66 "Cinecolor Gets New Capital for Expansion." *Film Daily* 12 Apr. 1946.
67 "7 Cinecolor Features Readied for Market." *Hollywood Reporter* 24 May 1946.
68 "Cinecolor Doubles Output Within Last Three Months." *Film Daily* 6 June 1946.
69 *Daily Variety* 2 April 1946.
70 *Ibid.*
71 Pullen, "Frank Orsino's Old Shocker Bought for Boris Karloff"; "Screen Guild Releasing 28 in '46, including 12 Hoppies." *Hollywood Reporter* 14 May 1946.
72 Handsaker, Gene. "In Hollywood." *Ironwood Daily Globe* (Ironwood, MI) 23 May 1946.
73 *Ibid.*
74 *Ibid.*
75 Weaver, Tom. Email to Gary D. Rhodes. 19 Feb. 2012.
76 *Scared to Death* pressbook. Screen Guild Productions, 1947.
77 *Ibid.*
78 *Variety* 3 April 1946.
79 "Screen Guild Releasing 28 in '46, including 12 Hoppies."
80 "Screen Guild Prods. Goes on National Basis." *Film Daily* 11 Feb. 1946.
81 *Variety* 2 Oct. 1946.
82 "Screen Guild Prods. Goes on National Basis."
83 "Screen Guild Releasing 28 in '46, including 12 Hoppies."
84 "Screen Guild's Board Meets in Chi. Today." *Film Daily* 9 May 1946.
85 "Lugosi to do P. A. Tour." *Hollywood Reporter* 19 July 1946.
86 Advertisement. *The 1946-47 Motion Picture Almanac*. Ed. by Terry Ramsaye. (New York: Quigley Publications, 1947); Advertisement. *Motion Picture Herald* 15 June 1946; Advertisement. *Daily Variety* 30 June 1946.
87 "Screen Guild Sets Seven to Fill 1946's Releases." *Film Daily* 23 July 1946.
88 *Daily Variety* 13 Aug. 1946.
89 "*Scared to Death*." *Film Daily* 19 Sept. 1946.
90 *Scared to Death* pressbook, 1947.
91 *Variety* 2 Oct. 1946.
92 *Daily Variety* 15 Nov. 1946, p. 6.
93 "Screen Guild Ahead of Sked on Eight Films." *Hollywood Reporter* 15 Nov. 1946.
94 "Screen Art to Produce 12 Pix for Screen Guild." *Film Daily* 6 Sept. 1946; "Screen Guild in Deal with Fortune Films." *Motion Picture Herald* 22 Feb. 1947.
95 "Screen Guild Conclave in Chicago on Oct. 11." *Film Daily* 3 Sept. 1946.
96 *Cape Girardeau Southeast Missourian* (Cape Girardeau, MO) 12 May 1947.
97 "Dr. Alice Wynekoop, Killer of Son's Wife, to be Freed Dec. 28." *Chicago Tribune* 1 Nov. 1947.
98 *Scared to Death* pressbook.
99 *Ibid.*
100 *Ibid.*
101 "*Scared to Death*." *Motion Picture Herald* 21 June 1947.
102 "*Scared to Death*." *Variety* 16 July 1947.
103 "Walter Winchell on Broadway." *Nevada State Journal* (Reno, NV) 22 June 1947.
104 *Cleveland Plain Dealer* 7 July 1947.
105 "Screen Guild." *Motion Picture Herald* 5 July 1947.
106 *Daily Variety* 15 July 1947.
107 Pullen, Glenn C. "Frank Orsino, Clevelander, Writes Film Biography of Tschaikovsky [sic] for Paramount." *Cleveland Plain Dealer* 29 Oct. 1946.
108 Pullen, Glenn C. "Derwent Prize Opens Door to Films for Ray Walston, Former Play House Actor." *Cleveland Plain Dealer* 17 May 1949.
109 "Cinecolor Thumbs Low-Budget Films." *Hollywood Reporter* 1 Oct. 1946.
110 "Hit Murder Pictures with Other Films." *Motion Picture Herald* 8 Feb. 1947.
111 "Fewer Psychological Mysteries on Screen in '47." *Film Daily* 26 Dec. 1946.
112 Schatz, *Boom or Bust: American Cinema in the 1940s*.

Lugosi in the late forties.

Chapter 3

FOR PETE'S SAKE

A total of 487 features were released in the United States in 1947, some 369 of which were produced domestically.[1] Lugosi appeared in only one of them, *Scared to Death*, and it had been shot the previous year. And so 1947 became something unique in Lugosi's American film career. After all, he had worked on a film set every single year since at least 1928, without exception.

Even in the late thirties, during the bleakest period of his horror film career, Lugosi appeared in the serial *SOS Coast Guard* (1937) and the feature film *Son of Frankenstein* (1939, which went into production in 1938). In every one of the nineteen years since 1928, there was always work on a film set, even if just for a few days.

Living in exile was nothing new to Bela Lugosi. He had to flee Hungary, the country of his birth, following a revolution in 1919 that left him, as he would later say, "on the wrong side." He first settled in Vienna, but quickly moved on to Berlin. All the while, the actor-in-exile had his sights firmly set on the United States, where he landed in 1921.

In a way, Lugosi's life in America was one of a cultural outsider. Though far from Hungary, his homeland dominated his personal life. Most of his friends were Hungarian expatriates. The food he ate, the sports he watched, and the causes he adopted were usually Hungarian. Such is the life of many an immigrant.

That said, Lugosi very definitely tried to forge a career that integrated him into the fabric of America. After staging some Hungarian-language performances in the early twenties, Lugosi eschewed ethnic theatre and struggled to find work in English-language plays. Broadway and the American cinema: once Lugosi began to conquer those, he never returned to Hungarian-language plays any more than he ever returned to Hungary.

But integration into the Hollywood film industry had been followed by disintegration. Lugosi had no film career in 1947. Instead of rapidly fleeing for his life to another country, he sat and watched his second exile happen slowly, sometimes even living within mere miles of the studios that no longer hired him. Aside from changing his management and hounding his friends and journalists, Lugosi could do little more than feed on dreams.

In 1946, Jimmie Fidler had conveyed Lugosi's desire to producers in print: cast him in non-horror film roles. Only one producer responded with a real project, and he wasn't making a movie. On February 8, 1947, Hedda Hopper – another columnist sympathetic to Lugosi – announced that Hunt Stromberg, Jr. had signed Lugosi for a new play written by Hugh Evans, *Three Indelicate Ladies*.[2]

Horror star Boris Karloff was also considered for an important role in *Three Indelicate Ladies* (1947). In this photograph, taken in San Francisco in ca. 1939, Karloff and Lugosi playfully intend to chop off Mischa Auer's head while John Sutton watches. (Courtesy of the Department of Special Collections, Davidson Library, University of California, Santa Barbara)

In it, Lugosi would portray a suave underworld figure with a somewhat convoluted background: Francis O'Rourke, an Irishman born in Finland. Lugosi had played gangsters and tough guys a few times onscreen, notably in *Postal Inspector* (1936), *SOS Coast Guard* (1937), *Black Friday* (1940), and *The Saint's Double Trouble* (1940), but O'Rourke was different than any of those, as was *Three Indelicate Ladies*. Here was a fresh kind of role in a witty and urbane comedy. Its ingredients included the crime and mystery genres, but it represented a concerted effort towards something different, something unique. Something, in other words, that Lugosi had long desired.

The story of *Three Indelicate Ladies* has its title characters – Kelly, Roberts, and Morgan – working for an eccentric old detective who has recently passed away. His bizarre collection features an array of memorabilia from famous murder cases, including an electric chair.[3] Now broke and in desperate need of work, the trio run an advertisement soliciting clients and end up being mistaken for detectives. A murder case leads them into contact with the "nutty killer" Francis O'Rourke, who quickly falls for the red-headed Morgan.[4] As *Variety* would later explain, the role gave Lugosi "no opportunity to capitalize on the horror angle which established him as a heavy."[5]

Curiously, in January 1947, the *New York Times* claimed that Stromberg was trying to hire Boris Karloff for a "major role" in *Three Indelicate Ladies* and that negotiations with the star were ongoing.[6] Presumably Stromberg wanted him to portray Francis O'Rourke, but Karloff didn't sign. In other words, Lugosi's opportunity for work and a new chance at Broadway seems to have come thanks to Karloff declining the role.

Stromberg – well-known in theater circles for such hits as *The Red Mill* and *The Front Page* – had purchased Hugh Evans' script for *Three Indelicate Ladies* in September 1946.[7] The producer spent months raising $45,000 in capital, $20,000 of which came out of his own pocket. Three of Stromberg's friends from Winoma, Kansas invested the rest of the money.[8]

Jed Harris, who was Stromberg's first choice as director, had earlier held the script option. At that time, it was titled *For Pete's Sake*.[9] Stromberg later said that he had kept his eye on the script for months "because Jed Harris' agent, who is also my agent, showed it to me just after Harris acquired it, and when I heard that he had given up the rights, I took it over at once."[10]

Stromberg brought in Thomas Spengler to be one of the associate producers. He also intended to begin casting in November 1946 after returning from a trip to Los Angeles in

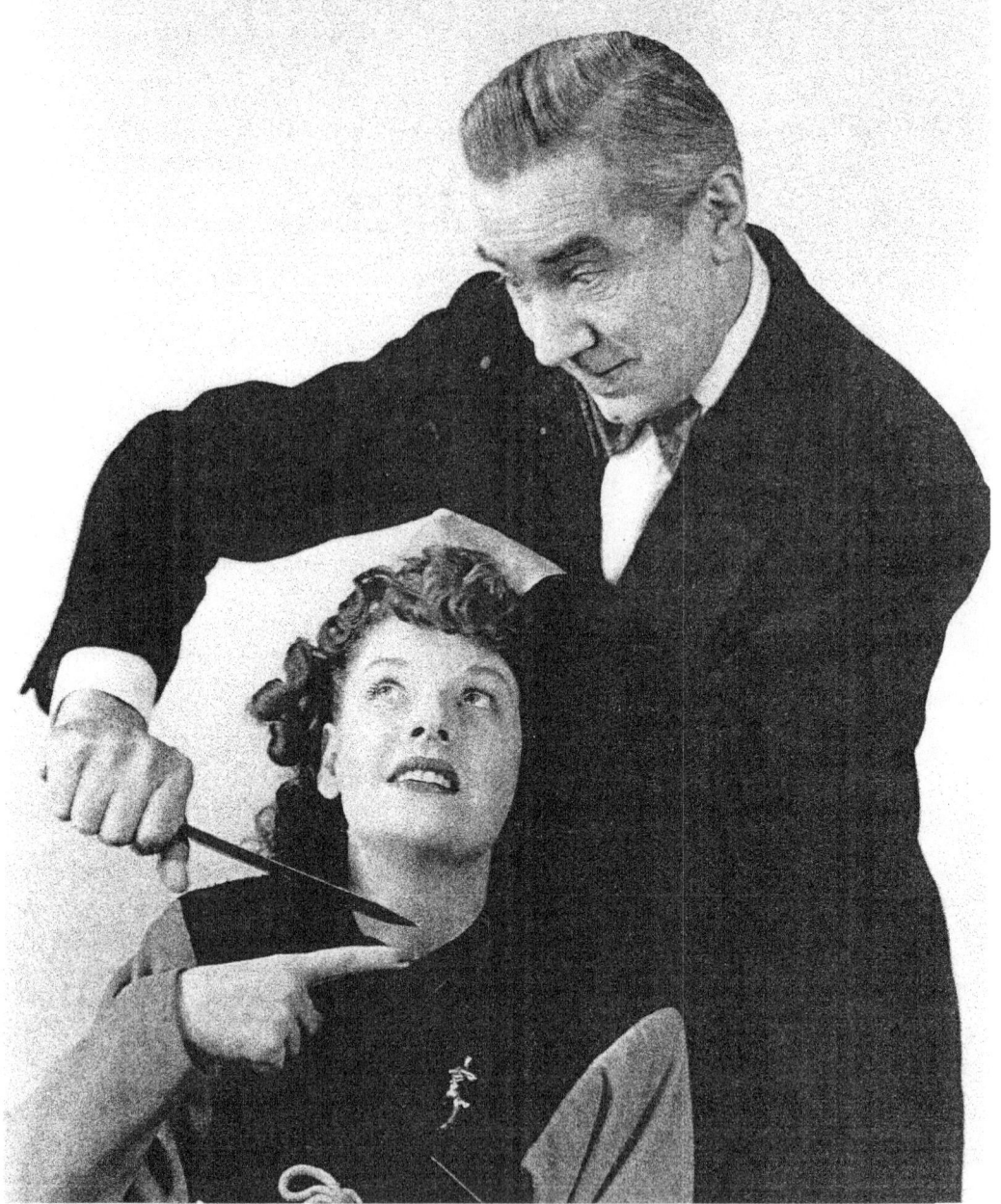

A publicity portrait for *Three Indelicate Ladies* (1947).

October, during which he hoped to secure a film deal.[11] Even before *Three Indelicate Ladies* had been staged, Stromberg was angling to transform it into a motion picture.

By early November, Stromberg announced that rehearsals for *Three Indelicate Ladies* would begin that very same month. Actors Jack Arnold, Thomas Walsh and Don Murphy were named, but of that group only Arnold would go on to appear in the play.[12] Stromberg also claimed H. C. Potter would direct the play, with an opening date in New York pushed forward to February of 1947.[13] The revised schedule meant that rehearsals would begin by the end of December 1946.[14]

But things changed yet again. In mid-January of 1947, Jed Harris became the director and planned rehearsals for later that same month.[15] An additional producer, Jack Cassidy, was added to the staff.[16] The industry press also claimed that Gloria McGhee, Jayn Fortner, and Sam Levene – one of the several individuals who had been offered the director's chair – would costar in the cast. Of that group, only Fortner would appear in the play.[17]

From the *New Haven Register* of April 6, 1947.

In addition to Lugosi, Stromberg signed Elaine Stritch and Ann Thomas as two of the "three indelicate ladies," with Fortner playing the third. Among those in supporting roles were Alexander Clark, Katherine Squire, Ray Walston, and Robert Schuler. The final contracts not only solidified the cast, but also the director, who turned out to be not H. C. Potter or Jed Harris, but instead Jesse Royce Landis. Like many of the others, Landis joined the play in February 1947. The actress-turned-director was in Cuba when she accepted Stromberg's offer and immediately flew to New York.

After signing his contract in early February, Lugosi left California for New York City. By February 21, the Lugosis arrived in Manhattan and stayed at the Gotham Hotel, which was then housing such notables as Martha Vickers and Gale Storm.[18] Not only did his arrival in New York mean a chance for Broadway, it also meant a possible return to the film industry, as Stromberg still had his eyes on a film version of the play.

In a second attempt to strike a movie deal, Stromberg returned to Los Angeles near the beginning of March. But he once again journeyed back to New York without success. To the press, he announced that the play would open on Broadway in March 1947, but that was at best wishful thinking.[19]

Rehearsals did not get underway until at least March 10, possibly even as late March 17 if one source is to be believed.[20] Years later, Ray Walston recalled, "during the rehearsals for *Three Indelicate Ladies*, one afternoon [Lugosi] was lying down on a bench, stretched out with his eyes closed. One of us in the group, I don't know which one it was, said 'Quick! Quick! Get a stake!'"[21]

Opening night finally came on April 10, 1927 at the Schubert Theatre in New Haven, Connecticut. Nearly two decades earlier, Lugosi had appeared at the same venue in *Dracula–The Vampire Play*, shortly before it moved to Broadway. All those years later, he was back at the same theatre, hoping yet again to appear on the Great White Way, but this time without the vampire along for the ride.

In advance of the opening, an article in the *Hartford Courant* noted that very fact:

> One of the great horror men of the films, Bela Lugosi, will change his medium when he takes to the stage as the star of *Three Indelicate Ladies*, a mystery-comedy which opens a 3-day engagement. ... the Hollywood

Published in the *New Haven Journal-Courier* on April 8, 1947.

Gary D. Rhodes | Bill Kaffenberger

Lugosi pictured here with all three of the "indelicate ladies."

star will not yield his unsavory reputation in the new play, although author Hugh Evans has refrained from making this his usual film-ogre self.[22]

In a subsequent article, the newspaper promised that Lugosi's character "manages to make things hum for the feminine agents of the law as bodies pop out of closets, precious jewelry is whisked out of thin air, and a bewildered district attorney wonders what goes on with his lady love."[23]

Recalling the early days of the play, cast member Stratton Walling said, "Bela was tremendous. His wife Lillian was there with him. I remember her wearing a gold bat on her dress. And they were having fun with the play and the cast, people like Elaine Stritch and Ray Walston. The mood changed a bit when the bad reviews came, and the writer even stormed out yelling."[24]

Sadly, opening night did not go particularly well, at least in the eyes of most critics. A review in *Daily Variety* admitted that the play's staging was "adequate insofar as script limitations permit" and that, "with added writing, script can emerge as a fair supporting film product." That said, the trade proceeded to lambast it for being "a routine whodunit, with not enough of any one element – comedy, mystery or menace – to sustain interest beyond a moderate stage."[25] A couple of days later, the weekly edition of *Variety* published a different review, with an even harsher assessment: "Hinterland ballyhoo on tryout of [*Three Indelicate Ladies*] has it listed as 'headed for Broadway.' For the time being, it might be well for it to slip quietly off the train at 125th and let it go at that."[26]

The Billboard was not much kinder. While admitting that Hugh Evans had written "a very funny play", reviewer Sidney Golly felt it needed "a lot of sprucing up" before it would be ready for Broadway.[27] Despite "many hilarious scenes," he noticed that first night viewers "found themselves stifling yawns between the guffaws."²⁸ As a result, Golly advised producers to rewrite Act I and to give Act III a new ending. But that wasn't all. In Golly's mind, Landis had "not done a particularly distinguished job of directing. The pacing was noticeably bad...."²⁹

Along with believing that Stritch and Fortner played their roles too broadly, Golly was left cold by Lugosi's performance, believing him to be "almost criminally miscast." To explain what he meant, Golly added "the cigar chewing, rough and tumble guy is not up Bela's alley, so the audience never once was able to give the character the response that a William Bendix would have received."³⁰ Such notices must have been particularly stinging to Lugosi, who was so eager to be freed from typecasting.

And so New Haven hardly paved the way to an eventual Broadway run. *Variety* noted that "at $3 (tax incl) top, four-performance gross slipped below estimated $3,000." The verdict: *Three Indelicate Ladies* in New Haven was "weak."³¹ Here seemed to be a repeat of the path that *No Traveler Returns* had taken.

By the time *Three Indelicate Ladies* reached its next destination, various alterations had been made to the script, either by Stromberg, Landis, Evans or some combination thereof. One of the most noticeable was Lugosi's character, whose name changed to "Turk the Jerk," thus erasing any hint of an Irish background. It was as if Golly's recommendations had become the template for the revisions.

Recalling the play and some of its troubles years later, Elaine Stritch said:

> The whole thing was very funny, and ridiculous in a way. The stage manager was Jack Cassidy, and I was in love with Jack Cassidy, and so that was a funny thing.
>
> Rewrites were happening quite a bit, and it was the night before we opened in Boston that they changed Lugosi's character name, which was Irish, and it was mentioned about 25 times in the play. Of course that Irish name for him was not to be believed. It was too funny to believe.³²

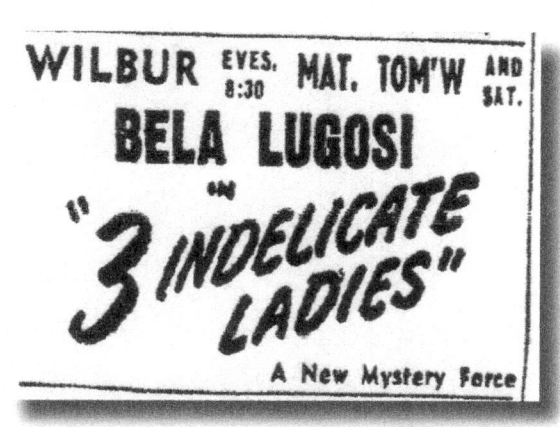

From the *Christian Science Monitor* of April 15, 1947.

Stritch added, "I loved Lugosi. He was a darling man, and he was a fine actor, and that play meant so much to him."

The play opened at Boston's Wilbur Theatre on April 14, 1947, with newspaper articles highlighting the fact that Lugosi's role was "quite different than those he has previously portrayed."³³ The following day, Elinor Hughes of the *Boston Herald*, told her readers, "I'll admit that I laughed frequently and so did the audience."³⁴

Edwin F. Melvin of the *Christian Science Monitor* offered a somewhat positive view of Lugosi and company, praising the actors while questioning the quality of the plot:

> The players were working hard at the Wilbur last evening, but Hugh Evans' new farce-melodrama... didn't seem to have the material to repay the effort. It's a well meaning enough attempt at light, warm-weather entertainment of the wacky sort. It needs more finesse, however, to attain its object.³⁵

In short, Melvin believed that the "laughter that is stirred seems to be generated more by the players than the play."

Cyrus Durgin at the *Boston Globe* was even more positive, claiming that the plot was "funny in

Another publicity portrait for *Three Indelicate Ladies*.

spots, suspenseful in others, but not designed for serious or sophisticated tastes. But if you like amiable corn mixed with the excitements of the whodunit, [this] may give you a relaxing evening at the theater."[36] He also had kind words for Landis, claiming her "flair for direction" helped to "sustain the purpose of kidding both farce and thrillers."

As for Lugosi, the critics were kinder than those who saw the show in New Haven. The *Boston Herald* said his appearance was a "pleasantly light touch."[37] The *Boston Traveler* called his "hardboiled" character "likeable" since Lugosi endowed him with a sense of "decency."[38] And the *Boston Globe* told readers that Lugosi was "both amusing and chilling as a crook who goes honest because he falls in love with Morgan (Ann Thomas)."[39]

Perhaps the new round of critical reviews rekindled everyone's hopes for a Broadway run. At any rate, Stratton Walling recalled that the cast was happy in Boston:

> In particular, I remember that in one scene of the play, someone punched their fist through Lugosi's hat. They went through this in rehearsals and then performances, so the busted hats started piling up. And in Boston, we saw this guy, we never knew who he was, who took out the busted Lugosi hats and went away. This happened more than once.
>
> Eventually we learned that it was a burlesque comic, a friend of an actor in the play named Joey Faye. Faye himself had done some burlesque I think. Anyway, after we learned this, Faye arranged for us all to go down to [The Casino] burlesque club where the hats were being used in a comedian's act.
>
> Lugosi was there, Ray Walston, and a few of us. And that was when the comedian got Lugosi to come up onto the stage. The audience wasn't told who he was, and so they may not have even known. But the comedian made him the butt of a few jokes, of course, because he was a comedian. And then, wouldn't you know it, he punched his fist right through Lugosi's hat!
>
> Lugosi of course was a very nice guy, and he took all of this in good humor. He was really enjoying himself the whole time of the play, I think.[40]

The Billboard covered Lugosi and Faye's burlesque show appearance, claiming that the duo "invaded the stage of The Casino during the Friday midnighter and gave an impromptu interpretation of the Fluegel Street bit [aka, the "Susquehanna Hat Company" or "Slowly I Turned, Step by Step, Bit by Bit" routine]."[41]

Lugosi received more publicity when Boston journalist Marjorie Adams interviewed him over dinner at the Ritz. As Lugosi enjoyed his order of "double lamb chops," he talked of many things, including how much his son – still in military school in California – missed his parents. Here was one of the problems of being on the road, so far from home. Adams commented on how the Lugosis spoke about their son with great affection, just as they did to one another. "Pop," Lillian called Lugosi, with him referring to her as "Lil."[42]

Adams also noticed that Lugosi still hesitated on "certain American words and sometimes fails to understand a modern slang phrase," but she had no trouble in understanding that he was appreciative of *Three Indelicate Ladies*, both for being cast in a "likeable role" and for the chance at employment. In her article, Adams wrote:

> Asked why no pictures of the shocking character are being made right now, Lugosi said it was because neither he nor Boris [Karloff] are under contract and, due to labor troubles, the film companies have cut down on the number of productions and are using their contract players to save money.[43]

And so Lugosi was in Boston, not Hollywood, and starring in a play that still had problems. Thankfully, Boston received Lugosi with open arms. Even before opening night, Lugosi attended

From the program for the play's run in Boston.

WILBUR THEATRE
DIRECTION — MESSRS. LEE AND J. J. SHUBERT

FIRE NOTICE: The exit indicated by a red light and sign nearest to the seat you occupy is the shortest route to the street. In the event of fire please do not run — WALK TO THAT EXIT.
Russell S. Codman, Jr., Fire Commissioner

SMOKING IS PROHIBITED IN ANY PART OF THIS THEATRE
Thoughtless persons annoy patrons and distract actors and endanger the safety of others by lighting matches during the performances and intermissions. This violates a city ordinance and renders the offender liable to a summons from the fireman on duty.

PLAYTIME PUBLICATIONS • 18 Tremont Street • Boston 8, Mass.
Edward S. Dangel, Publisher   Bowdoin 7825

Week beginning Monday, April 14, 1947   Matinees Wednesday and Saturday

HUNT STROMBERG, JR. and THOMAS SPENGLER
(In Association with IRVING COOPER)
present

BELA LUGOSI
in
"3 INDELICATE LADIES"
by HUGH EVANS
with

| Joey | Stratton | Ray |
| FAYE | WALLING | WALSTON |

and

| Ann | Jayn | Elaine |
| THOMAS | FORTNER | STRITCH |

Directed by
JESSIE ROYCE LANDIS

Setting and Lighting by
STEWART CHANEY

Gowns by Robert Lanza
Production Associate, Thomas Elwell

---

the "New England Modern Homes Show" along with Massachusetts Governor Bradford and Boston Mayor Curley. He did not perform, but instead watched some of the daily entertainment that included Emir the Wonder Dog, two orchestras, and a fashion show.[44] Then, in an effort to garner more local publicity for *Three Indelicate Ladies*, Hunt Stromberg, Jr. arranged a cast luncheon at Dinty Moore's Restaraunt on April 14. When Stromberg developed a case of the flu, co-producer Tom Spengler took the reins as a substitute host.[45] Lugosi attended, but he and some of the other cast members left early in order to participate in a Red Cross Show elsewhere in Boston.

A week later, the press announced that Lugosi would present a lecture on abnormal psychology to students at Boston University's College of Practical Arts and Letters. The *Boston Herald* told readers that Lugosi had "made a study of criminology and [would] impart some of his observations to B.U.'s psychology students."[46] University publications of the period make absolutely no reference to the event, which may well have been cancelled.[47] And the reason was likely the play, or – more specifically – what happened to the play.

Three Indelicate Ladies, originally scheduled to stay in Boston through April 27, 1947, ended prematurely on April 19, only a couple of days after Lugosi and the others had enjoyed themselves at The Casino. The press soon noted that, "Bela Lugosi and *Three Indelicate Ladies* will not try a Manhattan opening. After a Boston try-out, the show is closing for repairs."[48]

Elaine Stritch recalled the closing, noting how odd it was that the play closed on the day of a matinee performance. "It ended. And Lugosi wasn't happy about it. Of course. None of us were. But Lugosi and Joey Faye gave a party the night we closed."[49]

And so, despite Stromberg's hopes, *Three Indelicate Ladies* never reopened. There would be no film version, let alone a subsequent stage incarnation. By mid-May 1947, the *Oakland Tribune* wrote:

> Bela Lugosi's desire to get back on Broadway has come a cropper. *Three Indelicate Ladies* was closed before the New York engagement. That puts Boris Karloff at least one up on his horror colleague. Karloff, you'll recall, had quite a run for himself in *Arsenic and Old Lace*.[50]

Lugosi's feelings towards Karloff were likely complicated, evolving over the years and perhaps capable of changing within the course of a single day. But no one enjoys being forced into a rivalry, particularly one on public display in the Southern California press, the same region in which Lugosi could no longer get film roles.

During his Boston interview, Lugosi had told journalist Marjorie Adams that Hunt Stromberg Jr. had "led him out of the darkness and put him into a likeable role."[51] But within just ten weeks of signing his contract, the stage lights had to be dimmed so that the theatre could go dark.

(Endnotes)

1. "487 Feature Releases in 1947." *Film Daily* 12 Mar. 1948.
2. Hopper, Hedda. "Looking at Hollywood." *Los Angeles Times* 8 Feb. 1947.
3. "Stromberg Plans 3d Stage Offering, Co-Producer of Two Hits Will Present *Three Indelicate Ladies* in the Winter." *New York Times* 21 Sept. 1946.
4. "*3 Indelicate Ladies*." *Variety* 16 Apr. 1947.
5. *Ibid.*
6. Calta, Louis. "Jed Harris To Do Comedy By Evans, He Will Direct *Three Indelicate Ladies* – Boris Karloff is Sought for Major Role." *New York Times* 14 Jan. 1947.
7. "Stromberg Plans 3d Stage Offering."
8. "Parish Play Ends Its Run Tomorrow." *New York Times* 18 Apr. 1947.
9. *Ibid.*
10. "Hunt Stromberg, Jr. Has New Play in Boston." *Boston Herald* 14 Apr. 1947.
11. "Stromberg Plans 3d Stage Offering."
12. Calta, Louis. "Gielgud Tour Here Set For February, British Actor Will Appear in 2 Plays During 16-Week Run." *New York Times* 7 Nov. 1946.
13. *Ibid.*
14. Calta, Louis. "Garrett to Leave *Mister* on Jan. 4." *New York Times* 14 Dec. 1946.
15. Calta, "Jed Harris To Do Comedy."
16. *Ibid.*
17. *Ibid.*
18. Harris, Radie. "Broadway Runaround." *Daily Variety* 21 Feb. 1947.
19. Calta, Louis. "Cornell Will Play Cleopatra In Fall, Actress and Godfrey Tearle to Co-Star in Shakespeare Work for First Time." *New York Times* 11 Mar. 1947; *New Orleans Times-Picayune* 8 Mar. 1947.
20. *New York Times* 9 Feb. 1947; *New York Times* 26 Feb. 1947.
21. Weaver, Tom. "Ray Walston." In *I Was a Monster Movie Maker* (Jefferson, NC: McFarland, 2001).
22. *Hartford Courant* 30 Mar. 1947.
23. *Hartford Courant* 6 Apr. 1947.
24. Rhodes, Gary D. Interview with Stratton Walling. 20 Aug. 2005.
25. *Daily Variety* 14 Apr. 1947.
26. Bone. "*3 Indelicate Ladies*." *Variety* 16 Apr. 1947.
27. *The Billboard* 19 Apr. 1947.
28. *Ibid.*
29. *Ibid.*
30. *Ibid.*
31. "*Three Indelicate Ladies* Weak 3G, New Haven." *Variety* 16 Apr. 1947.
32. Rhodes, Gary D. Interview with Elaine Stritch. 28 Nov. 2011.
33. "Bela Lugosi Was Not Always a Vampire." *Boston Herald* 13 Apr. 1947.
34. Hughes, Elinor. "*Three Indelicate Ladies*." *Boston Herald* 15 Apr. 1947.
35. Melvin, Edwin F. "*3 Indelicate Ladies* Starring Bela Lugosi." *Christian Science Monitor* 15 Apr. 1947.
36. Durgin, Cyrus. "*Three Indelicate Ladies*." 15 April 1947.
37. Hughes, "*Three Indelicate Ladies*."
38. Eager, Helen. "Bela Lugosi Comes to Aid of 3 Indelicate Ladies." *Boston Traveler* 15 Apr. 1947.
39. Durgin, "*Three Indelicate Ladies*."
40. Rhodes, interview with Walling.
41. "Burlesque by Uno." *The Billboard* 3 May 1947.
42. Adams, Marjorie. "Bela Lugosi Glad of Respite from Horror-Inspiring Roles." *Boston Globe* 17 Apr. 1947.
43. *Ibid.*
44. Smith, Everett M. "Governor and Mayor Are Due To Visit Modern Homes Show." *Christian Science Monitor* 10 Apr. 10, 1947.
45. *Boston Globe* 15 April 1947.
46. "Lugosi in Boston University Talk." *Boston Herald* 17 Apr. 1947.
47. The *Boston University News* makes no mention of the Lugosi lecture, nor do volumes of the *Bostonia* for this time period.
48. Soanes, Wood. "Curtain Calls." *Oakland Tribune* 28 Apr. 1947.
49. Rhodes, interview with Stritch.
50. *Oakland Tribune* 14 May 1947.
51. "Bela Lugosi Glad of Respite."

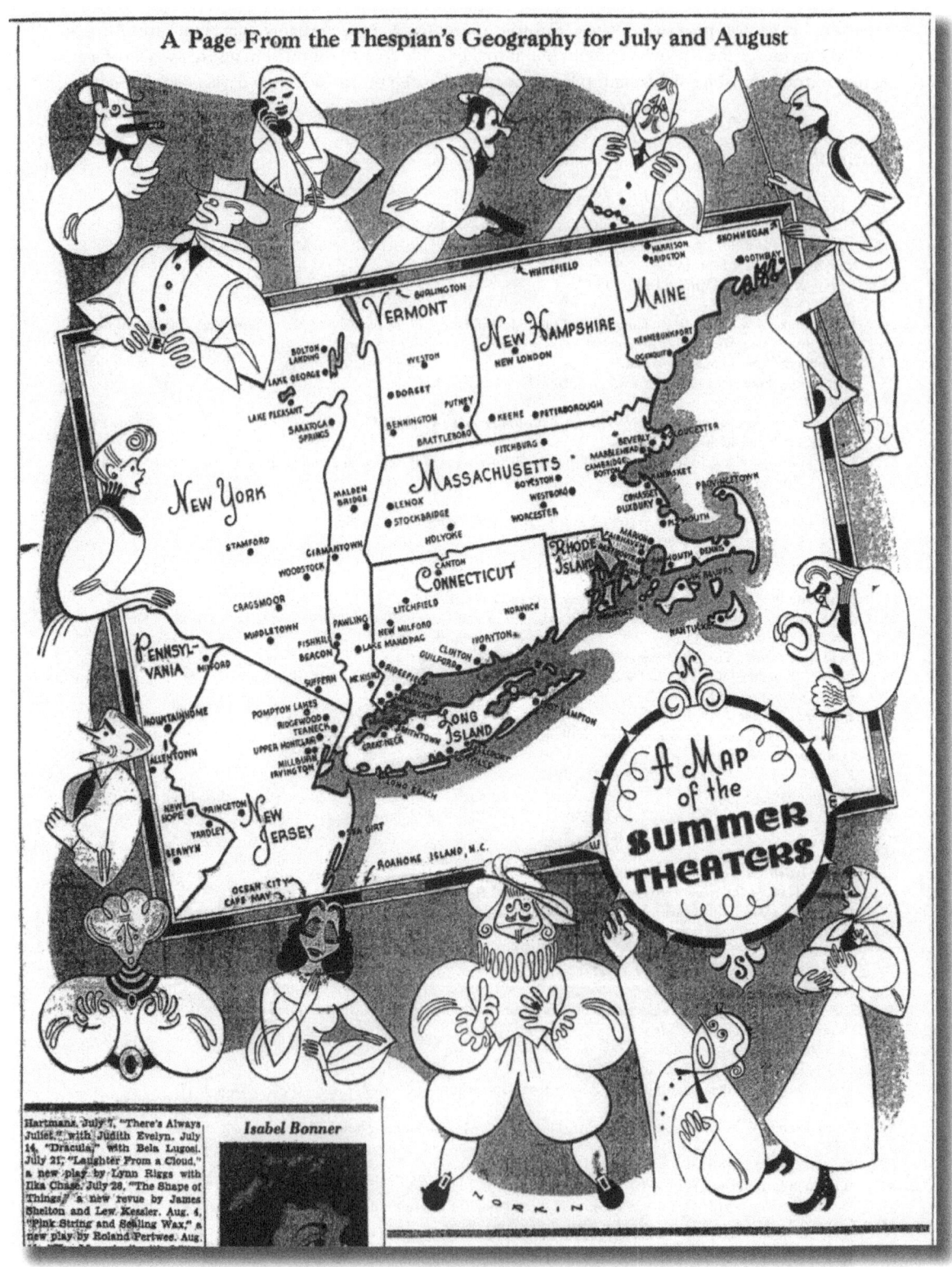

A newspaper artist's vision of the "straw hat" circuit of 1947.

Chapter 4
TWO STRAW HATS

On an autumn morning in 1947, Jack O'Brian searched for an appropriate topic for his Associated Press column that covered all things Broadway. He understood the theatre and, for that matter, the cinema. Whatever the subject, his columns regularly had a real impact on the entertainment industry. As the *New York Times* once claimed, his frequent negative opinions on famous persons "landed like bombshells."[1]

O'Brian knew the latest Broadway season like the back of his hand, and he was also well versed on summer theatre productions. However, for his latest column, he instead chose to write about an event that happened not at a theatre, but at Toots Shor's earlier that same year.[2] A New York landmark, Shor's restaurant and lounge was famed for its large circular bar and its even larger-than-life patrons, which included Frank Sinatra, Orson Welles, Marilyn Monroe, Ernest Hemingway, and – perhaps most commonly – a vast array of sports figures ranging from boxers and jockeys to baseball players like Mickey Mantle and Yogi Berra.

But on the night that O'Brian recalled in his column, an older gentleman appeared in the "favorite hangout of the sports mob." He seemed out of place, particularly when he was "bending over and kissing [O'Brian's wife's] hand in the approved continental style."[3] That's when O'Brian's memories took him back to the age of sixteen and to the balcony at his hometown movie theatre: back to when he was frightened by a vampire flickering on the screen.

As O'Brian wrote, "here was this tall and handsome elderly fellow... bestowing a highly unShorlike buss on my lady's paw. And despite the strangeness of the gentleman's behavior, I was delighted to have him around … he stirred up some wonderful old memories … a fellow who had, in fact, innocently caused me a great deal of trouble with my mother … when I had played hookey [to see *Dracula* in Buffalo, New York]." Mr. O'Brian proceeded to reveal that, "the continental character was, you see, Bela Lugosi, and his gentle solicitude of the moment was highly unexpected when you think of the times he'd scared heck out of me in his various film roles."[4]

In a subsequent column, O'Brian confessed, "I never take the villainy of Boris Karloff or Bela Lugosi seriously any more … I know the Lugosi lad, and he's a big lambie pie of a continental gentleman, a hand-kisser and dog-patter who couldn't possibly perform feats of skullduggery in real life...."[5] After all, O'Brian knew that there were two Lugosis. In real life, Lugosi kissed women's hands. In the theatre, he bit their necks. And starting in 1947, Lugosi found a new home for the latter, a home that O'Brian knew all too well.

Summer stock, or, as it would become fondly known, "the straw hat circuit." Historians debate

Gary D. Rhodes | Bill Kaffenberger   75

Lugosi as Jonathan Brewster during a wartime production of *Arsenic and Old Lace*.

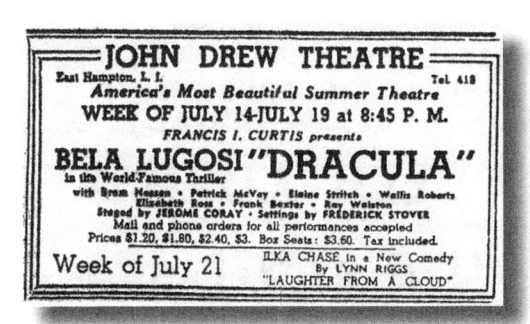

From the *New York Herald Tribune* of July 13, 1947.

whether it was actually a theatre movement that lasted from the 1920s to the 1960s, or whether it was simply a trend in which many new theatres were founded in a short space of time to take advantage of Americans who had – particularly in the post-war era – both discretionary income and leisure time during the summer. Whatever else it was, the era of summer stock represents, as scholar Martha Schmoyer LoMonaco has noted, an "American theatrical phenomenon."[6]

Summer stock theatres emerged across the United States, but most of the best-known venues were situated in the northeast. Many of them appeared in rural areas, sometimes presenting performances in school auditoriums or even converted barns. Between the months of June and September, they offered a number of different, usually well-known plays, many of them revivals of Broadway hits. They generally staged anywhere from eight to fifteen of them during a single summer, changing the bill on a weekly basis. In many cases, these plays featured famous stars in the lead role, with the rest of the cast supplemented from a stock company hired for the summer. Some of the actors were cast out of New York; others were locals. To keep costs under control, the theatres usually maintained and reused various props and backdrops as part of their "stock."

As the Director of the Cape Playhouse wrote in 1950, "Preparation starts in the spring as each player is signed. The play is read carefully, with the star in mind. ... when the star has originated the role and the pattern is more or less set, it is usually advisable to cast other parts to conform to the original interpretation."[7] Given the hectic schedules, rehearsals usually occurred before the star arrived and while the previous production was still underway. "There is no time for reading the play," the Cape Playhouse director said, adding, "There can be no experimentation at rehearsals ... for progress has to be made each hour." After all, each play represented a "production in seven days."[8]

With that general strategy already in place, summer stock theatres prepared for their 1947 season. In May of that year, Theron Bamberger, Director of the Bucks County Playhouse in New Hope, Pennsylvania, wrote that:

Program cover for the John Drew Theatre's production of *Dracula*.

Gary D. Rhodes | Bill Kaffenberger

Boston Summer Theatre
COOL—Air Conditioned—COOL
New England Mutual Hall
NOW PLAYING
★ BELA LUGOSI
"DRACULA"
For Tickets Call Ken. 2035
EVES. 8:30, $1-$3
MAT. Wed. & Sat. 2:30, 75c-$1.50 (Plus Tax)

CAMBRIDGE SUMMER THEATRE
(Brattle Hall, Harvard Sq.)
Week of July 28–Aug. 2
★ BELA LUGOSI
in the vampire thriller
"DRACULA"
For Tickets Call Tro. 1405
Mon. thru Thurs. Eve. 50c-$1.50. Fri. & Sat.
Eves. $1.00-$2.00 Sat. Mat. 50c-$1.00 Plus Tax

Above: From the *Christian Science Monitor* of July 23, 1947. Right: From the *Boston Herald* of July 27, 1947.

The summer stock season is just around the corner. The impresarios who guide the destinies of the converted barns, mills, churches, town halls and what not which house the rustic drama, have had their sleeves rolled up for weeks, selecting plays, interviewing actors, sending out publicity releases and performing the countless detailed chores which are essential in a branch of the entertainment business which is far more difficult than would appear to the naked eye.

... Now comes another year with conditions slightly changed. What, the impresarios are asking themselves and their colleagues, of 1947? They have occasional misgivings, as they speculate about the days ahead.... No longer are there hundred dollar bills in every lunch box. But in the final analysis the operators are only a little less optimistic than they were a year ago."[9]

Bamberger was quite optimistic that year, his schedule for the summer already in place.

And Bamberger enjoyed his work. He loved it, save for one thing. As he told *Theatre Arts* magazine, "You can't survive unless you are a penny pincher. I'm a fellow who likes to throw his dough around in a big way. But if you try to operate a barnyard temple of drama on that basis you wind up in bankruptcy – but quick."[10] After all, paying stars was an expensive enterprise, including in 1947, when Bamberger's plays featured such performers as Buddy Ebsen, and — in his summer stock debut — Bela Lugosi.

Lugosi's offer from Bamberger was certainly not the first he had received. In the spring of 1941, Chamberlain Brown approached the actor with the offer of a summer stock contract. He and his brother Lyman had long been friends with Lugosi; both of them also sometimes acted as Lugosi's theatrical representatives. But in 1941, Lugosi told Chamberlain Brown no, claiming:

SPA SUMMER THEATRE
SARATOGA SPRINGS, N. Y.
JOHN HUNTINGTON presents
★ BELA LUGOSI in
"ARSENIC and OLD LACE"
with LUCIA SEGER
TUES. THROUGH SUN.
Eves. 8:45, $1.00 to $2.50 Plus Tax
Mats. 2:45 Sat. and Sun. 50c to $2.00
Ticket Reservation Taken at Van Curler Music Store
525 STATE ST.   PHONE 4-5318

> In regards to your last letter I wish to inform you that my established film salary is $2,500 a week so you can appreciate that I couldn't be interested in playing summer stock.[11]

Three years later, Chamberlain Brown once again approached Lugosi about summer stock.[12] And once again

From the *Schenectady Gazette* of August 8, 1947.

78 NO TRAVELER RETURNS | The Lost Years of Bela Lugosi

> **KENLEY**
> **Deer Lake Theatre**
> R. 122 (Orwigsburg 6-3851)
> IN PERSON
> Hollywood's Horror Star
> **BELA LUGOSI**
> in the comedy hit
> *Arsenic and Old Lace*
> with DULCY COOPER and
> VIRGINIA GILBERT
> Don't Miss This Hilarious Comedy!
> Opening Tonight at 8:30 D. S. T.
> Bus Service from Pottsville

From the *Pottsville Journal* of August 18, 1947.

Lugosi turned him down. At that point, Lugosi could say no with relative ease.

By the time Lugosi appeared at the Bucks County Playhouse in 1947, he had changed agents. Now he was with the Virginia Doak Agency, Inc., apparently persuaded by promises of various kinds of work. Her office was located in Hollywood, not very far from a range of film studios, but none of them had any real interest in Lugosi. So the answer became summer stock, with Lugosi's first appearance staged over 2,700 miles from her office.

Lugosi was certainly not alone in 1947. In the summer of that year, movie stars like Constance Bennett, Ruth Chatterton, Lucille Ball, Elissa Landi, and many others invaded the stock theatres. As one newspaper article explained, "Ten years ago Hollywood celebrities looked at stock the way a duchess looks at the coachman's daughter. 'Now,' a Broadway sage observes, 'it has become a Hippodrome for old timers.'"[13] In short, Lugosi was not the only actor affected by post-war changes in the film industry.

The same article mentioned Lugosi's name. What property would suit him in summer stock? Not *Three Indelicate Ladies*, that was for certain, particularly after its failure. No, theatre managers quickly realized that two of his old plays were perfect for summer stock. One was *Dracula*, in which Lugosi had appeared on Broadway in 1927, and then in numerous revivals in Los Angeles, San Francisco, Oakland, and elsewhere. His deep identification with the role in the theatre and on the screen meant that it was a readymade success for the straw hat circuit.

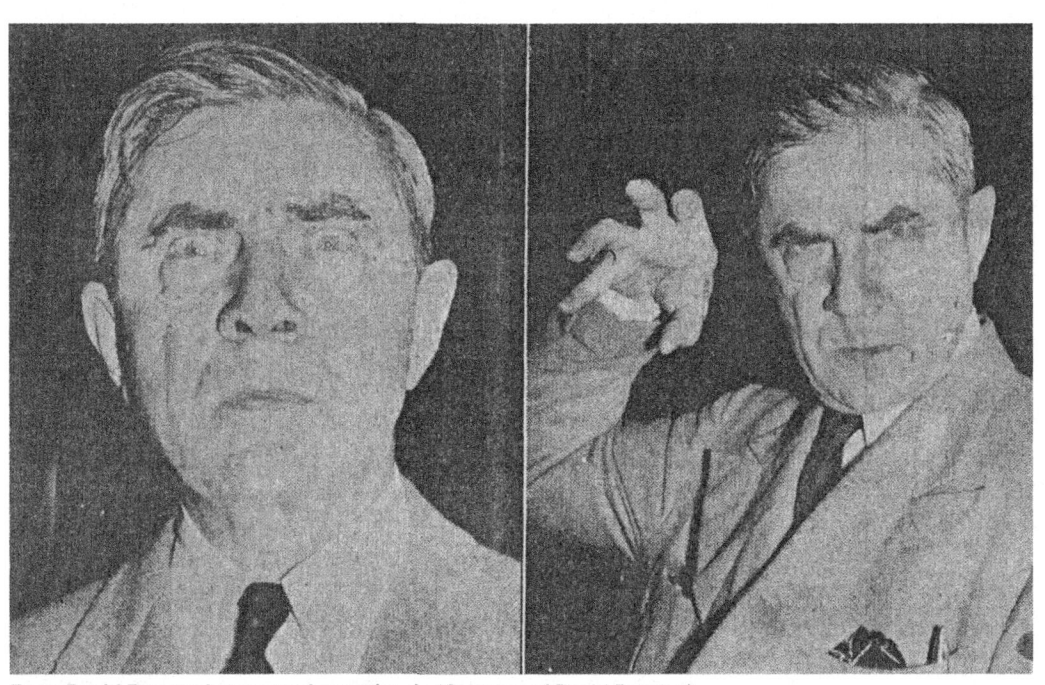

From David Durston's personal scrapbook. (Courtesy of David Durston)

From David Durston's personal scrapbook.
(Courtesy of David Durston)

And then there was *Arsenic and Old Lace*, the dark comedy that played on Broadway from 1941 to 1944. Its success on the Great White Way far exceeded *Dracula*'s. Boris Karloff created the role of the murderous Jonathan Brewster in the original production, but Lugosi's association with the same role dated back to at least September 1941, when Jimmie Fidler's column noted that he had been offered the chance to star in a roadshow version.[14] He turned it down, but subsequently appeared in the play in San Francisco and Los Angeles in 1943, and then again in a roadshow version in 1944.

Lugosi seems to have genuinely enjoyed *Arsenic*, telling a journalist in 1945 that, "just for a lark I'd … like to do the Karloff stage role in *Arsenic and Old Lace*. Replacing him on the screen as I did in *Frankenstein Meets the Wolf Man* [1943] was more in my line, of course."[15] Here his spin on history is interesting, as instead of "following" Karloff in those two important roles, he was instead "replacing" him.

At any rate, Lugosi needed *Arsenic* and *Dracula*. Badly. They became his signature shows in summer stock, which developed into his most reliable and respectable form of work between 1947 and 1950. Those two plays brought him admiration from fellow performers, applause from audiences who took him seriously, and at least some praise from critics. Those two straw hats also brought him money, with $750 being his standard fee for starring in them during the late forties.[16]

Of course the question was whether those two plays needed *him*. As Universal had shown with films like *Son of Dracula* (1943), *House of Frankenstein* (1944), and *House of Dracula* (1945), other actors could in fact portray the vampire count. And as for *Arsenic*, well, the 1944 Warner Brothers film version proved that the role of Jonathan Brewster (as played by Raymond Massey) didn't even need its originator, Boris Karloff, let alone Bela Lugosi.

In terms of summer stock in 1946, the Greenbush in Blauvelt, New York presented *Dracula*, and summer theatres in Skaneateles, New York; Suffern, New York; Keene, New Hampshire; and Westboro, Massachusetts staged *Arsenic*.[17] Lugosi appeared in none of those productions. But John Carradine – the man who played Dracula in *House of Frankenstein* and *House of Dracula* – played Jonathan Brewster twice in summer stock that year, in Cohasset, Massachusetts and Ivoryton, Connecticut.[18]

All of that changed in 1947, however. In the summer of that year, Lugosi dominated both plays. Over the course of roughly nine weeks, starting on July 1 and ending on September 7, Lugosi appeared in eight summer stock plays in eight different towns across four different states. Half of his appearances came in *Dracula*, and the other half in *Arsenic and Old Lace*.

In fact, Lugosi's summer stock debut came as Jonathan Brewster, rather than as Dracula. Theron Bamberger booked him for July 1-5 at his 600-seat Bucks County Playhouse, which was situated on Main Street in the small town of New Hope, Pennsylvania. As in Lugosi's earlier appearances in the role, the dialogue of Joseph Kesselring's play was amended slightly to accommodate him. Instead of

Jonathan claiming he murdered someone because "He said I looked like Boris Karloff," it was because he looked like "Bela Lugosi."

By June 25, 1947, Lugosi and wife Lillian checked into the Logan Inn so he could begin rehearsals with a cast that featured Viola Roache and Dorothy Sands as the "zany Brewster sisters" who poison sad old men to relieve them of their misery.[19]

But the play was not Lugosi's only work in the city. From July 3-5, Lugosi also made three evening appearances at the New Hope Street Fair, presumably after the curtain closed on *Arsenic* each night.[20] He "lent his talents" to the "Chamber of Horrors," one of forty exhibits that benefited the New Hope Recreation Center.[21] The fair was constructed on the grounds of the hotel where the Lugosis stayed.

Later, Lugosi returned to the fair after an evening performance of *Arsenic*. Illustrator and cartoonist Frank Godwin was there as well, sketching various members of the public. After one gruelling session that did not end until 4AM, Godwin looked up and saw Lugosi. The actor ordered 37 sketches. "That nearly killed me," Godwin later recalled.[22]

Lugosi and Harald Dyrenforth (as Van Helsing) in the Litchfield version of *Dracula*. (Photograph Taken by Samuel Kravitt; Courtesy of Mrs. Samuel Kravitt)

Another anecdote from his stay in New Hope had Lugosi still wearing his cape while entering a small luncheonette. Allegedly, Lugosi was concerned as to why he had not yet received a newspaper that he requested. In response, the owner allegedly told him, "You may have scared me once, Mr. Lugosi, but I'm not a kid anymore."[23]

After *Arsenic* ended, Lugosi had over a week's break before his next play opened. He and Lillian traveled 175 miles to East Hampton, Long Island. At the time, the area was a well-known artists' colony, catering to such luminaries as Jackson Pollock. There Lugosi would star in *Dracula* at the 360-seat John Drew Theatre. It became the first time in four years that he had appeared in the full, three-act version of the play.

According to theatre manager Francis I. Curtis, who had booked Lugosi in May of that year, the production represented a "revised version" of the play.[24] However, what – if anything – was changed is

Gary D. Rhodes | Bill Kaffenberger

From the *Hartford Courant* of August 31, 1947.

> The Litchfield SUMMER THEATER
> on West Street
> presents
> **BELA LUGOSI**
> in person
> **DRACULA**
> for SIX days
> Tues., Sept. 2 through Sunday, Sept. 7
> For Reservations phone Litchfield 943
> Tickets $1.50-$2.00 plus tax

unknown. The show opened on July 14, with seventeen-year-old technician Stephen Burg spending part of his week driving Lugosi to and from the theatre in his old Model-T Ford.[25]

The cast also featured Elaine Stritch, who had appeared with Lugosi only months before in *Three Indelicate Ladies*. Ray Walston, who had also appeared in *Three Indelicate Ladies*, portrayed Renfield. The two became friends, discussing the theatre over drinks and cigars. Lugosi even told Walston that he was the "best" Renfield that he'd ever known. Walston recalled Lugosi's insistence that real mice be used in the play, as opposed to a prop, but added that some real bats that somehow ended up in the theatre "troubled Lugosi a little bit." He also remembered:

> …an incident that happened on one of the performances. Toward the end of the play, when Dracula is staked, you didn't actually see Dracula lying there and somebody driving a stake in his heart, but you could hear the thuds. All the audience could see was a shadow – a show on the wall of a reclining figure, lying on its back, a stake at its breast, and this big, huge, hammer-like thing coming down on top of the stake. It was like the sound of someone knockin' a spike down with a sledgehammer or something. Each time it happened, Lugosi (who was on the other side of the stage) would let out some kind of a *rrrrrrrr-ooooooooo-owwwwwww* [groaning noises]. Well, they hit it, he let out one or two; they hit it, they hit it, they hit it, and he let out one or two more. And then there was no more hitting, but he kept going with the *rrrrrrrr-ooooooooo-owwwwwww*.[26]

To bring the prolonged death scene to a conclusion, Elaine Stritch screamed, "Hit him again, Bram, and hit him *hard*!"

After opening night, the *East Hampton Star* published a positive review of the play, claiming "The play is old, and seems more and more like a tale of a superstitious old crone as the years go on, but it does not lose any of its chilly power of attraction for the audiences, nor does it disappoint the morbidly curious for want of horror." The reviewer also believed that Walston's Renfield was the "stealer of many scenes."[27]

The Lugosis then traveled some three hundred miles to Boston so that he could appear in *Dracula* between July 21 and 26 at the 914-seat Boston Summer Theatre, which was touted as the largest of all summer stock theatres. Writer Lee Falk – best known as the creator of the comic strip heroes *The Phantom* and *Mandrake the Magician* – produced and directed the production, which costarred his wife Constance Moorehead as Lucy.

During the production, Elinor Hughes of the *Boston Herald* interviewed Lugosi about summer stock. Lugosi said he enjoyed it, "all of it except the weather," noting that even in air-conditioned theatres he used "up to three dress shirts every night." With regard to *Dracula*, he told Hughes that audiences were changing:

Dracula greets his new "friends" in England. From the Litchfield version of *Dracula*. (Photograph Taken by Samuel Kravitt; Courtesy of Mrs. Samuel Kravitt)

> Nowadays, to judge by my own experience, audiences are far more sophisticated, and, despite the screams and hysterical laughter that *Dracula* sometimes provokes, accept it only as a fairy story, a kind of make-believe which they enjoy as they might an animated cartoon.
>
> …If I do not [play the role as if I believe in it], then there is no illusion left; I must do it as well as I possibly can then people will still, I hope, have some sense of reality while the curtain is up. [28]

A review in the same newspaper underscored Lugosi's concerns about the changing audience. "Without Mr. Lugosi to lend it the authority of his presence, it would be hard to take, but with him, well, somehow you don't laugh."[29]

After the Boston run, the entire production — *Dracula*, Lugosi, Falk, Moorehead, and the others – moved to Cambridge's Brattle Hall for another five days. As in Boston, the cast performed *Dracula* in the evenings, as well as at Wednesday and Saturday matinees.

Recalling both productions, Constance Moorehead said that her husband had chosen *Dracula* specifically and made certain that Lugosi would play the title role. "Lugosi was weird," she said. "Weird onstage, and weird in person. Young kids wanted his autographs after those shows, and he would be nice about those kinds of things, but he was so *very* weird. He would even wear that white Dracula makeup out in public. I felt sorry for his wife."[30]

Lugosi had little chance to wear that makeup after closing night, however, because he had to rush to star in *Arsenic and Old Lace* at the 574-seat Spa Summer Theatre in Saratoga Springs, New York. One theatre critic in 1947 noted that the venue was situated in "about as beautiful a spot as could be imagined for a summer playhouse."[31]

The Lugosis arrived in Saratoga Springs on the morning of Monday, August 4. The next day meant both a rehearsal and opening night. Between Dracula and Jonathan Brewster, he had experienced only a two-day break, which included a 200-mile journey from Massachusetts to New York.[32] The theatre originally planned for him to appear in *Dracula*, but producer John Huntington had changed his mind.[33] The press reported the reason: "theatre audiences have evidenced a preference for comedy."[34]

Along with assuming the role of Mortimer Brewster, Ford Rainey directed *Arsenic*, which featured Broadway actress Lucia Seger as Abby Brewster and, at an early stage of his career, Richard Boone as

Dracula displays his hypnotic control over Renfield. From the Litchfield version of *Dracula*. (Photograph Taken by Samuel Kravitt; Courtesy of Mrs. Samuel Kravitt)

Officer O'Hara. The *Saratogian* believed the opening night featured some flaws, but believed that everyone involved would improve quickly:

> It isn't that anyone gives a bad performance. In fact, many of them are very good. But the production is spotty, gathering strength through a slowly-paced first act to a well-done third.
>
> Lines haven't been thoroughly learned by many characters and small bits of business seem awkward. It isn't up to the standard of direction of which Mr. Rainey showed he is capable earlier in the year. Perhaps it is too much both to direct and play a major part in such a play.
>
> Mr. Lugosi, after a slow beginning, works up until he is in full stride through act three. He ... may not have done *Arsenic and Old Lace* recently. At least, that's the impression one would get as he takes an act to get at home in the part of the sadistic Jonathan.[35]

Of course Lugosi had in fact played Jonathan Brewster only one month earlier in New Hope. Perhaps he was weary from the relentless schedule, or was still adjusting to appearing in plays in which he had little time to rehearse with new cast members.

At any rate, the *New York Post* reacted quite differently, claiming that, "the direction of Ford Rainey and the setting of Paul McGuire were slick and smooth."[36] Similarly, the *Albany Times-Union* told readers "the direction of Ford Rainey sparks the whole play with the realism of his acting. ... The entire production is very Broadwayish in the fidelity to the original."[37] The same reviewer added that, "Mr. Lugosi, with his thick foreign accent is ideal as the wandering brother, pointing up his performance through the subconscious groove which has been established in the minds of the members of any audience through his many horror films."

As the play finished, the Spa Summer Theatre prepared for Edward Everett Horton to star in *Springtime for Henry*. The *Saratogian* claimed that at the time Horton was the "biggest draw on the summer theatre circuit."[38] Whether Lugosi met him or not is unknown, but he did have several days of breathing room until appearing in his next play, staged approximately 300 miles away.

On August 18, Lugosi opened in *Arsenic and Old Lace* at Kenley's 500-seat Deer Lake Theatre near the tiny town of Deer Lake, Pennsylvania. The venue hosted an array of other stars that summer, including Conrad Nagel, Gloria Swanson, Jean Parker, Ruth Chatterton, Buddy Ebsen, and — once again appearing in his warhorse *Springtime for Henry* — Edward Everett Horton. Advertisements for the show referred to Lugosi as "Hollywood's Horror Star."[39] Some publicity also touted Dulcie Cooper, an Australian actress who had appeared in silent films and once upon a time had played opposite Edward Everett Horton. In this version of *Arsenic*, Cooper and Virginia Gilbert portrayed the Brewster sisters.

From Deer Lake, the Lugosis traveled some 350 miles to Fairhaven, Massachusetts and the 600-seat Fairhaven Summer Theatre to appear in yet another version of *Arsenic and Old Lace*. Once again, he had little time to relax between shows. The Deer Lake production ended on August 23 and the Fairhaven opened on August 25. Within two days, he had to make his way from Pennsylvania to Massachusetts and do whatever small amount of rehearsals were possible before opening in the new show.

Anthony Farrar (whose real name was Anthony Ferreira) directed this version of *Arsenic*, and the cast included David Durston as Mortimer. His appearance in the play would no doubt have delighted Lugosi, as they had earlier met in California when Durston was still a child. In fact, Lugosi had known Durston's father some three decades earlier in Europe.[40]

Speaking to a reporter from the nearby *New Bedford Standard-Times*, Lugosi took time to express the reasons why he enjoyed the opportunity to return to live theatre:

> You play directly to an audience and not to a battery of cameras and a gang of technical sound men, electricians, set men, and directors. On the stage, you can detect your shortcomings immediately and can make whatever changes in pace or style may be necessary to sustain a characterization or a mood.[41]

Nonetheless, Lugosi again complained that the summer heat was "terrible," and that the high temperatures were "a bit too much."

As usual with summer stock productions, the Fairhaven stock company staged *Arsenic* on five consecutive nights and at matinees on Wednesday and Saturday. In publicizing the event, the *Fairhaven Star* reminded reviewers of Lugosi's films, presumably having gotten their names from publicity material his agent had sent in advance to the theatre. Among the titles were *The Vampire*, *Werewolf of London* (1935), and *Dracula's Daughter* (1936).[42] The first never existed, and the latter two did not include Lugosi in their casts. It was not necessarily the case that Lugosi or his agents spread falsehoods about his Hollywood horror film credits: Lugosi just forgot their titles, or remembered being cast in films for which he was considered but did not finally appear.

As for *Arsenic and Old Lace*, a review in the *New Bedford Standard-Times* was positive in many respects, but did complain about the "noisy" audience. Of Lugosi, the critic echoed some of what had been said in Saratoga Springs:

the Litchfield summer theatre

NOW PLAYING THROUGH SUNDAY
DRACULA
starring
Bela Lugosi
in person
— o —
TUESDAY THRU SUNDAY. — SEPTEMBER 9 - 14.
The First Presentation of The Shakespearean Festival.
HAMLET
starring
JOHN CARRADINE
and
Sonia Sorel
Phone reservations: Litch. 943 $1.50 & $2.00 plus tax

From the *Litchfield Enquirer* of September 4, 1947.

Dracula shrinks from the crucifixes of Dr. Seward (left), Van Helsing (middle), and Harker (right) in the Litchfield version of the play. (Photograph Taken by Samuel Kravitt; Courtesy of Mrs. Samuel Kravitt)

He is effectively menacing and sufficiently nasty in a role that demands little more than those qualities. In the first act, we experienced a little trouble in understanding Mr. Lugosi's diction, but he became clearer as the evening progressed. Effective as he was in his performance, however, we kept wishing that he were doing Dracula instead – Count Dracula is a far juicier role.

Last night's production dragged on one or two occasions, but we suspect that these will be taken care of through the week.[43]

Fairhaven's *Arsenic* closed the theatre's summer season. Before the show completed its run, Lugosi made a personal appearance at the Fairhaven Town Hall. Photos taken of him that week show grayer hair than in photos taken earlier the same year. Perhaps he just hadn't dyed it due to his busy schedule, or perhaps it had in fact grayed further due to the hectic summer.

For September 2 to 7, Lugosi concluded his 1947 summer stock appearances in *Dracula* for a week at the Litchfield Summer Theatre in Litchfield, Connecticut. Once again, he had only 48 hours between one show closing and another opening. As much as any other summer stock town, Litchfield had quite a history, ranging from having the first law school in America to being the one-time home of Harriet Beecher Stowe.

Leonard Altobell directed the Litchfield *Dracula*, which featured Gene Lyons as Renfield and Saralie Bodge as Lucy. Bodge was not only the lead actress in the company, but she was also Altobell's wife. The two had opened the 325-seat theatre in 1940 and ran it together for some seventeen years.

Allan Jefferys, himself an actor and later a theater critic, constructed the *Dracula* set to conform to Lugosi's blocking, which Lugosi had sent in advance of his arrival. Jefferys remembered that:

Among other things, I built the set to meet Lugosi's needs. The result was my seven-door set (including a hidden door). Four were for him ... three for me.

Lugosi wasn't particularly talkative. It was actually a good thing that the Dracula role only had something like eight sides of dialogue, because he was pretty beat in those days. His wife was there, and, to help him not miss his cues to move out onto the stage, she gave him little nudges on the back. I remember seeing that from backstage.[44]

Capturing Jefferys' sets and Lugosi's vampire was noted photographer Samuel Kravett, who snapped a variety of pictures during the dress rehearsal. They remain the best images of all of Lugosi's many summer stock appearances as Dracula, but – as had been true in Fairhaven – they reveal an actor with grayer hair than ever before.

Publicity told ticket-buyers that seeing *Dracula* would be a great way to beat the summer heat. Altobell promised the theater would be "bloodchilled" and that "bloodchilling is much better than air conditioning" thanks to Lugosi, "that chiller of blood and giver of goose pimples."[45] Altobell also announced that he intended to take the play "all the way" by use of dog howls, screams and fog that would fill his theatre.[46]

When the show finally opened, Altobell's daughter Jayne sat excitedly in the audience. Meeting Lugosi that week, Jayne thought that he was "gentle and calm offstage," and she loved his performance. In particular, she found his "cape twirling technique mesmerizing as he made his entrances and exits."[47] Here is an effect that others would recall from his stage appearances, a use of the cape perhaps different than what he did in films like *Dracula* (1931) or *Abbott and Costello Meet Frankenstein* (1948).

Esther Bufferd of *The Litchfield Inquirer* praised Altobell, Bodge, Lyons, and Jefferys. Of Lugosi, she told readers that he was:

> … of course, perfect in the role. Mr. Lugosi is well acquainted with his characterization, if that's a compliment, and has an old-world stage poise and dignity which is good to see. He has wonderfully expressive hands, suitable for Dracula, and was so completely convincing that the next time I see a bat flying around (not soon, I hope), I shall accuse Mr. Lugosi, or Dracula – you pick the name.[48]

Speaking of the production as a whole, Buffered said, "I must admit I rather enjoyed the old-time horror story *Dracula*. … [It] is especially good as the company has kept the play from burlesque and melodrama."

After the Litchfield *Dracula* closed, Lugosi's summer officially came to an end. Biting people onstage; kissing hands offstage. Summer stock had meant respect, applause, and money. Shortly before it all had begun, Jack O'Brian met Lugosi at Toots Shor's in New York. After the summer was over, O'Brian finally took the time to craft his anecdote into a column. His story ended by noting that "Bela … bade us a pleasant, 'Goodbye, see you later!'"[49]

Lugosi said much the same as he left each of the eight towns in which he appeared on the straw hat circuit. It had been a busy summer, one that he may well have enjoyed, but one that he also viewed as "very hard work."[50] After all, by the time it ended, he was only weeks away from turning 65 years of age. And rather than retiring, he had to keep traveling.

(Endnotes)

1. "Jack O'Brian, 86, Columnist of the Entertainment World." *New York Times* 8 Nov. 2000.
2. O'Brian, Jack. "Broadway." *Sandusky Register-Star-News* (Sandusky, OH) 29 Nov. 1947.
3. *Ibid*.
4. *Ibid*.
5. O'Brian, Jack. "On Broadway." *Corsicana Daily Sun* (Corsicana, TX) 21 Jan. 1948.
6. LoMonaco, Martha Schmoyer. *Summer Stock! An American Theatrical Phenomenon*. (New York: Palgrave MacMillan, 2004).
7. Sircom, Arthur. "A Production in Seven Days." *Theatre Arts* June 1950.
8. *Ibid*.
9. Bamberger, Theron. "Straw-Hat Brigade Is Optimistic, Although Uncertainties Loom, Most Managers Appear Hopeful." *New York Times* 18 May 1947.
10. Bamberger, Theron. "Going Up!" *Theatre Arts* June 1950.

11. Lugosi, Bela. Letter to Chamberlain Brown 24 May 1941. [Available in the Chamberlain and Lyman Brown Papers, and Undated, Series II: Correspondence, Box 64, Folder F.9 at the New York Public Library/Lincoln Center for the Performing Arts in New York.]
12. Brown, Chamberlain. Letter to Bela Lugosi 29 Mar. 1944. [Available in the Chamberlain and Lyman Brown Papers, and Undated, Series II: Correspondence, Box 64, Folder F.9 at the New York Public Library/Lincoln Center for the Performing Arts in New York.]
13. "Movie Stars Going Rural to 'Keep Hand in' Rich Summer Theatrical Pie." *Coshocton Tribune* (Coshocton, OH) 21 June 1947.
14. Fidler, Jimmie. "In Hollywood." *Los Angeles Times* 2 Sept. 1941.
15. Johnson, Fred. "Dracula Sees Film 'Fear' as Escapism." *San Francisco Call-Bulletin* 10 Mar. 1945.
16. We base this claim on letters from the Brown Agency to Don Marlowe in 1948, in which $750 was consistently the amount offered to the actor to appear in one week of summer stock. It is possible on some occasions that Lugosi made as little as $500 a week or as much as $1,000 a week, the latter being a number that LoMonaco cites as a common fee for stars of the period. [Available in the Chamberlain and Lyman Brown Papers, and Undated, Series II: Correspondence, Box 64, Folder F.9 at the New York Public Library/Lincoln Center for the Performing Arts in New York.]
17. "The Summer Bills." *New York Times* 30 June 1946; "The Summer Bills." *New York Times* 28 July 1946.
18. "Goings On About Town." *New Yorker* 13 July 1946; "Goings On About Town." *New Yorker* 10 Aug. 1946.
19. *Variety* 25 June 1947; "Bela Lugosi in *Arsenic and Old Lace* at Bucks County Playhouse." Press Release. Bucks County Playhouse. 1947.
20. *Variety* 2 July 1947.
21. "Lugosi to Appear at New Hope Fair." *Trenton Evening Times* (Trenton, NJ) 3 July 1947.
22. "Illustrator to Sketch New Hope Fair-Goers." *Trenton Times-Advertiser* 26 June 26 1949.
23. "My Bela Lugosi Story." 1 Nov. 2009. Available at http://pattinase.blogspot.com/2009/11/my-bela-lugosi-story.html. Accessed on 10 Dec. 2012.
24. "*Open House* Due in Week of June 2." *New York Times* 22 May 1947; Curtis, Francis I. *Dracula*. Press Release. John Drew Theatre. 1947.
25. Rhodes, Gary D. Interview with Stephen Burg's widow. 2011.
26. Weaver, Tom. "Ray Walston." In *I Was a Monster Movie Maker* (Jefferson, NC: McFarland, 2001).
27. "Eerie Dracula Thrills Summer Theatre Goers." *East Hampton Star* (East Hampton, Long Island, NY). Courtesy of the East Hampton Historical Society.
28. Hughes, Elinor. "Bela Lugosi Now Playing First Year in Summer Stock." *Boston Herald* 24 July 1947.
29. "Two Popular Revivals." *Boston Herald* 27 July 1947.
30. Rhodes, Gary D. Interview with Constance Moorehead. 2006.
31. Rice, Vernon. "Summer Theatre: Spa's Successful Season; Youth in Bolton Landing." *New York Post* 12 Aug. 1947.
32. "Lugosi Flits Around Like Phantom." *The Saratogian* 7 Aug. 1947.
33. Eaton, Fred G., Jr. "Humor Survives Flaws in *Arsenic*'s First Night." *The Saratogian* (Saratoga Springs, NY) 7 Aug. 1947.
34. Armstrong, Shirley. "Spa Theatre Comedy Ably Presented." *Schenectady Gazette* (Schenectady, NY) 6 Aug. 1947.
35. "Humor Survives Flaws in *Arsenic*'s First Night."
36. Rice, "Summer Theatre: Spa's Successful Season; Youth in Bolton Landing."
37. Van Olinda, Edgar S. "Spa Players Score in *Arsenic and Old Lace*." *Albany Times-Union* 8 Aug. 1947.
38. "Horton Features Spa Play Next Week." *The Saratogian* 9 Aug. 1947.
39. Advertisement. *Pottsville Journal* (Pottsville, PA) 16 Aug. 1947.
40. Rhodes, Gary D. Interview with David Durston. 1996.
41. LaBrode, Melvin F. "Horror Man Lugosi Proud That He's Humanitarian." *New Bedford Standard-Times* (New Bedford, MA) 26 Aug. 1947.
42. "Summer Theatre Presents Lugosi." *Fairhaven Star* 21 Aug. 1947.
43. E. J. D. "Murder Made Hilarious in *Arsenic and Old Lace*." *New Bedford Standard-Times*. Courtesy of David Durston.
44. Jefferys, Alan. Phone interview with Gary D. Rhodes. 9 Feb. 2006; Email to Gary D. Rhodes. 10 Feb. 2006.
45. *Naugatuck News* 3 Sept. 1947.
46. *Ibid*.
47. Newirth, Jayne Altobell. Email to Gary D. Rhodes. 5 Apr. 2006.
48. Bufferd, Esther. "Litchfield Summer Theatre." *Litchfield Inquirer* (Litchfield, CT) 4 Sept. 1947.
49. O'Brian, "Broadway," *Sandusky Register-Star-News*.
50. LaBrode, "Horror Man Lugosi Proud That He's Humanitarian."

After Dracula is dispelled, Lucy Seward and Jonathan Harker are finally able to reunite. From the Litchfield version of *Dracula* in 1947. (Photograph Taken by Samuel Kravitt; Courtesy of Mrs. Samuel Kravitt)

Gary D. Rhodes | Bill Kaffenberger

Lugosi in *The Raven* (1935), a film in which he plays an obsessive fan of Edgar Allan Poe.

Chapter 5

A MIDNIGHT DREARY

By the time of the nickelodeon era, the American cinema had embraced Edgar Allan Poe, the legendary author who died in 1849. Long overlooked during his own lifetime, Poe's contributions to the genres of mystery, horror, and even science fiction are immeasurable. And with tales like *Murders in the Rue Morgue*, Poe helped to invent modern detective fiction.

For the film industry, Poe and his stories became an endless fount of ideas. Biograph released D. W. Griffith's biographical film *Edgar Allen* [sic] *Poe* in 1909. Griffith then returned to Poe for his movie *The Avenging Conscience* (1914), which featured Henry B. Walthall as the author. Believing him to be the very image of Poe, writer-director Charles Brabin cast Walthall as Poe in his own film, *The Raven* (1915).

Other Poe films emerged during the silent era, including two versions of *The Fall of the House of Usher* in 1928. James Sibley Watson and Melville Webber created the most memorable of the pair: an expressionist tour-de-force, their film attempted to capture the very essence of Poe's famous story. That same year, Charles Klein directed his own expressionist film, a wonderfully disturbing version of *The Tell-Tale Heart* (1928).

But as the silent era gave way to sound, another figure became linked with Edgar Allan Poe, far more than anyone else in the first half of the twentieth century, or – for that matter – until Vincent Price and Roger Corman assumed the mantle in a series of horror movies in the 1960s. That man was Bela Lugosi, and his continued relationship with Poe onscreen was second only to his irrevocable ties to Bram Stoker's vampire.

Lugosi's quartet of Poe movies not only remain important examples of the American horror film, but they also exemplify the struggle that Hollywood writers had in translating the author's work into feature-length scripts. Adding material to his short stories became a necessity. The question was whether the adaptation could retain the plot, theme, and/or essence of Poe's original tales.

Directed by Robert Florey and featuring dialogue contributions from John Huston, *Murders in the Rue Morgue* (1932) became Lugosi's first encounter with Poe. The often-overlooked classic features much to praise, ranging from its expressionist set designs to its memorable cinematography. Lugosi's character Dr. Mirakle was a Hollywood creation, part of the joint effort to create a menacing role for the actor and to transform Poe's detective story into a horror movie.

That said, the film retains various aspects of Poe's tale, from character names (L'Espanaye and Dupin) and plot devices (a corpse stuffed up a chimney) to a puzzling crime in which the police ini-

Ballyhoo stunt for *The Black Cat* (1934) promotes Lugosi, Karloff, and Edgar Allan Poe.

tially believe that a man — rather than an ape, or "Ourang-Outang" in Poe — is the murderer. However, it is in a particular scene that the film comes closer to Poe's original than most other Hollywood movies. A prefect questions German, Italian, and Danish residents of the building in which the L'Espanayes live. Believing the ape's "voice" to be human, each of them is convinced the man spoke a language other than their own, even though none of them are bilingual. Though it features minor variations from Poe's story, the comical scene faithfully brings the author's intentions to life.

Lugosi's second Poe film took a very different approach. Edgar G. Ulmer's *The Black Cat* (1934) paired the actor with Boris Karloff, who received top billing. Presenting a wonderfully strange tale of Satanism and sadistic revenge, the film became a classic of the thirties horror film. It also became the first sound film to do what would become common in later years: attach Poe's name and one of his story titles to a film that had little or nothing to do with him. In this case, the sheer appearance of a black cat – of which Lugosi's character has an abiding fear – attempts to link the film to Poe's tale.

Nonetheless, what is clear is that Lugosi was quite proud of his work in *The Black Cat*. Writing to his friend and theatrical representative Dr. Edmond Pauker, Lugosi noted that he played a "sympathetic part in it ... leaving Karloff as the fiend, as far as I can judge I am going to run away with the picture."[1] He urged Pauker to see the film when it premiered in New York, hoping that the "sympathetic" role might allow him to escape horror, whether or not Poe's name was involved.

The Raven (1935), Lugosi's third Poe film, again paired him with Boris Karloff, who again received top billing. Rather than attempt to be faithful to Poe (*Murders in the Rue Morgue*) or brazenly ignore him (*The Black Cat*), Louis Friedlander's *The Raven* opted for yet a third path, offering a bizarre celebration of the author in lieu of an adaptation. Lugosi dominates its story, playing a surgeon named Dr. Vollin who saves the life of a young woman and then becomes obsessed with her. But Vollin has another obsession: he is a Poe enthusiast and collector, to the extent that he has even constructed torture devices from such tales as *The Pit and the Pendulum* in his basement. Along with reciting lines from the poem *The Raven*, Vollin attempts to use devices that Poe had only conceived. "Poe, you are avenged!" he screams maniacally.

Returning to Poe in 1941, Universal Studios cast Lugosi in yet another version of *The Black Cat* (1941). Here he assumed the small role of Eduardo, a character who has little to do other than appear menacing during what is essentially an old dark house movie. Even though a black cat makes periodic appearances, *The Black Cat* seems aware of its very tenuous relationship to Poe; the film's credits make the appropriately cautious claim that it was merely "suggested" by the author's story.

Like Edgar Allan Poe, Lugosi experienced his fair share of career moments when money was in short supply. After the summer stock season of 1947 ended, Lugosi went from being employed regularly to being in need of work. That's not to say that his management wasn't trying to make deals. In August,

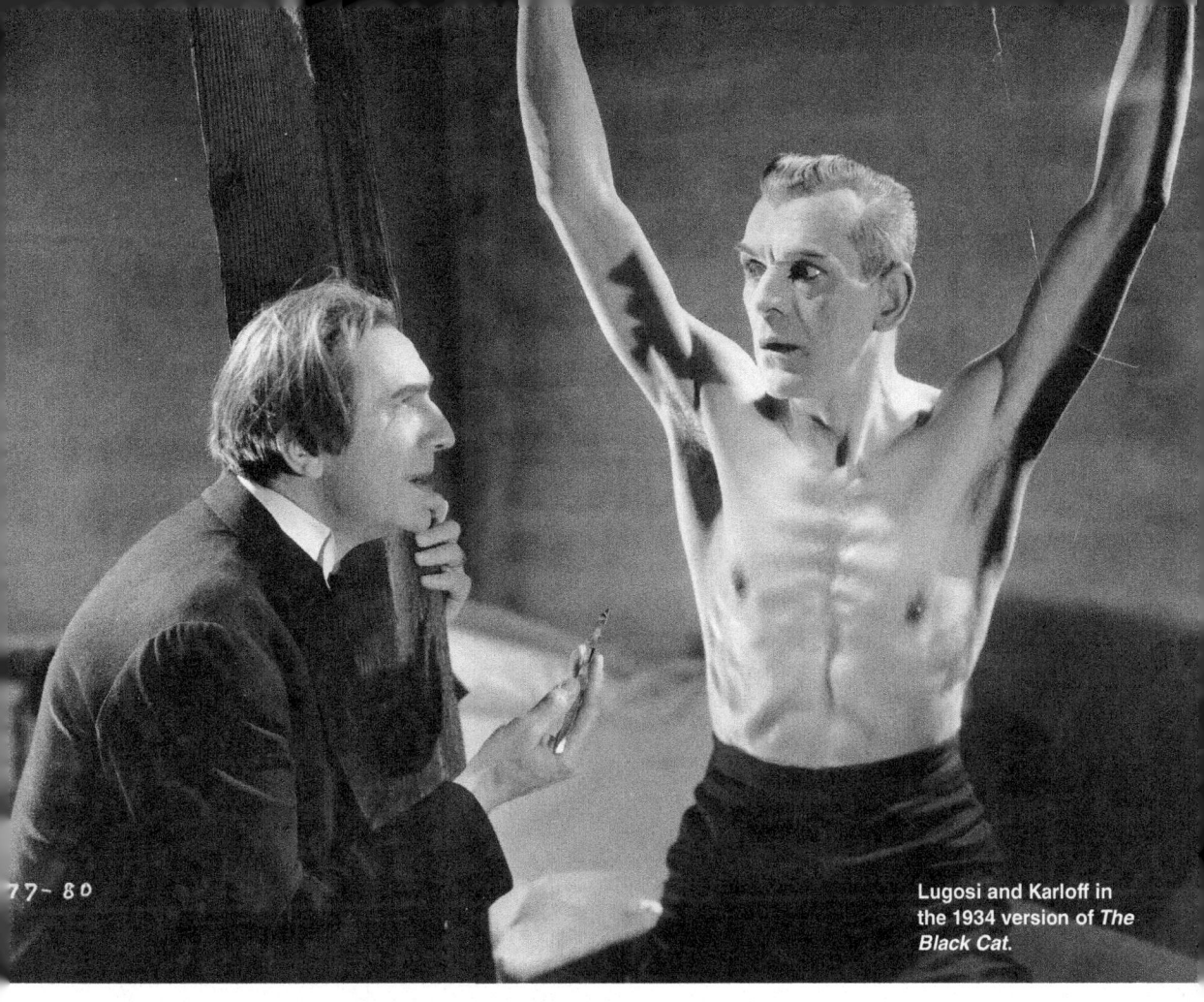

Lugosi and Karloff in the 1934 version of *The Black Cat*.

the Junior Chamber of Commerce of Hopkinsville, Kentucky announced plans to sponsor Lugosi in a performance of *Dracula* sometime in the autumn of that same year. The *Kentucky New Era* claimed that the organization had been "offered" the opportunity and planned to stage the show at the Hopkinsville High School Auditorium if there was "enough interest."[2] Apparently there wasn't.

Similarly, the *Lock Haven Express* of Lock Haven, Pennsylvania published a brief notice in August 1947 entitled "Kiwanis Brings Bela Lugosi." The organization's Board of Directors had met with a "representative of a New York theatrical producer" and decided to sponsor the stage version of *Dracula* with Lugosi, tentatively planning to open the show on October 8 of that year.[3] But as had been the case in Kentucky, the deal fell through.

Regardless, Lugosi had greater chances of landing work on the stage than in the cinema, and so he remained on the East Coast. Columnist Jack O'Brian mentioned that Lugosi took part in a roundtable discussion at the International Theatre in New York City in October 1947. Other participants included Alfred Drake, Onslow Stevens, and Edith Atwater (who had appeared in *The Body Snatcher* with Lugosi in 1945). The key issue was to address the fact that rising food prices had adversely affected attendance at live theatre, which as a result led to increased unemployment among technical staff and actors.[4]

As for Lugosi's own employment concerns, Edgar Allan Poe appeared in his life once again. And to be sure, Lugosi's connection to Poe had not ended with *The Raven*. In 1944, Monogram Pictures announced plans for Lugosi to appear in a film version of Poe's *The Gold Bug*, which was to be produced by Sam Katzman. Though that film did not materialize, another Lugosi-Poe project did in 1947: *The Tell-Tale Heart*.

But in 1947, Lugosi began discussions not for a film version of *The Tell-Tale Heart*, but instead for

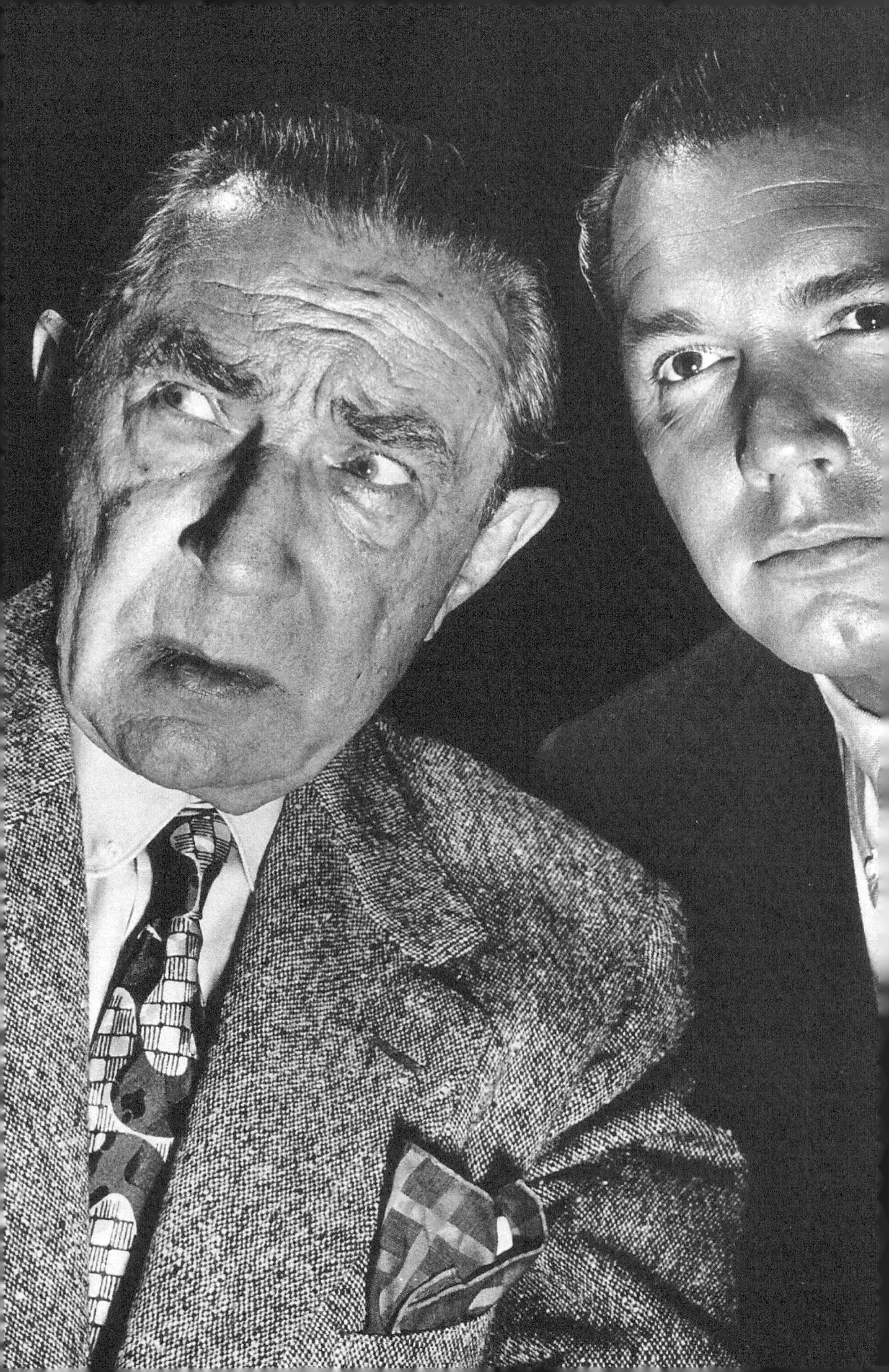

Bela Lugosi and Don Marlowe.

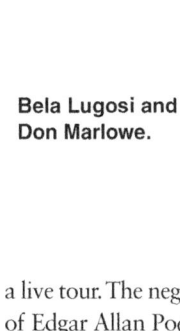

a live tour. The negotiations took place in October, an important month in the world of Edgar Allan Poe. The author's classic poem *Ulalume — A Ballad* takes place in October. In it, the "skies were ashen and sober," and the "leaves they were crisped and sere."

The contract for the show was finalized on November 1, 1947, after Lugosi struck one sentence regarding the number of performances he could be asked to give in a single day. That very day, *Motion Picture Herald* announced that Lugosi would undertake a *Tell-Tale Heart* tour. And, by the following day, details of the first performance began to appear in newspapers.[5] All looked well for a profitable and possibly lengthy tour.

As per Lugosi's contract, the opening performance would take place on November 19, with Lugosi receiving $1,000 per week against 18% of the top gross, in addition to transportation from New York to the first engagement, as well as transportation to all subsequent engagements, hotel rooms throughout the tour, and then transportation back to his choice of either New York or California.

His contract was with Don Marlowe, who was not only producing the *Tell-Tale Heart* show, but was also by that point acting in another capacity for Lugosi. On October 8, 1947, Lugosi wrote to his agent Virginia Doak, explaining matters to her at some length:

> The reason why I am putting the sugar on so thick in addressing you is to make you accept the bad news that on Sept. 18th I signed an exclusive contract with Don Marlowe, which naturally means that if he can't realize even one of his promises in four months that contract expires. It is easy for people that have a steady income from some source to be able to wait the help and achievement of their friend who is in the managerial business. But it is now close to two years that you have had so many prospects in view which unfortunately – naturally not your fault – did not realize. That would have been alright if I would have had money to cover my overhead expenses – which I didn't – and especially that I was not working for two years and getting very deep in the red. I had to borrow on my last collateral to escape from Hollywood and to try and cash in on my popularity and box office value in the East…I couldn't help signing with [Marlowe] … But I signed for motion pictures only … So as far as motion pictures are concerned he is entitled for full commission of anything he knows and is able to deliver but if you should know of anything which he does not – naturally you should receive full commission regardless of my obligations to Marlowe. So I would suggest, my dear, to cooperate with Marlowe for the time being and believe me I would not disappoint you. I need a job very badly and I am just human when I say that I do not mind who helps me to get my bread and butter I have to take it.[6]

Lugosi's letter reveals how bad his finances had been since Hollywood turned its back on him, as well as the intensity of his desire to get back into the movies.

95

The distinguished actor

Mr. Bela Lugosi

WHAT THE CRITICS SAY ABOUT

Bela Lugosi

"Bela Lugosi in 'Arsenic and Old Lace' proves himself a very amusing comedian"...Variety

"A versatile artist, indeed!"...Chicago Tribune

"One of the greatest actors ever to come to America"...Alan Dale

"Most electrifying performance I have ever witnessed"...Winchell

Exclusive Management
DON MARLOWE AGENCY
Hollywood, California

DON MARLOWE of OUR GANG COMEDIES
in scenes from some of his latest MOVIE + T.V. shows

- JACK WEBB — "DRAGNET"
- GIG YOUNG — "THREE MEN ON A HORSE"
- EDWARD EVERETT HORTON — "BACK DOOR TO HEAVEN"
- FRANCHOT TONE — "OH MEN OH WOMEN"
- LEO GORCEY — "CRASHING LAS VEGAS"
- BELA "DRACULA" LUGOSI — "THE TELLTALE HEART"
- DAN DURYEA — "CHINA SMITH"
- PATSY KELLY — "DEAR CHARLES"
- BASIL RATHBONE — "ALWAYS THE BUTLER"

Years later, Don Marlowe's publicity materials continued to refer to his work with Lugosi.

Who was Don Marlowe, the man who Lugosi believed could save his career? Born on October 23, 1919 in Duluth, Minnesota, his real name was actually Donald Paul Northrup. Sometimes he was a writer; sometimes he was a producer. At one point, he was employed at NBC television. As he grew older, he worked as an actor, nabbing a series of roles on episodes of various 1950s TV programs. Perhaps Marlowe's biggest part came in the 1960 independent film *Squad Car*, in which he received third billing.

Marlowe was also a manager and agent and promoter. A showman, and like so many showmen throughout film history, Marlowe's publicity for himself was sometimes built on falsehoods. He claimed to have been a child actor in the Our Gang film comedies, playing the role of Porky. He also claimed to have had a role in Lugosi's 1933 serial *The Whispering Shadow*. Neither statement was true. His autobiography – *The Hollywood That Was*, published in 1969 – also contained a number of inaccuracies and misstatements, including a reiteration of his claims about having been Porky.

On the one hand, Marlowe was a huckster, just like so many other producers and managers and promoters in the entertainment business. After Stan Laurel's death, he sold records of a private phone call that he had apparently taped without Laurel's permission. He also ran advertisements in magazines making the dubious claim that he possessed the 1931 test footage of Lugosi as the Frankenstein Monster.

Gary D. Rhodes | Bill Kaffenberger

Agreement or Contract

THIS INDENTURE, Made the __1st__ day of __November__, 19__47__.

BETWEEN   DON MARLOWE

, the party of the first part,

AND   BELA LUGOSI

, the party of the second part,

WITNESSETH: That the said party of the first part, in consideration of the covenants on the part of the said party of the second part, hereinafter contained, hereby covenant with the said party of the second part that the said party of the first part will pay the party of the second part the total sum of $1,000:00 per week against 18% of the top gross plus transportation from New York to place of engagement. Plus transportation during engagement and at close of engagement transportation to either New York or California. Plus all hotel bills incurred during engagement. Also party of the second part being an independent contractor shall receive monies due him net. This engagement shall begin November 19th, 1947, and the party of the first part agrees to pay the party of the second part every seventh day thereafter until close of said engagement.

AND the said party of the second part, in consideration of said covenants on the part of the said party of the first part hereinbefore contained, agree to and with the said party of the first part that the said party of the second part will enact the "Tell-Tale Heart" at theatre's where engagements are to be presented. ~~The number of performances~~ ■■. Further, upon wanting to close engagement, party of second part shall, if possible (not required) give the party of the first a three week notice.

AND for the true and faithful performance of all and every of said covenants the said parties to these presents bind themselves, each unto the other, in the penal sum of XXXXXXXXXXXX XXXXXXXXXXXXXXXXXXXXXXXXXXXXXXXXXXXXXXXXXXXXXXXXXXXXXXXXXXXXXXXX Dollars, lawful money of the United States of America, as fixed, settled and liquidated damages to be paid by the failing party.

IN WITNESS WHEREOF, the said parties have hereunto set their hands and seals the day and year first above written.

Don Marlowe
DON MARLOWE

Bela Lugosi
BELA LUGOSI

From the *Rockford Register-Republic* of November 15, 1947.

On the other hand, there can be no doubt that Marlowe actually was a friend of many actors from the Golden Age of Hollywood, including Stan Laurel. Richard Arlen wrote the foreword to Marlowe's book, and his friend Sam Peeples, a noted TV writer, later recalled how helpful and friendly Marlowe had been to a number of aging stars, as well as to many veterans' hospitals where he screened old films at no cost.[7]

Marlowe was not complicated; instead, he was something of the stereotypical used car dealer. And despite all the negative things said about him – usually by "historians" who have limited his biography to his admittedly untrue statements about being Porky – Marlowe provided Lugosi with what Virginia Doak and many of his other representatives could not. Time and again, Marlowe succeeded in getting work for Lugosi in the late forties, a period when the actor so badly needed what he once called his "bread and butter."

By the time of *The Tell-Tale Heart* tour, Lugosi had known Marlowe for well over two years, if not longer. On August 4, 1945, for example, *The Billboard* told readers that Lugosi would tour in a vaudeville act with Marlowe, who was also "working on [the] new routine" with him.[8] The same article added that the show was "pencilled in" on the schedule of the Loew's State in New York City. Given that the press did not mention it again, the act likely did not occur. The key reason was probably Lugosi's shooting schedule for RKO's *Genius at Work*, which began on August 18, 1945 and lasted until September 9. If Lugosi did go on such a tour, it would had to have been brief, as he was back at RKO for an additional day on *Genius at Work* in late November. At any rate, by 1947, Marlowe was back in Lugosi's life, and in a major way.

Why had Marlowe chosen *The Tell-Tale Heart*? It is difficult to know with certainty, but he may well have been aware of a successful TV broadcast of the same Poe story in late February 1947. Helen Carson directed the show, which was adapted by Bill Vance. Vance also starred in the lead role, with Bruno VeSota portraying the old man with the "evil eye." Broadcast over Chicago's WBKB, *The Tell-Tale Heart* received a positive, but tentative review in *The Billboard*. Praising its dramatic success, the trade also warned that "full-screen shots of a horrible looking eye, the sound and sight of a beating heart, screams and groans, and other weird sound effects" on television could be "upsetting."

Published in the *Rockford Morning Star* on November 20, 1947.

Gary D. Rhodes | Bill Kaffenberger

Advertisements from the *Minneapolis Star* of November 21, 1947.

to children. To prove his point, the reviewer noted that two kids in the live audience had started "crying with fright" during the broadcast.[9]

The Lugosi *Tell-Tale Heart* tour began in Rockford, Illinois, where the actor gave midnight performances of the show at the Coronado Theatre on November 19 and November 20, 1947. One early press account claimed that Lugosi was undertaking the show to celebrate two decades of being Dracula, an oblique reference to his playing the role for the first time on the stage in 1927.[10] Advance ads in Rockford promised that the "powerful dramatic sketch" – which would be paired with a screening of the 1931 film *Dracula* – would "thrill and chill" audiences.[11] The *Rockford Morning Star* told readers that *The Tell-Tale Heart* would open the city's autumn stage season, though the other shows named – such as Kay Francis in *State of the Union* – would be staged at the Palace Theatre.[12]

Marlowe and his wife Betty, who acted as the show's secretary, arrived in Rockford the week prior to the opening, using the time in an effort to bolster local publicity.[13] In a style typical of an entertainment promoter, he alleged that Lugosi's arrival in Rockford would "follow the closing of a stage play in New York, *Three Indelicate Ladies*."[14] In actual fact, that play – which had never been staged in New York – had closed on April 19, 1947, seven months earlier.

Along with announcing that the new show would go on a "nationwide tour," Marlowe also claimed that Lugosi had in fact performed a "short episode from the [*Tell-Tale Heart*] dramatization on a television broadcast," adding Walter Winchell's judgment that it represented "the most electrifying performance [he] had ever seen."[15] To help cash in on the growing local publicity, the Rex Theatre of Rockford scheduled a screening of *Scared to Death* (1947) on November 18.[16]

The Lugosis travelled to Rockford by train several days before the opening, arriving on November 14. Lugosi told the local press that he needed to "rest" for part of the week, a possible indication that he was not in good health.[17] Nevertheless, he did grant an interview to the *Rockford Morning Star* shortly after checking into his hotel. The journalist noted:

100   NO TRAVELER RETURNS | The Lost Years of Bela Lugosi

Published in the *Racine Journal-Times* on November 22, 1947.

Bela Lugosi, the king of horror, looked like a tired business man [*sic*] last night in his room at the Faust hotel with his shirt opened at the throat, wearing bedroom slippers and biting a big cigar as he slipped into an easy chair.

… Bela, as he likes to be called … talked freely about his past performances and about his 10-year-old son, Bela Lugosi II, who is a corporal at the Elsinore, Cal. Naval and military academy. The couple received a letter from the boy before they left New York and enclosed was his report card. Bela was proud of his son's marks and commented in his rich Hungarian accent, 'he received some good grades, too.'

… When his manager, Don Marlowe, stated that the weather gets pretty cold around these parts, Bela smiled and said, 'I like the cold weather and snow.'[18]

As was often the case, Lugosi's mind was on his son, and the fact that they were geographically so far apart.

Though they may well have enjoyed Rockford, the Lugosis certainly had a bad night on November 18. At 11:30PM, they notified the police that their hotel room had been burglarized while they were out for the evening. Their dresser drawer, suitcase, and trunk had been "thoroughly ransacked," with their "clothes … strewn over the floor." Lugosi reported that a fountain pen had been stolen, but nothing else. However, he had little time to do a thorough check, as he soon had to report to the Coronado Theatre for a midnight rehearsal of *The Tell-Tale Heart*.[19]

In his autobiography, Marlowe mentioned another anecdote about Rockford, Illinois. He claimed that, after having dinner, he and Lugosi strolled down the street until a ten-year-old boy asked for the actor's autograph. "Certainly," Lugosi said, pausing a moment before asking, "And, young man, what is my name?" The boy quickly replied, "Boris Karloff."[20]

As for *The Tell-Tale Heart*, the press announced that Lugosi's new live show would last 45 minutes, describing it as the "exposition of events involving two men, one attempting to kill the other who has an eye that never shuts. The victim is buried beneath the floor of a room, but his still beating heart resounds in the ears of the murderer. Sound effects add to the dramatic heights of the play."[21] The same article added that Lugosi's role was "strenuous," as he was the "only character" in the adaptation.

Years later, Marlowe noted that "for part of the show, I had written a short, modern version" of *The Tell-Tale Heart*.[22] In addition to updating the tale, Marlowe's approach meant that — unlike the original Poe — the text only needed one actor. It was written in such a way as to avoid actually showing the old man with the "evil eye" or the trio of police officers who later question the main character. That kept costs down, as well as perhaps the running time. According to Marlowe, the *Tell-Tale Heart* sketch was only "part" of the 45-minute show.

The *Rockford Morning Star* told readers that the Coronado sold a total of 1,500 tickets for *The*

Tell-Tale Heart's premiere, the result meaning that the theatre was at "near capacity."[23] An earlier article had promised that "autograph hounds" would have the opportunity to meet Lugosi after the performance, something that presumably happened after the November 20 show as well. Both nights were successful, which boded well for the tour that was to follow.

The Lugosis left Rockford in Marlowe's car, with the two couples apparently heading directly to Minneapolis.[24] When they arrived in the city, Lugosi was already there, at least in a sense. The city's RKO Pan was screening *Son of Frankenstein* (1939) and the Gopher was screening a double bill of *The Black Cat* (1941) and *Black Friday* (1940).[25]

On November 22, 1947, *Boxoffice* ran a small article originating from that city. It claimed, "Bela Lugosi is here from Hollywood to make personal appearances in a number of the territory's smaller situations operated by the Berger and Welworth independent circuits. The appearances are in connection with the showing of one of his pictures."[26] Both the Berger and Welworth circuits were headquartered in Minneapolis. The former owned theatres in Minnesota, Iowa, and Wisconsin; the latter owned theatres in Minnesota, North Dakota, South Dakota, and Wisconsin.[27] An article regarding the tour announced *The Tell-Tale Heart* would play those very states, but a careful search through newspapers of towns and cities with Berger and Welworth theatres reveals that Lugosi did not appear in any of them.[28]

Likely Marlowe was angling for more *Tell-Tale Heart* bookings, presumably for the final days of November and for all or part of December. After all, he had at least two commitments already lined up for the days following Rockford. The Marlowes and Lugosis left Minneapolis and headed to Racine, Wisconsin, where they staged *The Tell-Tale Heart* at a single midnight show in the Venetian Theatre on November 24, 1947. Along with the Poe story, ads promised that Lugosi would "hypnotize [the] Frankenstein Monster" on stage.[29] Rather than screening *Dracula* (1931), the Venetian booked *One Body Too Many* (1944).

In his autobiography, Marlowe recalled the Racine performance, though unfortunately he concentrates only on *The Tell-Tale Heart*, not mentioning the Frankenstein Monster sketch:

> …I dreamed up the idea that it would add realism to the play if we could reproduce the sound of a beating heart … I knew it would be impossible to get sound recordings in this part of the country. In a second-hand store I found an old drum which seemed to have just the right sound.
>
> Because we carried no stage-hands, I handled the sound effects on the drum myself. I did this until we reached the city of Racine, Wisconsin. I always stood as close to the stage as I could without being seen, in order to be able to hear Bela's dialogue. As I have already mentioned, the drum I was using was in poor condition, and as Lugosi was going through the lines of the Tell-Tale Heart that night, I was beating the drum softly at first, as usual. When Bela got to the part, "and the heart kept beating louder and louder and louder," I began to hit the drum harder and harder and harder. As we came to the climax of the vignette, my mallet broke into the drum. This threw me completely off-balance and I fell over the drum, past the curtain, and landed on the stage, practically at Lugosi's feet in full view of the audience.
>
> Bela looked down at me with an expression I had never before seen on his face, then very calmly announced:

Published in the *Racine Journal-Times* on November 24, 1947.

'Ladies and gentleman … my manager, Mr. Don Marlowe.'

I quickly recovered my composure and walked off-stage.

Lugosi, undaunted trouper that he was, went on with the performance as though nothing unusual had taken place.[30]

As much as anything else, Marlowe's anecdote underscores how inexpensive the production was.

From Racine, the Marlowes and Lugosis went to Lake Geneva, Wisconsin, where Lugosi made two different appearances in *The Tell-Tale Heart* at midnight on November 27, just as Thanksgiving Day came to an end. One was at the 705-seat Geneva Theatre, and the other was at the 405-seat Delavan Theatre on the opposite side of the lake, about twenty minutes away by automobile. The Geneva played the Lugosi film *Ghosts Break Loose* (presumably a retitled version of either *Spooks Run Wild* of 1941 or *Ghosts on the Loose* of 1943), and the Delavan screened *Return of the Ape Man* (1944).

Within the space of a single week, the tour seemed to be getting worse. Along with the rapidly dwindling quality of the accompanying films, Lugosi was appearing at smaller theatres and two of them at virtually the same time. To make the evening work, the live show presumably preceded the film at one theatre and followed the film at the other.

From Lake Geneva, the tour's schedule becomes hazy. Some press accounts claimed that *The Tell-Tale Heart* would make appearances at Minnesota theatres between November 22 and the Thanksgiving weekend, but that does not seem to have been the case. By contrast, it seems as if Lugosi was in Wisconsin for the days in question.

Then there was mention of a tour wrap up in Wisconsin and Michigan during the first two weeks of December. For example, December play dates included the 1,383-seat Capitol Theatre in Manitowoc, Wisconsin on December 3, the 864-seat Park Theatre in Waukesha on December 5, the 929-seat Vista Theatre in Negaunee, Michigan on December 8, and the 2,244-seat Capitol Theatre in Madison, Wisconsin on December 13.[31]

What Marlowe did not say in his autobiography was that the tour seems to have been cut unexpectedly short. On December 3, the *Waukesha Daily Freeman* announced:

Bela Lugosi, scheduled to present his dramatic sketch at the Park Theatre Friday night, will be unable to appear, Joe Baisch, city theater manager, said today. Baisch said Lugosi is ill with an aggravated attack of a recurrent malady. The regular feature, *Where There's Life*, with Bob Hope, will be shown.[32]

Another article in the same newspaper joked that Lugosi may have not been getting enough blood lately.[33]

What this means is that all of *The Tell-Tale Heart* dates from that day forward were cancelled. A search of relevant city newspapers for the December play dates makes this fact clear. At least one poster for the Negaunee appearance still exists, printed in advance for a show that was in fact never staged. Similarly, it is certain that the scheduled Madison, Wisconsin show on December 13 did not occur. In that city, his planned midnight appearance was replaced with filmed highlights of a

From the *Lake Geneva Regional News* of November 27, 1947.

Gary D. Rhodes | Bill Kaffenberger

A window card poster for a performance that was cancelled.

boxing match between Joe Louis and Jersey Joe Wolcott.[34] Nor did Lugosi do two planned shows at the Hollywood Theatre in Eau Claire, Wisconsin on December 23, despite a pre-printed poster that also still exists.

The key issue in doubt is the Manitowoc performance, which was to occur at the stroke of midnight on December 3, only hours before Marlowe announced that the tour was cancelled. The *Manitowoc Herald-Times* of December 2 clearly lists "Bela Lugosi on stage in a special midnight show."[35] The December 3 issue of the same newspaper makes no mention that the show was cancelled, but it also features no review or article or interview to prove that it went ahead. If it was cancelled, it was presumably cancelled at the last minute, sometime after the paper went to press on December 2.

And so, *The Tell-Tale Heart* tour had lasted two weeks or even less. The sheer fact that Marlowe was in Minneapolis angling for play dates after the Rockford show opened indicates that he was in desperate need for more bookings, and none of them materialized, certainly not from Berger or Welworth theatres. The tour may well have been little more than a handful of performances during the latter days of November, with most of them in Wisconsin.

Perhaps there is another explanation at to why *The Tell-Tale Heart* stopped beating. While Lugosi may have in fact been ill, Don Marlowe was definitely seeking other work for him. On November 15, 1947 – just four days prior to the Rockford premiere – *The Billboard* published a news item dated November 8: "Another new Elwell package stars Bela Lugosi, film horror expert, and Ann Thomas in a mystery show. Nelson Sykes is the writer."[36]

Tom Elwell had earlier been associated with Hunt Stromberg, Jr., and so he likely met Lugosi and Ann Thomas in the spring of 1947 during the run of *Three Indelicate Ladies*. In fact, the brief mention of a new "mystery show" sounds vaguely reminiscent of the earlier play. No subsequent articles mention this "package," so it likely did not occur. However, it does make clear that – even two weeks after signing *The Tell-Tale Heart* contract and only days before it opened – Lugosi and Marlowe were already looking for other work. Indeed, Marlowe likely encouraged and perhaps handled the negotiations.

More importantly, on December 10, 1947, *Variety* indicated quite clearly that Lugosi was abandoning a tour in the Midwest – presumably meaning *The Tell-Tale Heart* – to return to the East Coast for a new vaudeville act. The article added that Lugosi had signed with the Edward Sherman Agency, headquartered in New York. They promoted themselves as "Booking the Nation's Leading Independent Vaudeville Theatres." As for Lugosi, he would receive "$1,250 weekly for a skein of four-a-day stanzas in eastern vaudfilmers booked by Sherman. He opens at Adams, Newark, Dec. 18 and the week after has been set by Hippodrome, Baltimore."[37]

Why would Marlowe have agreed to such a change of plans when he had a signed contract with Lugosi? The answer is simple. Along with producing *The Tell-Tale Heart*, he was indeed Lugosi's manager, and as such, he would have profited from the actor's other live performances, including his work with the Sherman Agency. Instead of paying Lugosi $1,000 a week to appear in *The Tell-Tale Heart*, he could have made a commission from the new vaudeville act.

The change of plans would have been particularly enticing if the weekly costs of *The Tell-Tale Heart* outweighed any profit that it generated. To be sure, Marlowe may well have been hemorrhaging money due to *The Tell-Tale Heart*'s few bookings, and Lugosi may well have been increasingly upset by how rapidly the tour was deteriorating.

At any rate, *The Tell-Tale Heart* was over. Within a few weeks, the same would be true of the year 1947, a period of dreams and nightmares. Lugosi's Broadway ambitions with *Three Indelicate Ladies* had died, and he had obtained no new film work. Instead, the actor struggled his way through a hectic schedule in summer stock and then the all-too-brief Edgar Alan Poe tour. These were difficult times.

In Poe's poem *Ulalume*, the narrator sees autumn leaves that change from being "crisped and sere" to "withering and sere." Withering and sere. And he sees them near the end of what has indeed been his "most immemorial year."

Don Marlowe (right), pictured here some two decades after the *Tell-Tale Heart* tour with David Manners (left), Lugosi's costar in *Dracula* (1931).

(Endnotes)

1. Lugosi, Bela. Letter to Dr. Edmond Pauker. 24 Apr. 1934. [Available in the Edmond Pauker Papers, 1910-1957, Series I: Correspondence, 1915-1957, Box 42, Folder 11 at the New York Public Library/Lincoln Center for the Performing Arts in New York.]
2. *Kentucky New Era* (Hopkinsville, KY) 7 Aug. 1947.
3. *Lock Haven Express* (Lock Haven, PA) 22 Aug. 1947.
4. *Salamanca Republican-Press* (Salamanca, NY) 17 Oct. 1947.
5. "Appearance of Bela Lugosi Here to Open State Season." *Rockford Morning Star* (Rockford, IL) 2 Nov. 1947.
6. Lugosi, Bela. Letter to Virginia Doak. 8 Oct. 1947.
7. Peeples, Sam. Letter to Gary D. Rhodes. 14 May 1995.
8. "Bela Lugosi To Make PAs." *Billboard* 4 Aug. 1945.
9. Wagner, Cy. "*Tell-Tale Heart*." *Billboard* 8 Mar. 1947.
10. *Toledo Blade* (Toledo, OH) 29 Oct. 1947.
11. Advertisement. *Rockford Register-Republic* 15 Nov. 1947.
12. "Appearance of Bela Lugosi Here to Open State Season."
13. "Horror King Goes Dramatic in New Play; Premiere Here." *Rockford Morning Star* (Rockford, IL) 12 Nov. 1947.
14. "Lugosi Looks, That's Enough." *Rockford Register-Republic* 13 Nov. 1947.
15. "Horror King Goes Dramatic in New Play; Premiere Here." *Rockford Morning Star* 12 Nov. 1947.
16. Advertisement. *Rockford Morning Star* 18 Nov. 1947.
17. "Lugosi Looks, That's Enough."
18. "King of Horror Just Tired Businessman to Interviewer." *Rockford Morning Star* (Rockford, IL) 15 Nov. 1947.
19. "Thief Loots Movie Star's Hotel Room." *Rockford Morning Star* 19 Nov. 1947.

20 Marlowe, *The Hollywood That Was*. [In his book, Marlowe claims this anecdote happened while Lugosi was appearing in a roadshow version of *Dracula*. However, here his memory seems to be mistaken. He clearly indicates that the event took place in Rockford, Illinois in November. If so, his story must refer to the occasion when the two men appeared in the city for the *Tell-Tale Heart*.]
21 "Horror King Goes Dramatic in New Play; Premiere Here." [The fact that the show lasted for 45 minutes is confirmed in "Hayworth Is Coronado Star." *Rockford Morning Star* 20 Nov. 1947.]
22 Marlowe, Don. "Lugosi." *Classic Film Collector* Winter 1970.
23 "Near-Capcity Crowd Sees Coronado Show." *Rockford Morning Star* 20 Nov. 1947.
24 "Lugosi Looks, That's Enough."
25 Advertisements. *Minneapolis Star* 21 Nov. 1947.
26 "Bela Lugosi on Tour." *Boxoffice* 22 Nov. 1947.
27 Ramsaye, Terry, ed. *The 1945-46 International Motion Picture Almanac* (New York City: Quigley, 1945).
28 The Berger Amusement Company, headquartered in Minneapolis, owned theatres in Rock Rapids, Iowa; Duluth, Fergus Falls, Hastings, Minneapolis, St. Paul and St. Peter, Minnesota; and Mondovi and Superior, Wisconsin. The Welworth Theatres Company, also headquartered in Minneapolis, owned theatres in Minneapolis, Montevideo, New Ulm, Red Wing, and South St. Paul, Minnesota; Devils Lake, North Dakota; Sioux Falls, South Dakota; and La Crosse, Wisconsin.
29 Advertisement. *Racine Journal-Times* (Racine, WI) 24 Nov. 1947.
30 *Ibid*.
31 *Boxoffice* 22 Nov. 1947; *Manitowoc Herald-Times* 2 Dec. 1947; *Wisconsin State Journal* (Madison, WI) 16 Nov. 1947.
32 "Vampire Lugosi Sick, Cancels Show Here." *Waukesha Daily Freeman* (Waukesha, WI) 3 Dec. 1947.
33 "Up and Down Broadway in Waukesha." *Waukesha Daily Freeman* 3 Dec. 1947.
34 *Wisconsin State Journal* 13 Dec. 1947. [In addition to the boxing highlights, the day's advertised double feature was *Each Dawn I Die* with James Cagney and George Raft along with *Bad Men of Missouri* with Dennis Morgan and Jane Wyman.]
35 "Movie Guide." *Manitowoc Herald-Times* (Manitowoc, WI) 2 Dec. 1947.
36 "Foy-Cohan Package Set By Elwell." *Billboard* 15 Nov. 1947.
37 *Daily Variety* 10 Dec. 1947.

Enjoying a cigar during the production. (Courtesy of Buddy Barnett)

Chapter 6
ABBOTT AND COSTELLO MEET DRACULA

After interviewing Lugosi in 1947, a Boston journalist told readers that the "studios are being swamped with requests for Lugosi and Karloff pictures."[1] At first, given Lugosi's limited film output after World War II, it is tempting to view such a statement as nothing more than the actor's own wishful thinking and flair for publicity, channelled into the press thanks to a willing reporter. To be sure, Lugosi would have had little knowledge of how many letters the studios received on any subject.

That said, there seems to be a good deal of truth to the fact that many filmgoers in the late forties wanted to see Lugosi and Karloff and horror movies. And the simple fact is that they got them, with great regularity. No greater misconception exists about the history of horror films than the myth that they disappeared from the American movie theatre in the years immediately after World War II.

In reality, filmgoers were bombarded by a vast number of horror movies during the years 1947 to 1951. Some appeared in spotty releases, and some appeared only on spook show bills or at Halloween. However, a large number of horror movies had major releases throughout the United States during those years. And they included at least twenty-five Lugosi horror films. Twenty-five, in the space of just three years.

But none of them were new; they were all reissues. And the sheer number of them meant that in some ways Lugosi's greatest career obstacle was himself, or at least his screen self. The back catalogs of studios like Universal and Monogram saturated theatres with horror and Lugosi to the extent that they generally satisfied whatever demand existed for them, cheaply and efficiently. Why hire Lugosi and produce a new film when an old one would fit the bill?

Reissues were particularly appealing to studios in 1947 and in the years that immediately followed. As previously mentioned, the high tide of Hollywood's economic success in 1946 had indeed receded rapidly. According to Thomas Schatz, "the American movie industry went into an economic tailspin and a sustained fall from social grace."[2] Box-office receipts fell sharply due to declining attendance, with moviegoers spending an increasing percentage of their discretionary income on other kinds of leisure activities. The end result: the film industry felt great economic pressure.

At the same time, many exhibitors perceived a shortage of film product, something that led to a noticeable increase in the importation and distribution of foreign films. For example, many British films enjoyed great success at American theatres in the late forties. In fact, England's Eagle-Lion purchased the low-budget American company PRC in order to gain greater access to the US marketplace.[3]

Along with obtaining more and more product from other countries, studios realized that prof-

Published in the *Film Daily* on February 10, 1948.

Gary D. Rhodes | Bill Kaffenberger

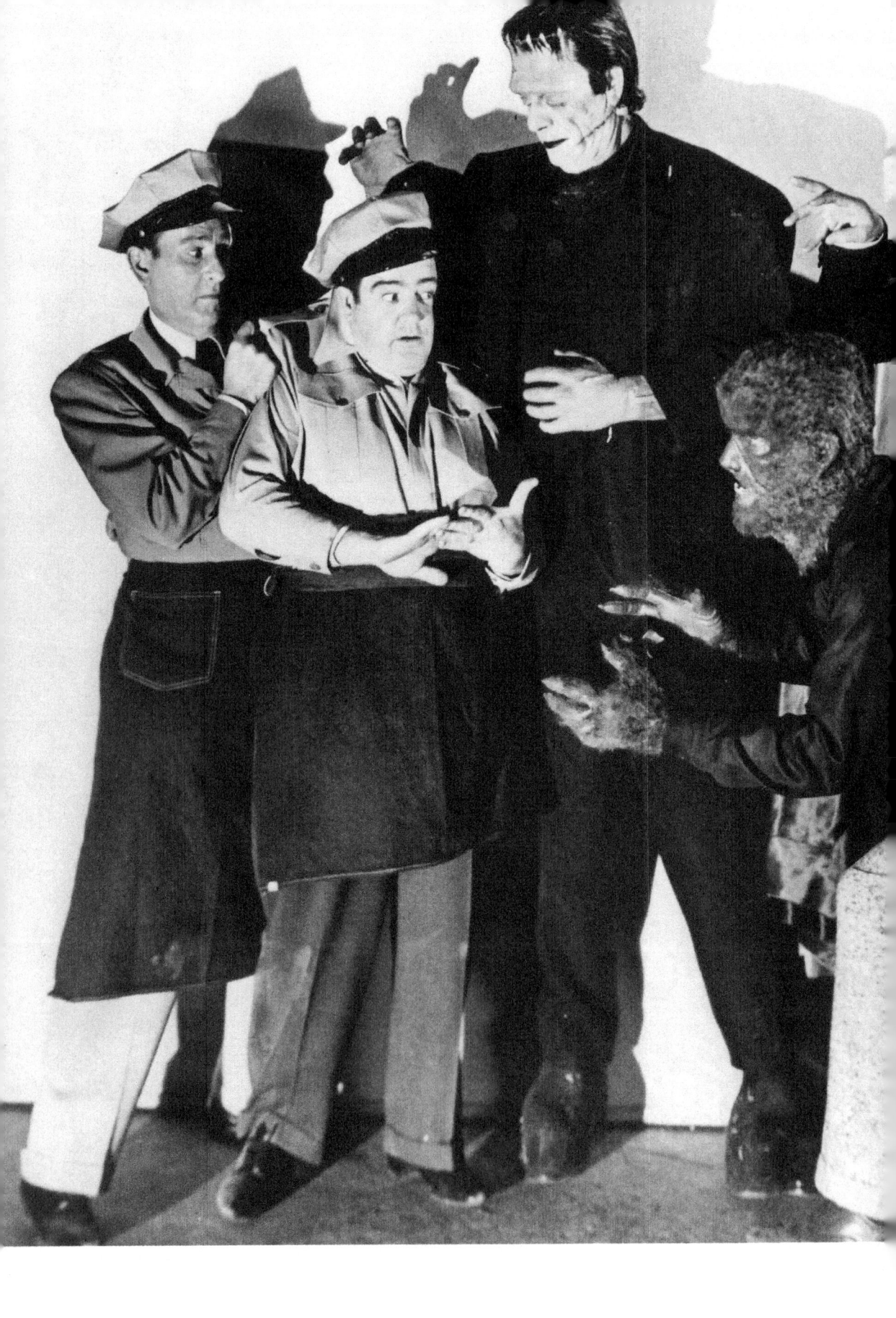

NO TRAVELER RETURNS | The Lost Years of Bela Lugosi

its could be had from reviving their own old films. It made good economic sense, at least in the short term. In April of 1947, for example, *Motion Picture Herald* reported that seven of the eleven producer-distributor companies – including MGM, Paramount, RKO, Twentieth Century-Fox, Universal, Warner Brothers, and PRC – would release 29 "hit pictures" from previous seasons in the weeks that followed.[4]

One studio executive noted that the "trend towards reissues [had] been brought about by the excessively high production costs which [had] practically doubled since 1941," adding that "the margin of profit from a reissue is sometimes even greater than that received from a new picture."[5] Universal's Vice-President agreed, deciding to re-release some old films as double features packages.

In March 1947 – the same month that one wire service article noted that ten "stock" film series, including "Frankenstein, Andy Hardy, and Dracula," were "out of production" – Universal announced that they would reissue *Dracula* (1931) and *Frankenstein* (1931) on a double bill.[6] It played Los Angeles in April of that year, and continued to appear on theatre screens throughout the summer and autumn. As one exhibitor reported:

> Played this double feature one day to capacity business. It will scare them, especially *Dracula*.
> –Roxy Theatre, Hinckley, Minn.[7]

At a number of theatres, the dual bill played as a midnight show.[8] And, curiously, at least a few theatres booked Dracula without Frankenstein.[9]

The success of such reissues brought even more of the same in 1948. In February of that year, *Hollywood Reporter* announced that Hollywood had scheduled 130 re-releases, the "greatest number of repeats for a single year's program in motion picture distribution history."[10] The practice continued in 1949, despite warnings from some in the indus-

Publicity still for *Abbott and Costello Meet Frankenstein* (1948), with the two famous comedians menaced by the Frankenstein Monster (Glenn Strange), the Wolf Man (Lon Chaney Jr.), and Dracula (Lugosi). (Courtesy of Jack Dowler)

From the *Los Angeles Times* of April 22, 1947.

try that reissues would eventually cause more problems than they solved.[11]

Hence the various Lugosi horror movies regularly appearing at American movie theatres. Realart Pictures, Inc. of New York City reissued many of his Universal films in 1948 and 1949. His Monogram films of the war era also returned to the screen. For example, the following breakdown provides a partial list of the Lugosi films screened in the post-war era:

1947: *Phantom Ship* (1935, aka *The Mystery of the Mary Celeste*), *The Human Monster* (aka, *Dark Eyes of London*, 1939), *The Devil Bat* (1941), *The Corpse Vanishes* (1942), *Ghosts on the Loose* (1943), *The Ape Man* (1943), *Return of the Ape Man* (1944), and *The Body Snatcher* (1945).[12]

1948: *Son of Frankenstein* (1939), *Black Friday* (1940), *The Wolf Man* (1941), *The Black Cat* (1941), *Ghost of Frankenstein* (1942), *Voodoo Man* (1944).[13]

1949: *Murders in the Rue Morgue* (1932), *The Raven* (1935), *Invisible Ghost* (1941), *Black Dragons* (1942), *Bowery at Midnight* (1942), *The Corpse Vanishes* (1942), *The Ape Man* (1943), *Frankenstein Meets the Wolf Man* (1943), *Ghosts on the Loose* (1943).[14]

In fact, Lugosi appeared so commonly on theatre screens during those years that his name was even advertised as starring in some old horror films in which he didn't actually appear. One 1947 advertisement credited him as the lead of *House of Dracula* (1945).[15] Perhaps more surprisingly, a 1950 ad for *Bride of Frankenstein* (1935) gave Lugosi second billing under Boris Karloff.[16]

In the midst of such reissues, Lugosi finally, and perhaps surprisingly, received an opportunity to star in a new movie. It was the chance to become the returning traveler, coming home to Hollywood in order to reclaim lost ground. And not just at any film studio, but at Universal, where he had starred in *Dracula* (1931).

However, Universal Studios in 1948 was different than any Universal that Lugosi had ever known. During 1945 and 1946, Universal became affiliated with International Pictures (an independent producing company that specialized in prestige films), and with United World Pictures (jointly owned by Universal, International and the British producer J. Arthur Rank). The collaboration coincided with – and was perhaps partially responsible for – Universal's extremely successful fiscal year in 1945.[17] By August 1946, in a deal orchestrated by Rank, Universal formally merged with International, with United World being consolidated into the new corporation.[18] Though Rank would have an important role

Bela Lugosi and Lou Costello. (Courtesy of Jack Dowler)

in the new company, the two men who had run International – Leo Spitz and William Goetz – would supervise all Universal productions.[19]

Spitz and Goetz quickly phased out all B-movie productions, planning to concentrate on approximately twenty-five films per year, as opposed to the fifty produced annually during World War II. Noting their elimination of low-budget productions, the *Hollywood Reporter* told readers that, "The new period being ushered in will be marked by a program of quality pictures."[20] In an effort to release prestige films, the studio also announced that nine of their 1946-47 releases would be shot in Technicolor.[21] Among the many results of the merger was that Universal-International began to distribute an increasing number of British-made films.[22] The studio also gained greater critical acclaim for its domestic productions.[23]

But such favorable response did not translate into box-office receipts. By November 1947, at the end of Universal-International's fiscal year, the studio's net profit had decreased by $1,335,202 from the previous fiscal year of 1946.[24] To the extent that particular divisions of the studio found success, it was in the distribution of J. Arthur Rank productions and from revenue from "new" 8mm and 16mm sales.[25] In terms of American film production, the Spitz-Goetz formula for success was not succeeding, but in fairness, much the same could have been said for many films at all of the studios in that bleak year.

At any rate, Universal-International's strategy helps explain the disappearance of horror films from their 1947 schedule, as well as other genre movies from their slate, including low-budget westerns. The exception was a project first announced in July 1947. *Variety* reported that comedy team Abbott and Costello would appear in a new film entitled *The Brain of Frankenstein*, slated to begin production under director Charles Barton in late October of that year.[26] In general, U-I did not actually view the film as an exception, because

Gary D. Rhodes | Bill Kaffenberger

Lugosi's son visits the set of *Abbott and Costello Meet Frankenstein* (1948). (Courtesy of Bill Chase)

– despite its title – they never described it as a horror movie, but rather as a comedy.[27]

Lugosi's involvement with the film came thanks to Don Marlowe. He had approached Lugosi about *The Brain of Frankenstein* in 1947, presumably in late summer shortly after it was announced, as it was one of the projects that convinced Lugosi to sign to Marlowe's "exclusive" management in September of that year.[28] Marlowe later told the story of his clinching the agreement with Universal-International only five days before shooting began, with his hard sell causing the studio to drop actor Ian Keith, whom they had allegedly already signed. As part of his tale, Marlowe claimed that he took no commission from Lugosi for the film deal.[29]

Though writer Arthur Lennig uncritically accepted and published Marlowe's tale in 1975, film historian Gregory William Mank rightly determined by 1990 that various features of it were problematic. It seems unlikely that Marlowe accepted no commission, though that fact remains unknown. At any rate, as Mank found, a cursory examination of the press reveals that Universal-International signed Lugosi to a contract on January 16, 1948, meaning at least twenty days before shooting began and at least fifteen days earlier than Marlowe had claimed.[30]

Father and son at Universal Studios. (Courtesy of Bill Chase)

Marlowe's memory of events featured obvious problems, and it was delivered with the kind of flair and self-aggrandizement not unexpected of so many Hollywood agents, managers, and promoters of the period. However, the cracks in his story do not cause its underlying structure to fall. In January 1948, as the *Player's Directory Bulletin* make clear, Lugosi was with the Don Marlowe Agency, phone number HO-8422. And Don Marlowe – who was in California while Lugosi was on the East Coast – made the deal that resulted in Lugosi's contract. Of that there can be no doubt. Marlowe even signed the contract on Lugosi's behalf.

Moreover, while there is no record that Marlowe was able to get Universal-International to drop Ian Keith in favor of Lugosi, it is certainly true that the studio was considering Keith. A studio memo dated September 9, 1947 had penciled in Keith for the role of Dracula.[31] Marlowe must have at least heard about Keith in 1947 or 1948, or otherwise he would not have been able to use his name in future stories. That said, Keith was not replaced at the last minute, and the changes possibly had nothing to do with Marlowe's skill as a negotiator.

But whatever he did or did not say to the Universal-International executives, whatever commission he did or did not take, and whatever inaccuracies are embedded in his later memories, Don Marlowe nabbed Lugosi the best role he had received in a Universal film since at least *Ghost of Frankenstein* in 1942. Indeed, it was the best film role Lugosi would receive for at least the last eleven years of his life.

Perhaps, as he was given to do in later years, Marlowe may well have used the hard sell approach of a used car dealer on Universal-International, even if it had little or no impact on their final decision to issue Lugosi a contract. Or perhaps, since he was telling Lugosi about the film prior to September

1947, Marlowe had been in regular touch with U-I for months. What is certain is that Marlowe did in 1948 what no one else could do in the post-war period: he made the deal that got Lugosi a major role in a major film.

Indeed, U-I announced signing Lugosi to the film on January 12, 1948, even though the final contract was dated January 16. His studio contract gave him four weeks of work at $2,000 per week.[32] According to the *Hollywood Reporter*, Lon Chaney Jr. (who would play the Wolf Man) and Glenn Strange (who would play the Frankenstein Monster) signed contracts that same day.[33] In both cases, Lugosi's fellow actors were back to portray characters that they had in earlier films, more times in fact than had Lugosi played Dracula onscreen. *The Brain of Frankenstein* marked Chaney's fifth portrayal of the Wolf Man, and Strange's third as the Monster. As for Lugosi, it would become only his second time in a feature film to essay the role for which he was most famous.

Lenore Aubert, who would play Dracula's consort "Sandra Mornay," was signed by January 20.[34] And by January 27, U-I had also issued contracts to actors Jane Randolph and Charles Bradstreet.[35] As the *Hollywood Reporter* wrote, the studio took on 1,000 employees in January 1948, and began issuing 2,200 weekly paychecks to the vast array of persons working on the studio's five new productions.[36]

After losing so much money in 1947, U-I may well have been looking for ways to save money on *The Brain of Frankenstein*. On January 30, only days before shooting began, the trade press announced that Bud Westmore would create masks for the Frankenstein Monster and the Wolf Man, thereby saving eight hours a day on makeup for both Chaney and Strange and, as a result, approximately 100 total hours of production time.[37] However, studio bosses quickly reversed themselves, allowing Barton to use makeup of a type comparable to earlier horror films.

Shooting began on February 5, 1948, with Lugosi's first day on the set coming on February 12.[38] By the end of the month, the film's title changed, though arguably it changed to three variants. The trade press began referring to the film by the title most identified with it: *Abbott and Costello Meet Frankenstein*. At the time of its release, studio publicity materials often referred to it as *Bud Abbott and Lou Costello Meet Frankenstein*. However, the film's opening credits opted for a third – and quite grammatically incorrect – title: *Bud Abbott Lou Costello Meet Frankenstein*, with the word "and" strangely absent.

Based upon memories of those present and a number of surviving film outtakes, the shoot was generally a happy one, with Abbott and Costello's friend Bobby Barber on the set to help keep everyone in a good mood. The comedy duo improvised a bit of their dialogue, but such changes seem minor in comparison to other script alterations and additions. For example, on February 12, after a week of shooting, producer Robert Arthur decided to change the ending, adding a cameo by the Invisible Man.[39] The *New York Times* announced on March 14 that Glenn Strange would provide the voice for the new character, though at some point those plans changed, as in the final film Vincent Price read the dialogue.[40]

Finding Lugosi in his dressing room "scrambling on the floor" in search of a missing shirt stud, a journalist reported that the actor was pleased to be in the film, particularly since the studio was not asking him to do anything "unbecoming to Dracula's dignity." Lugosi explained: "There is no burlesque

Here Lugosi, Bud Abbott, and Lou Costello clown around with Bobby Barber (center).

for me. All I have to do is frighten the boys, a perfectly appropriate activity. My trademark will be unblemished."[41]

Lugosi also seems to have enjoyed being back at Universal. One newspaper noted that he had lunch in the studio commissary with his son. Lugosi still had on his makeup, but "the kid isn't the least bit shocked. 'You sure got it on thick today, Pop,' is junior's comment."[42] Here was another reason to be happy. The film role not only returned Lugosi to the studio, but also to his son.

Lillian Lugosi later remembered that her husband took the behind-the-scenes antics of Abbott and Costello (and Bobby Barber) graciously. Director Charles Barton had positive memories of both Lugosi and his work ethic, but did recall that he avoided Abbott and Costello's epic pie-throwing battles.[43] Glenn Strange went even further, claiming Lugosi was "hard to get to know," and that he once admonished the comedians, "We should not be playing while we are working." Lugosi's remark only exacerbated the pranks, with Abbott and Costello later imitating his words and accent.[44]

Which of these represent Lugosi's actual interactions with his fellow actors? Probably all of them. Depending on the day and the prank, Lugosi seems to have responded differently, from engaging in some of the jokes – or at least laughing at them – to reacting with disdain. Indeed, surviving outtakes from the film reveal that very range of emotions, though they may tell only part of the story. In one of them, Bobby Barber secretly follows Lugosi down a staircase. When Lugosi realizes the joke, he appears visibly unhappy. The director had to shoot seven takes of the shot to get one that was usable. However, studio files indicate that Lugosi was one hour late to work that day, with the entire company left to wait on him. As a result, his apparent anger in the outtake may have been caused in part by other factors.[45] Indeed, that day was the second time Lugosi was late reporting to the set.[46]

The comedians might not have been the only persons at U-I with a knack for improvising. Studio publicists told the press that the bat prop used in the film "was built mainly out of airplane parts."[47] But even before that story appeared in some newspapers, the *New York Times* exposed the joke being played on reporters. Their journalist claimed that the bat was not "jet-propelled," as claimed, but was instead "nothing more than the conventional, though ingenious, wire controlled animal which has been gliding around the Universal stages for years."[48]

And then there was the question of the Dracula ring, which Lugosi wore in the new film. In the spring of 1945, the *Cleveland Plain Dealer* had told readers that "somewhere, somebody – presumably a man – is wearing an ornate gold and onyx ring with deadly crest of the legendary Count Dracula...."[49] The newspaper added that Universal rented the ring, first worn by Bela Lugosi and later by Lon Chaney Jr., from H. B. Crouch Jewelers of Los Angeles, a store that catereed to the film business. But the studio learned it had been sold when they attempted to rent it for John Carradine's Dracula in *House of Frankenstein* (1944).[50] Refusing to reveal the purchaser's name, Crouch created a duplicate ring and sold it to Universal.[51] In actual fact, Lugosi's ring in *Dracula* (1931) was a different ring. Presumably the ring he wore in the Abbott and Costello film was the ring purchased from H. B. Crouch.

Lugosi would later end up with the ring, or at least one that looked like it. In the 1950s, he told a friend that he borrowed the ring from Universal after the production was over and simply didn't return it.[52] But in 1948, Lugosi told a newspaper journalist something quite different. According to that version of events, Lugosi allegedly bought two copies of the ring from H. B. Crouch.[53] As a result, it is quite possible that the ring that Lugosi had in his possession in his later years was a different version of the ring seen in the Abbott and Costello film, or, for that matter, prior Universal horror movies.

At any rate, the production wrapped on March 20, 1948, with the final scene of the shoot being one in which the Wolf Man grabs Dracula on the castle balcony. However, some effects shots were filmed in late March, and U-I filmed a new scene with Jane Randolph on April 9.[54] *Abbott and Costello Meet Frankenstein* then went into post-production and was readied for release.

Admittedly, the film is not perfect, particularly in its post-synchronous dubbing. At times we hear the Wolf Man growling while we can very clearly see that his mouth not moving. And in a minor continuity error, Wilbur (Costello) seems not to pick up his costume for a masquerade ball after it drops on the ground. But these are minor quibbles regarding a film that continues to feel more fresh and exciting than several of the previous entries in either the Frankenstein or Abbott and Costello series. Or, for that matter, any film that Lugosi made after World War II.

In addition to consistently strong acting throughout and some brilliantly comedic moments, the film's strengths are many. The music score is superb, so much so that it is difficult to think of any Universal horror film score that was ever as closely timed to precise onscreen action as *Abbott and Costello Meet Frankenstein*'s opening credits. That is in addition to the joy of a cue specifically devoted to the moments when Dracula hypnotizes his victims.

Many strong visuals unfold thanks to highly atmospheric art direction and a judicious use of animation, both at the beginning of the film and in scenes that depict Dracula's transformation to and

Lugosi takes part in some of the antics of Lou Costello (left), Bobby Barber (middle), and Bud Abbott (right).

from bat form. Along with such obvious joys come more subtle but equally memorable images, as in the moonlight that shines through window blinds; it slowly, vertically ripples up Lawrence Talbot's (Chaney's) body while he is in London.

Together, the film's many pleasures make it easy to forgive a plot that is quite vague. While not in werewolf form, Lawrence Talbot attempts to put an end to Dracula and the Frankenstein Monster for reasons that we never learn. Talbot's dialogue "We meet again, Count Dracula," implies that he has been on their trail for some time. In the film, he follows them from Europe to America in an effort to stop them from doing something, but we don't know what. Though Dracula wishes to return the Monster to full strength, we have no idea why, or why he specifically wants to do so in America.

But at the same time, it is easy to overlook the film's subtle and fascinating invocation of World War II. Whether we take Talbot to be English or American, he calls from London to the United States at the beginning of the film to warn of imminent danger from – as the dialogue in film always suggests – "Europe." It is, for example, a "European agent" who has contacted McDougal (Frank Ferguson) of McDougal's House of Horrors.

And then there is the curious figure of Dr. Sandra Mornay (Aubert), who is traveling incognito. As a result, Mornay – a name that clearly suggests a French heritage – is likely not her real name, particularly given her accent. Instead, she seems Eastern European. Dracula's dialogue informs us that there is a "price" on Mornay's head as a result of her "curious operations" that "intrigued the European police." That she is a criminal is obvious. But in the context of 1948, such dialogue might well imply that she is a war criminal, whether a spy or a collaborator or – given her medical and scientific knowledge – a Nazi doctor. Treachery of that sort means that no audience member need shed a tear when the Frankenstein Monster hurls her out of a castle window to her death, a particularly fascinating moment given that this is meant to be a comedy film.

Abbott and Costello Meet Frankenstein also draws on the history of Hollywood horror films. As

From the *Film Daily* of July 21, 1948.

some modern writers have noted, it does ignore the plotlines of prior horror films, particularly the fact that all three monsters had been killed on more than one prior occasion. Nonetheless, the film echoes its predecessors in various respects. Dracula and the Monster successfully enter the United States in crates. Here the plot resembles Dracula's movements to England and Carfax Abbey in the 1931 film.

The vampire bat also evokes horror film history at Universal Studios. The film uses a physical prop to depict as Dracula in bat form for some shots, but it also uses animation to do the same in others. The disparity is obvious, though not necessarily problematic. Over fifteen years earlier, Universal's *Murders in the Rue Morgue* (1932), attempted much the same with Erik the Ape, who exists in the film at times as an actual ape and at times as a man in a costume.

In *Dracula* (1931), Mina (Helen Chandler) imitates Lugosi's Dracula, offering within the film's running time a parody of the vampire's voice. *Abbott and Costello Meet Frankenstein* offers something of the same order, but for all three of its monsters. On more than one occasion, Wilbur (Costello) mimics Dracula's use of the cape and his hand gestures, as well as the Monster's facial expression and his walk. Likewise, Chick (Abbott) wears a wolf's mask and – to help make his imitation complete – a dark shirt and trousers that closely resemble Lawrence Talbot's.

McDougal's House of Horrors also draws on prior films, offering specific exhibits that reference earlier Universal horror films, including *Murders in the Rue Morgue* (1932) and *The Mummy* (1932). However, other exhibits offer scenes of criminals like Bluebeard and a number of gangsters with machine guns. We also see a jail cell. Here it is as if McDougal uses a larger, more encompassing definition of the term "horror," just as the film industry and national press had since 1945.

Various torture devices are also on display at the House of Horrors. In this way, some exhibits resemble Latimer Marsh's personal collection of the same in RKO's *Genius at Work* (1946) with Brown and Carney. Indeed, it would be easy to suggest that Brown and Carney's two films with Lugosi were important precursors to *Abbott and Costello Meet Frankenstein*, as was *The Gorilla* (1939) starring the Ritz Brothers. In each case, a comedy team grapples with Lugosi and various horror film plot devices.

As for the specific character Dracula, Lugosi was proud of the fact that his "trademark" was "unblemished" by the film. He was correct, and his performance is perhaps as memorable as in the 1931 film. But the portrayals are different, and not merely because Lugosi is seventeen years older in the Abbott and Costello film. True, in some respects the character is the same, including to the extent that he must rely upon lackeys. Once bitten, Sandra becomes something of a Renfield character, even to the extent of calling Dracula "master."

However, while age may have changed Lugosi's physical appearance, it is the Dracula of *Abbott and Costello Meet Frankenstein* who is the more physically agile. In the 1931 film Lugosi's Dracula speaks and moves slowly, in a manner that befits royalty. Such methodical gestures serve to underscore the rare moments when he does move quickly, as when he sees a crucifix or a mirrored cigarette box.

By the time of the Abbott and Costello film, Dracula speaks more rapidly and with a less peculiar rhythm to his speech. He is somewhat less regal, including in the fact that he does not wear the medallion seen in the earlier film. He is also profoundly active, ranging from helping the Monster stand up to engaging in battle with the Wolf Man at the film's climax. In the 1931 movie, it would seem inconceivable for Dracula to run, to crash through a door, or to throw a flower pot, but he does all of those in the 1948 film.

If the earlier performance speaks, at least to an extent, of how Lugosi played the role on Broadway, the same might be true of the later performance and how Lugosi delivered his lines in summer stock. That said, the role also shows the influence of other films in which Lugosi did not appear. Whether it is the emphasis on showing the transformation to and from vampire bat or the more physically aggressive blocking, or, perhaps most noticeably, the character's interest in the Frankenstein Monster, Dracula in *Abbott and Costello Meet Frankenstein* bears the influence of *House of Frankenstein* (1944) and *House of Dracula* (1945).

In the Abbott and Costello film, Dracula uses the name "Dr. Lejos" as a cover story in his bid to purchase and assemble equipment that can restore the Monster's strength. To Lugosi, the name Lejos – at least as pronounced in the film, even if not in the spelling used in the script – would have quickly brought to mind two important figures in his life: his brother Lajos, as well as the towering figure of his first father-in-law, Lajos Szmik.

But in the film, it is Dracula's role as a "doctor" that is perhaps most fascinating. Aside from merely being a pseudonym, we hear the vampiric Sandra tell Wilbur, "I must obey my doctor's orders." And, more importantly, it is Dracula who takes control of the lab and turns on the electrical equipment in his mad quest to restore the Monster and give him a new brain. In 1931, Lugosi famously did not appear in the film Frankenstein, though he had undergone at least one, if not two, screen tests for the role of the Monster. Instead, Boris Karloff portrayed the character and another horror film icon was born. Later, Lugosi would comment that he had wanted to play the role of Dr. Frankenstein. All those years later in the Abbott and Costello film, it is as if Lugosi was able to portray both famous characters: Dracula and a permutation of Dr. Frankenstein.

Though Universal-International curiously did not copyright the

Lobby display at the Criterion Theatre on Broadway in New York City tested the "fear complex" of ticket buyers at the press of a button, the result indicating one of a dozen different scary topics.

Gary D. Rhodes | Bill Kaffenberger

Ballyhoo at a movie theatre in Miami, Florida.

film until August 1948, the studio released *Abbott and Costello Meet Frankenstein* on June 15 of that year. It was one of approximately 25 films that they released over a nine-month period.[55] Only two months earlier, Abbott and Costello's film *The Noose Hangs High*, also directed by Charles Barton, had made its premiere on American theatre screens.[56]

Critical reviews varied. The *Hollywood Reporter* decried the response of those New York critics, noting that many of the "BOO-geymen of Broadway" disliked *Abbott and Costello Meet Frankenstein*. For example, the *New York Sun* claimed that the story was a "grand idea, but it was too bad that it could not have been attended by persons capable of satire rather than pie-throwing comedy only." And the *New York World-Telegram* warned readers that if they didn't have a "taste" for Abbott and Costello's antics, the film would be a "painful experience."[57] Other New York critics used the film to make larger points. *The New York Herald-Tribune* claimed the film exposed the "innate absurdity of supernatural horror stories," and the *New York Post* believed the "one-shot giggle" revealed that Universal was "in disgrace with fortune."[58]

By contrast, generally positive reviews appeared in the industry press, including in the *Film Daily*, *Daily Variety*, *Harrison's Reports*, *Motion Picture Daily*, and – perhaps most enthusiastically of all – *Hollywood Reporter*.[59] Similarly, both *Photoplay* and *The Commonweal* promised readers that audiences would find the film funny.[60]

Such pronouncements seem to have been true. Despite the negative reviews, box-office receipts in New York City were extremely strong.[61] Other major cities experienced similar successes, including Chicago, where it grossed a "sensational" $40,000, and Boston, where the film had a "walloping seven days" and brought in $30,000.[62] In San Francisco, the film "gave Blumenfeld's Orpheum an almost unprecedented $26,700."[63] And in Los Angeles, the film was "nothing short of sensational," racking up $45,800.[64]

Theatre manager reports from across the United States were generally positive, except in cases where viewers interpreted it as a horror film rather than a comedy:

> One of the best and most entertaining in the Abbott and Costello series. A good draw and a pleased audience.
> – Gray Theatre, Gray, Ga.[65]

> A laugh riot from beginning to end. Liked by all. Did good midweek business.
> –The Gilbert, Okeechobee, Fla.

> Just about their best, I reckon, and lots of people came to see them. We played a midnight preview on this which also drew well.
> –Eminence Theatre, Eminence, Ky.[66]

> Very good at the box office. A little too scary for the little ones, but the high school kids really enjoyed it.
> –Grove Theatre, Blooming Grove, Texas.[67]

> I wonder if it is worth it – all those howling kids, screams, and broken seats. Did an above average business, but it wasn't Abbott and Costello at their best. Had more walkouts on this than any picture we've ever played. This is the last 'horror' picture we will ever book.
> – Williamette Valley Theatres, Albany, Ore.[68]

> The shrieks and screams could be heard in the street. Small children jammed the foyer. Babies cried. Women scratched all the skin from their husbands' hands and the PTA descended in mobs, demanding to know why we played a 'horror' picture on Saturday. If we get out of this one without bodily harm, we will be plain lucky. Spent most of my time drying tears and allaying hysteria among the children. Wow!
> – Shastona Theatre, Mount Shasta, Cal.[69]

Despite any difficulties experienced by particular theatres, the film became a major success, a triumph in what were dark economic days for Hollywood.

As a result, Spitz and Goetz at U-I planned more Abbott and Costello films, but not any horror films.[70] They had abandoned those, and did not return to them. After all, in the studio's eyes, *Abbott and Costello Meet Frankenstein* was a comedy. It had always been a comedy, even if some kids in rural towns fled from the sight of Dracula and the other monsters.

That's not to say that other studios did not release horror movies in 1948. They did, but they fell into an expanded definition of horror: intelligent and psychological, aimed at adult audiences. *Portrait of Jennie* (SRO), *Sorry, Wrong Number* (Paramount). *The Raven* (Westport International), and *The Spiritualist* (Eagle-Lion) appeared in American theatres, but none smacked of the Universal horror movie of the pre-1947 era. There were no monsters. No vampires.

Lon Chaney Jr. and screenwriter Curt Siodmak attempted to start their own production company in 1948 to produce films featuring characters "more horrible than any yet seen on the screen."[71] But nothing came of the venture. Likewise, Lugosi told the press that "there is enough material in the original novel [*Dracula*] for half a dozen pictures," but no studio produced any of them that year, or in the years that immediately followed.[72]

The Creeper (20th Century Fox) did provide a solitary example of the older style of horror film in

This 1948 lobby display at the Malco Theatre in Memphis, Tennessee featured lights and moving parts.

1948, unless one counts the potentially scary elements within *Abbott and Costello Meet Frankenstein*. The *New York Star* certainly did, but saw them as increasingly dated:

> ... it's heart-warming to see all our favorite monsters once more, each inexorably expressing his individuality, all at the same time. It's kind of like a class reunion. They look a little older now, and a little tired. Dracula seems to creak a bit with arthritis as he emerges from his coffin these days, and his bite has lost some of its depth.[73]

Perhaps the damning phrase in this review of the Abbott and Costello film is "once more," as if the subsequent disappearance of the monsters from the screen was a clear expectation.

Of course audiences who enjoyed such fare hardly needed to worry, as the reissue business kept the old horror movies on the screen. Lugosi was right there, larger than life, flickering alongside Karloff and Chaney Jr. on a regular basis in town after town, city after city.

But Lugosi the actor wasn't back in the studios after *Abbott and Costello Meet Frankenstein*. Likely that film had rekindled his hopes that he could mount a comeback in motion pictures, but if so, he probably did not gauge the affect all of those old reissues were having on his career. And so, he once again had to leave his son and hit the road, the trip to Hollywood being just a temporary stop on a journey that was far from over.

(Endnotes)

1 Adams, Marjorie. "Bela Lugosi Glad of Respite from Horror-Inspiring Roles." *Boston Globe* 17 Apr. 1947.
2 Schatz, Thomas. *Boom or Bust: American Cinema in the 1940s* (Berkeley: University of California Press, 1997).
3 *Ibid.*

4. "Seven Majors Releasing 29 Reissues This Season." *Motion Picture Herald* 26 Apr. 1947.
5. *Ibid.*
6. "Better Movies." *Seattle Times* 9 Mar. 1947.
7. "Universal." *Motion Picture Herald* 25 Oct. 1947.
8. *The Record-Argus* (Greenville, PA) 7 November 1947.
9. *Kingsport News* (Kingsport, TN) 11 Nov. 1947. [In another curious example of theatre programming, the West End in Chicago booked *Dracula* (1931) on a double bill with *House of Frankenstein* (1944) in September 1947. See: *The Garfieldian* (Chicago, IL) 11 Sept. 1947.]
10. "Industry Schedules 130 Re-Releases for this Year." *Hollywood Reporter* 9 Feb. 1948.
11. "Reissues Are Bad Policy, Says Broidy." *Motion Picture Herald* 29 Jan. 1949.
12. *Naugatuck Daily News* (Naugatuck, CT); Advertisement. *Gastonia Gazette* (Gastonia, NC) 6 Dec. 1947; *Corsicana Daily Sun* (Corsicana, TX) 16 Oct. 1947; *Albuquerque Journal* (Albuquerque, NM) 1 June 1947; *Dallas Morning News* 2 Feb. 1947; *Berkshire Evening Eagle* (Pittsfield, MA) 22 July 1947.
13. *Dallas Morning News* 24 Aug. 1948; *Cleveland Plain Dealer* 14 May 1948; *Dallas Morning News* 31 Oct. 1948; *Dallas Morning News* 20 May 1948; *Dallas Morning News* 7 Sept. 1948; *Daily Hayward Review* (Hayward, CA) 30 Oct. 1948.
14. "Reissues." *Boxoffice* 3 Dec. 1949; "Favorite Films"; *Dallas Morning News* 1 July 1949.
15. *Freeport Facts* (Freeport, TX) 30 Jan. 1947.
16. *Lima News* (Lima, OH) 20 Oct. 1950.
17. "Univ. Nets Record $3,910,928." *Hollywood Reporter* 29 Jan. 1946.
18. "U-Int'l Production Merged." *Film Daily* 31 July 1946.
19. "Univ. Int'l $60,000,000 Slate." *Hollywood Reporter* 31 July 1946.
20. "U-I Merger Papers Being Inked Today." *Hollywood Reporter* 12 Nov. 1946.
21. "U-I Will Spend $40,000,000 on 25 Pix, 9 in Technicolor." *Hollywood Reporter* 14 Aug. 1946.
22. Schatz, *Boom or Bust*.
23. *Ibid.*
24. "Univ. 47 Gross $64,958,405; Net Drops More Than Million." *Hollywood Reporter* 29 Jan. 1948.
25. "U 1947 Profit Is $3,230,017." *Motion Picture Daily* 29 Jan. 1947.
26. "A-C's Next, *Brain*." *Variety* 20 July 1947.
27. Brady, Thomas F. "Hollywood Digest." *New York Times* 14 Mar. 1948.
28. Lugosi, Bela. Letter to Virginia Doak. 8 Oct. 1947.
29. Lennig, Arthur. *The Count: The Life and Films of Bela "Dracula" Lugosi* (New York: G. P. Putnam's Sons, 1974).
30. Mank, Gregory William. "Production Background." *Abbott and Costello Meet Frankenstein*. Ed. by Philip J. Riley. (Absecon, NJ: Magicimage Filmbooks, 1990).
31. Furmanek, Bob, and Ron Palumbo. *Abbott and Costello in Hollywood* (New York: Perigee, 1991).
32. Brady, Thomas F. "Trio Signed by U-I for New Comedy." *New York Times* 13 Jan. 1948. Brady wrote this article in Hollywood on January 12.
33. "Abbott and Costello to Have Aid of Monsters." *Hollywood Reporter* 13 Jan. 1948.
34. *Abbott and Costello Meet Frankenstein*, studio papers at the University of Southern California. Courtesy of Gregory William Mank.
35. *Ibid.* See also: "Casting News." *Hollywood Reporter* 29 Jan. 1948.
36. "U-I Takes on 1,000 Employees in Jan." *Hollywood Reporter* 9 Feb. 1948.
37. "U-I Will Use Monster Masks to Save Make-Up." *Hollywood Reporter* 30 Jan. 1948.
38. *Abbott and Costello Meet Frankenstein*, studio papers at the University of Southern California. Courtesy of Gregory William Mank.
39. "Invisible Man Returns." *Hollywood Reporter* 13 Feb. 1948.
40. Brady, "Hollywood Digest."
41. *Ibid.*
42. Heffernan, Howard. "Out Hollywood Way." *Canton Repository* (Canton, OH) 24 Mar. 1948.
43. Mank, "Production Background."
44. Strange, Glenn. Count Dracula Society Banquet. 22 Apr. 1972.
45. *Abbott and Costello Meet Frankenstein*, studio papers at the University of Southern California. Courtesy of Gregory William Mank.
46. *Ibid.*
47. Heyn, Howard C. "Hollywood Property Men Reap Varied Harvest from War Surplus." *Hartford Courant* 4 Apr. 1948.
48. "Anything Doesn't Go." *New York Times* 7 Mar. 1948.
49. *Cleveland Plain Dealer* 8 Apr. 1945.
50. *Ibid.*
51. *Ibid.*
52. Sheffield, Richard. Email to Gary D. Rhodes. 18 Oct. 2011.
53. *The Desert News* (Salt Lake City, UT) 5 Sept. 1948.
54. *Abbott and Costello Meet Frankenstein*, studio papers at the University of Southern California. Courtesy of Gregory William Mank.
55. "Universal Plans 24 in 9 Months." *Motion Picture Herald* 21 Feb. 1948.
56. "Noose Hangs High Given Brush-Off by N.Y. Reviewers." *Hollywood Reporter* 4 June 1948.
57. "*Frankenstein* Gets Gold in N.Y. Despite Notices." *Hollywood Reporter* 2 Aug. 1948.
58. *Ibid.*

Boris Karloff purchases a ticket to *Abbott and Costello Meet Frankenstein* (1948).

59   "*Abbott and Costello Meet Frankenstein.*" *Film Daily* 28 June 1948; "*Abbott and Costello Meet Frankenstein.*" *Daily Variety* 28 June 1948; "*Abbott and Costello Meet Frankenstein.*" *Harrison's Reports* 3 July 1948; "*Abbott and Costello Meet Frankenstein.*" *Motion Picture Daily* 6 July 1948; "A and C's *Frankenstein* a Hilarious Brainstorm." *Hollywood Reporter* 28 June 1948.
60   "*Abbott and Costello Meet Frankenstein.*" *Photoplay* Sept. 1948; Hartung, Philip T. *The Commonweal* 6 Aug. 1948.
61   "*Frankenstein* Gets Gold in N.Y. Despite Notices."
62   "*Lady in Ermine* Sets Bright Pace in Otherwise Dull Loop." *Hollywood Reporter* 8 Sept. 1948; "Key City Grosses," *Motion Picture Daily* 18 Aug. 1948; "Boston Figures on Upswing, Holdovers Do Most Business." *Hollywood Reporter* 14 Sept. 1948.
63   "Pinch Off in San Francisco: *Frankenstein*, *Judy* Lead." *Hollywood Reporter* 10 Aug. 1948.
64   "*Island*, *Largo*, *Frankenstein* Setting Los Angeles Pace." *Hollywood Reporter* 27 July 1948.
65   "Universal." *Motion Picture Herald* 2 Oct. 1948.
66   "Universal." *Motion Picture Herald* 25 Dec. 1948.
67   "Universal." *Motion Picture Herald* 11 Dec. 1948.
68   "Universal." *Motion Picture Herald* 18 June 1949.
69   "Universal." *Motion Picture Herald* 19 Feb. 1949.
70   "Universal Plans 24 Next Season." *Motion Picture Herald* 21 Aug. 1948.
71   Thomas, Bob. "Hollywood Blows Hot for Chillers." *Oakland Tribune* 3 Mar. 1948.
72   *Ibid.*
73   "*Frankenstein* Gets Gold in N.Y. Despite Notices."

Pressbook page from *Abbott and Costello Meet Frankenstein* (1948).

Gary D. Rhodes | Bill Kaffenberger

Lucy (Rande Carmichael) in Dracula's clutches.
(Courtesy of George R. Snell)

Chapter 7

THE BARN EMPORIUMS

Writing in the *New York Post* in 1948, Vernon Rice worried openly about the fate of summer stock theatres. Much of their growth and success had depended on the use of famous stars to garner audiences. Rice recalled that various "fugitives from the films" had invaded the straw hat circuit in 1946, but was concerned that their numbers were rapidly increasing.[1]

Due in part to Hollywood's troubles, Rice understood that the year 1948 saw "more stars off screen than on," and he warned that overuse of them in summer theatres represented "daring speculation." Certainly the situation was helpful to out-of-work stars who returned to live theatre and made "handsome" salaries. Speaking sarcastically, Rice mocked this kind of actor:

Nothing pleases him so much as the smell of grease paint, the flies in his dressing room and the apprentices stealing his big scenes.

Of course he is only getting $3,000 a week plus percentage, he claims, but one really has to make sacrifices in life, doesn't one? And if one has to make sacrifices, why shouldn't they be made for the Theatre?

Off he goes muttering these weighty words to stumble over the stage furniture and to get lost in his lines while showing his well-capped teeth.

The horrifying thing about all this is that the audience will love it.[2]

Aside from his personal disdain for the practice, Rice was indeed nervous about what problems it would cause. "What's going to happen," he asked, "when screen stars are no novelty?" Audiences might grow weary of them, and so "this year's attraction may become next year's prize turkey."

Several of the stars in 1948 were "more or less new to the rural circuit," including Jackie Cooper, Ida Lupino, Walter Abel, Kay Francis, Sylvia Sidney, and Ilona Massey.[3] It wasn't uncommon for some of them to receive upwards of $4,000 per week, though many were making as little at $500 for the same amount of work.[4]

Despite Vernon Rice's objections, such stars played a major role in the summer stock boom. However, the increasing number of new stars in 1948 may have had an adverse affect on those stars who

Gary D. Rhodes | Bill Kaffenberger

Don Marlowe

AGENCY

6331 HOLLYWOOD BOULEVARD
HOLLYWOOD 28, CALIFORNIA

Telephone
HOllywood 8422

May 14, 1948

Mr. Lyman Brown
145 W. 45th St.
New York City, New York

Dear Mr. Brown:

Many thanks for your letter.

Mr. Lugosi is interested only in a new play with Broadway probabilities and is not interested in appearing in "Arsenic and Old Lace" or "Dracula" at any figure.

Many thanks for your offer, and if you can possibly find a new play, I could guarantee that he will be most anxious to accept.

Most sincerely,

DON MARLOWE

DM:hr

---

had appeared in stock the prior year: new competition could well have limited the number of offers they received.

For Bela Lugosi, the straw hat circuit had been a major success in 1947. And by late spring of 1948, he likely hoped the same would be true of the forthcoming summer. The problem was that he remained tied to just two productions: *Dracula* and *Arsenic and Old Lace*. Other actors, including those associated with horror, seemed to have greater ease in branching out. For example, during the summer of 1948, John Carradine appeared in *20th Century* at the Cape Playhouse in Dennis, Massachusetts and the Lakeside Theatre at Lake Hopatcong, New Jersey; he also starred in *A Bill of Divorcement* in Watkins Glen, New York and *The Imaginary Invalid* in Rehoboth Beach, Delaware.[5]

As late as May 14, 1948, Lugosi's manager Don Marlowe responded to a letter from theatrical representative Lyman Brown, who had already begun to line up opportunities for Lugosi to star in summer stock. Marlowe told him: "Mr. Lugosi is interested only in a new play with Broadway possibilities and is not interested in appearing in *Arsenic and Old Lace* or *Dracula* at any figure."[6] Here we can see what may well have been maddening at times for Marlowe and other representatives. Lugosi refused work even when he needed it badly, apparently in a doomed effort to escape from typecasting.

One week later, Brown wrote again, claiming he understood that Lugosi had a new play and offered to send it to three stock companies.[7] But further discussion of a new play disappeared just as quickly as Lugosi changed his mind. He agreed to do *Dracula* in summer stock in 1948, just as he agreed to do *Arsenic*. But having initially turned down such work, Lugosi unwittingly limited his number of possible bookings.

In theory, being linked with two plays should not have posed any difficulty. After all, Edward Everett Horton continued his straw hat success in the summer of 1948 with *Springtime for Henry*. But there was a clear difference between Horton and Lugosi. Summer theatre managers generally did not attempt to stage *Springtime* without Horton, whereas they regularly produced versions of *Dracula* and *Arsenic and Old Lace* without Lugosi. Consider 1948: versions of *Arsenic* appeared in Jennerstown, Pennsylvania, Mashpee, Massachusetts, and Whitefield, New Hampshire, all of them without Lugosi.

And so Lugosi would have a summer stock career in 1948, but not to the extent of the previous year. Three of his four summer stock appearances that year would be in *Dracula*. It is possible that Lugosi's appearance as Dracula in *Abbott and Costello Meet Frankenstein* may have led managers of summer theatres to program the play *Dracula*, rather than, say *Arsenic and Old Lace*, which was generally the more popular of the two in the late forties.

At any rate, summer stock meant leaving California and his son once again. It also meant leaving Lake Elsinore, where he not only had a home, but where he also had some investments. In the spring of 1948, Hedda Hopper reported that Lugosi had invested in seven homes that were built near the lake.[8] Later, a newspaper article in June 1948 claimed that Lugosi would be involved in twenty more "popular-priced homes on his own subdivision" at Lake Elsinore, and that he hoped to have the project finished by August 1 of the same year, by which time he would be in the middle of the summer stock season.[9]

Lugosi's first 1948 appearance at the "barn emporiums," as they were sometimes called, came in Denver, Colorado. Given the concentration of high profile summer theatres in the East, the Denver appearance at first seems unexpected. However, the city was home to Elitch's Gardens, touted as the "oldest summer theatre in America." In the late forties, Norris Houghton, director of that venue, explained in *Theatre Arts* magazine that the "majority of Denverites' principal acquaintance with the new plays comes through Elitch's presentations."[10] And Houghton had at

From the *Denver Post* of July 6, 1948.

> CAN YOU TAKE IT?
> —Some of Last Night's Audience Were Shocked Out of Their Wits
>
> ARTISTS REPERTORY THEATRE
> Presents
>
> **BELA LUGOSI**—*in person* *Master Character Actor*
> in
> **"DRACULA"**
> —The Greatest Horror Play Ever Written.
> For Fun and Excitement DON'T MISS IT
>
> **PHIPPS AUDITORIUM**
> Tonight Thru Tuesday—Special Saturday Matinee
> Seats Going Fast—Phone FLorida 0044 for Reservations
> Tickets on Sale at May Co. Box Office, AComa 0911
>
> Prices: $2.40 and $1.20 Evening, $1.80 and $1.00 for Matinee

Published in the *Denver Post* on July 9, 1948.

least one thing in common with Vernon Rice: he despised the reliance many summer theatres had on visiting stars.

Not surprisingly, then, the historic Elitch Gardens did not book Lugosi. Instead, Denver's newly-formed Artists Repertory Theatre starred Lugosi in *Dracula*. Philip Tonge directed, and Oscar Hobman designed the sets. Along with Lugosi, the group booked New York actress Marjorie Lytell to portray Lucy. Members of the resident company played the other key roles. For example, Harry Lowery played Renfield, Jim Herrick played Dr. Seward, and — in a last minute change due to another actor's illness — Frank Mosier "stepped into the very difficult role of Professor Van Helsing."[11]

The Artists Repertory Theatre was a theatre company, but not an actual theatre. The group staged their summer stock plays at Denver's 960-seat Phipps Auditorium, located in the City Park. Working on a different schedule than most other summer theatres, the Artists Repertory Theatre opened *Dracula* on a Thursday night, staging six performances and a Saturday matinee between July 8 and July 13, 1948.[12]

Lugosi's friend David Durston also worked on the play, warmly recalling the experience decades later:

> There were a couple of great stories about Denver. For example, I remember after the Saturday matinee, Bela gave me the old nudge. Lillian wasn't there that day, so Bela was kind of lonely, and he always wanted companionship. So he said we should go over to the Brown Palace and have something to drink and eat. And so we were there, and he had his Napoleon brandy.
>
> Finally this young lady ran over to the bar, and she said, 'Oh, Mr. Lugosi! Oh, can I have your autograph?' And he looked down at this pretty little face, and she was rather well-endowed. He said, 'Of course my dear.' So he wrote on the program, 'With all my love, Bela Lugosi.' And he handed it to her, you see, and she said, 'Oh Mr. Lugosi, I just wish there was something I could do for you.' And Bela looked at her and said, 'There is, my dear. I would love to kiss you around the world.' And the little girl, being very naïve, said, 'Oh, Mr. Lugosi, I don't think my family will let me travel that far.' *(Laughs)*
>
> Now, the other thing was that Bela was a big spender, and he loved to enjoy people, but at that time in his career, he was hurting financially. And so one day, Bela said, 'I'm going to take all of you out to dinner. There is a wonderful Hungarian restaurant

> ARTISTS REPERTORY THEATRE
> *presents*
>
> LAST THREE TIMES — Tonight Through Tuesday
> **BELA LUGOSI** IN PERSON
> **"DRACULA"** Greatest Masterpiece of Horror Ever Written
> THERE ARE STILL GOOD SEATS LEFT for Remaining Performances
> PHONE AComa 0911
> MAY CO. BOX OFFICE
>
> COMING THURSDAY — July 15th Through July 20th
> **SYLVIA SIDNEY** IN PERSON
> (Glamorous Film Star) in
> **"KIND LADY"** Featuring Edward Ashley
>
> Phipps Auditorium--City Park
> Seats Now on Sale—May Co.
> $2.40-$1.20 Evenings; $1.80-$1.00 Matinees
> Call FLorida 0044 for Last-Minute Reservations

From the *Denver Post* of July 11, 1948.

(Courtesy of George R. Snell)

here.' It was me, some of the principals, and Sylvia Sydney [who was in the city to star in *Kind Lady*, the next production at the Phipps] came along. There were six of us. Well, when Bela Lugosi walked into a Hungarian restaurant, I mean, the proprietor went up and hugged him, and the music played a Hungarian rhapsody, and my god, you'd have thought he was the President of the United States.

Bela said, 'Order whatever you want,' you see, and then we had Napoleon brandy afterwards, and I'm thinking, Bela really can't afford this, or shouldn't, because he needs the money. Now, during the dinner, the proprietor kept coming over and interrupting, but Bela was very gracious about it. And when it was all over, he came over again and asked if everything was okay.

So Bela stood up, in all his grandeur. He enveloped the man in his arms, and said, 'How wonderful of you to compliment this meal. I shall never forget it! I shall speak about your restaurant everywhere I go!' *(Laughs)* The restaurant owner was a little bit stunned; he didn't know what to do or say. And so we walked out without paying a dime, all six of us!

Afterwards, Bela explained that the owner had gotten his money's worth with all of his regular customers getting to see a famous actor, as well as the stories he would be able to repeat year after year.[13]

In terms of the production, Durston noted that he never knew of Lugosi using drugs. He added that, while Lugosi did drink a great deal of alcohol, it did not seem to have any affect on him, and certainly not on his performance.

Reviewing the Denver version of *Dracula*, the *Rocky Mountain News* concentrated on Lugosi's portrayal: "His vocal delivery was sing-song, his gestures composite of stylized evil. His famous wicked eyes glowed and leered with all their fabled hypnotic force."[14] The newspaper also spoke well of the sets, advising readers that some lighting difficulties on opening night would soon be resolved by a "dimmer now in transit."

Lugosi playfully attempts to steal a radio at the Philco dealer's party. From the *Burlington Hawkeye-Gazette* of July 16, 1948.

The *Denver Post* praised such performers as Lowery, Herrick, Mosier, and Ion Paleo, who played Butterworth. Though offering some background history on Lugosi, the *Post* did not comment on his performance. However, the newspaper did say, "as theatregoers entered the auditorium from the foyer, they were told 'faint' tickets would be issued; anyone who fainted from the 'frightful' stage show would be issued a ticket to return another night.... No one fainted."[15]

The final newspaper advertisements for the play told readers that "there are still good seats left," which was sadly true. *Variety* later said that the original intent of Artists Repertory Theatre was to present a long series of dramas. However, "... it ran five weeks and closed. Some of the productions paid off, but others, notably *Dracula*, lost enough money to close the deal."[16] The trade added, "It was a case of too much competition and not enough advance ground work."[17] And more than anything else, *Dracula* took the blame for the entire company having to shut down.

While Lugosi may well have noticed empty seats, he and Lillian had little time to worry about them. The morning after the final performance, Lillian drove their convertible Buick coupe 400 miles to an overnight stop at Hastings, Nebraska.[18] The journey likely took about nine or ten hours. The next morning, on July 15, the couple headed another 450 miles further east to Burlington, Iowa.[19]

Burlington was not chosen without good cause. In addition to staying at the Hotel Burlington, the Lugosis were Guests of Honor at the Philco Dealer's dinner and party.[20] Approximately 150 dealers had descended on Burlington to inspect the latest Philco radio models, and – as a bonus – to mingle with the "film horror man."[21] Along with signing autographs, Lugosi engaged in a publicity stunt for the *Burlington Hawkeye-Gazette*, playfully pretending to steal a tabletop model Philco from a display table.

The newspaper also interviewed Lugosi, with journalist Cort Klein claiming that he "... looks like anything but a horror man, and he acts like just what he is – a happy American husband and father. He and his wife are very proud of their son, Bela Jr., their 10-year-old son now attending Elsinore Naval and Military Academy at Lake Elsinore, California."[22] Apparently unaware of the rocky relationship that marked some points in the Lugosis' relationship, Klein added that the actor "... has been married to his wife for 15 years, and they're a good example of the opposite of Hollywood's marital rifts and divorces. His wife ... matches her husband's quiet and courteous manner with a personality that brims over, especially when she talks about her husband or her son."[23]

Telling Klein about the first time she met Lugosi, Lillian recalled that she was "thunderstruck" when he clicked his heels and kissed her hand.[24] Klein added that Lugosi grinned when hearing his wife's memory, but denied that it had been love at first sight.[25] Lillian countered by insisting that Lugosi asked her to marry him at their third meeting.[26] While checking her wristwatch, she added that the two had been "married exactly 15 years, 7 months, 16 days and 10 hours." Explaining his devotion to her, Lugosi said, "I wanted someone to help me make a home ... she is a wonderful wife and mother. Her mother is the best cook in the world and on my first visit I ate a triple dinner. I don't do that anymore."[27]

When Klein asked him whether frightening people was an art form or just a bit of fun, Lugosi re-

PARK LANE — Denver

July 2, 1948

Lyman Brown
New York, N.Y.

My dear Lyman:—

I am now in Denver doing stock and want to give you my line up and hope that you can set a few for me too.

Week of July 19 — Green Hills Th. Mohnton, Pa. "Dracula"
July 26
Aug 2 — Norwich Sum. Th. Norwich, Conn. "Dracula"
Aug 9 — Sea Cliff Sum. Th. Seacliff, L.I., N.Y. "Arsenic & Old Lace"
Aug 16
Aug 23
Aug 30

Joe Magee of the Wm Morris office set the above. Will you notify me immediately if you can fill in the idle weeks. I will be at the above hotel until the 14th AM.

With kindest regards.

Sincerely,
Bela Lugosi

From the *Reading Eagle* of July 18, 1948.

plied, "Well, it is both. You see the funny part of my kind of acting is you can't scare the kids. You only frighten the grownups. The kids just look at you and say 'come on boogy man, make some more faces'."[28]

After the interview ended, the Lugosis retired to their hotel room. The next day, they traveled to Mansfield, Ohio, a distance of about 500 miles. The *Mansfield News-Journal* told readers, "Mr. and Mrs. Bela Lugosi, Hollywood stars, stopping at the Mansfield-Leland Hotel for the night [Friday, July 16] and leaving early today for the east."[29] Riding another 400 miles, the two finally arrived at their destination: the Abraham Lincoln Hotel in Reading, Pennsylvania.

Rehearsals for another version of *Dracula* quickly began at the Green Hills Theatre, located five miles south of the city. Producer George R. Snell originally intended to stage evening performances from July 19 to 24 at the 400-seat theatre, but after it became a sell out, he added a Saturday matinee, the first in the theatre's history.[30] Publicizing the show, the *Reading Eagle* claimed that *Dracula* would be the "most difficult production ever staged at the Green Hills. It entails specialized scenic and lighting effects, as well as use of the stage wagons for rapid changes of the three sets."[31]

Snell quickly befriended Lugosi, enjoying his company and eating breakfast with him on more than one occasion. After the dress rehearsal, Lugosi even asked Snell for an important favor. Snell later recalled:

Lugosi's *Dracula* approaches the vulnerable Lucy (Rande Carmichael) in George R. Snell's production. (Courtesy of George R. Snell)

'George,' he said, 'the cape I wear is very sentimental to me since it is the original I wore in the motion picture and ever since. Not to demean your theatre security, but it would be a tragedy if something happened to it during the night. I would greatly appreciate it if you could take it to your home in West Reading each night, and, of course, return it for the next performance.'

My response without hesitancy, 'It would be a pleasure and no trouble at all.'

So after the opening night's performance concluded when we all departed the theatre and went our way, I arrived at my garage (about a city block away from my home) and removed the cape from the car and a question arose. How to treat this huge cape without getting it wrinkled? Aha! Wear it on my shoulders. One problem: Bela was over 6 feet tall, and I was 5'8 and a half. So, I hiked the bottom up so it wouldn't drag the sidewalk, and walked up the street.

Since Snell walked home after midnight, no one seems to have noticed him wearing the famous vampire cape.

Given all of his other duties at the theatre, Snell did not have time to direct *Dracula*, so that job went to William C. Cragin. Snell remembered:

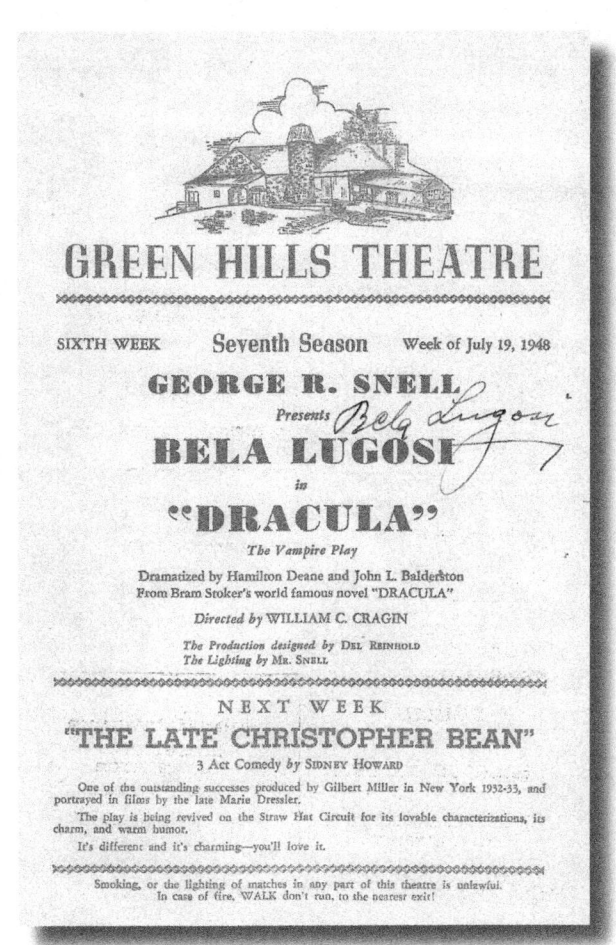

Program cover to the production of *Dracula* at the Green Hills Theatre. (Courtesy of George R. Snell)

My talented director had no difficulty with Bela. He was amenable to any departure from the way he wanted to interpret the role to suit the better good of the play and the other actors. And of course his every movement was so credible and yet creepy. Along with that deep commanding voice.

As I had observed the original film many times, his hands and fingers appeared enormous, making one think he had some sort of mechanical extensions. But no, these were his God-given storytelling hands. And they also produced a warm but firm greeting and handshake.

He was so easy to know and work with on *Dracula*. We all felt it, and we all agreed he was such a dignified gentleman. All of that fit perfectly with his philosophy of life that he told me about, which was an old Hungarian proverb: 'You can't receive with a tight fist.'[32]

Snell added that – despite the horrifying role Lugosi played – the audience felt his "warmth."

Attending the premiere, a critic from the *Reading Eagle* also gave Lugosi a positive response:

Bela Lugosi is a great artist, a star of the first magnitude, a Dynamic Presence on the stage. … It's a modest appraisal to say that the largest Monday night crowd to date was held spellbound by Mr. Lugosi's interpretation of Count Dracula … Only a truly great actor could create about himself the aura of evil which Lugosi conjures up in his role of the blood-sucking vampire.…

George R. Snell's production of *Dracula*. From left to right are Richard Malek (Harker), Rande Carmichael (Lucy, seated), Jacques Aubuchon (Dr. Seward), Maury Hill (Van Helsing), Lugosi, Lloyd Jones (Miss Wells), and Greg Rodgers (Renfield), and Robert McLean (Butterworth). (Courtesy of George R. Snell)

Mr. Lugosi and the rest of the cast received an enthusiastic demonstration after the final curtain. Quite as thrilling as anything in the performance was an original and surprising fillip that Mr. Lugosi gave to a brief curtain speech. We can't give it away, of course, and can only say of it that it was a stroke of good theatre that climaxes a highly satisfying evening.[33]

He also witnessed Lugosi's popularity among the kids at the theatre, who " just loved the guy."

A review in the *Reading Times* was equally impressed with *Dracula*, calling it "first rate in every way." The critic praised the use of green lights and the "soft but crunchy sound when the stake strikes through the vampire's heart." He also said that Lugosi instilled such "reality to the part that several women in the audience were seen furtively to be examining their pretty necks for a vampire's toothmarks during the intermissions." His review concluded with yet another reference to Lugosi's curtain speech, telling readers "it would be unfair to give it away, but it's a whammy."[34]

While in Reading, Lugosi was the special guest at a Rotary Club luncheon, where his speech recounted Dracula's origins in superstitions and folklore. Then, after the Saturday evening performance, Lugosi attended a cast party. Snell recalled the actor keeping others "spellbound" with his stories, adding, "The one point I will never forget, when it was time to leave, he said goodnight to my wife, Dottie, and gave her a proper kiss. I remarked, 'Gee, Bela, thanks for not drawing blood!' Lugosi and everyone broke into gales of laughter."[35]

And then there was a bit of unplanned publicity when Lugosi went out for a walk one evening at about 6PM, some two and a half hours before the evening performance. If a newspaper clipping is to be believed, a "chap" spotted Lugosi, without recognizing him, and decided to singe his hair with a packet of pocket matches, a common and allegedly harmless prank at that time. Lugosi – the "singee," as the journalist called him – "took it all in the spirit of good, clean fun and stood still for the operation."[36]

That same summer, John Carradine arrived at the Green Hills Theatre to star in *20th Century*.[37] By then, the Lugosis were long gone. But Lugosi did not forget George R. Snell, as the two had discussed various other projects, including Lugosi's desire to return to the Green Hills in 1949 to play the lead role in a production of *Harvey*. Despite having agreed finally to do *Dracula* and *Arsenic* that summer, Lugosi was still yearning for a chance at a different play.

After leaving Reading, the Lugosis traveled over 250 miles to reach Norwich, Connecticut. Between Monday August 2 and Saturday August 7, Lugosi would appear in seven performances of *Dracula* under the auspices of Herb Kneeter's Norwich Summer Theatre, which staged its plays in the local – and "aircooled" – Masonic Temple.[37] The Saturday matinee featured the added bonus of the cast serving "fresh refreshments" to the audience after the show.[38]

The Norwich cast revealed a side of summer stock that was lost in Vernon Rice's newspaper diatribe. The theatre managers did hire film stars for lead roles, but the rest of the cast was usually comprised of young, budding talent. Many of them had only brief careers in the theatre, but others became famous in the years that followed, something true of the Norwich version of *Dracula*. For example, Simon Oakland portrayed Van Helsing; he was still years away from roles in *I Want to Live!* (1958), *Psycho* (1960), and *West Side Story* (1961), and the television series *Kolchak: The Night Stalker*. And then there was Richard Kiley – later famed for being Broadway's original *Man of La Mancha* – in the role of Jonathan Harker.

As for *Dracula*, the cast rehearsed even while the prior play, *George Washington Slept Here*, was still being staged. On Saturday night – just two days before the Lugosi show opened – a real bat appeared in the theatre during show time. In an amusing adlib, actor Ernest Truex quipped, "You're not due here until next week."[39] The same bat returned during a Sunday dress rehearsal for *Dracula*, but was never seen again.[40]

Ted Post directed *Dracula*, recalling that his first meeting with the Lugosis was awkward. Post noticed a degree of strain between the two of them, with Lillian doing most of the talking. Though Post believed he finally connected with Lugosi, he never felt that Lugosi was receptive to his direction:

> On opening night, before the curtain went up, I asked him to pick up the tempo a bit. I said, 'It will help make the moments a little more exciting, a little more vibrant, just by doing that.' He said, 'I'll do it, Ted.' And then he did it *slower*. I went backstage after the first act and I told him, 'Bela, please, it's gotten slower.' He said, 'I thought I *picked up* the tempo.' I said, 'No, Bela, it went slower. And what's happening is, the scenes are flattening out. They're becoming less interested by doing it with that slow pace. He said, 'I'll pick it up in the second act.' So he went back on stage, and it was *even slower*, the second act. Afterward, I went back again to his dressing room, and his wife was there, putting a needle into his arm.
>
> I thought it was heroin. So he was taking a lot of drugs, and I didn't know it. I opened the door, to his dressing room, and there she was, his wife, doing that. He was not shocked by my entrance, and neither was she. I guess they assumed that everybody knew this about them. I said, 'I'll come back later' – but I didn't. I didn't talk to him again that night, after seeing that. After seeing what I saw, I knew I was wasting my breath.[41]

Post also recalled that some of the cast members were puzzled by Lugosi's slow-paced performance.

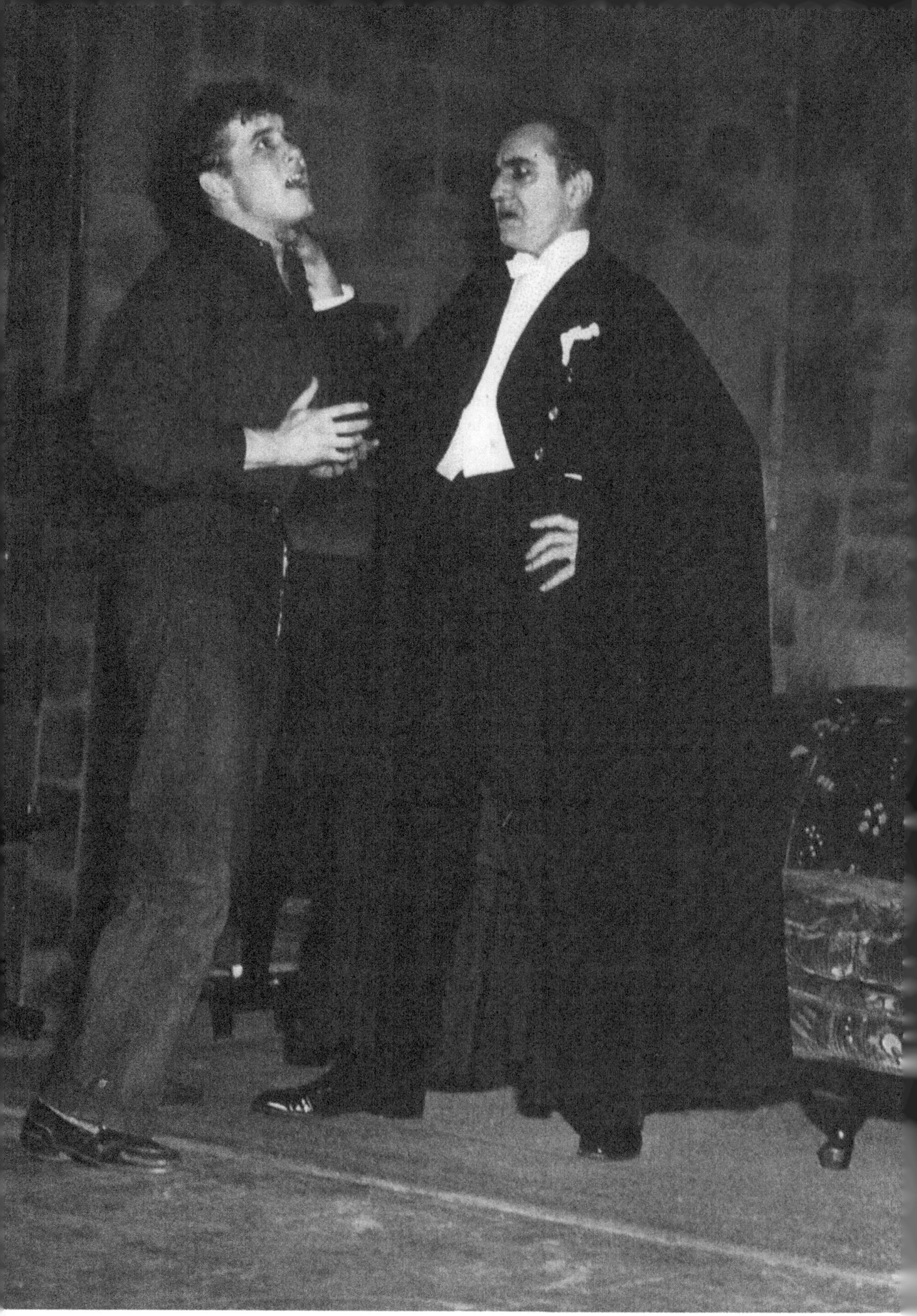

But that does not seem to have been something Simon Oakland believed. When interviewed in the 1970s, Oakland spoke of Lugosi as being "generous" and "patient" in Norwich. Of the rehearsals, Oakland recalled:

> I was supposed to struggle against his will until the very last second and then break the spell by turning away with my hand covering my eyes. When his fingers got to within a few inches of my face, I broke up. I just couldn't help myself. The harder I tried to control myself, the louder I laughed. Pretty soon, we were both laughing and I apologized for ruining the scene. It was so uncanny watching Bela doing his thing in a sports shirt that it was funny.[42]

Oakland believed that Lugosi was "understanding" about his laughter, even if also a bit "perturbed."

Another cast member was Howard Jessor, who played Butterworth. He remembered that Lugosi was:

> … a friendly gentleman. He was very nice, and he and his wife were very pleasant. He seemed very elderly to the rest of us, but of course many of us were pretty young.
>
> I think he gave a pretty satisfying performance, though I wasn't really evaluating him. Along with my role, I was also an apprentice to the stage designer as well. As for the play, well, Ted Post did some directing, but a lot of the movement and so forth was pre-ordained.

Lugosi's Dracula chokes Renfield (Greg Rodgers) while Van Helsing (Maury Hill) tries to stop him. (Courtesy of George R. Snell)

Gary D. Rhodes | Bill Kaffenberger

Harker (Richard Malek) prepares to strike the stake held by Van Helsing (Maury Hill) while Renfield (Greg Rodgers, center) and Dr. Seward (Jacques Aubuchon, left) watch. (Courtesy of George R. Snell)

My main memory of Lugosi was seeing him between acts. He would be sitting backstage, and I would see those hands of his. He kept them in a bucket of ice cubes. I don't know what he accomplished by that, but it must have worked for him.[43]

Jessor recalled absolutely no evidence of Lugosi's drug use during his week in Norwich.

At any rate, after the first night's performance, Jack Cruise of the *New London Evening Day* reviewed *Dracula*:

> The part of Count Dracula seems to have been created especially for Bela Lugosi, who brings to the role every bit of gruesome characteriza-

From the July 24, 1948 issue of the *Reading Eagle*.

144   NO TRAVELER RETURNS | The Lost Years of Bela Lugosi

tion needed to insure a convincing portrayal of the master vampire. While Lugosi's curtain speech at the finale indicates he is a mild man, his action in the play is one that creates awe for the audience.[44]

Cruise also praised Simon Oakland, Ralph Longley, Gloria Hoye, and Howard Jessor.

The *Norwich Bulletin* also published a review, lauding not Oakland or Kiley, but instead Ralph Longley, who played Renfield, and Howard Jessor. Speaking of Lugosi, the newspaper said:

> ...the veteran blood-curdler seemed to be really enjoying himself as he crept about the stage hypnotizing people, flapping his long black cape, and in general behaving like a first-class bogeyman. One young patron, when asked what he thought of Lugosi's performance, could only whisper through his chattering teeth, 'G-g-g-olly!' And the number of sweat-soaked programs lying around afterwards with the edges chewed off testified to the success of this venture into the world of horror.[45]

The newspaper added that Lugosi made an "ap-

> POLICE DEPT. (Convention Division)—It happened in front of the Abe Lincoln about 6 o'clock Tuesday afternoon. A police convention delegate, probably a visitor, who was well along in his cups spied a chap coming across the street and decided his hair was too long, or something. Anyway, the delegate stopped the man and proceeded to singe his hair with a packet of pocket matches. The singee took it all in the spirit of good, clean fun and stood quite still for the operation. Apparently the happy copper didn't recognize his singe-customer as Bela Lugosi, the famous actor who's playing at Green Hills Theatre this week...

(Courtesy of George R. Snell)

NORWICH SUMMER THEATRE
MASONIC TEMPLE

TELEPHONE NORWICH 376 and 623
Your Nearest Summer Theatre, Playing a Guest Star Each Week

TONIGHT AND ALL THIS WEEK
H. L. KNEETER PRESENTS

BELA LUGOSI in "Dracula"
The Master of Horror in a Spine Chilling Drama!

Eves. $1.00 to $2.00, plus tax. Sat. Eve. only, $1.00 to $2.50, plus tax
SAT. MAT.—Bal. $1.00, plus tax. Orch.-Loge $1.50, plus tax
Box Office Now Open for Phone or Mail Reservations, or on Sale at Crocker House Newsstand or Mohican Hotel Newsstand
Mystic or Groton Long Pt.—Bliven's; Stonington—Keene's Newsstand

COMING NEXT WEEK JANET BLAIR FRANCIS LEDERER in "FOR LOVE OR MONEY"

From *The Day* (New London, CT) of August 3, 1948.

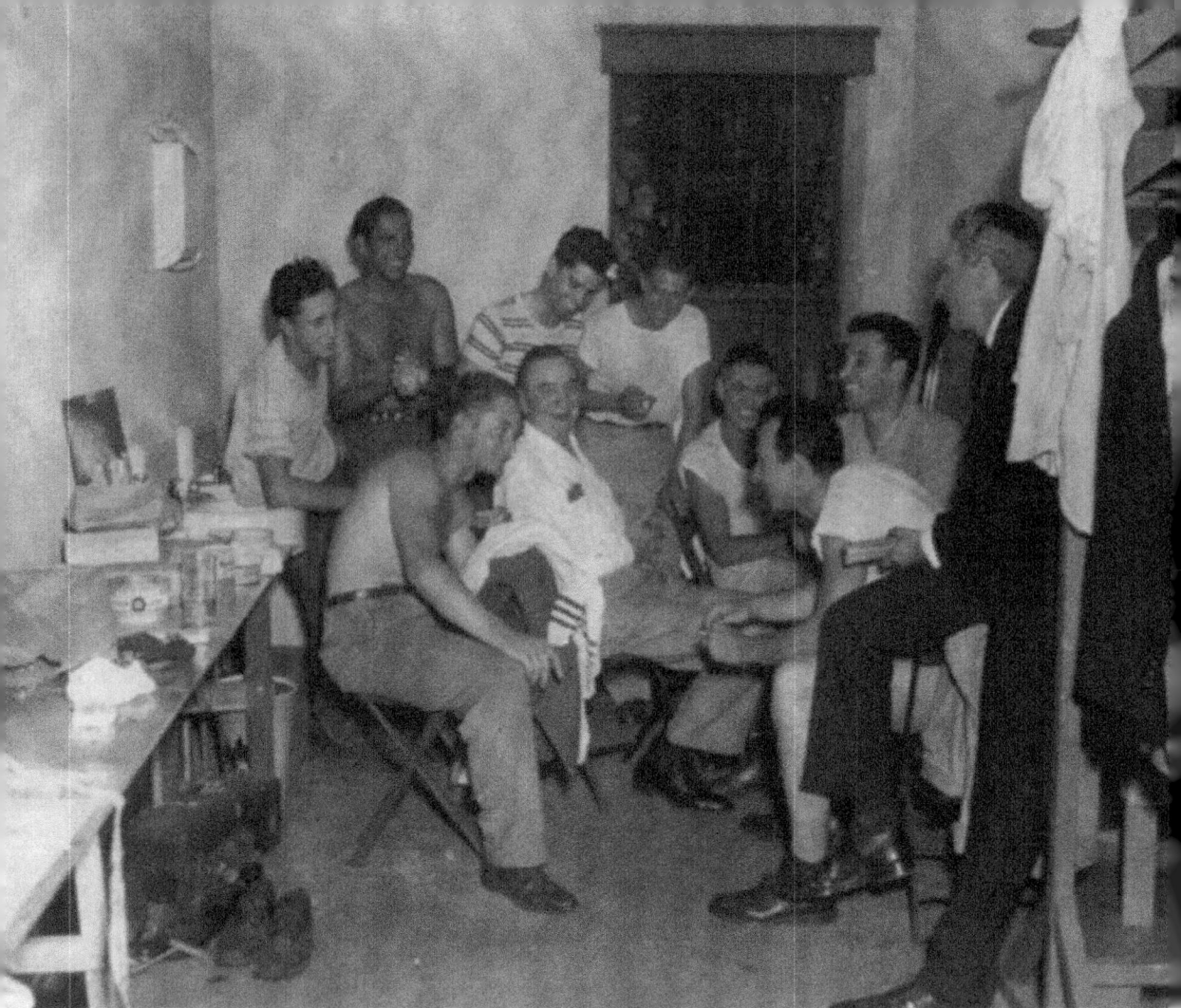

Lugosi with some cast and crew members of the Norwich, Connecticut production of *Dracula*. (Courtesy of Howard Jessor)

propriate curtain speech that had everyone feeling nervously as they left for the two telltale marks on their throats."

Despite Post's concern over Lugosi's pacing and drug use, two critics – and, based upon the *Bulletin*'s review, many audience members – had reacted favorably. Perhaps Lugosi's age and the long road he traveled that summer might explain why Ted Post encountered such a very different Lugosi than the one George Snell worked with in the same play only a week earlier. Indeed, Snell never saw any indication of Lugosi's poor health or drug use.

While in Norwich, Lugosi made two live appearances, the first at the Elks Fair on August 6.[46] Then, he attended a local Lion's Club luncheon as guest of honor, sitting at the head of the table with Ted Post at his side. The room was packed, and at a given point Lugosi gave a speech, completely off the top of his head. Post recalled:

> *Well...* he knocked everybody for a loop. He was *so* brilliant, *so* funny, *so* satirical, *so* insightful. He spoke so beautifully, and in such a comical, ironic way [about current events and the entertainment industry] that everybody was in tears with laughter. I never forgot that.[47]

Lugosi received so much applause that Post had some difficulty in getting him back to a rehearsal on time.

Lugosi during his stay in Norwich, Connecticut. (Courtesy of Howard Jessor)

The actor also received a good deal of applause at the end of each performance of *Dracula* in Norwich, but only from what Post recalled as being "half a house." By the time *Dracula* came to an end, Francis Lederer had arrived in Norwich, where he would appear in *For Love or Money*; a decade later, Lederer would play the vampire count in *The Return of Dracula* (1958).[48]

The Lugosis then traveled to New York and to the Sea Cliff Summer Theatre on Long Island, where he made $750 for one week of work.[49] The play was *Arsenic and Old Lace*, which was also being staged that very same week at another summer theatre. The Westchester Playhouse in Mount Kisco, New York produced a stock version featuring famed actress Estelle Winwood, who had costarred with Lugosi in his first English-language play in America, *The Red Poppy* (1922).[50]

Richard and Alex Gordon, British émigrés to the United States, attended one of the performances. Both were struggling to get a foothold in the American entertainment industry. Richard Gordon later wrote:

> Alex and I went to see the performance [in Sea Cliff], and to meet him after the show. Instead of giving us a few minutes of his time backstage, Bela generously invited us to join him and his wife Lillian for dinner in a nearby restaurant which started a friendship that lasted until his unfortunate death.
>
> I remember at the restaurant Bela holding up a glass of red wine that he had ordered and saying very matter-of-factly, 'I like red wine because it is the color of blood.'[51]

From the August 8, 1948 issue of the *New York Herald Tribune*.

Gary D. Rhodes | Bill Kaffenberger

The Lugosis meet Alex Gordon (left), and (to the right of Lillian) Richard Gordon and William K. Everson. (Courtesy of Buddy Barnett)

onderful to be together Bela & Brian

Recalling the same event, Alex Gordon noted that the venue was a Hungarian restaurant, where Lugosi immediately became the "center of attraction, the owner being thrilled to see him."[52]

Lugosi apparently felt an immediate kinship with the Gordons. In Sea Cliff, Lugosi told the two brothers that he was exasperated by a lack of film offers. He was disappointed that he did not get more work in summer theatre in 1948, and that, when he did, he was relegated to the same two roles: Dracula and Jonathan Brewster. As a result, he made clear to them that he was not "altogether satisfied" with his manager, which presumably meant Don Marlowe.[53] However, what he didn't say was that his initial reluctance to play Dracula and Jonathan Brewster was more to blame for his lack of summer stock bookings than anything that Marlowe did or didn't do.

But the larger and lasting problem of that summer may well have been how the industry viewed box-office receipts for the *Dracula* productions that did occur. It was not good to have half of the seats empty in Norwich. However, it was much worse to have *Variety* describing in print that *Dracula* was a key reason that the Artists Repertory Theatre went out of business. That fact may not have been enough to prove Vernon Rice's arguments against employing film stars in summer stock, but it might have been enough to suggest that staging *Dracula* with Lugosi could be a financially dangerous proposition.

(Endnotes)

1. Rice, Vernon. "Summer Theatres." *New York Post* 22 Aug. 1948.
2. *Ibid.*
3. Bamberger, Theron. "Straw Hat Serenade." *New York Times* 23 May 1948.
4. *Ibid.*
5. "Along the Straw Hat Theatre Trail." *New York Times* 13 June 1948; "Along the Rustic Trail." *New York Times* 20 June 1948; "The Straw Hat Trail." *New York Times* 27 June 1948; "Along the Straw Hat Trail." *New York Times* 25 July 1948; "The Straw Hat Trail." *New York Times* 8 Aug. 1948; "The Straw Hat Trail." *New York Times* 15 Aug. 1948.
6. Marlowe, Don. Letter to Lyman Brown. 14 May 1948. [Available in the Chamberlain and Lyman Brown Papers, and Undated, Series II: Correspondence, Box 64, Folder F.9, at the New York Public Library/Lincoln Center for the Performing Arts in New York.]
7. Brown, Lyman. Letter to Don Marlowe. 21 May 1948. [Available in the Chamberlain and Lyman Brown Papers, and Undated, Series II: Correspondence, Box 64, Folder F.9, at the New York Public Library/Lincoln Center for the Performing Arts in New York.]
8. Hopper, Hedda. "Looking at Hollywood." *Chicago Tribune* 9 Mar. 1948.
9. Heffernan, Harold. "Hollywood." *Long Island Star-Journal* (Long Island, NY) 22 June 1948.
10. Houghton, Norris. "A Director's Viewpoint." *Theatre Arts* June 1950.
11. "*Dracula* Offers Loads of Horror." *Denver Post* 7 July 1948; "Lugosi in *Dracula* Opens Thursday." *Denver Post* 8 July 1948.
12. Advertisement. *Denver Post* 6 July 1948.
13. Rhodes, Gary D. Interview with David Durston. 18 Mar. 1996.
14. Gaskie, Jack. "Lugosi Leers Effectively in *Dracula* Here." *Rocky Mountain News* 10 July 1948.
15. "*Dracula* Opens for Denver Run, Lugosi Heads Cast." *Denver Post* 9 July 1948.
16. *Daily Variety* 25 Oct. 25 1948.
17. *Ibid.*
18. *Burlington Hawkeye-Gazette* (Burlington, IA) July 16, 1948.
19. Klein, Cort. "Dracula and Wife Here." *Burlington Hawkeye-Gazette* (Burlington, IA) 16 July 1948.
20. *Ibid.*
21. *Ibid.*
22. *Ibid.*
23. *Ibid.*
24. *Ibid.*
25. *Ibid.*
26. *Ibid.*
27. *Ibid.*
28. *Ibid.*
29. *Mansfield News-Journal* (Mansfield, OH) 17 July 1948.
30. Rhodes, Gary D. Interview with George R. Snell. 7 Apr. 2006.
31. "Green Hills Slates Lugosi in *Dracula*." *Reading Eagle* 18 July 1948.
32. Rhodes, interview with Snell.
33. "Lugosi Leaves Crowd Limp in Classic of Horror Plays." *Reading Eagle* 20 July 1948.
34. E.M.S. "Bela Lugosi Horribly Good in Dracula at Green Hills." *Reading Times* 20 July 1948.

35 Rhodes, interview with Snell.
36 Clipping exists in the scrapbook of George R. Snell.
37 "Summer Theatre Notes." *Hartford Courant* 1 Aug. 1948.
38 Advertisement. *Norwich Bulletin* 6 Aug. 1948.
39 *New London Evening Day* (New London, CT) 2 Aug. 1948.
40 *Ibid.*
41 Weaver, Tom. "Ted Post on Bela Lugosi" in *Eye on Science Fiction: 20 Interviews with Classic SF and Horror Filmmakers* (Jefferson, NC: McFarland, 2007).
42 Cremer, Robert. *Lugosi: The Man Behind the Cape* (Chicago: Henry Regnery, 1976).
43 Rhodes, Gary D. Interview with Howard Jessor. 1 Oct. 2011.
44 Cruise, Jack. "Native Bats Missing, but Lugosi and Cast Combine to Thrill Audience in *Dracula*." *New London Evening Day* 3 Aug. 1948.
45 "Night of Thrills Given Monday at Summer Theatre." *Norwich Bulletin* 3 Aug. 1948.
46 "Bela Lugosi to Appear at Elks' Fair Tonight." *Norwich Bulletin* 6 Aug. 1948.
47 Weaver, "Ted Post on Bela Lugosi."
48 Advertisement. *Norwich Bulletin* 7 Aug. 1948.
49 Brown Agency. Letter to Don Marlowe. 14 May 1948. [Available in the Chamberlain and Lyman Brown Papers, and Undated, Series II: Correspondence, Box 64, Folder F.9, at the New York Public Library/Lincoln Center for the Performing Arts in New York.]
50 "Goings On About Town." *New Yorker* 7 Aug. 1948.
51 Gordon, Richard. Letter to Gary D. Rhodes. 20 Aug. 1986.
52 Gordon, Alex. "My Favorite Vampire." *Fantastic Monsters of the Films* (Vol. 1, No. 5, 1963).
53 Gordon, letter to Rhodes.

In the late forties, Lugosi signed this photo of himself for the Redpath Bureau. (Courtesy of the Records of the Redpath Lyceum Bureau, University of Iowa, Iowa City, Iowa)

Chapter 8
PHANTOMS

On December 1, 1948, Lugosi and Lillian drove into the little town of Deming, New Mexico, staying overnight before heading back to California.[1] Decades earlier, in 1881, Deming was the location of the driving of the Silver Spike, which commemorated the joining of the Southern Pacific Railroad with the Atchison, Topeka, and Sante Fe. It was a good omen: the coming together of travelers and the paths they took. And Lugosi's seemed to be taking him home.

A journalist at the local newspaper covered the Lugosis' unexpected visit to Deming:

> If you saw a strange-looking character wandering through the streets of Deming Wednesday night, it was none other than 'Frankenstein' himself. Mr. Bela Lugosi, the movie 'Frankenstein', accompanied by his wife, was a guest at The Roundup Lodge Wednesday night, according to Mr. DeBord, manager of The Roundup.
>
> ... The movie star amazed other guests at The Roundup by his unusual manner of drinking his beer. When he couldn't get a bottle of beer at room temperature, he asked that it be held under hot water until warm enough to suit his taste. He chased the beer with a double Scotch.[2]

While Lugosi had portrayed the Frankenstein Monster in one film, *Frankenstein Meets the Wolf Man* (1943), it was hardly the role with which he most identified. It was as if he had been recognized and yet confused once again with Boris Karloff. Regardless, after a brief stay, the Lugosis returned to their automobile. This time it was over six hundred miles on a stretch of road that took them through Arizona and finally back to Los Angeles and back to their son.

During the final days of 1948 and for the first six-odd months of 1949, Lugosi lived in California. It became his longest sojourn in the state from 1945 to 1951. And it was a sojourn, a temporary stay during which Lugosi reconnected with his wife and son, far from the hectic schedules of vaudeville and summer stock, and far from the lonely and seemingly endless highways of post-war America.[3]

But geography alone could not return Lugosi to the life he led before 1945. During those months in California in 1949, Lugosi heard about various projects from his representatives, but few of them came to be. In many respects, this was hardly unusual for an actor, particularly one who was not under a contract at a major studio. Projects were regularly discussed, but most of them did not materialize. They were like phantoms in the night, disappearing from view almost as soon as they were noticed.

For example, in April 1949, *The Billboard* announced that Lugosi would appear in a road company tour of *Dracula* with actor Hampton White. After it ended, the two actors would costar in *Strange*

BELA LUGOSI

The Famous "DRACULA" of Stage and Screen in an evening of CHARACTER SKETCHES.

Mr. Lugosi, who has given command performances before the King of England, is considered to be one of the Greatest of Shakespearean Actors.

His varied program consists of excerpts from "Hamlet," "King Lear," "Richard III," Edgar Allen Poe's "The Tell-Tale Heart" and others from his extensive repertoire.

Don Marlowe's advertising brochure for Lugosi's planned live appearances on the waning "Chautauqua" market in the Midwest. (Courtesy of the Records of the Redpath Lyceum Bureau, University of Iowa, Iowa City, Iowa)

Deception, the "first feature film to be made in third dimension."[4] Neither project got off the ground, nor did another play that Lugosi discussed in a letter to a theatrical representative in May of 1949. In it, Lugosi wrote that he would have to be in Los Angeles in mid-August of that year in order to "start rehearsals in a new play opening in September at the El Capitan."[5]

Later in 1949, the press claimed that Lugosi would likely star in Dorothy Waring and Ann Baldwin's play *Now Really, Peter*, which covered the exploits of a "Hungarian quack analyst who sets up offices on Park Ave."[6] Having temporarily shelved her plans for *The Searching Heart*, a musical play about Edgar Allan Poe's life, Waring concentrated on the new play. But here again is an example of a role that Lugosi did not get to portray. *Now Really, Peter* was never staged.

Lugosi's problem was not that all of these projects did not occur: he couldn't have possibly had time to play every role offered to him during his career. No, his problem in the post-war period was that the ratio of projects that did occur versus those that did not became increasingly skewed against him. By the time he left Deming and arrived in California, he was plagued with far more phantoms than he was with solid offers of real work, particularly when it came to the cinema. Hence his inability to remain permanently in California: the traveling actor had to keep on the move.

His other problem was that he remained forever unsatisfied with his representation, frequently changing his agents and managers in pursuit of another kind of phantom: a representative who was honest and who could deliver on all promises. And yet Lugosi was himself not always completely honest with his agents and managers, sometimes complicating his affairs by allocating authority to more than one representative at the same time. Perhaps this was his strategy to increase his employment opportunities, or perhaps it was simply the result of his impatience and exasperation.

Consider for example his shift from Virginia Doak to Don Marlowe in 1947. When he told Doak of his decision, it was in a letter dated three weeks after he signed with Marlowe. He intentionally delayed informing her, as many of his other surviving letters from the same time period indicate that he usually responded to business communications rapidly, even while he was on the road. Furthermore, in this instance, it is clear that Lugosi had already been relying on Marlowe to at least a small degree for months. A surviving letter dated May 1947 has Lyman and Chamberlain Brown informing Marlowe – not Doak – about an offer for Lugosi to star in a summer stock version of *Arsenic and Old Lace* in Rehoboth Beach, Delaware.[7]

Then, in order to keep his options open, Lugosi told Doak that his agreement with Marlowe was for "motion pictures only," telling her that Marlowe promised him such projects as "an MGM picture" and "the Columbia Chandu serial." As a result, he agreed to take any non-cinematic work that Doak could find for him. And yet, in the very same letter he also reveals that his agreement with Marlowe was "exclusive," and that Marlowe was indeed attempting to get him non-cinematic work as well, including an eight-week guarantee to play *Dracula* onstage in London or – if that didn't come to pass – a version of *Dracula* in New York and also for an American tour.[8]

None of those projects came to pass, but that was not necessarily Marlowe's fault. The Columbia Chandu serial was never produced, and so no one starred in it. And it does seem that Marlowe was able to make arrangements for a British tour of *Dracula*. On the heels of earlier press announcements, *Daily Variety* told readers on December 15, 1947 that Lugosi was to sign pending contracts for a London revival of the stage play. The actor was to sail to England on the *Queen Elizabeth* on March 4, 1948, with the play opening on April 3.[9]

Then, on February 2, 1948, *Daily Variety* reported that Lugosi would travel to London by plane on March 18 and star in four weeks of *Dracula* with the West End Varieties Company, which would then be followed with four weeks of *Harvey*.[10] The filming of *Abbott and Costello Meet Frankenstein* (1948) initially interrupted these plans, which later fell apart completely in April 1948 after producer Sir Lew Grade learned that Lugosi did not hold the exclusive rights to *Dracula–The Vampire Play*.[11]

Nevertheless, Marlowe's efforts on Lugosi's behalf extended to many other projects. One of them promoted Lugosi in an evening of character sketches. A surviving advertising brochure declared:

The Famous 'DRACULA' of Stage and Screen in an evening of CHARACTER SKETCHES. Mr. Lugosi, who has given command performances before the King of England, is considered to be one of the Greatest of Shakespearean Actors. His varied program consists of excerpts from *Hamlet*, *King Lear*, *Richard III*, Edgar Allen [sic] Poe's *The Tell-Tale Heart* and others from his extensive repertoire.[12]

An additional advertising herald from this period (distributed by the "Don Marlowe Agency") announced the availability of "the distinguished actor Bela Lugosi" for such live appearances.[13]

Marlowe apparently aimed the evening of character sketches at the waning "Chautauqua" market in the Midwest, specifically targeting the Redpath Bureau. Focusing initially on religious and educational activities, the Chautauqua movement morphed over the years to focus on bringing cultural activities – including lecturers, musicians, actors and famous personalities of the day – to rural cities.

Lugosi with Boris Karloff in San Francisco, circa 1939. Plans for them to costar in the 1948 film project *The Strange Case of Malcolm Craig* never materialized. (Courtesy of the Bancroft Library, University of California, Berkeley)

Bela Lugosi & Boris Karloff

Performances primarily took place under the cover of a huge tent.[14] Agencies eventually formed to sign the talent for various locations. For example, the Midwest regional location for the Redpath Bureau (originally operated by Keith Vawter and headquartered in Cedar Rapids, Iowa) booked talent for Chautauquas in Iowa, Minnesota, the Dakotas, Nebraska, and Missouri.[15] But no evidence indicates that the proposed Lugosi-Redpath events were ever staged.

In November 1947, Marlowe excitedly told the press that Lugosi would appear in a biographical film based on the life of Rudolph Valentino.[16] Lugosi was likely disappointed that it didn't happen, as even in the post-war era he had brief moments in which he was solely interested in non-horror roles. That was true in January 1948 when he told Hedda Hopper that *Abbott and Costello Meet Frankenstein* would be his last horror film; in May of that same year, he instructed Don Marlowe that he did not wish to appear in *Dracula* or *Arsenic and Old Lace* in summer stock.[17] Instead, he announced his intentions to star in such plays as *Harvey*.[18]

But in a confusing turn of events, Lugosi seemed eager to appear in *more* Dracula-related projects at given moments between January and May of 1948. In March of that year, he told columnist Bob Thomas that Universal-International was considering two different films based on his Dracula role. "There is enough material in the original novel for a half a dozen pictures," he said.[19] That same month, Dorothy Kilgallen's column announced that Lugosi would appear in a film with his "young son, who will play a brat-aged Dracula."[20] And in May – the very month he told Marlowe that he no longer wished to appear in *Dracula* in summer stock – Erskine Johnson's column claimed that Lugosi would appear in a remake of the 1931 film version of the same.[21]

Lugosi's occasional unwillingness to play horror characters may have been admirable from an artistic standpoint, but it can hardly have helped his career, and it likely posed difficulties for representatives like Don Marlowe. Though many of Marlowe's projects did not materialize, he was able to succeed in obtaining some horror-related work for the actor. And Marlowe's most publicized failed efforts also fell into the horror genre. In various editions of the *Player's Directory Bulletin*, he announced that Lugosi would appear in Universal-International's film *Invisible Man* in 1948, as well as in MGM's *Inner Sanctum* in 1949.

Here again Marlowe cannot be blamed for these projects not becoming Lugosi films. MGM did not produce *Inner Sanctum*; instead, it became a low-budget film produced by M.R.S. Pictures and released through Film Classics.[22] And U-I never produced a version of the *Invisible Man* in the late forties, no more than it produced any of the Dracula films that the press described in 1948. As part of their ongoing strategy in the late forties of producing fewer films, U-I announced only 24 features for the 1948-49 season. None of them were horror movies.[23]

The only Universal-International film that might have been suitable for Lugosi, at least in the eyes of studio execs, would likely have been the project mentioned in December 1948 as *Abbott and Costello Meet the Killers*.[24] In September of that year, Lugosi had in fact told the press that he expected "to go into another mystery comedy with Abbott and Costello."[25] But in the end, the film's title went from the grammatical plural to the singular. It became *Abbott and Costello Meet the Killer, Boris Karloff* (1949, aka *Abbott and Costello Meet the Killer*), and there was simply no role in it for Lugosi. And, as with its predecessor, the studio viewed it as an Abbott and Costello comedy, not a horror movie.

In mid-February 1948, while *Abbott and Costello Meet Frankenstein* was in production, Marlowe did engineer a term contract for Lugosi at 20th Century Fox. *Hollywood Reporter* and *Variety* covered news of this development, with the latter noting that it would likely have a negative impact on Lugosi's ability to travel to London for the revival of *Dracula*.[26] Trade publications did not offer subsequent details, and it is clear that Lugosi made no films for that studio in 1948 or in the years that followed. Though the actual contract has not surfaced, it would seem likely that it became null and void after a given period of time during which Fox did not cast him in any productions.

Undaunted, Marlowe continued his efforts to find other work for Lugosi, the most intriguing of which was *The Strange Case of Malcolm Craig*, a film set to reunite him with Boris Karloff. Announced in June 1948 and mentioned again in August of the same year, Film Classics intended to produce and release *The Strange Case of Malcolm Craig* as part of their schedule of 34 new movies for 1949.[27] Film Classics had produced only ten movies in 1948, and was intending to increase its output. But only two months after announcing those 34 films, the number dropped to 26, and then, eventually a lower number, to the point that *Malcolm Craig* was never made.

Drawing on the same marketing strategy, another Karloff-Lugosi project was announced during the summer of 1948. Newspapers claimed that the two actors, along with Peter Lorre, would make joint stage appearances. The idea was that they would give a live presentation after theatres screened clips from their old movies.[28] But like so many other projects, it simply faded away.

And so Lugosi grew impatient, and particularly unhappy that no film work had followed in the wake of *Abbott and Costello Meet Frankenstein*. In the summer of 1948, when he told Richard and Alex Gordon that he was not satisfied with his representation, he may not have mentioned that it had undergone a transition. Lugosi was still with Don Marlowe, but Marlowe's status had changed. On May 1, 1948, *The Billboard* announced that the McConkey Music

Gary D. Rhodes | Bill Kaffenberger

159

Corporation had "increased its business potential" by acquiring, among others, Marlowe and the clients he represented.[29] McKonkey concentrated on one-night stand appearances by musicians and other performers. Here is likely the reason that Marlowe increasingly placed emphasis on booking live appearances for Lugosi instead of pursuing film roles.

And yet not all of Lugosi's live appearances materialized either, such as his planned appearance at the New Orleans Municipal Auditorium during their 1948-49 season.[30] Nor did the three-act play *Magic*, which Lugosi mentioned in September 1948 while he was in Springfield, Massachusetts. He hoped to star in *Magic* on Broadway, but the plans came to nothing.[31]

That Lugosi would express unhappiness over Marlowe is hardly surprising given his long history of doing the same about other managers and agents. As early as 1929, Lugosi wrote to his longtime friend and theatrical representative Dr. Edmond Pauker of New York regarding one of Pauker's associates. In it, he complains:

> Before I arrived to Hollywood, I got in touch with Lichtig. I had been playing Dracula for two months successfully: and Lichtig had not done anything about it. But in the fifth month – when I had stopped playing for 2 months – he asked me to give him pictures that he would show the *casting director*!
>
> I have been out of work for a while now. Lichtig, who represents you, is incompetent, and you are 3000 miles from here, and I need to eat: so I'm asking you to break this contract, which has no point or base to it.
>
> I am glad you are doing well. If you could do something in N.Y for me, I'd be thankful. I did let Lichtig know that I would ask to break our contract, which he thought was natural after this [situation].[32]

Here Lugosi had little compunction about complaining to Pauker, or about breaking a contracual agreement with a representative.

Lugosi repeated this same approach over and over again in the years that followed. In America, he never relied solely on any individual as a representative. Even while Marlowe was his agent and manager in late 1947 and in 1948, Lugosi continued to depend on Chamberlain and Lyman Brown – two brothers who were New York theatrical representatives – for his summer stock bookings. For example, on May 3, 1948, Lugosi asked Marlowe to contact the Browns to announce that he was available for summer stock if they could "do anything for him."[33] They responded with two dates, one being a version of *Dracula* in Woodstock, New York that did not come to pass.[34]

It was a logical move, and it was hardly unusual for a film actor's agent to work with other representatives. In addition to the Browns, Marlowe was also working with Joe Magee of the William Morris Agency to arrange Lugosi's summer stock schedule. However, by July 2, 1948, while appearing in *Dracula* in Denver, Lugosi clearly bypassed Marlowe, writing a letter directly to Lyman Brown. In it, he detailed his three upcoming summer stock engagements, leaving blanks beside dates that were still open. He told Brown that Magee had booked his three scheduled shows, but was hoping that Brown could book more.[35]

Perhaps Lugosi believed that Marlowe simply had not tried – or tried hard enough – to get bookings from Brown, or perhaps he believed that he could avoid paying Marlowe a commission by communicating directly with Brown. After all, Brown responded directly to Lugosi, effectively keeping Marlowe out of the loop, even though he must have known that Lugosi's initial unwillingness to star in *Dracula* and *Arsenic and Old Lace* was the real problem, not Marlowe's representation.[36]

By 1949, Lugosi's association with representatives grew far more convoluted, perhaps due to his increasing disenchantment with Marlowe and Marlowe's increased emphasis on live appearances. On February 18, 1949, Marlowe wrote to Chamberlain Brown inquiring about possible summer stock bookings. His letter made sense, as many summer stock shows were booked in the springtime. If anything, he was trying to be particularly timely.[37] Brown responded on February 23, agreeing to "look after Mr. Lugosi," but adding that he wished "Lugosi could think of another play" since "*Arsenic* has been done [in] nearly every place."[38]

Marlowe responded that at that time Lugosi had "no other plays – just *Dracula* and *Arsenic*."[39] Brown apparently did not write again until March 30, telling Marlowe that the summer theatres were "just on the fire," but would "really start to pop" in terms of bookings in April.[40] It was in the days that followed that the confusion occurred. For one, Marlowe signed a deal on Lugosi's behalf with another theatrical representative, Olga Lee, who immediately started to book Lugosi for summer stock.

Lugosi must have known about Lee, especially given that she sent him (via Marlowe) a copy of the play *Shop at Sly Corner* for him to consider using in summer stock along with *Dracula* and *Arsenic*.[41] But the question remains as to *why* the change, particularly given that Lugosi had worked with the Browns off and on for a number of years. Regardless, Marlowe informed Lyman Brown about Olga Lee on April 23, 1948, writing, "I did not hear from you for over a period of five weeks so I took it for granted you were no longer interested."[42]

Chamberlain Brown's response to Marlowe came quickly, claiming that he couldn't "understand" what had happened, as he *had* expressed his interest and that he had "five dates for Mr. Lugosi."[43] That Marlowe was writing at times to Chamberlain Brown and at times to Lyman Brown about the same issue may have been an intentional effort to confuse matters. Nevertheless, Marlowe wrote to Lyman Brown on April 27, noting, "As I told you in my last letter I already gave an authorization to Olga Lee on Bela Lugosi, so please contact her if you have any dates for him. That is all settled – maybe next year on Lugosi."[44]

Whatever Marlowe did or did not understand about the Brown brothers' level of interest in representing Lugosi – and whatever Lugosi did or did not ask Marlowe to do – the number of Lugosi representatives continued to grow. On April

29, 1949, the Hollywood film agent Charles Beyer sent Lyman Brown a letter stating that he had Lugosi available for summer stock.[45] Only days later, Beyer sent an apparently baffled Brown yet another letter, reassuring him:

> I am definitely Bela Lugosi's agent and I am handling all deals for him. Therefore, any deals should be made through me.
>
> Will you kindly let me know the dates and places for Mr. Lugosi so I can arrange his time accordingly [as well as] the price you have set for him [?][46]

Lugosi had in fact signed a contract with Beyer on March 15, 1949, but it only gave Beyer an authorization to pursue film roles. The first paragraph of their agreement clearly reads: "This contract is limited to the motion picture industry and to contracts of the Actor as an actor in such industry...."[47]

And so here the question arises as to why Beyer attempted to act as Lugosi's agent in the matter of summer stock, and how he even knew to contact Lyman Brown, as opposed to any number of other theatrical representatives involved in summer stock. The likely answer is that Lugosi told Beyer about Brown. If so, that meant Lugosi was using Beyer to deal with the Browns at the very same moment that he was using Marlowe to deal with Olga Lee. At any rate, Brown obviously believed Beyer, telling him on May 5, 1949 that he was "glad to learn [he was Lugosi's] exclusive agent, for now I can go ahead and pick up where I left off."[48]

But Lugosi's own letter to Lyman Brown on May 10, 1949 made matters all the more chaotic. From Lake Elsinore, he wrote:

> Since it is again 'summer stock' season [I] felt it might be wise to contact you and advise you that I am available for bookings. I am writing you regarding this as you have been booking me for the past two years and would like you to continue to do so.
>
> I also wish to advise you that I am not under contract with any agent for summer stock work and that my agent for motion pictures *only* is with Mr. Charles Beyer, consequently you will get full commissions on any bookings you may make.[49]

Rather than playing agents off of one another, perhaps Lugosi was simply trying to rein in Beyer, who was clearly overstepping his bounds. At any rate, Lugosi's actions could hardly have inspired Beyer to work harder on behalf of his film career.

Then, only a few days later, Olga Lee wrote to Lugosi, telling him that she believed the "wisest thing" for her to do was to "withdraw from the picture." Lee told Lugosi that she would keep "all that [he] wrote confidential," which she did to the extent that his communication to her does not seem to exist. Apparently he had tried to explain away the confusion, perhaps speaking negatively about his other representatives. Lee did implore Lugosi to respect the one summer stock booking she had made on his behalf, and added that she would continue to search for a new play for him to use "for Broadway in the Fall."[50]

It is very likely that all of this confusion caused Lugosi to lose possible summer stock dates in 1949. On May 14, 1949, Lyman Brown wrote to Lugosi with offers to do *Dracula* in Hoboken, New Jersey and *Arsenic and Old Lace* in Matunuck, Rhode Island.[51] Both came with offers of $750 each, guaranteed. But for reasons unknown, Lugosi did not appear in either city.[52] Nonetheless, Lugosi continued to place much trust in the Brown brothers.

For the rest of the summer of 1949, Lugosi seems to have dealt directly with Lyman Brown. As late as June 14, he wrote to Brown regarding contractual details and publicity materials for upcoming straw hat performances.[53] And as for Charles Beyer, their association was limited. Lugosi grew tired

July 26th 1938

Dr. Edmon Pauker
1639 Broadway
New York City

My dear Eddy:-

Up until to date I have not heard from you and would like you to know that I am very eager to play a part on the stage either in New York or London.

I understand that Gilbert Miller will produce the "Tragedy of Man" at the New York Fair. I played both leading parts in the original (in hungarian) and was directing it in Hungary as far as 25 years ago and in 1923 I produced, directed and acted in the Lexington Opera House (in hungarian). But regardless of the above please try to dig up something for me.

Gratefully yours

Béla

January 29, 1937

My dear Edmond:

I was very happy that you bothered me as it has been a long time since I have heard from you. I am glad the matter about "A FEJEDELEM" has been cleared. I am still very interested in it and whenever you get a revised script from the author please send me one immediately.

I am getting rather stale in Hollywood and if you could secure an interesting engagement for me on our past business basis I would appreciate it. Stage, film or radio.

With best wishes to you and family, I remain

Sincerely yours,

Béla

BL:VM

Mr. Edmond Pauker
1639 Broadway
New York, New York

of Beyer more quickly than he had with many of his other agents, including Marlowe. In November 1949, Lugosi signed a new agreement for motion picture representation, this time with the William Morris Agency.[54]

In some respects, Lugosi's actions can be explained by his impatience, which may have heightened while he was largely out of work in California during the first half of 1949. So much spare time may well have intensified his exasperation. But his actions also speak to another feature of his approach to business. The fact that he so regularly insinuated himself into negotiations — rather than letting representatives speak for him — is likely the result of a man who had in fact been a producer and director. Shortly after arriving in America in the 1920s, for example, Lugosi produced a number of Hungarian-language plays.[55] Then, in 1935, he had unsuccessfully tried to form his own production company.[56]

When he was generally unemployed during 1937 and 1938, Lugosi returned to the same basic idea. Writing to Edmond Pauker, Lugosi indicated his interest in staging an English-language version of Viktor Kelemen's *A Fejedelem* (*His Majesty*).[57] When nothing came of the plans, Lugosi sent Pauker another letter, noting that he would be "very happy" for any work Pauker could help him find for the "usual 10% reimbursement."[58]

By the summer of 1938, an increasingly desperate Lugosi wrote to Pauker again, having heard that Gilbert Miller planned to stage a version of Imre Madách's Hungarian classic *The Tragedy of Man* at the New York Fair. He reminded Pauker that he had produced, directed, and starred in the same play in 1923.[59] Pauker assured Lugosi that he could get him "one of the leading roles" in it, adding that he would try to persuade Miller to let Lugosi assist in directing the play.[60] But then came the bad news that Miller was not going to produce the play.[61]

Lugosi contacted Pauker again in 1939, asking for copies of English translations of Erno Szep's play *Majus* (*In May*) and Kelemen's *Fejedelem*. He told Pauker that he would "try to place these stories for radio or screen."[62] Here again Lugosi was attempting to make negotiations on his own in an effort to control his career and the kind of roles he would play.

Such an approach may have been wise on occasion, but at times it seems to have interfered with the careful negotiations that his representatives were undertaking on his behalf. At any rate, he proceeded to do much the same during the post-war era. For example, in 1948, Lugosi negotiated at length with summer stock director George R. Snell about a possible *Dracula* tour. Snell recalled:

> At one point when discussing his future plans, I approached the subject of a world tour of *Dracula*. As these discussions continued, he became positive and enthused. Over the next winter, I met with potential investors. However, it all came to a screeching halt with world conditions and the growing possibility of our encountering military conflicts in some places.
>
> We decided to shelve the project, which was unfortunate, and I always regretted that outcome.[63]

During all of their talks, Lugosi represented himself, rather than rely on Don Marlowe or anyone else.

It is difficult to determine whether Lugosi was actually good at representing himself in these situations or not. But it is clear that his often overlapping and ill-defined relationships with representatives could hardly have helped him obtain work when he needed it most. True, some of them may have had their own difficulties, ranging from large egos to tendencies to exaggerate, but such would have been common currency among many entertainment agents and managers. Whatever their faults, Lugosi could well have been his own worst enemy in finding new roles to portray.

And then there is simply the fact that so much of what is talked about in the entertainment business is just that, talk. Most films and plays do not materialize. Whether it was in California during the first half of 1949 or at any point during his "lost years," Lugosi regularly heard about so many projects that did not occur. They were little more than apparitions, phantoms that vanished just as he tried to grasp them in his hands.

(Endnotes)

1. "Likes Hot Beer and Strong Scotch, Frankenstein Guest At Roundup." *Deming Headlight* (Deming, NM) 3 Dec. 3, 1948.
2. *Ibid.*
3. Cremer, Robert. *Lugosi: The Man Behind the Cape* (Chicago: Henry Regnery, 1976).
4. "Ink Hampton White for *Dracula* Lead." *The Billboard* 23 Apr. 1949.
5. Lugosi, Bela. Letter to Lyman Brown. 25 May 1949. [Available in the Chamberlain and Lyman Brown Papers, and Undated, Series II: Correspondence, Box 64, Folder F.9 at the New York Public Library/Lincoln Center for the Performing Arts in New York.]
6. "*Now Really, Peter*." *Brooklyn Eagle* 20 Dec. 1949.
7. Brown, Lyman and Chamberlain. Letter to Don Marlowe. 14 May 1947. [Available in the Chamberlain and Lyman Brown Papers, and Undated, Series II: Correspondence, Box 64, Folder F.9 at the New York Public Library/Lincoln Center for the Performing Arts in New York.]
8. Lugosi, Bela. Letter to Virginia Doak. 8 Oct. 1947.
9. *Daily Variety* 15 Dec. 1947.
10. *Daily Variety* 2 Feb. 1948.
11. *Daily Variety* 14 Apr. 1948.
12. Available in MSC 150, Series I, Talent, Box 197 of the Redpath Chautauqua Collection at the Special Collections Department of the University of Iowa Libraries (Iowa City).
13. *Ibid.*
14. "What Was Chautauqua?" Available at http://sdrc.lib.uiowa.edu/traveling-culture/essay.htm. Accessed 25 Sept. 2011.
15. Records of the Redpath Chautauqua Collection, Organization History, http://sdrc.lib.uiowa.edu/traveling-culture/inventory/MSC150.html. Updated 4 Oct. 2006. Accessed 14 Sept. 2011.
16. "Horror King Goes Dramatic in New Play; Premiere Here." *Rockford Morning Star* (Rockford, IL) 12 Nov. 1947.
17. Hopper, Hedda. "Looking at Hollywood." *Chicago Tribune* 31 Jan. 1948; Marlowe, Don. Letter to Lyman Brown. 14 May 1948.
18. "Looking to Hollywood."
19. Thomas, Bob. "Hollywood News." *Indiana Evening Gazette* (Indiana, PA) 3 Mar. 1948.
20. Kilgallen, Dorothy. "Voice of Broadway." *Schenectady Gazette* (Schenectady, NY) 19 Mar. 1948.
21. Johnson, Erskine. *Portland Press Herald* (Portland, ME) 16 May 1948.
22. "MRS Pictures Start First *Inner Sanctum* July 7." *Film Daily* 18 Oct. 1948.
23. "U-I Skeds 24, with Six in Color." *Hollywood Reporter* 8 Sept. 1948. [In addition to these 24 features, U-I also distributed other films during its 1948-49 season.]
24. "Universal to Release 28 Top Features in 1949." *Film Daily* 27 Dec. 1948.
25. "Films' Dracula Comes to Town." *Springfield Union* (Springfield, MA) 15 Sept. 1948.
26. "Termer for Lugosi." *Hollywood Reporter* 20 Feb. 1948; *Daily Variety* 19 Feb. 1948.
27. "Classics Sets 34 New Films for 1949, Against 10 in 1948." *Motion Picture Daily* 24 June 1948; "Film Classics to Have 26 Pictures." *Motion Picture Herald* 7 Aug. 1948.
28. *Pittsburgh Press* 9 Aug. 1948.
29. *The Billboard* 1 May 1948.
30. *New Orleans Times-Picayune* 19 Sept. 1948.
31. "Films' Dracula Comes to Town."
32. Lugosi, Bela. Letter to Edmond Pauker. 22 Oct. 1929. [Available in the Edmond Pauker Papers, 1910-1957, Series I: Correspondence, 1915-1957, Box 42, Folder 11 at the New York Public Library/Lincoln Center for the Performing Arts in New York.]
33. Marlowe, Don. Letter to Chamberlain and Lyman Brown. 3 May 1948. [Available in the Chamberlain and Lyman Brown Papers, and Undated, Series II: Correspondence, Box 64, Folder F.9 at the New York Public Library/Lincoln Center for the Performing Arts in New York.]
34. Brown, Chamberlain and Lyman. Letter to Don Marlowe. 12 May 1948. [Available in the Chamberlain and Lyman Brown Papers, and Undated, Series II: Correspondence, Box 64, Folder F.9 at the New York Public Library/Lincoln Center for the Performing Arts in New York.]
35. Lugosi, Bela. Letter to Lyman Brown. 2 July 1948. [Available in the Chamberlain and Lyman Brown Papers, and Undated, Series II: Correspondence, Box 64, Folder F.9 at the New York Public Library/Lincoln Center for the Performing Arts in New York.]
36. Brown, Lyman. Letter to Bela Lugosi. 7 July 1948. [Available in the Chamberlain and Lyman Brown Papers, and Undated, Series II: Correspondence, Box 64, Folder F.9 at the New York Public Library/Lincoln Center for the Performing Arts in New York.]
37. Marlowe, Don. Letter to Chamberlain Brown. 18 Feb.1948. [Available in the Chamberlain and Lyman Brown Papers, and Undated, Series II: Correspondence, Box 64, Folder F.9 at the New York Public Library/Lincoln Center for the Performing Arts in New York.]
38. Brown, Chamberlain. Letter to Don Marlowe. 23 Feb. 1949. [Available in the Chamberlain and Lyman Brown Papers, and Undated, Series II: Correspondence, Box 64, Folder F.9 at the New York Public Library/Lincoln Center for the Performing Arts in New York.]
39. Marlowe, Don. Letter to Chamberlain Brown. 29 Feb. 1949. [Available in the Chamberlain and Lyman Brown Papers, and Undated, Series II: Correspondence, Box 64, Folder F.9 at the New York Public Library/Lincoln Center for the Performing Arts

40 Brown, Chamberlain. Letter to Don Marlowe. 30 Mar. 1949. [Available in the Chamberlain and Lyman Brown Papers, and Undated, Series II: Correspondence, Box 64, Folder F.9 at the New York Public Library/Lincoln Center for the Performing Arts in New York.]

41 Lee, Olga Lee. Letter to Don Marlowe. 3 May 1949. [Available in the Chamberlain and Lyman Brown Papers, and Undated, Series II: Correspondence, Box 64, Folder F.9 at the New York Public Library/Lincoln Center for the Performing Arts in New York.]

42 Marlowe, Don. Letter to Lyman Brown. 23 Apr. 1949. [Available in the Chamberlain and Lyman Brown Papers, and Undated, Series II: Correspondence, Box 64, Folder F.9 at the New York Public Library/Lincoln Center for the Performing Arts in New York.]

43 Brown, Chamberlain. Letter to Don Marlowe. 25 Apr. 1949. [Available in the Chamberlain and Lyman Brown Papers, and Undated, Series II: Correspondence, Box 64, Folder F.9 at the New York Public Library/Lincoln Center for the Performing Arts in New York.]

44 Marlowe, Don. Letter to Lyman Brown. 27 Apr. 1949. [Available in the Chamberlain and Lyman Brown Papers, and Undated, Series II: Correspondence, Box 64, Folder F.9 at the New York Public Library/Lincoln Center for the Performing Arts in New York.]

45 Beyer, Charles. Letter to Lyman Brown. 29 Apr. 1949. [Available in the Chamberlain and Lyman Brown Papers, and Undated, Series II: Correspondence, Box 64, Folder F.9 at the New York Public Library/Lincoln Center for the Performing Arts in New York.]

46 Beyer, Charles. Letter to Lyman Brown. 3 May 1949. [Available in the Chamberlain and Lyman Brown Papers, and Undated, Series II: Correspondence, Box 64, Folder F.9 at the New York Public Library/Lincoln Center for the Performing Arts in New York.]

47 Lugosi, Bela. Contract with Charles Beyer. 15 Mar. 1949. [Available in the Chamberlain and Lyman Brown Papers, and Undated, Series II: Correspondence, Box 64, Folder F.9 at the New York Public Library/Lincoln Center for the Performing Arts in New York.]

48 Brown, Lyman. Letter to Charles Beyer. 5 May 1949. [Available in the Chamberlain and Lyman Brown Papers, and Undated, Series II: Correspondence, Box 64, Folder F.9 at the New York Public Library/Lincoln Center for the Performing Arts in New York.]

49 Lugosi, Bela. Letter to Lyman Brown. 10 May 1949. [Available in the Chamberlain and Lyman Brown Papers, and Undated, Series II: Correspondence, Box 64, Folder F.9 at the New York Public Library/Lincoln Center for the Performing Arts in New York.]

50 Lee, Olga. Letter to Bela Lugosi. 13 May 1949. [Available in the Chamberlain and Lyman Brown Papers, and Undated, Series II: Correspondence, Box 64, Folder F.9 at the New York Public Library/Lincoln Center for the Performing Arts in New York.]

51 Brown, Lyman. Letter to Bela Lugosi. 14 May 1949. [Available in the Chamberlain and Lyman Brown Papers, and Undated, Series II: Correspondence, Box 64, Folder F.9 at the New York Public Library/Lincoln Center for the Performing Arts in New York.]

52 A thorough check of newspapers in the same (and nearby) towns and cities makes clear that Lugosi did not appear at them in 1949.

53 Lugosi, Bela. Letter to Lyman Brown. 13 June 1949. [Available in the Chamberlain and Lyman Brown Papers, and Undated, Series II: Correspondence, Box 64, Folder F.9 at the New York Public Library/Lincoln Center for the Performing Arts in New York.]

54 Lugosi, Bela. Contract with the William Morris Agency. 10 Nov. 1949.

55 For more information on these plays, see Gary D. Rhodes' *Bela Lugosi: Dreams and Nightmares* (Narberth, PA: Collectables, 2007).

56 For more information on Lugosi's planned production company, see Gary D. Rhodes' *Lugosi* (Jefferson, NC: McFarland, 1997).

57 Lugosi, Bela. Letter to Edmond Pauker. 29 Jan. 1937. [Available in the Edmond Pauker Papers, 1910-1957, Series I: Correspondence, 1915-1957, Box 42, Folder 11 at the New York Public Library/Lincoln Center for the Performing Arts in New York.]

58 Lugosi, Bela. Letter to Edmond Pauker. 22 Sept. 1937. [Available in the Edmond Pauker Papers, 1910-1957, Series I: Correspondence, 1915-1957, Box 42, Folder 11 at the New York Public Library/Lincoln Center for the Performing Arts in New York.]

59 Lugosi, Bela. Letter to Edmond Pauker. 26 July 1938. [Available in the Edmond Pauker Papers, 1910-1957, Series I: Correspondence, 1915-1957, Box 42, Folder 11 at the New York Public Library/Lincoln Center for the Performing Arts in New York.]

60 Pauker, Edmond. Letter to Bela Lugosi. 20 Aug. 1938. [Available in the Edmond Pauker Papers, 1910-1957, Series I: Correspondence, 1915-1957, Box 42, Folder 11 at the New York Public Library/Lincoln Center for the Performing Arts in New York.]

61 Pauker, Edmond. Letter to Bela Lugosi. 30 Sept. 1938. [Available in the Edmond Pauker Papers, 1910-1957, Series I: Correspondence, 1915-1957, Box 42, Folder 11 at the New York Public Library/Lincoln Center for the Performing Arts in New York.]

62 Lugosi, Bela. Letter to Edmond Pauker. 5 Sept. 1938. [Available in the Edmond Pauker Papers, 1910-1957, Series I: Correspondence, 1915-1957, Box 42, Folder 11 at the New York Public Library/Lincoln Center for the Performing Arts in New York.]

63 Rhodes, Gary D. Interview with George R. Snell. 7 Apr. 2006.

To Lillian – Bela

Lugosi in a publicity still circulated in the late forties. (Courtesy of George R. Snell)

Chapter 9

EASTERLY

After Lugosi enjoyed a relatively quiet spring in California, the summer stock circuit of 1949 beckoned. Once again Lillian would drive their Buick convertible coupe, but for this trip the couple had an additional passenger. For the first time, their son Bela Jr. went on the road with them. And it was a long road, starting in Lake Elsinore, California around June 27 and moving east, always east.

A few days and over 1,600 miles later, the Lugosis passed through Carroll, Iowa. As so often happened, the locals recognized the actor. The *Daily Times Herald* proudly told readers that "Count Dracula" ate breakfast in their town. Wrongly crediting him as the star of *I Walked with a Zombie* (1943), a journalist explained that one of the diners had recognized Lugosi. Word spread quickly, and Lugosi soon began autographing meal checks for employees and customers.[1]

Over 500 miles further down the road, the Lugosis stopped near Warsaw, Indiana. The *Warsaw Daily Times* reported:

> A movie actor almost passed through Warsaw Friday night. But a Frankenstein fan spotted Bela Lugosi, the batman in the Frankenstein pictures, at the Cedar Lawn Tourist Camp, a mile west of Warsaw, where Lugosi and his family were spending the night.[2]

The newspaper added that the Lugosis were on their way to Buffalo, New York.[3] At that point, they still had nearly 500 more miles ahead of them.

After traveling for a few more hours, the Lugosis stopped in Cairo, Ohio. Not content with just resting or eating, Lugosi insisted on exploring the town. That was the day when Robert Ray "Bob" Edgington spotted a mysterious person playing ball with his children, Bob Jr. and Carolyn. Edgington had lived a fascinating life and had witnessed many strange things, but he had never expected to see Dracula appear on his front lawn.

Describing the event, the *Toledo Blade* reported that Edgington initially "thought the heat had affected his vision."[4] Concerned for the safety of his children, he then:

> ... went out and made an investigation and found that quite by accident he had become momentary host to a Hollywood star. His visitor turned out to be Bela Lugosi. ... Lugosi turned out to be anything but a villain, however, and signed autographs for the entire Edgington family and numerous townsfolk who appeared when word got around the community of the star's presence. It seems Lu-

Robert Ray "Bob" Edgington.
(Courtesy of Carolyn Edgington Anderson)

gosi, his wife and son were en route by motor to a vacation in the East. The quiet shade of the Mayor's lawn and the presence of the Edgington children there playing ball prompted the Lugosis to stop and rest for a brief interval.[5]

While Lillian and Bela Jr. visited a nearby restaurant, Lugosi stayed at the Edgington home.

Carolyn Edgington, who played ball with Lugosi that day, recalled, "Our home was right beside the Cairo restaurant, which meant many different cars, trucks, and other vehicles parked in front of our home. As we were growing up, my Mom and Dad were always warning us not to go up to any of these cars or trucks, no matter how nice the people acted." Despite the warning, however, Carolyn and her brother Bob Jr. were somehow drawn to the stranger. "I remember [Lugosi] playing ball with me on our sidewalk and in the yard," Carolyn later wrote.[6]

For Lugosi and his family, the stop was a brief respite from the trek east. For the Edgingtons, the afternoon became one of the most memorable days of their lives. Decades later, Robert Edgington recalled how the road led Bela Lugosi to his home:

> I was born in Lima, Ohio, but I spent quite a bit of my younger days in Plymouth, Indiana on the farm during the Depression. Later on then my Dad moved back to Ohio. I spent six months in the Civilian Conservation Corps back in 1936. I'm a World War II veteran of the Air Force – England and North Africa – 8th and 12th Air Forces – and I was in the Battle of Kasserine Pass in Africa. And I was a Technical Sergeant.
>
> [I was the mayor of Cairo for] one term, two years. My neighbor next door was a member of the Democratic Party. The mayor that was didn't want to run for another term. [He thought,] 'There's a young guy across the street. Maybe we ought to have some young blood.' And I said, 'Well, I've never been a mayor, and I wouldn't know anything to do,' and he said, 'We'll train you.' And I said, 'Well, have I got a chance?' And he said, 'Well, in this town, you will be elected.' So it was true. I was the Mayor in '48 and '49, and it was quite an experience.
>
> [As far as Lugosi goes], I had seen some of his films. [My favorite was] *Dracula*. I saw several of his [television] shows, but I don't remember what they were. I don't remember him being on

the radio. I liked him. I liked what he did. His shows were scary and all, and I just enjoyed him, so much.

His eyes! The eyes! They were piercing. ... But as we got to talking, that real piercing look faded into a warm friendly face. As we talked and just got acquainted there, he just kind of relaxed and smiled and that look [the piercing eyes] disappeared. Just somebody relaxing there for a few minutes.

[It was] right around noon when people started going into the restaurant to eat – Oh yeah, [the weather] was hot! – I'll tell you, I was sitting on the porch with my two kids, my older daughter was four and my little boy was two. A car stopped in front of my home. A man got out, walked around to the sidewalk. A lady was in there also. I looked at him as he stood up on the sidewalk. I thought, 'Do I know him? He looks familiar. How can you know him? He just pulled up!' And I said, 'My land, I'm dreaming here.' This just could not be who I thought it looked like. I said, 'It *can't* be.'

It was only about 30 feet from my front porch to the sidewalk. And my little son and daughter were playing ball, tossing the little ball back in the yard. And he just stood there and watched from the sidewalk. I said, 'It's warm!' He smiled, 'Yes it is!' I felt like I was meeting a friend. I told him, I said, 'Are you who I think?' He interrupted me, he said, 'Yeah, I'm him!' I'll never forget that. I said, 'Well, come on up and sit on the porch.' And he said, 'You don't mind?' I said, 'Heavens no! Come on up here!'

We come up, and we got chairs out there, and we sat down. He had a big hankie, and he wiped his forehead. I said, 'You want a drink of ice water?' He said, 'I'd appreciate that very much.' I got him a big glass of ice water, and we sat there and talked. It was about the weather, just general information. He asked me about the town, and the size and the people, this kind of stuff. As the little kids were playing ball when he came up on the porch, he picked up the ball and tossed it back and forth to the kids for a little bit.

... I said, 'It's so wonderful that I can be able to meet you, a person of your stature, and the things that you do.' I said, 'It's very appreciated that you're talking to me and doing this kind of thing.' He said, 'I'm enjoying myself. Looks like you have a nice little town. What do you do otherwise?' I said, 'Well, I work in a factory, and I'm also the mayor of the town.'

He talked to me for a while. Some people started to coming up. His wife ... she never actually came up, but she went to the restaurant out of the car. She kind of waved cause we were sitting on the porch. She could see us, and it was 35, 40 minutes anyhow, and she came back, and she just kind of waved, and she got back in the car. And I don't know whether she said something in the restaurant or what, but people started kind of collecting around, you know, just one or two, then three or four. And he just came out in the yard, and he was talking and he said, 'Well' – he kind of paused – 'I'm going to have to go!' I said 'Why?' He said, 'The crowd is coming!' So far there was only about ten or twelve people there.

And so he said, 'You have a nice little town here,' and he looked at me and he said, 'Thank you, Bob!' He called me by my first name, and I was thrilled to pieces. And I told him to call me that. He said, 'You've been very pleasant. I enjoyed our visit,' he said, 'I really enjoyed our visit.' Then he said, 'Looks like I must leave.' He picked up my kids – one at a time – gave them a hug. 'Nice family,' he said. He shook my hand. Placed his hand on my shoulder, 'And it's been swell,'

Another snapshot of Robert Ray "Bob" Edgington. (Courtesy of Carolyn Edgington Anderson)

he said. He gave me his autograph, smiling. 'I won't forget how nice you treated me.'

I walked with him out to his car. The lady would be driving. He entered, looked, smiled, [and] waved as they slowly drove away. It was a special day to meet him. What a gentleman. As he smiled, it offset his eyes, which now looked so warm and friendly. I have never forgotten him. Never forgot him. Dracula playing ball with my kids!

I asked him, 'You're traveling?' He said, 'We're on a vacation. We're going east on a vacation.' I said, 'Well, the next little town you go through will be Beaverdam, Ohio.' We didn't discuss any of his business. He was so friendly, and so down to earth, so warm to talk to. It was just like I had known him for twenty years. He gave me a hug, he put his arm around me, and I walked with him. His arm was around me, and I walked with him to the sidewalk, he had his arm around me and he shook hands and he said, 'It's been great!'

The biggest part of it was, after he's gone the crowd came. 'Did Bela Lugosi stop at your house?" I says, 'Yeah!' 'Well, where's he at?' Well, I says, 'You've missed him. He's gone; he left!' 'Already?' I says, 'Yeah.' I says, 'I guess he don't like crowds or something, you know.' Oh, they were disappointed! One guy says, 'Oh gosh, too late!'

In just that short visit, I never forgot him. He just had some kind of a magnetic attraction. Just, you know, you just see him and you just loved him! The way he talked, who he was, and he just forgot that 'I'm Mr. Bela Lugosi,' he's a big movie star. [Instead, it was as if] 'I'm just a friend here talking to a friend'. Like I'd known him for twenty years![7]

After their conversation ended, Edgington's new friend had to leave Cairo. The Lugosis were on a family vacation. But they were also on a business trip, and Lugosi needed to reach his first summer stock engagement of 1949. So it was back to the car. Back to endless city streets, county roads, and two-lane state highways. And back to the relentless hum of the tires spinning against the pavement, intermittently accompanied by the sound of a wheel hitting a hole in the blacktop, or by a small piece of gravel bouncing underneath the car.

That was Lugosi's life after the war, at least a good part of it: a brief stop, and then it was time to get moving again.

(Endnotes)

1 *Daily Times Herald* (Carroll, IA) 30 June 30 1949.
2 "Movie Star in Warsaw." *Warsaw Daily Times* (Warsaw, IN) 6 July 1949.
3 *Ibid.*
4 *Toledo Blade* (Toledo, OH) 6 July 1949.
5 *Ibid.*
6 Anderson, Carolyn. Letter to Bill Kaffenberger. 7 Oct. 2011.
7 Kaffenberger, Bill. Interview with Robert Ray Edgington. 22 Sept. 2011.

Lugosi and his son on the road in 1949. (Courtesy of Bela G. Lugosi)

Chapter 10
RETURN ENGAGEMENTS

From Cairo, Ohio, Lugosi – together with Lillian and Bela Jr. – traveled to Buffalo, New York, apparently staying in the city for a brief time before moving onward to Syracuse and the actor's first straw hat appearance of 1949. According to the *New York Times*, approximately 156 summer theatres would operate that summer, employing approximately 1,000 actors. That was as opposed to roughly 129 "barn emporiums" operating the year before.[1]

In 1949, one journalist declared that audiences at summer stock performances were among the most dedicated and enthusiastic that could be found anywhere:

> No other audience struggles so hard just to get to the theatre. The drive is liable to be anywhere from the breadth to the length of Long Island. On arrival there is a snarl of stalled or parked cars along country lanes suitable for one wagon and one horse to pass abreast. Broadway theatres can never equal the shock of confronting an actress in full war paint and between dress-house and playhouse. You sit behind a pillar or aft of a beam on benches straight from the Puritans.
>
> ... this audience is a loyal and sentimental one, recalling older stars in famous vehicles regardless of vintage. Here *Springtime for Henry* [with Edward Everett Horton] is forever summer.[2]

As for those older stars, another article noted that many of the "rustic impressarios" from prior summers would return to the straw hat circuit, as would a number of newcomers like Bramwell Fletcher, who had appeared in such horror films as *Svengali* (1931) and *The Mummy* (1932).[3]

The continued emphasis on stars brought more condemnations of the same. Melville Burke (of the Lakewood Theatre in Skowhegan, Maine) implored fellow managers to forego stardom and instead consider the merits of particular plays that would appeal to their audiences. Burke predicted, "it is my belief that summer stock companies may be ruined in the next decade by their concentration on stars. This wholesale destruction may descend on the rustic circuit unless summer theatre companies realize that their theatrical firmament is greater than any stars therein."[4]

Ignoring such warnings, theatre managers returned to many of the same stars and plays of previous seasons, including *Dracula*. However, in the summer of 1949, Lugosi was noticeably absent from the cast of that play. The Pittsford Summer Theatre's *Dracula* in July featured Robert Bride as the vampire.[5] Robert Carricart took the title role of *Dracula* at the Lakeside Theatre, and J. Edward Bromberg did the same at the Robin Hood Theatre.[6] Nor did Lugosi appear in productions of *Dracula* at the Penn-Mill Theatre in Pennsylvania or the Major Vail Playhouse in Vermont.[7]

Lugosi's absence from *Dracula* in summer stock that year might have been due in part to having other commitments the same week that it commenced on a given stage. And some of it may also have been because given theatres might not have been able to afford him. But a third possible reason is the fact that theatre managers likely knew that *Dracula* with Lugosi had bombed in Denver in 1948, and that its poor showing was a key reason the Artists Repertory Theatre went out of business.

Lugosi was also unable to branch out into new summer stock productions in 1949. He did not star in *Harvey*, as he had hoped. Nor did he receive any new roles in other horror stage plays. At least four theatre managers scheduled *The Bat* for their 1949 seasons; three others staged *The Cat and the Canary*. Lugosi starred in none of them.[8] He also did not appear in the Ocean City Playhouse's production of *The Thirteenth Chair*, though he had in fact appeared in a 1929 film version of that very play.[9]

Newspaper advertisement dated July 8, 1949.

Paul Lukas and Lugosi together in Fayetteville, New York in 1949.

Unlike the summer of 1948, when Lugosi originally hoped to avoid horror plays at the straw hat theatres, it is clear that he wanted to embrace them in 1949, even if only because of financial reasons. On April 29, 1948, Charles Beyer — who was ostensibly handling only Lugosi's film career, but who for some reason entered into stock negotiations — wrote to theatrical representative Lyman Brown: "Bela Lugosi is available for summer stock. He could do *Dracula*, *Arsenic and Old Lace*, or any other good play they would like him to do."[10]

And so, Lugosi's summer of 1949 depended on the only play that "they" wanted him to do: *Arsenic and Old Lace*. Boris Karloff had appeared in an adaptation of the play on the *Ford Television Hour* in April of that year.[11] For Lugosi, there would no broadcast event, but instead five different versions at five different venues. Only five, out of what were in fact at least thirteen productions of *Arsenic* at summer theatres in 1949.[12] And of those five, two of them came thanks to return engagements at theatres he had played in previous summers. Lugosi's rapport with their managing directors had paved the way for his return.

176   NO TRAVELER RETURNS | The Lost Years of Bela Lugosi

Lugosi had originally hoped to appear in some of these plays with his friend Harald Dyrenforth, a German actor who had worked on Broadway and on various radio programs. When Lugosi played in *Dracula* onstage in Litchfield in 1947, Dyrenforth had appeared as Van Helsing. Writing that he "would most certainly welcome" the chance to work with him again, Lugosi encouraged Dyrenforth to contact Lyman Brown.[13] After all, Dyrenforth was also able to work as Lugosi's front man, traveling to stock theatres in advance of rehearsals to help stage the productions. To Brown, Dyrenforth offered that service, as well as his acting: "In *Dracula*, [Lugosi] wants me to do my old stand-by of Van Helsing. In *Arsenic*, I would like to play Dr. Einstein, but Bela thinks I would be a wonderful Teddy Roosevelt."[14]

From the *Syracuse Herald-American* of July 10, 1949.

But there is no evidence that Lugosi and Dyrenforth reunited onstage that summer. Perhaps Brown did not lobby on Dyrenforth's behalf, or — more likely — the summer theatres simply did not need him, preferring to cast their own actors or use members of their own stock companies. The Lugosis decision to travel with their son may also have made another person unnecessary. At any rate, it would be Lillian driving Lugosi to the five versions of *Arsenic*, not Dyrenforth, with Bela Jr. along for the journey.

The first of the *Arsenic* quintet came near Syracuse, New York, at the Famous Artists Playhouse in Fayetteville, where Lugosi received $750 for the week, plus 10% of the net over costs.[15] The Lugosis arrived in the town on July 4, staying at the Fayetteville Inn. Rehearsals began immediately thereafter.[16] To help cash in on Lugosi's appearance, the nearby North Drive-In Theatre scheduled a Thursday night "Super Spook Show" double bill of *Bride of Frankenstein* (1935) and *Son of Frankenstein* (1939).

As for Lugosi, the stay at Fayetteville was less hectic than some of his other summer stock appearances, his early arrival in the town coming one week before *Arsenic* premiered. Fellow Hungarian Paul Lukas was then starring at the Famous Artists in another play, *Accent on Youth*. The two actors socialized together, with a Syracuse photographer snapping a picture of Lugosi visiting Lukas backstage.[17]

On the Saturday before opening night, the *Post-Standard* told readers that Lugosi

Program cover for the production of *Arsenic and Old Lace* in Fayetteville, New York.

Gary D. Rhodes | Bill Kaffenberger

was a "gentleman" for paying a special visit to Vinnie Shelton, a war veteran who lived in the area. Eschewing formality and his horror image, Lugosi wore a blue and white checked shirt with a red and yellow-striped bow tie.[18] The newspaper described Shelton as a "twice-wounded veteran... paralyzed from the waist down by a sniper's bullet on Leyte."[19] The two men talked at length, with the actor remarking on the sacrifice Vinnie had made for his country. He also commended Mrs. Esther Shelton for being such a "loyal wife." Presenting the couple with free tickets to the show, Lugosi assured them that he would have the manager find a place where Shelton could comfortably view the play from his wheelchair.[20]

David Yellin directed *Arsenic* and also portrayed the comical Officer Klein; John Larson, managing director of the Famous Artists company, played Mortimer Brewster.[21] Stage veteran Catherine Cosgriff appeared as Abby Brewster, with Florenz Ames taking the role of Dr. Einstein.[22] Ames – who would go on to have three decades of Broadway experience, including over four years in the cast of *Oklahoma!* – was a member of the Famous Artists resident company in 1949.[23]

Herbert Cheyette, who worked as an apprentice

Promotional brochure for the Lakeside Summer Theatre's 1949 season. (Courtesy of the Lake Hopatcong Historical Museum of New Jersey)

Lugosi with his son at Lake Hopatcong in 1949. (Courtesy of Bela G. Lugosi)

on the Fayetteville production, later recalled:

I was in college at the time, and I had always dabbled in acting. My father was in the music department at Syracuse, and he was my contact with one of the producers of the Famous Artists, a man called Murray Bernthal.

As for Lugosi, well, I have to say he was one of the most superstitious people I've ever encountered. His wife told me that if certain things seemed out of place, he'd refuse to get up.

One funny incident happened as we prepared for the play. If you remember in *Arsenic and Old Lace*, the men who get poisoned are buried in the cellar. One of the jokes is that at the end of the show, the deceased elderly gentleman come out and

Advertisement for Lugosi's appearance at the Lakeside Summer Theatre. (Courtesy of the Lake Hopatcong Historical Museum of New Jersey)

take a bow. The question became where are you going to get the old men to come out and take a bow, so I suggested to Mr. Bernthal that there was a Jewish home for the aged, and maybe the residents there would enjoy playing the old men. 'We can't do that!' Bernthal said to me. 'The audience will think we're anti-Semitic.' Anyhow, they finally got members of the fire department [which was one of the play's sponsors].[24]

Cheyette also recalled that the Famous Artists' version of *Arsenic* was successful, playing to full houses.

Arsenic premiered on July 11, 1949 at the auditorium of the Fayetteville High School, with the production running five nights and – counting matinees on Wednesday and Saturday – seven performances.[25] The cast had a break on Tuesday night, as a school district meeting meant the stage was unavailable. By that time, a review had appeared in the nearby Syracuse *Post-Standard*:

> Last night's Famous Artists Country Playhouse audience gleefully discovered new angles for laughs in the old chilling farce *Arsenic and Old Lace* ... The Lugosi play, for after all, it is Lugosi who is the arch criminal of the piece, pleased everybody....[26]

The same review praised John Blankenship's stage settings, on which Burry Fredrik also worked, as well as John Larson's performance as Mortimer.

From the *Atlantic City Press* of August 8, 1949.

Gary D. Rhodes | Bill Kaffenberger

George Snell's telegram confirming that he would postpone his version of *Arsenic and Old Lace* in Reading, Pennsylvania to enable Lugosi to star in the same play in Atlantic City, New Jersey.

After the Fayetteville performance closed, the Lugosis traveled some 200 miles to Lake Hopatcong and the Lakeside Theatre at Landing, New Jersey. Hopatcong had a long history as a summer resort for the middle and upper classes. It grew in popularity to the extent that it featured more than forty hotels and rooming houses as well as an amusement park. The summer theatre staged both old favorites and "summer tryouts" hoping to get to Broadway.[27] Its 1949 season featured not only Lugosi, but also such stars as John Loder, Vivian Blaine, Ann Dvorak, and Ann Harding.[28]

Arriving in the area, the Lugosis resided at the beautiful lakeside Bon Air Lodge, which boasted of being the "most exclusive hotel on Lake Hopatcong," featuring "all social and athletic activities, varied and thrilling aquatic sports, [and] superb Jewish-American cuisine."[29] While in the area, Lugosi was able to enjoy some free time with his son. Bela G. Lugosi later remembered:

> One summer when I was 11, I went East with my parents for summer stock. Even though Dad was busy with rehearsals, performances, and reading scripts continually, he was as interested in teaching me as he himself was in learning. He taught

From the *Reading Eagle* of August 21, 1949.

me the fundamentals of canoeing on a lake in New Jersey where we stayed, because he thought it was important for me.

During the drive East, he spent a good part of the time in the car trying to improve my understanding of things around us. He would talk about the local geology, the strata of rocks, the history of towns we passed through, or any one of a thousand things that came into his mind. As a young boy, I failed to appreciate this wealth of experience my father was offering me, although now I do; and I know what a remarkable man he was.[30]

Lugosi's son also recalled, "Dad was above all a family man who placed my mother and me at the top of his list."

The Lakeside Theatre's management originally planned to feature Lugosi in *Dracula*, but changed their plans, opting instead for *Arsenic and Old Lace*.[31] As always, Lugosi portrayed Jonathan Brewster, receiving $750 for the week.[32] Lakeside favorite Elwyn Harvey played Abby Brewster.[33] The cast also included Richard Stevens, who owned the theatre, and Eddie Hyans, who not only played Teddy Brewster, but also directed the show.

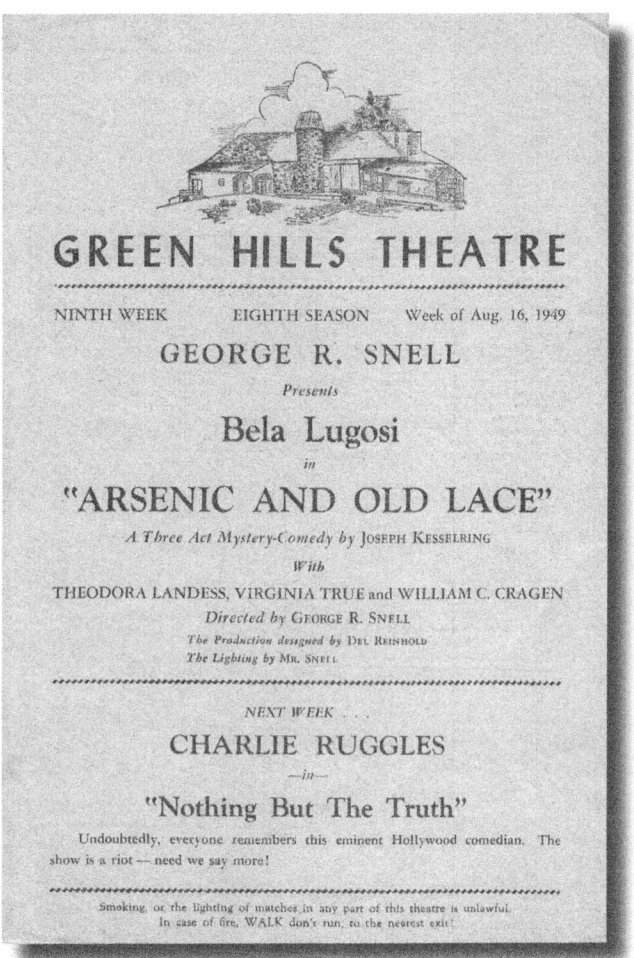

Program cover to George R. Snell's production of *Arsenic and Old Lace* with Lugosi. (Courtesy of George R. Snell)

Arsenic ran at the Lakeside Theatre from Tuesday July 26 through Sunday July 31, 1949. A critic from nearby Morristown, New Jersey praised the production, drawing particular attention to Harvey, Stevens, and Hyans. Of Lugosi, she said, "He was hailed enthusiastically by the audience."[34]

Cast member Paul J. Phillips warmly recalled Lugosi, remembering that he was a "wonderful" man:

Unlike a lot of stars who were very temperamental, Lugosi was genuinely nice. You could feel that from him, though we also knew that he was ill. By the end of the show, he seemed very ill.

His wife was with him, and she would always coach him and cue him on his lines. He did a couple of rehearsals with us, and then the shows, and he was always on time. His performance was wonderful. He would wear green lipstick to add a hint of mystery to his appearance, and he would drink from a tiny little bottle before going on stage.[35]

Phillips also recalled that Lakeside audiences "loved Lugosi, and he had a lot of followers that bought tickets."

Actress Theodora Landess (aka, Helen Richman, as Abby) and Virginia True (as Martha) with Lugosi in Snell's production of *Arsenic and Old Lace*. (Courtesy of George R. Snell)

Lugosi looks at William C. Cragen (Mortimer Brewster) in Snell's production of *Arsenic and Old Lace*.
(Courtesy of George R. Snell)

From New Jersey, the Lugosis traveled approximately 130 miles to Litchfield, Connecticut and a return engagement at Litchfield Summer Theatre, where the actor had appeared in *Dracula* in 1947. The Altobells, who ran the theatre, had experienced great success with Lugosi and were happy to see him return in *Arsenic and Old Lace*. Promoting the event, one newspaper claimed, "He returns to Litchfield due to many requests received by the management to star him in another play."[36]

This version of *Arsenic* ran from August 1 to August 6, 1949. A critic for the *Hartford Courant* told readers that the play was one of the "best of the season," adding that it held "the attention of the audience from the very opening ... through the third act. ... The entire production was well-cast."[37] Similarly, a notice in the *Litchfield Inquirer* said that the play received an "enthusiastic and heavy response" on opening night.[38]

Leonard Altobell experienced absolutely no problems with the actor. As Altobell's daughter Jayne Newitch, recalled, "Despite ill health at that point in his life, and disparaging rumors surrounding his lifestyle, my father found Lugosi to be a thorough professional. He showed up on time for rehearsals, knew his lines, and endeared himself to the cast of *Arsenic and Old Lace*."[39]

After Litchfield, the Lugosis headed over 225 miles away to Atlantic City, where he appeared in a version of *Arsenic* at the 1,450-seat Ocean Playhouse on the Steel Pier from August 9 to 14, 1949. At that time, producer Robert S. Courtney operated the Playhouse. He had leased the venue that summer to bring "legit" theatre to the Boardwalk, in part to re-establish the city as a location for Broadway try-outs. The result became something of a variation on typical summer stock theatres. Unfortunately, by the end of July 1949, Courtney's plans seemed in jeopardy, as box-office receipts had been poor.[40]

In addition to their standard 9PM evening performances, the cast performed special late night shows on Friday and Saturday in lieu of matinees. According to the *Atlantic City Press*:

Snell's *Arsenic and Old Lace*. From left to right are two unidentified actors, Virginia True (as Abby), Theodora Landess (aka, Helen Richman, as Martha), Lugosi, and William C. Cragen (as Mortimer). (Courtesy of George R. Snell)

> Bela Lugosi and his supporting company (30 in all) are coming intact from their tour of the Summer theatres and he brings along with him many of the players who appeared with this comedy-mystery on Broadway a few years ago.[41]

Given that no program has surfaced, it is difficult to determine who else worked on this production. It is possible that the reference to other summer players could mean actors from Litchfield or Fayetteville, but those theatres – as well as most other barn emporiums – were still producing other plays, meaning that most of their own repertory companies would have been obligated. More likely, Courtney cast the other actors out of New York.

From the Steel Pier, the Lugosis journeyed over 100 miles to Reading, Pennsylvania, and to another return engagement, this time at the Green Hills Theatre. Like Leonard Altobell, Lugosi's friend George R. Snell was happy to book the actor again, adding a ninth week to what was originally planned as an eight week season in order to stage *Arsenic and Old Lace*.

Originally, Snell announced that Lugosi would appear in *Arsenic* one week earlier. According to the local press, a heat wave caused the delay; Snell allegedly couldn't risk the danger of suffocation to the "bodies" stuffed into the window seat. In actual fact, Snell postponed his own version of *Arsenic* so that Lugosi could appear in Atlantic City.

Snell and Lugosi had discussed the actor's return visit for *Arsenic* the prior summer, a production that Snell saw as more viable than Lugosi's plan to star in *Harvey*. At any rate, the Litchfield and Reading productions of 1949 illustrate how Lugosi did not rely solely on his representation for work, but

Lugosi with Theodora Landess (aka, Helen Richman). (Courtesy of Kristin Dewey)

was at times actively involved in promoting himself to producers.[42]

After the passage of one year, Snell found Lugosi to be a bit "heavier" than he had been, but otherwise in good health and eager to give a great performance. Once again the Snells socialized with the Lugosis, finding the couple quite happy with one another and with their son. Snell saw absolutely no hint of drug use or of marital problems.[43]

Arsenic played evening performances at the Green Hills from August 16 to August 21, 1949, with Snell scheduling only one matinee. Snell remembered:

What a pleasant surprise in [Lugosi's] ability to do comedy. For this presentation, I directed. It was fun. It was rewarding. Since Bela and I were good friends by that time, he said, 'George, you are the director. It is your interpretation. Forget that I have previously performed in this play. Tell me what to do, where and how to move, what lines to hold for effect.'

Gary D. Rhodes | Bill Kaffenberger

Lugosi in Snell's production of *Arsenic and Old Lace*, with Virginia True (as Abby) and Theodora Landess (aka, Helen Richman, as Martha). (Courtesy of George R. Snell)

>That was a true talent. Compare that to many other stars who tried to run the theatre. No, with Lugosi, the cast and I were able to present a vehicle richly enjoyed by our audiences.[44]

Snell's relationship with Lugosi was much the same as the previous year: warm and friendly, and simultaneously professional.

Cast member Helen Richman – who played one of the two old Brewster aunts under her stage name Theodora Landess – later recalled:

>The first time I saw Bela in person, my girlfriend (who was playing the other old lady) and I were standing on a country road and he was walking towards us. And I thought, 'There he is, and I must not be frightened.' I had nothing to be scared of; he was charming and warm, not pretentious at all. But, even off stage, he had tremendous presence.

>… I remember his son was with him – young, only 13 or 14, I think, but no wife. … It was during [a change of costume in the dark] that I felt Bela's lips running up and down my back while I was in the process of changing costumes. … I was in utter shock. Nothing like that had ever happened to me before. I decided to put it from my mind and I concentrated doubly hard on my role.

Bela never spoke of our 'brief encounter' afterwards. For several nights we did the play, and I rehearsed for the next one in the mornings. As I recall, Bela came and watched the rehearsal several mornings and we had lunch afterwards. And I'll never forget exactly what he said: 'I would like you to tour with me as Lucy in *Dracula*.' And before I could say yes or no: 'Of course, you would have to be my baby.'[45]

Richman's memories are an important component of the oral history surrounding Lugosi's second appearance in Reading, but she is incorrect about Lillian, who was definitely present.

Wiliam C. Cragen – who had directed Lugosi in the 1948 Green Hills production of *Dracula* – co-starred in *Arsenic* as Mortimer Brewster, and Del Reinhold was the production designer, just as he had for *Dracula*.[46] One critic claimed that Lugosi's "return to Reading after his 1948 success in *Dracula* was greeted with cheers," with the entire cast giving *Arsenic* the "Number One treatment."[47] Another said:

> ... it scared the hell out of us. It makes nearly everyone jumpy to watch this play for the first time. But you don't get really jittery until, like ourselves, you've seen the ninth or tenth performance.
>
> The house was packed for this show, and the crowd applauded generously, so that should make it evident that the audience was well pleased.
>
> ... William C. Cragen, who directs most of the Green Hills plays, has the part of the dramatic critic. You'll like him quite as much as you'll like Bela Lugosi....[48]

Ending the review, the critic gave his overall impression: "What did we think of *Arsenic and Old Lace*? Oh, it was swell."

Interviewed during his summer stock season of 1949, Lugosi told one journalist that he "never goes to the movies and views his own pictures just to see if he can improve his acting." He added that he planned "to return to Hollywood September 1."[49] By that time, his work in summer stock would be over, and so traveling west would be the next order of business.

But the combination of a lack of film roles and steady opportunities for more work in the east meant that Lugosi did not return to Hollywood. His son would journey back to California for another year, but he could not. In fact, Lugosi would be based out of the New York area until April of 1951, almost two years later. And month after month, his father would spend a great deal of his time on the road.

(Endnotes)

1. "The Rustic Trail." *New York Times* 12 June 1949.
2. "Theatre in the Straw." *New York Times* 6 June 1949.
3. "Summer Activity for 155 Theatres." *New York Times* 18 June 1949.
4. Burke, Melville. "Danger Sign Sighted on the Rustic Trail." *New York Times* 18 Sept. 1949.
5. *Dracula*. Pittsford Summer Theatre Program. 14-23 July 1949.
6. *Dracula*. Lakeside Summer Theatre Program. 6-11 Sept. 1949; "Along the Rustic Trail." *New York Times* 7 Aug. 1949.
7. "Along the Rustic Trail." *New York Times* 19 June 1949.
8. "Along the Rustic Trail." *New York Times* 10 July 1949; "Along the Rustic Trail." *New York Times* 24 July 1949; "Along the Rustic Trail." *New York Times* 31 July 1949; "Along the Rustic Trail." *New York Times* 14 Aug. 1949; "Along the Rustic Trail." *New York Times* 21 Aug. 1949.
9. "Along the Rustic Trail." *New York Times* 17 July 1949.
10. Beyer, Charles. Letter to Lyman Brown. 29 Apr. 1949. [Available in the Chamberlain and Lyman Brown Papers, and Undated, Series II: Correspondence, Box 64, Folder F.9 at the New York Public Library/Lincoln Center for the Performing Arts in New York.]
11. "Radio and Television." *New York Times* 21 Mar. 1949.
12. "Along the Rustic Trail." *New York Times* 19 June 1949; "Along the Rustic Trail." *New York Times* 24 July 1949; "Along the Rustic Trail." *New York Times* 31 July 1949; "Along the Rustic Trail." *New York Times* 14 Aug. 1949.

13 Lugosi, Bela. Letter to Harald Dyrenforth. 19 May 1949. [Available in the Chamberlain and Lyman Brown Papers, and Undated, Series II: Correspondence, Box 64, Folder F.9 at the New York Public Library/Lincoln Center for the Performing Arts in New York.]
14 Dyrenforth, Harald. Letter to Lyman Brown. 21 May 1949. [Available in the Chamberlain and Lyman Brown Papers, and Undated, Series II: Correspondence, Box 64, Folder F.9 at the New York Public Library/Lincoln Center for the Performing Arts in New York.]
15 Brown, Lyman. Letter to Bela Lugosi. 14 May 1949. [Available in the Chamberlain and Lyman Brown Papers, and Undated, Series II: Correspondence, Box 64, Folder F.9 at the New York Public Library/Lincoln Center for the Performing Arts in New York.]
16 *The Post-Standard* (Syracuse, NY) 10 July 1949.
17 *The Post-Standard* 6 July 1949.
18 *The Post Standard* 10 July 1949.
19 *Ibid*.
20 *Ibid*.
21 "Lugosi Heads Fayetteville Cast for *Arsenic and Old Lace*." *The Post Standard* 10 July 1949.
22 "Lugosi Heads New Playhouse Offering Opening Monday." *The Eagle-Bulletin* (Fayetteville, NY) 8 July 1949.
23 "Theatre Artists Arrive This Week." *The Eagle-Bulletin* 17 June 1949.
24 Rhodes, Gary D. Interview with Herbert Cheyette. 26 Oct. 2011.
25 "Fayetteville Summer Playhouse Opens at High School July 4." *The Eagle-Bulletin* 27 May 1949.
26 Tabor, Thola Nett. "Country Playhouse Audience Finds New Angles on Laughs." *The Post-Standard* 12 July 1949.
27 "A History of Landing, Morris County, New Jersey: The Lake Becomes A Summer Resort." 2009. Available http://www.landingnewjersey.com/history.htm; "Your Letters (Well, Emails): Lakeside Summer Playhouse and Editor Response." 18 Feb. 2009. http://www.landingnewjersey.com/letters.htm. Accessed 24 Feb. 2012.
28 Lakeside Summer Theatre, Season of 1949. Theatre Program.
29 *Lake Hopatcong Breeze* (Lake Hopatcong, NJ) 27 August 1949.
30 Lugosi, Bela G. "Biography." Available at http://www.lugosi.com/biography.html. Accessed 21 Dec. 2011.
31 Brown, Lyman. Letter to Bela Lugosi. 14 May 1949. [Available in the Chamberlain and Lyman Brown Papers, and Undated, Series II: Correspondence, Box 64, Folder F.9 at the New York Public Library/Lincoln Center for the Performing Arts in New York.]
32 *Ibid*.
33 "Famed *Arsenic* at Landing Theatre." *The Daily Record* (Morristown, NJ) 27 July 1949.
34 Mishkin, Esther. *The Daily Record* 27 July 1949.
35 Rhodes, Gary D. Interview with Paul J. Phillips. 11 Feb. 2012.
36 *Naugatuck News* (Naugatuck, CT) 29 July 1949.
37 *Hartford Courant* 4 Aug. 1949.
38 Frank, Stanley. *Litchfield* Inquirer (Litchfield, CT) 4 Aug. 1949.
39 Newirth, Jayne. Email to Gary D. Rhodes. 23 Oct. 2011.
40 "Steel Pier Legit Fate Hangs in the Balance." *The Billboard* 30 July 1949.
41 "Bela Lugosi Himself in *Arsenic and Old Lace*." *Atlantic City Press* (Atlantic City, NJ) 8 Aug. 1949.
42 Rhodes, Gary D. Interview with George R. Snell. 7 Apr. 2006.
43 Rhodes, interview with Snell.
44 *Ibid*.
45 Orrison, Katherine. "Bela's Baby Leading Lady." *Cult Movies* 16 (1995).
46 For reasons unknown, William C. Cragen spelled his last name with an "e" in 1949. The prior year he spelled it with an "i," as in "Cragin."
47 E.M.S. "Bela Lugosi in Mad Comedy, Pleases Green Hills Audience." *Reading Times* 17 Aug. 1949.
48 L. J. M. "*Arsenic and Old Lace* Potency Again at Green Hills." *Reading Eagle* 17 Aug. 1949.
49 *The Post-Standard* 10 July 1949.

Bela G. Lugosi while on vacation with his parents in the summer of 1949. (Courtesy of Bela G. Lugosi)

A photograph that Lugosi inscribed to Les Rohde, bandleader at the Olympia Theatre. (Courtesy of Michael Rohde)

Chapter 11

THE BELA LUGOSI COMPANY

In the spring of 1950, Bela Lugosi picked up the phone and called the famous vaudeville performer Jackie Bright. Known as the "Krazy Auctioneer," Bright built his career on rapid-fire delivery and an act that relied on audience participation. According to *The Billboard*, Bright:

… was home with a sick baby, resentful at phones and brusque to all callers, when the phone rang… 'Hello? Jackie Bright? This is Bela Lugosi. Can you tell–' 'Lugosi, eh! Why doncha drown yourself.' And hung up.

A few minutes later the phone rang again. 'Mr. Bright? This is Bela Lugosi. I was told to call you…' 'Look, Lugosi,' roared Bright, 'I got news for you. I saw you in *Dracula* and you still stink. Now get off and stop bothering me.'

Two days later Bright was told it wasn't a rib, that the caller was Bela Lugosi, who was referred to him for some information. Bright immediately sent off a letter of apology and explanation. He's now wondering what to say if he meets Lugosi.[1]

Why Lugosi phoned Bright remains unknown, but he likely had vaudeville on his mind.

Vaudeville thrived from the 1880s to the early 1930s, offering different acts on balanced programs to audiences throughout the United States. Comedians, acrobats, magicians, musicians, trained animals, and many other performers populated vaudeville stages. After the rise of cinema, theatres often paired vaudeville with films. For many celebrities, ranging from famous boxers of the late nineteenth century to film stars of the Great Depression, vaudeville provided an important source of income.

Lugosi's entry into vaudeville came in 1933, shortly after he left the cast of a Broadway play entitled *Murder at the Vanities*. The timing was interesting for another reason as well. Many vaudeville historians view 1932 – when New York City's Palace Theatre eliminated live acts in order to concentrate solely on movies – as the beginning of the end. But vaudeville's death would come slowly, very slowly, over the period of many years.

The inaugural Bela Lugosi vaudeville act revealed the limitations that all of his future acts would face: duration. In the space of some ten minutes, more or less, whatever Lugosi did had to start *and* end, allowing little time for the creation of mood or atmosphere, let alone for extended adaptations of plays like *Dracula*. And whatever he did would be sandwiched between other acts and/or films that usually had nothing to do with horror.

His first vaudeville show opened at the Loew's Gates in Brooklyn and ran from December 5 to 7, 1933, before moving onto the Loew's State in New York, the Loew's Stanley in Baltimore, and then Loew's Fox in Washington, D.C. A review of the Fox appearance indicates the show's content and something of the template that Lugosi would follow in future years:

> Bela Lugosi headlines the vaudeville goings-on in a condensed version of *Dracula*, which naturally loses much of the sustained suspense ... of the longer play. Mr. Lugosi is still the ominous figure of the personified vampire bat ... a considerable measure of horror still clings to the Bram Stoker drama.[2]

Another review indicated that Lugosi broke character at the end of the act with a humorous closing speech: audiences thus saw fleeting minutes of Lugosi as Dracula combined with a bit of the actor playing himself.[3]

After his brief series of 1933 performances, Lugosi did little vaudeville during the thirties and early forties, the key exception being a 1940 package show called *Stardust Cavalcade*. Organized by Ed Sullivan, the acts included Lugosi, Arthur Treacher, Marjorie Weaver, Helen Parrish, Douglas McPhail, Betty Jaynes, Vivian Fay, and Peg Leg Bates. As with the 1933 show, the brief tour was financially successful, something that Lugosi may well have remembered during the final days of World War II.[4]

When the play *No Traveler Returns* came to a close and no film work seemed to be on the horizon, Lugosi signed for a vaudeville tour that was set to play North Dakota and Minnesota from April 23 to May 19, 1945. Cities included Fargo, Duluth, and Minneapolis.[5] But as newspaper advertisements in those locations make clear, the announced tour did not happen. The same was apparently true of a vaudeville tour that Don Marlowe attempted to schedule for Lugosi during the second half of 1945.

The difficulty in documenting all of Lugosi's vaudeville appearances is the short duration of some of the tours, as well as varied descriptions of them in period publications. For example, according to *Daily Variety* of December 10, 1947:

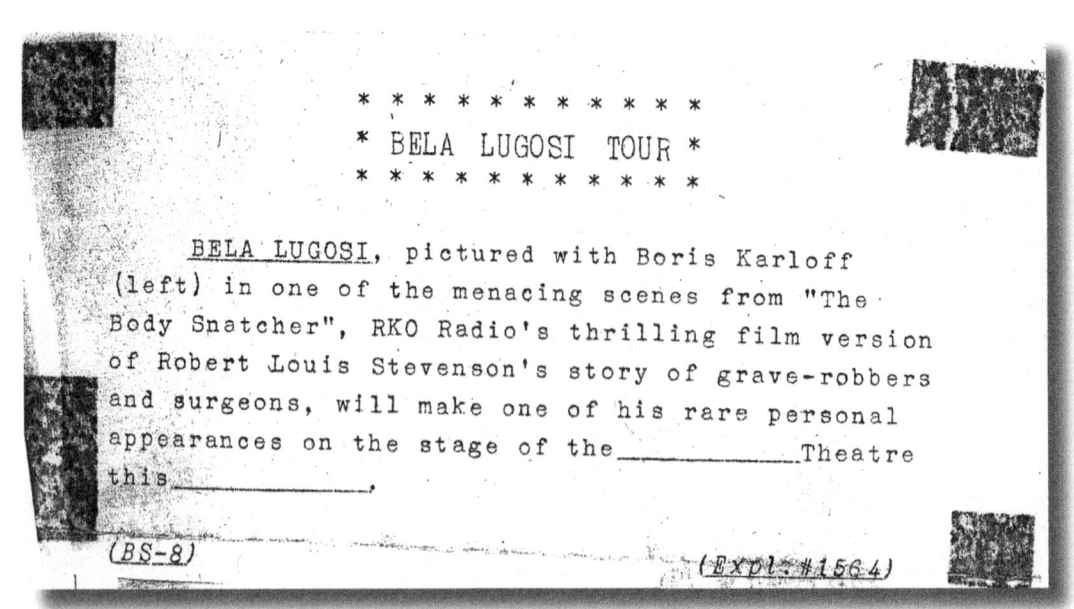

```
* * * * * * * * * *
* BELA LUGOSI TOUR *
* * * * * * * * * *

    BELA LUGOSI, pictured with Boris Karloff
(left) in one of the menacing scenes from "The
Body Snatcher", RKO Radio's thrilling film version
of Robert Louis Stevenson's story of grave-robbers
and surgeons, will make one of his rare personal
appearances on the stage of the_____Theatre
this_____.

(BS-8)                                    (EXPL #1564)
```

Label on the back of a publicity still used for a Lugosi vaudeville tour.

Newspaper photograph of Lugosi taken circa 1947.

Bela Lugosi, in taking his 'spook act' out of the barnstorming one-night circuit and into four-a-day standard vaude, is sacrificing coin. For the last two months the vet film menace has been touring the mid-west putting on midnight shows in film houses, booking himself in at 50-50 slice of gross, charging $1.50 per head and unspooling a print of the old Universal release, *Dracula*. Midway in picture, Lugosi inserted an eight-minute act, in which he used a girl partner and re-enacted a chill sequence from the footage. The actor himself rented the print from Universal, and on this stunt has been netting around $4,000 weekly....[6]

Based upon the description, Lugosi played Dracula in the act, with wife Lillian likely being the "girl partner." But the show could not have lasted two months, as late November would have been devoted to the ill-fated *Tell-Tale Heart* tour.

Another reporter told readers that Lugosi made a personal appearance tour of "the South and Texas" at what would have been roughly the same time frame. A newspaper column claimed "his act called for women to step onto the stage while he drew out their blood, vampire fashion. There were more volunteers than he could handle."[7] If it actually occurred, this "tour" might well be the same one described in *Daily Variety*.

At any rate, Lugosi's "standard vaude" routine transformed into a show packaged by the Sherman Agency. It opened on Christmas Day, 1947 at Baltimore's 2,100-seat Hippodrome Theatre. Robert Alda – "Sensational Motion Picture Star and the man who portrayed George Gershwin in *Rhapsody in Blue* [1945]" – headlined the bill, which was advertised as arriving "Direct from Hollywood!" Lugosi took second billing, with singer and actor Gordon MacRae listed as the "Extra Added Attraction!"[8] Rounding out the program were tap dancer and comic actor Lou Wills, Jr., "Comedy Songstress" Ann Russell, Jo Lombardi's Hippodrome Orchestra, and the feature film *I Love Trouble* (1948) with Franchot Tone and Janet Blair.[9]

Robert Alda's son, actor Alan Alda,

From the *Baltimore Sun* of December 24, 1947.

recalled that, "Lugosi didn't have a real act." He added:

> A classically trained actor known in this country for horror movies, [Lugosi] sat with my father and Beetlepuss [George Lewis, Alda's partner] in their dressing room and said he wished he had more to offer the audience.
>
> Beetlepuss thought about it and came up with an idea for him. The singer in the show [Ann Russell] was a young woman, who would introduce Bela to the audience and he would go on stage and do a joke with her – a line about bats, or maybe he would ask if you can get a good glass of blood at the local diner.
>
> Then she'd laugh and say 'Oh Bela, you kill me.' And he'd look at her hungrily and say, 'In due time, my dear.'[10]

From the August 18, 1948 issue of the *Detroit News*.

Alda concluded by saying, "In those days, this was close enough to funny to seem like an act."

While in Baltimore, Lugosi made an appearance at the city's Variety Club. Originating in Pittsburgh, Variety Clubs were private organizations run by showbiz people for showbiz people. When passing through a city with a Variety Club, performers often put in appearances at them. In this case, "Bert Claster brought the Hippodrome show to the Variety Club ... Bob Alda, Bela Lugosi and Gordon MacRae. Members also enjoyed the fine voices of the *Carousel* cast."[11] The group apparently staged an impromptu version of their vaudeville acts.

The Hippodrome show closed on December 30, 1947, which also seems to have brought a close to Lugosi's association with the Sherman Agency that booked it. Landing the role of Dracula in *Abbott and Costello Meet Frankenstein* (1948) meant that Lugosi shelved other vaudeville shows for what seems to have been several months.

After his summer stock season for 1948 ended in Sea Cliff, New York, Lugosi headlined a vaudeville program at Detroit's 3,367-seat Broadway-Capitol Theatre. Others on the bill included jazz singer Rose Murphy, novelty singer Harry Babbitt (with whom Lugosi had appeared in the 1940 film *You'll Find Out*), comedian Barney Grant, and the Four Evans, an act that featured two hoofing parents and their two hoofing children. One of their kids, daughter Maryetta, also did an "acro contortion bit," which *The Billboard* called "sensational."[12] In addition to the vaudeville company, audiences saw the popular house orchestra of Larry Paige and His Pages of Melody, as well as two films, *Train to Alcatraz* (1948) and *King of the Gamblers* (1948).[13] The show opened on August 20, 1948, and closed on August 26.

While in Detroit, Lugosi renewed his acquaintance with magician Loring Campbell, whose stage names were "Kim Key" and "Alexander the Great."[14] Along with being noted for such tricks as the Chinese Linking Rings, Campbell's act featured ventriloquism. The two ate dinner at a Hungarian restaurant, where Lugosi's fame quickly drew a crowd. Campbell later remembered:

The proprietor came and told us everything was ready in the backroom for us to eat so we went back. It was just a few minutes later that he came back with a policeman and said the policeman was complaining that the whole street was jammed with cars.

The kids had found out Mr. Lugosi was in there and they wanted to see him. There were 60 to 100 kids out there chanting, 'We want to see Dracula! We want to see Dracula!'

So Bela turned to Mr. Hevesi [the manager] and said, 'Bring me an overcoat or a raincoat – but dark.'

So the manager brought him one and he put it over his shoulders. 'I will get rid of them,' he said.

I went to do the door and slowly opened it. He walked out, part of his face covered with the coat. He said, 'I am Dracula, and I'm going to get every one of you! I am after your heart!' He opened his coat like a vampire.

Pretty soon you couldn't see a kid anywhere and the traffic could move.[15]

The two resumed their dinner, with Campbell pitching the idea that the two of them should tour in a midnight spook show. Lugosi was receptive, but the idea never came to pass.

As for the Detroit vaudeville show, Al Weitschat of the *Detroit News* wrote that, "nothing could be said against the ... new bill on the score of abundance. ... but like so many big packages, the quantity is heavy and the quality light."[16] Of Lugosi, Weitschat said:

Temporarily done with the business of spreading goose pimples among movie fans, Bela Lugosi comes out to indulge in a bit of uncomfortable chit-chit and then re-enact a *Dracula* scene, which is more humorous than horrifying.[17]

A review of the same show in *Variety* offered a similar critique, claiming that Lugosi offered some "colorless chatter which leads up to a skit in which the chillmaster of the screen falls short of winning the audience. It's mild and unconvincing."[18] It was also not particularly different than his original 1933 vaudeville act.

From Detroit, the Lugosis traveled over 1,300 miles to Miami, Florida, where the ac-

Loring Campbell and Bela Lugosi.

tor headlined yet another vaudeville bill, this time at the 2,500-seat Olympia Theatre. Likely Don Marlowe acted as Lugosi's representative. Whoever packaged the performers together had a keen eye towards the old vaudeville method of creating balanced programs, meaning a group of acts that were quite different from one another.

When Lugosi opened on September 1, 1948, he was at the top of a bill that included Johnny Woods (who acted as emcee and offered his own bit), Ada Lynn (a comedienne who did imitations of Martha Raye and Betty Hutton), Tato and Julia (a Latin dance duo), and the LaVernes (two men and two women who did an "roughhouse Apache routine" that included some "pistol shooting" and "knife throwing").[19] These acts were in addition to Les Rohde's house orchestra and a screening of the film *The Emperor Waltz* (1948) with Bing Crosby and Joan Fontaine. The Olympia presented the show four times daily, the first performance at 1:25PM and the last at 10PM.

From the *Detroit News* of August 23, 1948.

Recalling the show, Ada Lynn spoke of the Olympia Theatre and of meeting Bela Lugosi:

The Olympia was very beautiful, but very old. Dressing rooms were on different floors, and you had to walk up stairs to get to some of them.

I was still very young, probably about 17 or 18 years old. I would have been booked by my agent in New York. My mother traveled with me to Miami. She made my costumes, and she was very careful to make sure I only met the nice people. She was over protective.

We all had rehearsals, but I don't really remember if Lugosi attended them. But I do remember him well.

He was a very charming and gentle man, and by that time, his movie career wasn't as it once was. He would come out onstage dressed as a pseudo-scary man, and as I remember it, he did a scene out of one of his movies, wearing his cape.

The audience loved him, because he was in their memories and to see the man in person, a very soft-spoken man, but one who could do that terribly scary laugh that he did. But afterwards, as part of his act, he would make some sort of joke about his laugh.[20]

Lynn also recalled that many adults rushed backstage after the performances to get Lugosi's autograph. While in Miami that week, the Lugosis were treated like royalty. On September 1, after the 10PM show at the Olympia, the couple were special guests at the Club Bali.[21] Then, two days later, they

OLYMP
ON THE SCREEN ROLLICKING TECHN
BING CROSBY JOAN FONTAINE "THE
ON THE STAGE BELA LUGOSI DRACU
ADA LYNN-LA VERNES TATO & JULI
CONDITIONED
NOW PLAYING
BELA LUGOSI
ON THE STAGE

were guests at the Five O'Clock Club along with Mickey Keats, who had acted with Lugosi years earlier in the 1929 film *Prisoners*. There the trio enjoyed watching a Rhumba contest (featuring a $50 prize), as well as the talents of dancers Del Carmen and Nino (The Great) Yacovino.[22]

Writing in the *Miami News*, journalist Grace Wing described meeting Lugosi while he was in Florida:

> Dracula – or Bela Lugosi to give him his own name – had heard that people don't die here. 'I onnerstand Mee-ah-mee has no cemeteries,' he murmured in a menacing Blue Danube accent, going on to explain that it is one of his hobbies to collect epitaphs of tombstones. The reporter was too loyal to explain that it actually is Miami Beach which has no cemeteries.
>
> ... Instead of the sinister black cloak in which Dracula enfolds his fainting victims, Lugosi was sporting a baby-blue shirt and a red polka-dot bow tie. 'What kind of blood's in circulation these days, with meat prices the way they are?' he was asked. Lugosi raised one eyebrow, the way you've seen him do, and said he hasn't been sampling any lately, he's taken up cigars. And he pulled a long stogie out of his vest pocket, and lighted it....

Wing added that someone asked Lugosi about his hands and the way he "crook[ed] his fingers. 'Oh those... I am dobble-jawnted!'" he laughed.[23]

The same newspaper also reviewed the vaudeville bill, paying particular attention to Lugosi's act:

> Lugosi, unlike most Hollywood personalities who make personal appearance tours, really gives his admirers their money's worth. He comes out in his traditional Dracula costume – black clothes and flowing cape – and, after a short chat with Bandleader Les Rohde, gives a dramatic skit with all the thrill of a suspenseful movie scene. It [is] a fine performance.[24]

The Olympia at the time of Lugosi's 1948 vaudeville appearance.

Gary D. Rhodes | Bill Kaffenberger

Of the rest of the performers, the critic claimed that they were "routine – though excellent."[25]

However, a critic from *Variety* who saw the same show was not nearly as kind, writing:

> Bela Lugosi, marquee lure for the package, offers the Hollywood personal, complete to the uninteresting reminiscing and a 'scene' which in this case is supposed to be a scary bit, but which just doesn't come off, inspiring giggles instead. In fact, the aisle-sitters seemed to be looking for laughs rather 'horror character' stuff done straight.[26]

From the *Miami News* of September 2, 1948.

Perhaps Lugosi's recent role in *Abbott and Costello Meet Frankenstein* had paved the way for the unintended laughter. At any rate, the critic reserved the greatest praise not for Lugosi, but for Ada Lynn, observing that she 'brightens what would otherwise add up to an average vaude layout which sags perceptibly in the topliner spot.'[27]

After Miami, the Lugosis traveled to Springfield, Massachusetts where Lugosi headlined yet another vaudeville show, this time at the Loew's 1,730-seat Court Square Theatre. Opening on September 16, 1948, the talent performed three times daily for four days. The rest of the bill consisted of Mann and Ross (acrobats), Julia Cummings (an impressionist), the Burns Twins and Evelyn (dancers), Patsy Garrett (comic singer), and Cavicco "The Marimba King."[28] Barney Grant – who had appeared with Lugosi at Detroit's Broadway-Capitol – was a featured attraction, as was the film *The Timber Trail* (1948) starring Monte Hale.

The day prior to the show's opening, the Lugosis lunched with the local press. One journalist assured readers that Lugosi was:

> … not a bogeyman at all. Actually he is a pleasantly [and] quietly humorous man who dotes on his ten-year-old son, now at military school, and defers to his charming wife with attentive gallantry.
>
> He created *Dracula* twenty years ago in New York and not without storm and stress that almost caused him to lose the part. He was engaged in the role, then 'fired.' Sunk in despondency he went home engulfed in defeat from which he was eventually rescued by being given another chance.[29]

From the *Springfield Union* of September 16, 1948.

The reporter concluded the story by noting that the very scene from *Dracula* that Lugosi used to audition for the role would constitute his vaudeville act.

One audience member who attended the Springfield show later recalled, "[Lugosi] walked out onto the stage dressed in full Dracula garb and slowly pulled his cape over his face. Just then all the lights were turned off! (Part of the act!) The bloodcurdling screams from the audience filled the auditorium. ... Did I scream too? No! I was too frightened to scream!"[30]

The Lugosis then made their way to Atlantic City, New Jersey. There he topped a bill called "The Bela Lugosi Company" at the 2,500-seat Steel Pier Music Hall; the troupe played only two days: September 25-26, 1948.[31] The *Atlantic City Press* drew attention to the fact that it would be Lugosi's first "shore appearance."[32] Other acts included soprano Marilyn Frechette, comedian and hoofer Sonny Sparks, and the Four Elgins (comical jugglers who did "hat tricks and Indian club manipulations").[33] Aside from Lugosi, the most

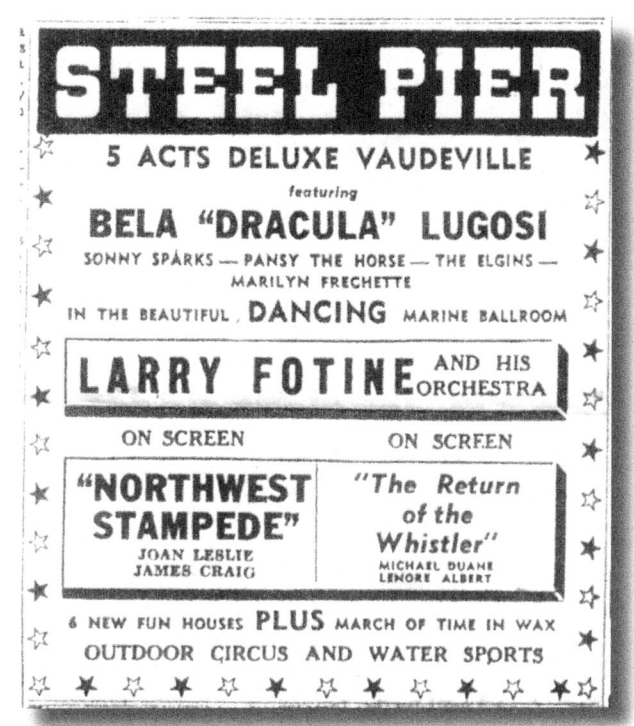

From the *Atlantic City Press* of September 25, 1948.

The Dewey Sisters, who appeared on a vaudeville bill with Lugosi in Holyoke, Massachusetts in 1948.

famous act on the program was "Pansy the Horse," two comics inside a horse costume. Pansy's greatest success had come in the 1941 Broadway musical *Banjo Eyes* with Eddie Cantor, after which the character remained popular in vaudeville. One review of the Pansy act called it "a real winner as far as the juveniles in the house were concerned."[34]

The following month, Lugosi worked in what may have been the worst show of his vaudeville career. He headlined the "Vodvil" bill at the Loew's in Bedford, New York on October 11. It wasn't so much that the films were a problem: Paul Muni in *Commandos Strike at Dawn* (1942) and Laurence Olivier in *Invaders* (1941, aka *49th Parallel*) were just fine. It was the rest of the program that might have been embarrassing, as they were all "Amateurs."[35] At any rate, he would have had little time to reflect on that point. Only one day later, he gave another vaudeville performance, this time at the Loew's

Gary D. Rhodes | Bill Kaffenberger

Triboro in Astoria, New York.[36]

Soon thereafter, Lugosi opened at the Valley Arena Gardens in Holyoke, Massachusetts on October 24, just four days after his 66th birthday.[37] The other acts included the Dewey Sisters (Charlotte and Evelyn, who sang and danced), Helene and Howard (comical acrobats), Barney Grant (who had appeared at the Broadway-Capitol in Detroit with Lugosi earlier in the year), and the famed Gene Krupa Orchestra.[38] The acts performed matinees at 2:30PM, and then two evening shows at 7 and 9PM.[39] In this case, Krupa took top-billing, relegating Lugosi to second place in the advertisements.

At the end of the month, on Friday, October 29, 1948, Lugosi played one night at the 968-seat Manhasset Theatre in Manhasset, New York; comedian Sonny Sparks was also featured. Only days later, Lugosi worked at the Binghamton Theatre with four other acts, including Ted and Art Miller (who presented the comical sketch *Fun on the Bouncing Pad*), and Jerry Rinsko and Nina ("juggling jesters").[40] Ventriloquist Terry Bennett also performed on the bill; in the late fifties, he would become a noted horror film host in Chicago.[41] The company presented their acts three times on November 4, and then four times daily on November 5 and 6.[42]

In February 1949, Lugosi wrote to his good friend Dr. Edmond Pauker and made clear his intention to continue working in vaudeville:

From the *Holyoke Transcript* of October 20, 1948.

It just occurred to me that while Laszlo Bekeffy is in New York if you would try to get from him a couple dozen cabaret sketches which are suitable for vaudeville and night club [*sic*]. Keeping in mind what the general public expects from me. It is either mystery or horror, which may end in a comedy situation enabling the people to laugh off the horrible or different ones which you judge spectacular or even burlesque. I would read them immediately in Hungarian and return those I consider right to be translated into English.[43]

Despite Lugosi's hopes of reworking his vaudeville act, there is no evidence that Bekeffy wrote new material for him.

And so Lugosi returned to vaudeville at the Loew's theatre circuit in New York, likely using the same material as he had in 1948. He starred in "Vodvil" at the Loew's at Coney Island on September 9, 1949, alongside the films *The Great Gatsby* (1949) and *Slightly French* (1949).[44] On September 20, he returned to the Loew's Triboro Theatre in Astoria.[45] On September 23, he made another return

From the *Binghamton Press* of November 2, 1948.

202   NO TRAVELER RETURNS | The Lost Years of Bela Lugosi

engagement, this time to the Loew's in Bedford, headlining the "Vodvil" show on a bill featuring the films *Rope of Sand* (1949) and *Calamity Jane and Sam Bass* (1949).[46] Then, on October 14, he played the Loew's Hillside Theatre in Queens.[47]

Of all of Lugosi's work for the Loew's theatres, one of the most interesting is his appearance at the Melba Theatre on September 16, 17, and 18, 1949. The "Vodvil" program also featured comedians Stuart and Taylor, performers Bud and Sissy Robinson, and xylophonist George Guest.[48] Years later, one moviegoer remembered seeing Lugosi at the Melba, claiming he performed a brief sequence from the play *Dracula* and then joked about coming out into the audience to "get some blood."[49] The moviegoer recalled that the show took place in 1946, but it is quite possible that she was actually referring to this 1949 performance.[50]

Lugosi's next work in vaudeville came when he headlined at the 5,037-

From the *St. Louis-Post Dispatch* of November 17, 1949.

From the *Oswego Palladium-Times* of March 2, 1950.

seat Fox Theatre in St. Louis from November 16 to November 22, 1949.[51] F&M Stage Shows, Inc. of New York City placed small advertisements in *Variety* during 1949, announcing that the Fox Theatre was reinstating vaudeville.

A critic from *The Billboard* visited the act. More than perhaps any other surviving document, his review provides insight into how Lugosi's act unfolded as part of a larger vaudeville bill:

> The current bill at this 5,000-seater moves at a neat clip. The curtain-raiser, the Four Strongs, rope spinners, showed plenty of dexterity and manipulation.
>
> On in the No. 2 spot was Hal Menkin and Madlyn. Menkin is a smooth tap dancer who picks 'em up and lays 'em down cleverly. He did some tricky stair routines. Madlyn, a

Gary D. Rhodes | Bill Kaffenberger

From the *Torrington Register* of March 11, 1950.

shapely blonde, around chiefly for decorative purposes, was okay for sight stuff.

Minda Lang offered a whistling routine and got a nice hand from the payers. The girl's attractive and sells to good results.

Edward Brothers (3) did some plain and fancy aero work and presented some amazing feats of tumbling and hand balancing. One of the boys had had polio when a child and the theatre brought in groups of polio victims as guests of Edwards. The promotion was intelligently handled.

Fastest act on the bill, by far, was the Three Appletons, adagio act, consisting of Charles Appleton, his wife, Mitzie, and blond Virginia Tribbet. The hectically paced act had the crowds on edge of seats and closed to a terrific mitt.

The hefty gal, Aunt Jemima, did songs in the Sophie Tucker style, and garnered plenty chuckles with her dancing hats.

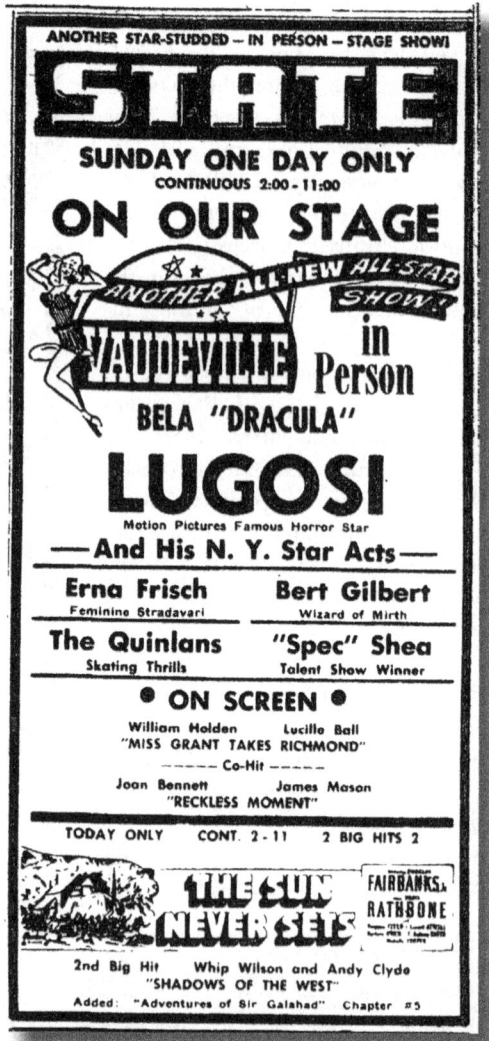

Undoubtedly one of the biggest laugh-getters on the show was Steve Evans. His take off on a Polish drunk was excellent.

Closer was Bela Lugosi. He did a scene from *Dracula* with his wife playing the part of [a] maid. It got a nice hand from the horror fans.[52]

Frank Panus' house orchestra provided the music, with the western film *Brimstone* (1948)

Erna Frisch, the "Feminine Stradivari," who appeared on a vaudeville bill headlined by Lugosi in Torrington, Connecticut.
(Courtesy of Anne Ponticelli)

starring Rod Cameron completing the bill.[53]

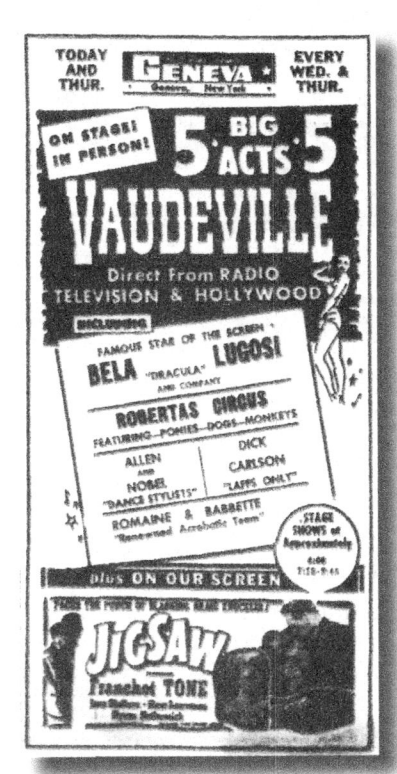

Lugosi's last known vaudeville work in 1949 came in Wichita, Kansas at the 1,659-seat Orpheum Theatre. He opened on November 23, one day after the St. Louis show closed. That meant the Lugosis faced a long, 450-mile drive in between two rigorous bookings. Five of the acts on the Wichita bill had appeared with Lugosi in St. Louis: 3 Edwards Brothers, Menkin and Madalyn, Aunt Jemima, Steve Adams, and the 3 Appletons.[54]

The following year, Lugosi headlined the vaudeville show at the Oswego Theatre in Oswego, New York. In addition to four other acts was the film *Red Light* (1949) with George Raft and Virginia Mayo. Lugosi played the theatre for two days only, March 2 and 3, 1950, giving three performances per day.[55] A local critic told readers:

Lugosi received a warm welcome as the Hollywood headliner, attired in full Count Dracula costume, [he] repeated one of the most thrilling scenes from the picture of the same name. The master scare artist sent shivers down the spines of the younger patrons as he placed the nurse attending one of his planned victims under his hypnotic spell. Lugosi actually turned out to be a suave comedian, in spite of impressions gleaned from his screen roles, and his experience resulted in one of the most entertaining acts seen here this season.[56]

While it is problematic to place too much emphasis on any single review, it is possible that many of Lugosi's vaudeville acts during this period were also well-received and popular with audiences.

Soon thereafter, Lugosi headed to Torrington, Connecticut for a program at the State Theatre. Advertisements billed the show as "Bela 'Dracula' Lugosi and His N. Y. Star Acts."[57] The other four performers were Bert Gilbert (a comedian), the Quinlans (trick skaters whose act included Zippy the Chimpanzee), and Erna Frisch, a female violinist from Vienna who wore beautiful gowns and sometimes danced while she played.[58] The show played one day only, March 12, 1950.[59]

Later that same month, Lugosi played the Schine's Geneva,

From the *Geneva Daily Times* of March 27, 1950.

From the *Amsterdam Evening Recorder* of April 14, 1950.

Gary D. Rhodes | Bill Kaffenberger

205

From the *Amsterdam Evening Recorder* of April 15, 1950.

a 1,868-seat theatre in New York, appearing at three shows daily on March 29 and 30. Advertisements promoted "Vaudeville featuring Bela Lugosi, the Original Count Dracula of the Movies." In large measure, the rest of the bill smacked similar to prior Lugosi vaudeville shows: Allen and Nobels ("Dance Stylists"), Dick Carlson ("Laffs Only"), and Romaine and Babbette ("Renowned Acrobatic Team"). However, the show became the only known occasion on which Lugosi worked with an animal act: "Roberta's Circus," which featured ponies, dogs and monkeys.[60]

Then, in one of his final vaudeville acts, Lugosi played the Rialto Theatre in Amsterdam, New York. Ads featured him towering over the other acts, which included Deval, Merle & Lee ("Comedy Dancing Trio"), Caldwell and Hunter ("A Song Festival"), Dick Shawn ("Master of Laughs"), and Carlton & Dell ("Dancing Darlings of Broadway").[61] Opening on Thursday, April 13, 1950, the company played for three days alongside the film *Mother Didn't Tell Me* (1950) with Dorothy McGuire. The first night featured the added attraction of a "Tri-City Talent Quest" with entrants competing for the chance to appear on Ted Mack's television show.[62]

For Lugosi, vaudeville hardly held the appeal of summer stock, where he received more money and more respect. In fact, Lugosi once told a reporter that "From a practical standpoint, that of earning the most money for the least work, I like radio; after that pictures, plays, and finally vaudeville."[63] In short, it was at the bottom of his list, which is hardly surprising. Vaudeville meant tough schedules in which he often had to perform in several shows a day, with tours sometimes requiring arduous trips between theatres.

But working in vaudeville wove Lugosi into the fabric of a special American entertainment form, and one that predated television, radio, and even the cinema. To work alongside comedians and dancers and even animal acts may have not seemed all that respectable by some standards, particularly during vaudeville's slow and painful death. However, vaudeville gave performers a sense of immediacy and connection to their audience that was not possible in legitimate theatre plays.

And that wasn't all. Vaudeville provided Lugosi with an important source of income between 1947 and 1950. It's little wonder that he phoned vaudevillian Jackie Bright in 1950. Or that he phoned back even after Bright hung up on him.

(Endnotes)

1. *The Billboard* 22 Apr. 1950.
2. *Washington Post* 23 Dec. 1933.
3. *Variety* 12 Dec. 1933.
4. Details of *Stardust Cavalcade* can be found in Gary D. Rhodes' *Lugosi* (Jefferson, NC: McFarland, 1997).
5. *The Billboard* 28 Apr. 1945; *The Billboard* 5 May 1945; and *The Billboard* 12 May 1945. While these brief notices mention no producer for the tour, it is interesting to note that the schedule included locations played by Don Marlowe on his own vaudeville appearances.
6. *Daily Variety* 10 Dec. 1947.
7. Plumlee, Denney. "A Texan in Hollywood." *Amarillo Daily News* (Amarillo, TX) 19 Mar. 1948.
8. Advertisement. *Baltimore Sun* 24 Dec. 1948.
9. "Hipp Offers Fine Holiday Program." *Baltimore Guide* 23 Dec. 1947.
10. Alda, Alan. *Never Have Your Dog Stuffed and Other Things I've Learned* (New York: Random House, 2005).
11. *Boxoffice* 3 Jan. 1948.

12 "Olympia, Miami." *The Billboard* 10 Nov. 1945.
13 Advertisement. *Detroit News* 23 Aug. 1948.
14 Windley, Charles. Email to Gary D. Rhodes. 15 May 2006.
15 Blankenhorn, Richard. "The Great Lugosi, as Remembered by Alexander the Great." *Famous Monsters of Filmland* 132 (Mar. 1977).
16 Weitschat, Al. "The Screen in Review." *Detroit News* 21 Aug. 1948.
17 *Ibid.*
18 "Broadway-Capitol, Detroit." *Variety* 25 Aug. 1948.
19 "Palace, New York." *The Billboard* 17 Sept. 1949.
20 Rhodes, Gary D. Interview with Ada Lynn. 5 Sept. 2011.
21 *Miami Daily News* 3 Sept. 1948.
22 *Miami Daily News* 2 Sept. 1948
23 Wing, Grace. "City 'Disappoints' Lugosi – 'People Don't Die Here.'" *Miami Daily News* 3 Sept. 1948.
24 *Miami Daily News* 2 Sept. 1948.
25 *Ibid.*
26 "Olympia, Miami." *Variety* 8 Sept. 1948.
27 *Ibid.*
28 Advertisement. *Springfield Union* 15 Sept. 1948.
29 "Films' Dracula Comes to Town." *Springfield Union* (Springfield, MA) 15 Sept. 1948.
30 Available at http://ww.wethepeoplenation.com/showthread/php?265-Whoopie-Goldberg%92s-Race-Card-Ignorance. Posted 24 July 2011. Accessed 12 Dec. 2011.
31 *Variety* 22 Sept. 1948.
32 "The Steel Pier Continues Week-End Dancing, Vaudeville." *Atlantic City Press* (Atlantic City, NJ) 25 Sept. 1948.
33 "Loew's State, New York." *The Billboard* 12 Oct. 1946.
34 "Fox, St. Louis." *The Billboard* 1 Oct. 1949.
35 Advertisement. *Brooklyn Eagle* 11 Oct. 1948.
36 Advertisement. *Long Island Star-Journal* (Long Island, NY) 12 Oct. 1948.
37 *Variety* 20 Oct. 1948.
38 "Night Club Reviews." *The Billboard* 1 Nov. 1947; "Paramount, New York." *The Billboard* 19 Mar. 1949.
39 Advertisement. *Springfield Union* (Springfield, MO) 28 Oct. 1948.
40 "Dracula in Person Here." *Binghamton Press* (Binghamton, NY) 2 Nov. 1948.
41 "Terry Bennett & Joy." Available at: http://www.chicagotelevision.com/bennett.htm.
42 "Movie Timetable." *Binghampton Press* 5 Nov. 1948; "Movie Timetable." *Binghampton Press* 6 Nov. 1948.
43 Lugosi, Bela. Letter to Dr. Edmond Pauker. 15 Feb. 1949. [Available in the Edmond Pauker Papers, 1910-1957, Series I: Correspondence, 1915-1957, Box 42, Folder 11 at the New York Public Library/Lincoln Center for the Performing Arts in New York.]
44 Advertisement. *Brooklyn Eagle* 9 Sept. 1949.
45 Advertisement. *Brooklyn Eagle* 20 Sept. 1949.
46 Advertisement. *Brooklyn Eagle* 23 Sept. 1949.
47 Advertisement. *New York Times* 14 Oct. 1949.
48 Corby, Jane. "Screen." *Brooklyn Eagle* 13 Sept. 1949.
49 See Gary D. Rhodes's *Lugosi* for a discussion of this appearance.
50 Examinations of the relevant newspapers for 1946 have not uncovered any Lugosi-Melba appearance.
51 *Boston Globe* 14 Oct. 1949.
52 Morris, Abie L. "Fox Theatre, St. Louis." *The Billboard* 17 Dec. 1949.
53 Advertisement. *St. Louis Post-Dispatch* 17 Nov. 1949.
54 *Variety* 23 Nov. 1949.
55 "At the Theatres." *Oswego Palladium-Times* (Oswego, NY) 2 Mar. 1950.
56 "Count Dracula Is Featured in Vaudeville Show." *Oswego Palladium-Times* 3 Mar. 1950.
57 Advertisement. *Torrington Register* (Torrington, CT) 11 Mar. 1950.
58 Rhodes, Gary D. Interview with Anne Ponticelli., Erna Frisch's daughter. 7 Nov. 2011.
59 "Bela Lugosi at State Tomorrow." *Torrington Register* 11 Mar. 1950.
60 Advertisement. *Geneva Daily Times* (Geneva, NY) 27 Mar. 1950.
61 Advertisement. *Amsterdam Evening Recorder* (Amsterdam, NY) 12 Apr. 1950.
62 *Ibid.*
63 Hughes, Elinor. "Bela Lugosi Now Playing First Year in Summer Stock." *Boston Herald* 24 July 1947.

Lugosi with an unknown actor inside what appears to be a recording studio.

Chapter 12
ALMOST MUSICAL

No single characteristic of Bela Lugosi ever became more recognizable than his voice. The film *Dracula* (1931) goes so far as to have Mina (Helen Chandler) imitate the sound and cadence of his voice in front of the smitten Lucy (Frances Dade), much in the same way that comedians would do during the decades that followed.

Over the years, many authors have attempted to describe Lugosi's voice, no easy task given that the written word can only go so far in depicting sounds on paper. Of all of these efforts, columnist Jack O'Brian's remains one of the most fascinating. When he told readers about meeting Lugosi at Toots Shor's in 1947, O'Brian wrote that his voice was "almost musical."[1]

It was a unique description, and one that placed emphasis on Lugosi's voice above all else. O'Brian understood that the remarkable sound of Lugosi's accent could stand alone quite memorably from his physical presence. And he was not the only person who believed that was true.

For example, in July 1946, *The Billboard* reported that Musicraft Records would produce a series of eight different 12-inch records featuring narration by Bela Lugosi, perhaps in conjunction with MCA. The proposed series title was *Mysterioso*, with individual records featuring radio show-style scripts written by Merwin Gerard and Seeleg Lester. The trade publication added that they would be "horror tales, each one dealing with another phase of violence, chills or sudden death. Lugosi narration should be backed by theme music in keeping with spine-chilling format...."[2]

Unfortunately, the Musicraft series did not occur. But the company's plans may not have been unique. In the 1980s, Lugosi's friend Richard Sheffield described a record that he once owned; it featured Lugosi reading Edgar Allan Poe's *The Tell-Tale Heart*. Here was yet another connection between Lugosi and Poe.

Sheffield recalled the record as being a 16-inch transcription disc of the type radio stations used in the 1940s. In the 1960s, Sheffield gave the record to horror film collector Forrest J Ackerman. When film historian Gary D. Rhodes contacted Ackerman about the record in the 1980s, he had no memory of it. Given the use of the Poe story, Rhodes and Sheffield speculated that the recording might well have been made in conjunction with Lugosi's *Tell-Tale Heart* live tour of 1947.

Then, in the late summer of 2002, Ackerman's friend Lee Harris discovered *The Tell-Tale Heart* in Ackerman's record collection, slipped safely but anonymously into the sleeve of his wife's copy of Sir Thomas Beecham conducting the London Philharmonic Orchestra. It was actually recorded on two, 12-inch discs at 78rpm.

The typed labels simply note *Tell-Tale Heart-Poe* as the "Program" and mention Lugosi's name. The

The label on Side 1 of the mysterious *Tell-Tale Heart* recording. (Courtesy of Lee Harris)

label also has the pre-printed information "Recorded by WCAX" and "Burlington, Vermont." It does have a space for the recording date to be listed, but the typist regrettably left that line blank. The recording features Lugosi's voice, but no music, sound effects, or opening and closing credits.

Some horror fans have suggested that the recording was aired in 1945 on WPEN's radio show *With Book and Pipe*, but various factors make that explanation problematic. It is true that the show — more regularly referred to in newspaper radio listings of the period as *Man with Book and Pipe* – did air a version of *The Tell-Tale Heart* on July 9, 1945. The program was fifteen minutes in length, with the Lugosi recording being roughly thirteen minutes. Theoretically, that could have allowed for the Lugosi recording to be aired with additional credits and sponsor information added live.

But at the same time, anyone reading that particular Poe story would likely read it in less than fifteen minutes, so the sheer length of the Lugosi recording is not an indication of anything. Instead, it

From the *Philadelphia Evening Bulletin* of July 9, 1945.

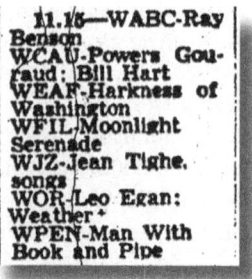

From the *Philadelphia Inquirer* of July 9, 1945.

210 NO TRAVELER RETURNS | The Lost Years of Bela Lugosi

is easier to seize on such questions as *why* Lugosi would have recorded a WPEN show in Burlington, Vermont, when *Man with Book and Pipe* originated out of Philadelphia, Pennsylvania. Furthermore, the program does not seem to have regularly featured celebrity guests; by contrast, it relied on a consistent Philadelphia-based narrator. Indeed, the Philadelphia papers that list the July 9, 1945 episode make no mention of Lugosi's name. That includes the *Philadelphia Evening Bulletin*, a newspaper that *owned* WPEN.

Then there is the fact that the Lugosi recording is not only devoid of credits and music, but even the simplest of sound effects, such as the beating of the old man's heart. Also strange is the fact that, having been recorded at 78rpm, the two discs feature the tale on four sides. As a result, the sides would had to have been changed three times during a broadcast, creating either awkward pauses or a rather high number of station breaks for a thirteen-minute recording. Indeed, rather than Disc 1 featuring Sides 1 and 3, and Disc 2 featuring Sides 2 and 4 (which would have allowed a radio station with two turntables to keep the story going without interruption), whoever cut this recording did so in such a way that *requires* three interruptions for side changes.[3]

If stations breaks were the intent, the change from side two to side three comes at a particularly awkward moment, as Side 3 begins with the dialogue "At length it ceased." Any break from the narrative would have made that line's meaning difficult to understand, as listeners would likely not have remembered what noun the word "it" referred to.

That is all in addition to the important and yet overlooked issue of the very words that Lugosi reads. *Man with Book and Pipe* offered spoken literature over the airwaves, bringing to life the exact words of famous authors for its radio audience. But the Lugosi recording of *The Tell-Tale Heart* features numerous changes to Poe's original story. Words like "Hearken" are replaced with less antiquated words like "Listen," and entire phrases and sentences are deleted, such as a description of the "perfect suavity" with which the investigating police officers enter the home. For the Lugosi recording, it is clear that *The Tell-Tale Heart* was changed with an eye towards eliminating at least some outmoded words or expressions, but not its overall length, which is little different than Poe's original.

Side 1 of the disc for Lugosi's *Mystery House* radio show. (Courtesy of Buddy Barnett)

If *The Tell-Tale Heart* was not intended for *Man with Book and Pipe*, the question remains as to why and when it was made. Perhaps Lugosi recorded the story at Burlington station WCAX when he was in Vermont in the summer of 1950, appearing in summer stock at St. Michael's College in Winsooki Park. That marks Lugosi's only known work in the Burlington area, and so this is the most plausible explanation.

Or perhaps Lugosi did visit Burlington in November or December of 1947 either immediately before or during his live tour in *The Tell-Tale Heart*. After all, the changes to Poe's story seem similar to what Don Marlowe did when he wrote the script for the live show: alter the language in an effort to update it.

Given the lack of any credits, music, or sound effects, as well as the lack of any program information on the original discs, as well as being recorded at 78rpm on four sides of two discs, it is unlikely that this version of *The Tell-Tale Heart* was meant for radio airplay. Instead, it may well have been recorded as a demo for a record company, something not unlike the proposed Musicraft series. After all, Lugosi owned the discs that later ended up in Ackerman's hands. Lugosi possessed no copies of his radio shows, but did own these particular records.

At any rate, the sheer possibility that *The Tell-Tale Heart* might have been broadcast invokes a discussion one of the most fascinating aspects of Lugosi's American career: his work in radio, with his "almost musical" voice disembodied from his physical appearance for the sake of his listening audience. To be sure, the very medium of radio was ideally suited for an actor associated with horror, as it represented audio moving mysteriously through the air and into homes across a broad geographical region. Spectral sounds and voices from the void: in its early years, radio epitomized what scholar Jeffrey Sconce has called a form of "haunted media."[4]

(Courtesy of the Wisconsin Center for Film and Television Research)

But for Lugosi's American career, radio held the potential for something far more than metaphors. While he was never a major presence on American radio, his work in the medium gave him a broader platform for his talents than either the cinema or the stage. In addition to starring in horror and non-horror dramatic tales, Lugosi found numerous opportunities to use his comedic abilities on radio. While the same could be said of his work in other entertainment forms, Lugosi was also able to explore the world of nonfiction on radio. Much of this was in the form of live interviews about his career, but on more than one occasion (including once with William S. Gailmor), Lugosi had the opportunity to engage in a political discussion.[5]

It is difficult to determine when Lugosi first spoke over the American airwaves. Certainly his earliest known radio show came in the late twenties for a broadcast of *Dracula–The Vampire Play*. He performed in an abbreviated version of the Broadway play over Newark's station WJZ on the afternoon of March 30, 1928.[6] At that time, the powerful WJZ could be picked up by radios in various parts of the US, far outside the confines of New Jersey.[7] And so Lugosi's Dracula had invaded the mass media of radio a few years before he did the same in the cinema.

Once Lugosi became a horror film star, he was simultaneously present and absent on some radio shows, another sign of the medium's haunted capabilities. For example, in March 1932, Universal Studios sent abbreviated scripts of *Murders in the Rue Morgue* (1932) to theatre managers screening the film so that they could "locally air the picture" with an actor playing Lugosi's role as Dr. Mirakle. As a result, theatres could publicize the film over the airwaves.[8]

While most of Lugosi's radio shows do not exist, those that do survive reveal his talent for the "theatre of the air." Certainly his most famous role came on CBS's *Suspense* on February 2, 1943, an episode well remembered not only because of the ongoing fame of *Suspense*, but also due to its commercial release on a trio different LP records during the 1970s and 1980s.[9]

As of January 26, 1943, the episode's title was *The Boomerang*.[10] Within the space of a week, however, the revised script bore a new title: *The Doctor Prescribed Death*. Lugosi's role of Antonio Basile offered him an intriguing variation on his usual mad doctor roles. Here he stars as a psychologist with a theory that a person's impulse towards committing suicide can be redirected towards committing murder. After an editor scoffs at his theory, Basile proceeds to test it. His experiment proves successful, but he suffers a horrible end when he jumps off a 17-story building to evade arrest. As the Man in Black narrator explained to listeners, Basile's theory worked perfectly … "in reverse."

Lugosi's performance as Basile was wonderful, but so were some of his lesser-known radio appearances. Consider for example his guest shot on the *George Jessel Show* (aka, *The Vitalis Program*) of October 13, 1939. In it, Lugosi exchanged comedic banter with the show's famous host:

JESSEL: Come on, Bela. Don't be frightened. That's the microphone right there.

LUGOSI: It isn't the microphone that bothers me.

JESSEL: Well, it certainly can't be me. I'm Georgie Jessel.

LUGOSI: Oh, George Jessel. Thank goodness! For a minute, I thought you were Boris Karloff in a new kind of makeup!

JESSEL: Well, that's very good. Tell me something, Bela. Did you and Karloff ever meet face to face?

LUGOSI: Yes. It was terrible.

JESSEL: What happened?

LUGOSI: We both fainted.

The sketch reveals Lugosi's masterful sense of timing and the use of various inflections and dynamic range of his voice to create comedy. And all of it occurred during a live broadcast.

With regard to Lugosi's limited radio career during and after the year 1945, it is easy to share his own discontent. In 1947, his representative Virginia Doak actively tried to arrange radio work for him, but she had little success. His relatively small number of radio appearances after World War II is particularly unfortunate given that – as opposed to the shrinking number of new horror movies – horror radio shows remained popular and common, so much so that a 1947 article in *The Billboard* noted fears that they might be "overdone."[11]

Most disappointing of all was Lugosi's own ill-fated program *Mystery House*. While historians normally date it as being from the year 1944 (due to a plug in the closing credits for the 1944 film *Bluebeard*), a surviving disc of the pilot episode exists in the collection of Buddy Barnett. Both of its typed labels indicate a date of June 11, 1945. Either the typist made two identical typographical errors, or the show was recorded – or at least promoted or even planned for airplay – in 1945. The label's abbreviation "MBS-Net" suggests a connection (or at least hoped connection) to the Mutual Broadcasting System. In any event, the show was intended to promote a publisher called Mystery House and introduce them into a variety of other mediums, not only radio, but also movies, thanks to hopes for a Mystery House film series with Lugosi at Universal Studios.

Entitled *The Thirsty Death*, the pilot features Ken Carpenter as the announcer, with star Bela Lugosi joined by guests John Carradine and Lurene Tuttle. In a story set in "darkest Africa," Lugosi plays Francois, a jealous doctor. His wife Eve (Tuttle) stops at Rene's (Carradine's) house when her servant leaves her all alone in the jungle. Though it is an impromptu and innocent visit, we learn that Eve loved Rene years earlier in Paris. Insane with suspicion, Francois soon locks Eve and Rene in Rene's home. He then claims that he has injected one of them with hydrophobia (the "thirsty death"), going so far as to leave a knife in the room so that the one without the affliction can kill the other. Eve meets a horrible end, after which Francois confesses that he hadn't injected anyone with anything. But his lie has led to the death of his innocent spouse.

DRACULA WALKS
Look out, Billie O'Day!
From the *Miami Daily News* of September 3, 1948.

The Thirsty Death is stellar, every bit the equal of *The Doctor Prescribed Death*, if not its superior. Lugosi attacked his role with relish, his performance easily besting Carradine, who stumbled at least twice while reading his dialogue. In fact, Lugosi's performance recalls his role in *The Raven* (1935), a story in which he played yet another doctor who gleefully tortures victims trapped in a house from which they cannot escape.

The lack of precise information about the *Mystery House* pilot and *The Tell-Tale Heart* recording underscores the issue of how much information on Lugosi's radio career remains unknown. For example, in August 1945, Erskine Johnson's syndicated newspaper column referred to an occasion on which Lugosi "showed up for a radio show with a mild case of hiccups. He begged someone to scare him out of it."[12] Exactly what program this anecdote refers to – or whether it was in fact little more than a concocted joke – is hard to determine.

Unconfirmed reports suggest that Lugosi acted on an episode of the Mutual program *Human Adventure* in approximately 1947, but no proof has yet surfaced. Similarly, we know that Lugosi *might* have worked on the CBS program *Which is Which?* on February 14, 1945. Ken Murray hosted the thirty-minute quiz show, during which contestants guessed whether the famous voices they heard actually belonged to the real celebrities or were merely being imitated by other actors. Lugosi's voice was

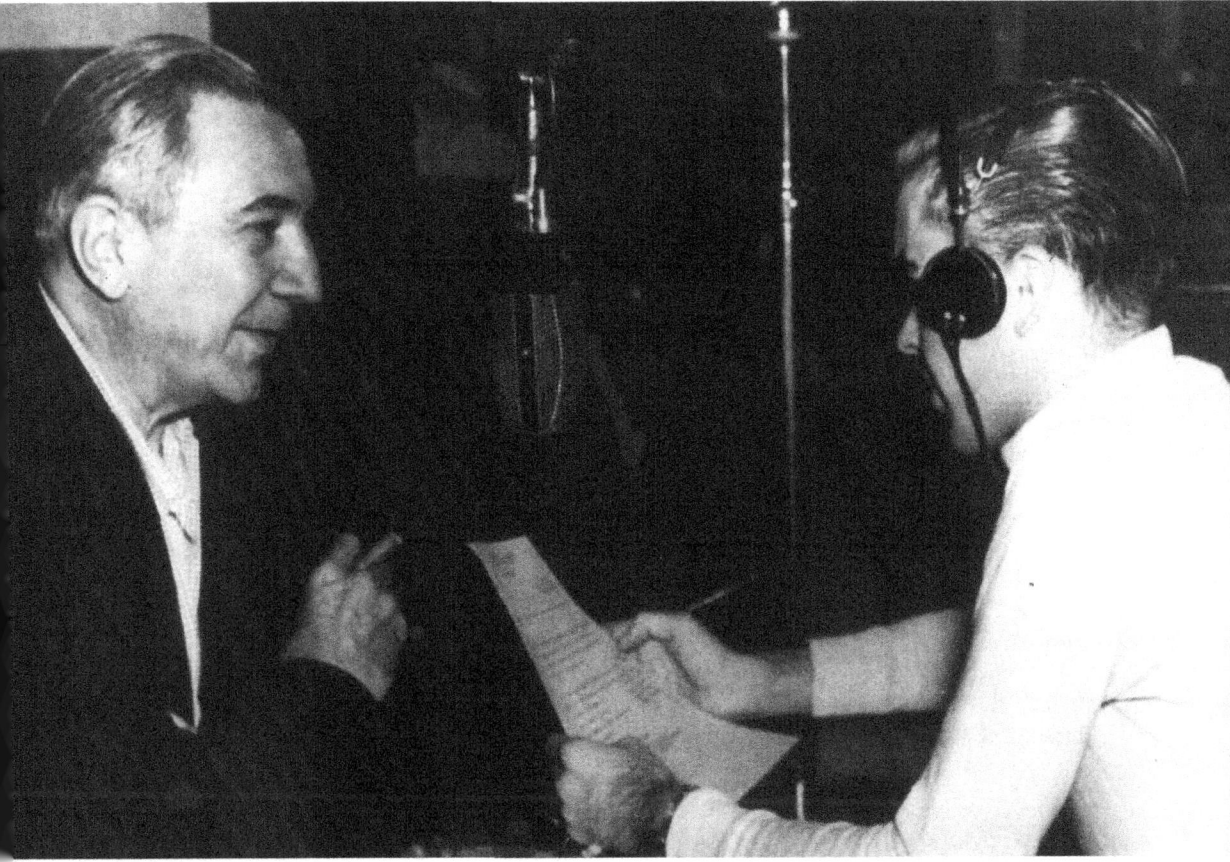

Lugosi being interviewed on the radio in the late 1940s. (Courtesy of Bill Chase)

definitely heard on that Valentine's Day, as were the voices of Jerry Colonna, Bonnie Baker, Ida Lupino, and Bert "The Mad Russian" Gordon. However, it is unknown whether Lugosi himself spoke his dialogue or whether an imitator spoke "his" voice.[13]

Then, on January 3, 1951, Lugosi was scheduled for *The Buddy Rogers Show*, broadcast over WOR in New York City.[14] However, on that very same day, Lugosi cancelled a live tour due to an illness. As a result, it is quite possible that he cancelled this appearance as well.

And then there are questions surrounding some shows on which Lugosi definitely did appear. On November 22, 1948, Lugosi guest-starred on CBS' *Herb Schriner Time*, as did the Raymond Scott Quintet.[15] But what Lugosi actually did on this program is hard to determine. Given that it was a variety show, he could have done anything from a fictional horror or comedy sketch to a nonfiction interview.

Nonfiction would certainly be the best description for many of Lugosi's radio shows in the post-war era. For example, on August 7, 1947, he was interviewed on a radio program in Saratoga Springs, New York while starring in a summer stock version of *Arsenic and Old Lace*.[16] Just over a year later, he appeared on WOR's *Martha Deane Program* in New York.[17] In September 1948, he gave an interview to Billie O'Day on her Miami, Florida-based radio show on station WIOD.[18] Then, in February 1950, Lugosi and singer Mindy Carson stopped by WWSW in Pittsburgh to promote their respective nightclub acts in the city.[19]

More notably, though, Lugosi gave interviews on a handful of nationally famous programs, such as

5-18-47

-25-

ROBERTS: Now for our big race - the Helbros Derby. We've already tested our guests' on their powers of recognition and now we check their powers of observation. We do this in a tabloid mystery play, in which we've invited one of your favorite personalities to set the stage for us. He is the famous Hollywood star - Mr. Bela Lugosi. The contestant who first arrives at the correct solution to our problem will be awarded $_____. And now it is my great pleasure to introduce the man who has frightened you in a hundred pictures: Mr. Bela Lugosi.

(MUSIC: .... _ _)

(APPLAUSE)

LUGOSI: Thank you very much, ladies and gentlemen, and thank you, Mr. Roberts.

ROBERTS: Well, it's a great pleasure to have you here on QUICK AS A FLASH, Mr. Lugosi, because ever since Dracula, you've provided us with more chills and thrills than any other character I can remember.

LUGOSI: I wish you wouldn't harp on that. I don't think anybody has been as misrepresented to the public as I have. When you say the name "Bela Lugosi", what do you think of?

ROBERTS: I hate to tell you.

LUGOSI: That's just the trouble. People think of me as a monster, which is absolutely unfair. Even my first name proves it. Do you know that "bela" means beautiful?

vr

A page from the script to the *Quick as a Flash* episode featuring Lugosi. (Courtesy of the American Heritage Center, University of Wyoming, Laramie, WY)

when he discussed the role of Dracula on *Art Linkletter's House Party* in October 1949. Then, on February 7, 1951, he appeared on ABC's *Johnny Olson Luncheon Club*, with advance publicity claiming he would "discuss his career, emphasizing the role that brought him to fame, that of Count Dracula."[20]

Perhaps Lugosi's most unusual nonfiction radio show came thanks to ABC's *Betty Crocker Magazine of the Air* (aka, *The Betty Crocker Show*) on January 29, 1951. According to a review in the *Dallas Morning News*, Lugosi "discarded his Dracula outfit for a kitchen apron" in order to tell the "hostess and the air audience of several Hungarian delicacies – also of how he and Mrs. Lugosi now celebrating their 18th anniversary first met."[21]

In terms of Lugosi's work in fiction, it is odd that he was unable to get work on horror radio shows of the period, an outcome that seems particularly surprising not only in terms of his distinctive voice, but also his famous ties to the horror genre. At most, it seems that during the post-war era he guest-starred on what would be best described as a few mystery programs. For example, on March 19, 1947, Lugosi was the "guest armchair detective" on an episode of CBS' *The Adventures of Ellery Queen* (aka, *Ellery Queen*) entitled *Adventure of the Specialist in Cops*.[22]

Two years later, Lugosi performed on another CBS program, *Tales of Fatima* (aka, *Tales of Adventure*), which starred Basil Rathbone. Broadcast on September 10, 1949, the episode *The Man in the Shadows* featured Rathbone as the black sheep of a prominent London family. Abetted by a mysterious accomplice (presumably Lugosi), the title character "follows a bizarre career of crime, stemming from his inexhaustible need for pounds and shillings."[23]

Regrettably, the *Ellery Queen* and *Tales of Fatima* episodes do not seem to exist, but a third mystery story does, at least in the form of a script on file at the American Heritage Center at the University of Wyoming. On May 18, 1947, Lugosi worked on Mutual's radio quiz program *Quick as a Flash*, which featured a unique format in which contestants weighed clues from mystery sketches and hit buzzers when they were prepared to solve the crimes. On the Lugosi episode, after a bit of light banter with the announcer, Lugosi starred as Hungarian detective Dr. Heggi in a sketch entitled *A Severe Case of Murder*.

In the episode, character Harry Sutton receives a phone call from a man threatening to kill him. His wife Sylvia suggests they should tell the authorities, but he refuses. Harry is soon murdered, with the killer leaving Sylvia alive but bound in ropes. After she phones Dr. Heggi for assistance, the police apprehend a young man. But he proclaims his innocence, telling police that Sylvia actually paid him to threaten Harry and to tie her up. Further suspicion falls on Sylvia when the young man reveals that she had a "load of [insurance] policies."

After weighing the various clues, contestants needed to determine who really killed Harry. As the announcer would later reveal, those clues could only lead to one correct conclusion: Sylvia had murdered her husband. As for Lugosi, though he had relatively few lines of dialogue, the episode seems to mark the first time he was able to play a Hungarian character on a radio program.

In 1949, Lugosi played another Hungarian character on the radio. For the series *Crime Does Not Pay*, which was based on a series of MGM movie shorts of the same name, Lugosi acted in an episode entitled *Gasoline Cocktail*. Rather than being a live broadcast, the show was recorded and then aired on at least a few occasions, first in December 1949 and then again February 1951, at which time the press incorrectly publicized it as a "new" show.[24]

In it, Lugosi's character Nick Szegedin is a Hungarian living in New York. He is so thrilled by the sight of fires that he rushes to them whenever he hears the sounds of nearby sirens. Szegedin's wife has tired of his mania, which is one reason that he is cheating on her with a younger woman named Edna. But Edna spurns him after realizing he cannot marry her. To exact his revenge, Szegedin hurls a "gasoline cocktail" into Edna's apartment, the resulting conflagration killing both her and her friend.

Szegedin flees, eventually hiding up at an apartment house in New Jersey. There he shares his love of fires with the landlady's daughter:

Gary D. Rhodes | Bill Kaffenberger

BROADCASTS:

Horror Man In New Air Crime Series

Listeners who like their radio fare well sprinkled with murders, individual or gang-style, with various and sundry other law violations thrown in for good measure, will be well satisfied when they hear Saturday's *Crime Does Not Pay* (WFAA-570, 9 p.m.). Starring in this week's drama of the gun and laboratory will be Bela Lugosi, famous for movie horror roles, who will play an arsonist in "Gasoline Cocktail."

Based on the movie shorts of the same name, *Crime Does Not Pay* is adapted for radio each week with the technical guidance of former Kings County (N.Y.) Prosecutor Burton Turkus.

Two girls are killed in the fire started by Nick Szegedin, but that's a small number compared with the usual casualties in a Lugosi horror vehicle.

From the *Dallas Morning News* of February 17, 1951.

Fires are never too high, Lina. Watch the flames. See? It's like a dance, so light so graceful, but such power. Such strength in the flame, Lina. Even from a little match. The whole house sometimes, from a single, little match.

But then Szegedin grows angry with his new companion, and readies another gasoline cocktail just before the authorities arrive. Though he threatens to explode it, a policeman shoots him in the shoulder so that he can be taken alive.

Lugosi closed the show out of character, blaming not only Szegedin, but also a society that must share some of the guilt for not helping the arsonist find proper education and training. "It comes back to us," Lugosi said, "the responsible citizens of our community." With that, the episode comes to an end. His performance on *Crime Does Not Pay* was magnificent, offering a broad range of emotions in well-delivered and well-timed dialogue. For a man who once told the press he would not let his son "listen to crime radio programs," his work in the genre ranks among the very best of numerous radio appearances.[25]

In addition to dramatic roles like Nick Szegedin, Lugosi continued to portray comedic characters on radio in 1945 and the years that followed. For example, just days before the end of World War II, Lugosi starred on ABC's comedy program *County Fair*, which was hosted by Jack Bailey. On it, Lugosi was "scheduled to saw a woman in half."[26] Here is yet another fascinating example of the wonders of old-time radio: Lugosi performed a comedic magic trick, but one that could be seen only in the minds of listeners.

Then, on July 16, 1946, Lugosi appeared on the Armed Forces Radio Service program *Command Performance* in a Superman sketch with Bob Hope as the superhero and Paulette Goddard as Lois Lane.[27] Lugosi costarred as the evil Dr. Bikini, aided by his assistant Professor Atoll (Sterling Holloway), both of their names evoking the nuclear age. Their victims on the program were the famous King Sisters.

Though Superman finally wins the day, Bikini attempts to transform the King Sisters into cakes of soap, knowing full well that, however one slices them, they will only make "eight to the bar." When Lugosi read his dialogue, "Do you know what we can do with those girls?", he received one of the biggest laughs he would ever get on a radio show. Holloway followed with a simple but knowing, "Yeah," which served to keep the laughter going.

Only months later, in October 1946, Lugosi costarred with Billie Burke in a sketch on *The Rudy Vallee Show* in an effort to give radio audiences a bit of horror-inspired humor during the Halloween season. In it, Lugosi played a vampire working to create life, a curious amalgam of Dracula and Dr. Frankenstein:

LUGOSI: I think you will be interested in my experiments, Miss Burke. I take parts of people and put them together.

BURKE: You mean you manufacture people like Ford manufactures Chevrolets, or does he?

LUGOSI: I'm building a human being!

BURKE: Oh, you're in production! Well, how nice. Any shortage of materials?

LUGOSI: All I need is a brain!

BURKE: Well, don't feel badly. We can't all be Quiz Kids.

Here again Lugosi reveals excellent comedic timing and seems to be enjoying himself a great deal, so much so that, when he takes Burke into his laboratory, he nearly breaks up with laughter.

Lugosi's most famous comedic appearance on radio came two years later on the *Abbott and Costello Show*. Broadcast on ABC on May 5, 1948, the show was likely intended to promote *Abbott and Costello Meet Frankenstein* (1948), though no direct reference is made to that film. The horror-themed sketch features Bud Abbott naming Lou Costello as the new sheriff of Encino, California. That leads both of them to investigate the strange goings-on at Lugosi's home.

Though the sketch is fun, Lugosi stumbled while delivering a few of the punchlines, which was likely the cause for the generally unenthusiastic audience response. For example, he leaves the word "if" out of a joke about "a strange man should suddenly appear" and offer to cut Costello's throat. Later, after hearing the suggestion that he should use ketchup on a rattlesnake burger, he responds "What? *To* get heartburn?", rather than the more likely dialogue "*And* get heartburn?" He also falls short trying to give a punchline about a dead renter being "paid up until June first" by accidentally saying "paid up until *fir*– June first."

And then, perhaps most problematically, he made another mistake after a lengthy build up to his final joke:

LUGOSI: Well, Sheriff Costello. I've got to go now before I get into trouble with the police.

ABBOTT: Are you afraid of the police because you killed those nine people last week?

LUGOSI: No, it's not that.

ABBOTT: Are you afraid of the police because of the dastardly crimes you've committed.

LUGOSI: No, it's not that.

ABBOTT: Then why are you afraid of the police?

COSTELLO: Yes, why? Why do you have to leave here so suddenly?

Lugosi on an unknown CBS radio show in the late forties.

LUGOSI: Well, I just remembered I left *a my* car parked in a one hour zone, and you know those Los Angeles cops.

By awkwardly saying "I left *a my* car parked," his timing is thrown completely, with the studio audience unable to muster very much laughter.

Though not entirely disappointing, Lugosi's work on Abbott and Costello's program did not go as well as it could have. Perhaps Lugosi was unwell, or perhaps Abbott and Costello's penchant for improvising and making derivations from written scripts threw him a bit. Lugosi's appearance hardly shows off the kind of comedic skill that he displayed so well on programs with the likes of George Jessel, Billie Burke, and Sterling Holloway.

While most of Lugosi's radio work in 1945 and the years that followed fit neatly into the categories of fiction (comedy and drama) and nonfiction, he worked on two fascinating programs that are intriguing in large measure because they attempted to blend elements of both, thus blurring the lines between fact and fantasy.

On March 9, 1947, he starred on an episode of *Exploring the Unknown* entitled *Jungle Death*. Originating on the Mutual Broadcasting System, this thirty-minute series concentrated on a broad range of science topics, ranging from man's struggle against disease to the fight against racism. Mutual pitched the program as something akin to a documentary series, but the stories were fictionalized, sometimes to the extent that they belonged as much in the horror genre as in any nonfiction category.

Regrettably *Jungle Death* does not seem to exist, but Lugosi's other main foray into the realm of what would later be referred to as "mockumentaries," "docufictions," and "reality" programming does. In 1950, he guest-starred on Allen Funt's *Candid Microphone*, pretending to be the owner of a curio shop selling "shrunken heads, oddly fashioned skulls, [and other] ghoulish knick-knacks." But a female customer entering the store didn't recognize him, instead believing he really was what he claimed he was: a collector selling "odd things" like human bones.

Lugosi played the role straight, but with a wry sense of black comedy. After showing her his wares, Lugosi tries to entice the woman into leaving him her own skull when she dies, so that he can make something "practical out of it." Again it is possible to hear his masterful timing at work as he suggests keeping tobacco in her skull, so that every time he stuffs his pipe he can be reminded of her. Then, when he reveals who he really is and she says she doesn't believe him, Lugosi threatens to bite her on the neck. Though it is not apparent on the recording, a newspaper columnist went so far as to claim that she "ran from the store" in horror, which suggests again the porous boundary between fact and fiction, as she seems to have been more frightened by Lugosi's vampire persona than she was his allegedly "real" occupation as a store owner.[28]

Whether it was fiction or nonfiction or some strange combination of the two, radio became an important facet of Lugosi's American career. His surviving radio shows not only place emphasis on his extremely distinctive and memorable voice, but also highlight his skill at using particular inflections, pauses, and dynamic range to inspire horror or cause laughter.

Perhaps Lugosi's voice was "almost musical," but it would be another performer who would profit from him in the world of music. Humorist Abe Burrows regularly sang a "love song" entitled *Bela Lugosi* at live events and on the radio during 1947 and 1948:

>Bela Lugosi!
>In the Argentine means,
>'I love you.'
>
>Means skies above you.
>Bela Lugosi!
>
>Bela Lugosi!
>In the Argentine
>That magic phrase,
>Puts me in a magic daze.
>Bela Lugosi![29]

Lugosi himself would have no record releases in the post-war era, either from Musicraft or any other company. Nor would he have his own radio program, or even a steady stream of work in the medium. His name in Burrows' comical love song speaks to his ongoing celebrity value in the late forties, but also perhaps to how much radio show programmers and the overall entertainment business misunderstood him.

(Endnotes)

1. O'Brian, Jack. "Broadway." *Sandusky Register-Star-News* (Sandusky, OH) 29 Nov. 1947.
2. *The Billboard* 20 July 1946.
3. Harris, Lee. Email to Gary D. Rhodes. 9 Feb. 2012.
4. Sconce, Jeffrey. *Haunted Media* (Durham, NC: Duke University Press, 2000).
5. Lugosi's political discussion with Gailmor can be heard on the bonus audio disc that accompanied the DVD release of Gary D. Rhodes' *Lugosi: Hollywood's Dracula* (Spinning Our Wheels, 2000).
6. "Brooklyn Station Ends Iowa Squeal." *New York Times* 22 Mar. 1928. (Along with Lugosi – whose name was incorrectly spelled "Lugosa" in the *New York Times* coverage of the WJZ broadcast – the radio cast included Terrence Neill, Dorothy Peterson, and Edward van Sloan. The broadcast occurred at 3:30PM EST. In addition to the initial announcement, the broadcast was listed in the "Today on the Radio" column in the *New York Times* on March 30, 1928.)
7. See, for example, "Takes Steps to Curb WJZ Radio Station." *New York Times* 17 Feb. 1926.
8. "Radio Script." *Variety* 14 Mar. 1932.
9. These three LP records were: *Boris Karloff/Bela Lugosi* (Command Perforamnce LP-5, 1974), *Suspense/Bela Lugosi* (Mark 56 Records 611, 1975), and *Bela Lugosi Meets Alfred Hitchcock (On the Radio)* (Radiola Records MR-1162, 1987).
10. Two original scripts for this program exist in the William Spier and June Havoc Papers, 1931-1963 at the Wisconsin Center for Film & Theatre Research of the Wisconsin Historical Society in Madison, Wisconsin.
11. "Commercials, Horror Shows Seen Overdone." *The Billboard* 8 Mar. 1947.
12. Johnson, Erskine. "In Hollywood." *Wisconsin Rapids Daily Tribune* (Wisconsin Rapids, WI) 24 Aug. 1945.
13. "*Which is Which* to Get De-Gagging So Ken Murray Is Ex." *The Billboard* 20 Jan. 1945, p. 6.
14. "On the Radio." *New York Times* 31 Jan. 1951.
15. "Programs on the Air." *New York Times* 22 Nov. 1948.
16. "Lugosi Flits Around Like Phantom." *The Saratogian* (Saratoga Springs, NY) 7 Aug. 1947.
17. "Programs on the Air." *New York Times* 9 Aug. 1948.
18. Wing, Grace. "City Disappoints Lugosi – 'People Don't Die Here.'" *Miami Daily News* (Miami, FL) 3 Sept. 1948.
19. *The Billboard* 25 Mar. 1950.
20. "On the Air." *Rockford Morning Star* (Rockford, IL) 7 Feb. 1951.
21. Bailey, Clay. "Theatre-of-the-Air." *Dallas Morning News* 30 Jan. 1951. [This article incorrectly spells Lugosi's name as "Logosi."]
22. "On the Air." *The Canton Repository* (Canton, OH) 19 Mar. 1947.
23. "On the Airlanes Tonight." *Portsmouth Times* (Portsmouth, OH) 9 Sept. 1949.
24. "Radio Programs." *Brooklyn Eagle* 12 Dec. 1949; "Broadcasts: Horror Man in New Air Crime Series." *Dallas Morning News* 17 Feb. 1951. [The *Gasoline Cocktail* episode of *Crime Does Not Pay* was also aired over CJOB in Canada in October 1952. See *Winnipeg Free Press* 31 Oct. 1952.]
25. Upchurch, C. Winn. "Lugosi Assails Crime Comics, Radio Dramas." *The Independent* (St. Petersburg, FL) 16 Mar. 1950.
26. "Woman'n Half by Bela Lugosi on Radio Fair." *Dallas Morning News* 31 July 1945.
27. This appearance has regularly and incorrectly been identified as having been broadcast in 1944. Confirmation of the correct date can be found in "Armed Forces Radio Service." *Hollywood Reporter* 17 July 1946.
28. Ames, Walter. "Movie Writer Likens Video, Film War to Weather; Bela Lugosi Fails *Candid* Stunt." *Los Angeles Times* 7 Aug. 1950.
29. For example, Burrows sang this song on CBS's *The Abe Burrows Show* on September 6, 1947 and April 10, 1948.

THE MOVIE STARS HAVE MOVED

...AND THEIR NEW ADDRESS IS WDOS!

YES, STARTING TODAY—YOU'LL BE HEARING STARS! WHEN YOU DIAL 1400, THAT IS... FOR FROM NOW ON ALL THE BELOVED STARS OF METRO-GOLDWYN-MAYER WILL BE SENDING YOUR WAY, VIA WDOS AND THE MUTUAL BROADCASTING SYSTEM, AS FINE ENTERTAINMENT AS YOU'VE EVER HEARD... ANYWHERE! TEN WONDERFUL NEW SHOWS... HUNDREDS OF GREAT STARS, OLD AND NEW... ALL ADD UP TO THE BIGGEST PLUS IN RADIO ENJOYMENT YOU'LL EVER FIND!

...JUST LOOK
AT THIS LINEUP OF GREAT NEW PROGRAMS FOR YOUR EVENING LISTENING PLEASURE!

MONDAYS—
AT 8:00 P. M. ...
"WOMAN OF THE YEAR"
Starring Bette Davis!
AT 8:30 P. M. ...
"CRIME DOES NOT PAY"
Tonight Starring Donald Buka!

TUESDAYS—
AT 8:00 P. M. ...
"THE BLACK MUSEUM"
Starring Orson Welles!
AT 8:30 P. M. ...
"THE STORY OF DOCTOR KILDARE"
Co-Starring Lionel Barrymore And Lew Ayres!

WEDNESDAYS—
A FULL HOUR FROM 8:00 to 9:00 P. M. ...
"THE MGM MUSICAL COMEDY THEATRE OF THE AIR"
Starring Popular MGM Musical Personalities in an Hour of Exciting Entertainment!

THURSDAYS—
AT 8:00 P. M. ...
"The Modern Adventures of Casanova"
Starring Errol Flynn!
AT 8:30 P. M. ...
"THE GRACIE FIELDS SHOW"
Starring England's Most Popular Comedienne!

FRIDAYS—
AT 8:00 P. M. ...
"THE ADVENTURES OF MAISIE"
Starring Ann Sothern!
AT 8:30 P. M. ...
"THE HARDY FAMILY"
Starring Mickey Rooney!

SATURDAYS—
A GREAT HOUR FROM 8:30 to 9:30 P. M. ...
"THE MGM THEATRE OF THE AIR"
Starring the Biggest Names in Hollywood... This Week Van Heflin as Johnny Eager!

REMEMBER... FROM NOW ON THE STARS' ADDRESS IS WDOS... 1400 ON YOUR DIAL... MUTUAL IN ONEONTA!

VAN · ROBERT TAYLOR · BELA LUGOSI · NANCY KELLY · SIDNEY BLACKMER · ORSON WELLES · ALAN BAXTER · MICKEY ROONEY · LEWIS STONE · FAY HOLDEN · GRACIE FIELDS · LIONEL B.

RING OUT THE OLD 1951 — HAPPY NEW YEAR — **RING IN THE NEW 1952**

WDOS, ITS ADVERTISERS AND THE MUTUAL NETWORK SEND GREETINGS WITH THESE

SPECIAL HOLIDAY SHOWS

TODAY

1:15- 1:30 P. M. SPORTS THRILLS OF 1951
—Sponsored by Oneonta Diner
Recalling the heart-stopping moments when sports history was made in the past 12 months.

9:00- 9:30 P. M. 1951 PASSES IN REVIEW
—Sponsored by Wright's Electric Co.
The news events and the music that made headlines during the year now ending.

9:30-10:00 P. M. GUY LOMBARDO SALUTES THE NEW YEAR
—Sponsored by The Windsor Hotel
The Royal Canadians give a "royal" welcome to the little fellow in the short pants.

10:15-11:00 P. M. TWELVE TOP TUNES OF 1951
—Sponsored by Oneonta Area Merchants
Felicitations and good wishes from your business friends who have been served you so well this year.

11:00- 3:00 A. M. NEW YEAR'S DANCING PARTY
—Sponsored by Angellotti Brothers
Four hours of music by the nation's foremost orchestras inspire dancing at your holiday House Party.

TOMORROW

8:00- 8:30 A. M. UPSTATE NEW YORK YEAR-END NEWS REVIEW
—Sponsored by Oneonta GLF Co-Op. and Norton's Farm Service
The biggest news stories in the Empire State in 1951.

11:45-12:15 P. M. MAYORALTY INAUGURAL
—A WDOS Public Service Presentation
Ceremonies at the Municipal Building during which Mayor-Elect Roger G. Hughes and City Judge, Supervisors, Aldermen and Assessors are sworn in. The new mayor will speak; the Oneonta High School Mixed Ensemble will sing.

1:15- 1:30 P. M. HERE COMES TOMORROW
—Sponsored by City Drug Store
A thought-provoking program with predictions for the New Year.

2:15 P. M. 'GATOR BOWL FOOTBALL GAME
—Mutual Broadcasting System
Clemson College vs. Miami University in the annual Florida gridiron classic.

WEDNESDAY

9:05- 9:30 P. M. SALUTE TO 1952's FIRST BABY
—WDOS and Cooperating Merchants
A Radio Package of Gifts, Music, and Interviews of Parents in our Best Bedside Manner.

1400 On Your Dial   **WDOS**   **1400 On Your Dial**

MUTUAL BROADCASTING SYSTEM

Here Lugosi receives brief mention in a radio advertisement published in the *Oneonta Star* (Oneonta, NY) on December 31, 1951.

Lugosi in the late 1940s.

Chapter 13

THE GREAT UNKNOWN

Writing in the *Motion Picture Herald* of April 9, 1949, George Schutz editorialized on the growth and power of television, which he referred to as the "great unknown." Acknowledging the concerns of "faltering [film] exhibitors," he wrote:

> Despite some effort to develop a prospect of television as a tool of the theatre, the fear of it recognizes its greatest field of service as an instrument of the home. Television is motion pictures that can be exhibited anywhere. To attempt to obscure that simple fact is not to deal with the fear very helpfully.
>
> … The real issue is: *Will television in the home give people what they seek when they go to the theatre?*[1]

Such fears were not without merit. By the time that Schutz wrote his article, the film industry had suffered through two years of terrible box-office receipts. Several reasons were to blame, with television increasingly becoming one of them.

Some exhibitors shrugged off the TV threat, believing that audiences would always want to attend films screened in theatres. But others believed the answer to Schutz's question could all-too-quickly become a resounding "Yes," and that television *could* replace the theatre, at least in some measure:

> It's obvious that when television is commercially accessible to theatregoers, they'll be stay-at-homers for the same show.
>
> – Jim Porter, Gallipolis, Ohio[2]

> Unless the movies improve, people will feel that can get just-as-good or better entertainment for cheaper at home.
>
> –Marjorie Pierce, La Grande, Oregon[3]

> Many persons, I find, already are rejecting a night at the movies in favor of remaining home with their television sets — and this when the programming is still exceptionally poor!
>
> –Paul Kosene, Perth Amboy, New Jersey[4]

Gary D. Rhodes | Bill Kaffenberger

Others saw the television threat as being more specific, believing that it was likely to "push the so-called 'B' picture off theatre screens."⁵ B-movies: they had been the lifeblood of Bela Lugosi's film career during World War II.

During the late forties, television not only seemed to pose a threat to the cinema, but also to live performances of all kinds, ranging from music events to dramatic theatre, including summer stock. But at the same time, TV presented great opportunities, not only to young talent, but also to older stars. Exiled from Hollywood filmmaking, an actor like Bela Lugosi might find a new home in television. The Great Unknown could open up new vistas for work.

And in some respects, Lugosi had long ties to television. In the comedy movie *International House* (1933), he portrayed one of several persons bidding on the rights to a new invention, a "Radioscope" that required "no broadcast station" to deliver images captured from around the world onto a screen. As its inventor explains, "it can materialize anything, anywhere, at any time."

Two years later, Lugosi starred in *Murder by Television* (1935), a low budget mystery in which he played two roles: brothers who look alike, but who have very different relationships with the law. Here is Lugosi's first appearance on television, at least of sorts, as the opening credits frame his face inside artwork of a TV screen. As for the film's plot, Professor James Hougland (Charles Hill Mailes) is murdered while talking oncamera for an experimental broadcast. At the film's conclusion, one of Lugosi's two characters speaks dialogue that aptly describes the earliest days of television: "Even though the eyes may see, the mind will not believe."

Lugosi as framed inside a faux TV set for the credits of *Murder by Television* (1935).

Television continued to surface in Lugosi films during the 1940s. Remembering a TV exhibit at the World's Fair of 1939, screenwriter Gerald Schnitzer wrote the invention into his script for *Bowery at Midnight* (1942). Here Lugosi's character uses a TV monitor for surveillance, spying on other characters from afar. There is no broadcast station or even cameras. Like the "Radioscope" of *International House*, this TV seems capable of displaying images without relying on any other technology. Borrowing from Schnitzer's idea, the Lugosi film *Voodoo Man* (1944) features a similar invention.

And so Lugosi was no stranger to television, even years before he made his first visit to a TV studio. The Great Unknown, which – like radio before it – represented an example of "haunted media."⁶ Fleeting images and sound from the sky illuminated on screens in viewers' homes, appearing out of thin air, much like ghosts or spirits. Even though the eyes may see, the mind will not believe. What better place for a horror actor to occupy?

Lugosi's television debut apparently came on the premiere episode of the program *Backstage at the Spa Theatre*. Broadcast on August 7, 1947, the show featured Lugosi alongside John Huntington, manager of the Spa Summer Theatre at Saratoga Springs, New York, where Lugosi was then starring in a stock version of *Arsenic and Old Lace*. The ten-minute show was filmed at General Electric's television studio and broadcast over WRGB at 7:20PM EST.⁷

Backstage at the Spa Summer Theatre was only the first of several Lugosi TV interviews. For example, television pioneer Guy Lebow claimed to have interviewed Lugosi on his television show near the release of *Abbott and Costello Meet Frankenstein*, placing it sometime in the summer or autumn of 1948. Lebow recalled Lugosi telling viewers that his favorite role was Santa Claus.[8] Then, Lugosi appeared on *The Bill Slater Show* on June 6, 1950, along with Fred Vandeventer and Roger Price.[9] He was scheduled for Slater's show again in early January 1951, with the other guests being Richard Arlen and Arch Oboler.[10] Even Lugosi's wife Lillian gave a TV interview, appearing on *Okay Mother* with Dennis James on December 28, 1950.[11]

For the premiere of his *Little Old New York* television show, Ed Sullivan interviewed Lugosi. The show was broadcast over WPIX on June 1, 1950.[12] In his newspaper column, Sullivan described the Lugosi episode:

Guy Lebow, who interviewed Lugosi on television in 1948.

> Bela Lugosi delighted me by confessing that the slump in horror pictures had driven him and Boris Karloff eastward, with Karloff switching from ghouls to Peter Pan... Lugosi revealed something that I never knew: that he was chosen as *Dracula* as the result of playing a romantic lead in *Arabesque*. He played the part of a sheik, and the use of his hands attracted the attention of Horace Liveright and director John B. Williams, who were searching for a male vampire.[13]

While it was not a national program, *Little Old New York* could be seen in a number of states in the New York region.

More than interviews, television variety shows dominated Lugosi's work in the medium during the late forties. Scant records and the lack of surviving kinescopes makes it difficult to determine the exact content of Lugosi's appearances on some of these programs, though general information about them would suggest that he acted in short sketches as part of longer shows that included other kinds of acts. Such programs were a kind of televised vaudeville. While their writers might have created scenarios for Lugosi, at least some of them presumably drew upon the kinds of material he used in vaudeville: scenes from (or, more likely, inspired by) *Dracula–The Vampire Play*, and/or comedic variations of them.

His first variety show was probably the *KTSL-TV Variety Show*, broadcast from Los Angeles-station KTSL on August 18, 1948. Producer Don Lee and the *Los Angeles Examiner* served as hosts for a "television party" celebrating a new business relationship that they forged with KTSL. Billed as the "largest variety show yet to be televised" on the West Coast, some 150 invited guests viewed it on the same day that they toured Don Lee's new building.

From the *Long Beach Independent* of February 3, 1950.

Lugosi approaches Milton Berle on a 1948 episode of the *Texaco Star Theatre*.

Given Lugosi's schedule, he did not attend the live event, but it is clear that he was one of the featured performers on the 90-minute broadcast, his segment likely being filmed in advance and on the East Coast. Others on the program included Garry Moore, Mickey Rooney, Evelyn Knight, Edgar Bergen, Eddie Bracken, and Helen Forrest.[14] Abbott and Costello also appeared, which suggests that – while there is no indication that they were in the same sketch as Lugosi – the casting of all three may have stemmed in part from the then-current release of *Abbott and Costello Meet Frankenstein*.

One year later, Lugosi became one the guests on *Surprise Theatre*, with the others being Zasu Pitts, Billie Burke, Sterling Holloway, and Pinky Lee.[15] As early as July 14, 1949, *Variety* published the first of what became several articles on the half-hour program, which was packaged by the William Morris Agency.[16] Their goal was the "obtaining of a kinescope print for sale purposes," meaning that potential sponsors only needed to "handle incidental costs."[17] Even the talent waived their standard high fees to help make the program possible.

In the end, KNBH – an NBC affiliate in Los Angeles – picked up *Surprise Theatre* for thirteen-to-fifteen weeks, with William Morris using the resulting kinescopes. Lugosi starred on the fourth program of the series, which was apparently broadcast on August 31, 1949.[18] Nothing is known about the content of Lugosi's sketch, but his affiliation with *Surprise Theatre* may well have led to his signing a long-term agreement with the William Morris Agency, which he did on November 10, 1949.

It is difficult to determine exactly how many times Lugosi acted on such television variety shows, though they definitely formed the core of his work in the new medium. A possible clue to his next performance came in a January 14, 1950 wire service column penned by George Hamilton. In it, Hamilton spoke about TV studios in New York, which he claimed were "so crowded and overworked that a visiting professor on a forum show fell into the arms of Bela Lugosi, who appeared the proceeding half-hour. Lugosi was frightened."[19]

Shortly after that anecdote was published, Lugosi worked on *Celebrity Time* on January 22, 1950. Actress and singer Lisa Kirk, who was then starring in *Kiss Me Kate* on Broadway, was a guest on the same show. One newspaper item joked that their joint appearance meant that viewers would see "two types of vampires together."[20] Hosted by Conrad Nagel, *Celebrity Time*'s guests that day also included Arlene Francis and John Daly. Though the show had originally been a quiz program with guests identifying film clips, it had transformed into a general variety show by the time of the Lugosi episode.

In fact, *Celebrity Time* was not altogether different from *Versatile Varieties*, on which Lugosi guest-starred only days later. Broadcast on January 27, 1950 to celebrate the show's "first anniversary," *Versatile Varieties*' other guests included Anne Russell and the Kay Gorham Girls, a group of four dancers. Emceed by Harold Barry, the program was set at a nightclub, with actors and other performers entertaining an onscreen audience, which itself sometimes included celebrities. The question here is whether Lugosi offered a scene from *Dracula* or some horror-comedy skit, or if he was simply an onscreen celebrity guest watching someone like Russell.[21]

Within four months, Lugosi appeared on another variety show, *Starlit Time*. Bill Williams and Phil Hanna were the emcees, and Cy Coleman and Reggie Bean provided the music. The show made its debut on the DuMont network on May 9, 1950, with Lugosi performing on the third installment, which was aired on May 21.[22] Early episodes lasted two hours. In addition to various guests, the show – which only lasted until November 1950 – featured a regular cast of performers that included Bibi Osterwald, Sandra Lee, Sam Steen, and Reggie Bean.[23] But what Lugosi did on the show remains unknown.

By contrast, a good deal is known about Lugosi's appearance on *The Robert Q. Lewis Show* on Christmas Eve, 1950. Pre-recorded on December 15, 1950, the 15-minute program was broadcast at 11PM EST over WCBS in New York City.[24] Lugosi was the main guest, though the show also briefly included a choir and someone dressed as Santa Claus. A surviving script reveals that Lugosi was able to engage in both some horror humor and an interview.[25] In their sketch, Lugosi joked that Lewis was such a "young man" to have died:

LEWIS: What do you mean, 'Die'? I'm right here. I'm living.

LUGOSI: (LOOKS AROUND) You call this living?
(FEELS LEWIS' FACE...NOSE, CHIN, ETC.)
(PLEASED) Horrible...horrible...do you think I might have a picture of you?

LEWIS: Oh, I'd be delighted. How would you like me to sign it?

LUGOSI: Oh, that doesn't matter...I just want to use it to scare my children.

After a couple minutes of such banter, the two went into a straight interview, after which Lugosi wished everyone a "Merry Christmas." He also shook hands with Santa Claus and, in a final bit of humor, sneaked away with Santa's hat.[26]

A fair amount of information also exists about Lugosi's work on the October 2, 1950 episode of *The Paul Winchell Show* (aka, *The Paul Winchell-Jerry Mahoney Show*).[27] Ventriloquist Winchell later recalled:

My first guest of the new season [1950-51] was turned down by almost every TV show. It was Bela Lugosi, whose price was shamefully low because he had fallen on hard times since his days at Universal when he played Dracula. ... In keeping with Bela's mystique, my writers came up with a story in which Jerry's school assign-

Lugosi jokes with Berle on the *Texaco Star Theatre*.

Gary D. Rhodes | Bill Kaffenberger

Lugosi attempts to hypnotize Berle on the *Texaco Star Theatre*.

ment was to find a certain tombstone in a local cemetery [Jerry Mahoney being one of Winchell's dummies].

Simultaneously, a bank robber who happened to resemble Dracula was hiding loot in the graveyard. As we began to rehearse, Lugosi found he was having difficulty with a line.

'Who would ever think of looking for it here?' he began. 'Who would ever *for* looking *of it–*.' He stopped and looked at me apologetically, then tried again and stopped again. He excused himself for a moment and walked to the other end of the room. I watched him as he read the line several times in Hungarian.

He was translating the words in order to comprehend their meaning. 'Okay, I got it!' he announced and returned to try it again. Now with self-assurance, he said, 'Who would ever think of linking for it? Wait, please, I will get it. Who would ever look of think? Wait, wait!' I tried to convince him that the line was unimportant, and that he could improvise. He might say, 'Who would find it here?', or even, 'Nobody will find it here.'

Honestly, the line was insignificant, but the poor guy got stuck on the grammar. Now he had to prove himself.

'Wait, wait. I will get it,' he insisted and tried again. We did our best not to laugh, but Bela wouldn't quit. Then, in desperation, he said to me, 'Look, I have Dracula's full dress suit with the red ribbon on it. Why couldn't Dracula rob that bank and hide the money there?'

Since he just couldn't say the line, he decided to change the story. It was transparent that Bela would do anything not to have to say that line. His suggestion was the last straw in an hour of repressed laughter. Fortunately, even Bela, realizing the absurdity of the situation, joined us in our laughter. We finally convinced him that the line was trivial and he could say it any way that felt comfortable. When we went on the air, he was fine and smooth as silk.[28]

Lugosi's problem with the dialogue calls to mind his grammatical problems on the *Abbott and Costello Show* on radio in 1948, though in this instance it seems as if his mistakes were not broadcast.

Likely Lugosi's most viewed TV show in the forties came on NBC's *Texaco Star Theatre*, popularly known and remembered as the *Milton Berle Show*. Though Berle was the star, his program was itself a variety show. Indeed, Lugosi was one of several guests on September 27, 1949, the others being Billie Burke, Jackie Robinson, Bill "Bojangles" Robinson, and Olsen and Johnson, who provided a surprise ending by emerging from a mummy's sarcophagus along with a dwarf. Ed Cashman produced and directed, with the Al Roth Orchestra providing the music.

Given surviving clips of the episode, it is possible to see Lugosi at work on live television in a comedy sketch. Dressed in his Dracula attire, he tries to hypnotize Berle. The brief act disappoints in large measure because the two actors are working on very different wavelengths. Lugosi's comic timing was often near perfect, as films like *International House* (1933) and *The Gorilla* (1939) exemplify. And he was quite capable of utilizing his comedic skills in live broadcasts, as his guest shot on the *George Jessel Show* of 1939 makes very clear.

At times, though, Lugosi had difficulties with comedians who improvised, as well as with scripts containing words or phrases with which he was unfamiliar. On the *Texaco Star Theatre*, for example, Lugosi seems ill at ease, and he clearly flubbed the words *Otchi Chornya*, a reference to a popular song of that name featured on records and in the 1945 film *Wonder Man* with Danny Kaye. As a result, Berle jabbed at Lugosi's lack of comedic skill, claiming "You kill people on the screen; you also kill jokes."

But in some ways, Berle's work on live television was founded not only on improvisation, but also on an insult-style of meta-humor: looking into the camera and making jokes about jokes. In other words, though viewing the footage today seems to put Lugosi in an embarrassing situation, viewed in the context of its time and Berle's particular approach to TV comedy places the appearance in a somewhat different light.

```
8:30-WCBS-TV—Arthur Godfrey Talent Scouts
    WNBT—Howard Barlow Orchestra, Lily
        Pons, Soprano, Guest
    WABD—Al Morgan Show: Music, Variety
    WJZ-TV—Author Meets the Critics:
        Irwin Ross, James F. Murray
    WPIX—Murder and Bela Lugosi
    WATV—Finals of Miss Television, 1950,
        Contest
```

From the *New York Times* of September 18, 1950.

Indeed, period reviews of the show were positive. Claiming the episode came off "well," *Variety* noted that a "hoke-horror bit with Bela Lugosi ... provided a good deal of yocks."[29] *The Billboard* was also impressed:

> Berle should make it a must to get one wild sketch into each show, the sort of slapstick, cornball idiocy built around Bela Lugosi on this show. It's almost Keystone cop-like in its flavor; provides a wonderful pace for the show and provides ample opportunity for Berle's own antics. Which the people want.[30]

Indeed, this critic saw the Lugosi segment as one of the highlights of the show, as opposed to, say, the Jackie Robinson bit, which was "poorly handled." Such reactions were quite different than how modern viewers generally respond to the same sketch.

The sheer number of Lugosi's variety show performances suggests that – much like his vaudeville work and his appearance in *Abbott and Costello Meet Frankenstein* – his brand of horror was increasingly dependent on being played for comedic purposes. Lugosi seemed to understand this transition, believing that television was "one of the factors [responsible] ... for the changes in the art of blood chilling." Speaking to a newspaper journalist, he said, "When you walk right into a person's living room through the medium of the television screen, you have to use the subtle approach. The old-fashioned horror actor would evoke nothing but gales of laughter."[31]

And so Lugosi hoped to capitalize on what he perceived to be the comical value of horror. In 1948, Don Marlowe actively tried to get CBS to sign the actor for a program entitled *The Bela Lugosi Show*.[32] Speaking to one reporter, Lugosi claimed it would be a comedy program, produced by Tom Elwell and costarring Ann Thomas. Both Elwell and Thomas had been slated to work with Lugosi in a 1947 live production that never materialized.[33] The reporter added:

> ...his wife spoke up and said, 'If his public can imagine Bela in a comedy.'

With actor Romney Brent on the October 11, 1949 episode of *Suspense*.

To which Bela replied, 'Charley [sic] Chaplin wants to do *Hamlet*, so why can't I go into comedy?'[34]

Lillian added that her husband had a great sense of humor. But he never had a chance to explore it in his own TV program. *The Bela Lugosi Show* never came to be.

Nor did *any* Lugosi television show apparently. New York's WPIX did broadcast what was called the "premiere" episode of *Murder and Bela Lugosi* on September 18, 1950 at 8:30PM EST. It sounds tantalizingly like a dramatic TV show starring Lugosi, and certainly WPIX did air numerous original programs, including some that lasted for only a single episode. However, *Murder and Bela Lugosi*'s hour-long running time suggests that it was more likely one of his old films, some of which were cut down in length for 60-minute broadcast slots.[35]

During his career in television, Lugosi rarely had the chance to offer dramatic scenes of horror.[36] His key opportunity came only months before he described TV's negative effect on the genre. After having years of success on CBS radio since 1942, the popular program *Suspense* made its debut on CBS television in 1949, even as the radio version continued. Just as Lugosi created one of his most memorable radio show characters during *Suspense*'s first season on radio, he would do the same during the program's first season on TV.

Here Lugosi would return once again to the grotesque and arabesque world of Edgar Allan Poe, starring in a thirty-minute adaptation of *The Cask of Amontillado*. Produced and directed by Robert Stevens, the program was sponsored by Electric Auto-Lite. Broadcast on October 11, 1949, the show exemplifies not only the perceived need to expand upon Poe's original stories, but also the changing horror landscape of the post-war years.

Just as films like *Scared to Death* and *Abbott and Costello Meet Frankenstein* featured allusions to World War II, so too did this version of *The Cask of Amontillado*, to the extent that it was far more explicit than the others. Set in Italy, two American soldiers – one of them played by Ray Walston, with whom Lugosi had appeared onstage in two plays in 1947 – take the testimony of an Italian count (Romney Brent) inside the very castle he once owned. The count describes a murder committed in the catacombs beneath them, a murder that he committed himself during the war.

A flashback finds the count tormented by a Fascist Italian general (Lugosi) who was once the count's stable boy. But times have changed. The general seizes the count's castle, and takes his sister for his wife. After the sister's death in an "accident," the general has an affair in Rome with the count's wife. Then he returns to the castle to murder the count. Understanding what is about to happen to him, the count offers the general some Amontillado stored in the catacombs. Understanding what is about to happen to him, the count offers the general some Amontillado stored in the catacombs. The two journey down the old castle steps, with the count finally managing to confiscate the general's gun. He shoots the Fascist villain before walling him up alive. *In pace requiescat!*

Adapted by Halsted Welles, the story – which was retitled *A Cask of Amontillado*, perhaps simply out of carelessness – indicts the Axis powers on the basis of their cruelty, but not through references to invasions of particular countries or to the Holocaust. Instead, Welles explores the vile excesses of Fascism by dramatizing the repeated abuses of an alcoholic general to the man who once employed him and even paid for his education. The general takes the count's property, his sister, and his wife. And then he tries to take the count's life.

Taunting Romney Brent's character on *Suspense*.

Such personal excesses offer a powerful metaphor, but they take the story far from Poe, whose tale never reveals the specific reasons why its narrator walls up the ironically-named Fortunato. No, for Poe, it was enough to suggest that Fortunato had inflicted a "thousand" unnamed injuries on the narrator, and then "ventured upon" an unstated insult. But in a brief bit of dialogue, Welles tries to reconnect his adaptation with Poe's literary world by claiming the general installed "torture devices" at the castle. Such words bring to mind Poe's *The Pit and the Pendulum*, and perhaps by extension, Lugosi's character in the film *The Raven* (1935).

That said, Welles was unable to limit himself to such lofty goals. He gives Lugosi the double entendre line, "I have the whole afternoon to kill," which seems more suited to a horror-comedy vaudeville act than to a serious condemnation of Fascism. Then, in what seems to have been a clumsy effort to conjure images of Lugosi's vampire roles, Welles has the count describe some red wine by saying it "glowed and gurgled like blood."

The Billboard published what seems to have been the only major review of the program, claiming on October 22, 1949:

> [*Suspense*] is still characterized by good story material expertly adapted for tele, facile production and, except in one instance on the show, caught good performances.

Stopping to drink on the way down to the catacombs. The fake wall behind Romney and Lugosi is revealed to be nothing more than a stage curtain when the two walk past it.

Gary D. Rhodes | Bill Kaffenberger

Lugosi as the alcoholic fascist on *Suspense*.

...Bela Lugosi was ... the show's greatest weakness for he failed to bestow an iota of reality on what appears to have been a fine and meaty part. The entire story points to that moment when the general is forced to place his wrists in chains suspended from a wall while the count prepares to turn mason. Lugosi seemed to walk into the spot with alacrity, and the tension which had been established in the chase down to the cellar was vitiated.

What may have added to the ineffectual quality of Lugosi's job was the commanding and immaculate performance turned in by Romney Brent, the sort of work which delivers much satisfaction in observing the work of a master craftsman.[37]

Noting only a couple of other minor concerns, the critic believed the show was overall "grade 'A,' all the way."

Recalling the episode, Ray Walston once claimed that director Robert Stevens was a "very nervous man ... who was in the wrong place at the wrong time." Walston added that the show was "so bad because [Lugosi] couldn't remember his lines. He was bad about that; it was hard for him to remember his lines. He had a hard time on that half-hour show."[38]

But examining the episode calls into question much of what has been said about it. At no point does Lugosi ever seem to grope for his dialogue or verbally stumble in any way that suggests he was forgetting his lines. By contrast, it is Romney Brent who makes a noticeable mistake when describing his sister's marriage to the general; aurally, it is clear that he starts to call the character his "daughter" before correcting himself.

Not only does Lugosi seem to deliver his lines with no problem, his performance is quite strong. Dressed in military apparel, with his hair often dishevelled and his shirt's top button open, Lugosi seems to relish his role as a drunken Fascist, guzzling wine and wooing another man's wife. Indeed, this role seems like a logical extension of the Axis villains he had portrayed in such films as *Black Dragons* (1942) and *Ghosts on the Loose* (1943).

Why then would *The Billboard*'s critic and costar Ray Walston remember things so differently than what the surviving kinescope reveals? Likely it is because of the program's conclusion. Though we do not see the count fire the gun, he does shoot the general before walling him up. We hear the sound effect of a gun, and shortly thereafter the general's dialogue indicates that he has been shot. The problem is that we do see Lugosi at the moment the count pulls the trigger, and he does not react as if he has been shot. Aurally, it seems as if the sound effect comes from somewhere other than the prop gun, perhaps from a backstage source; indeed, we have already heard the same audio-visual disconnect when the general fires the same gun at some birds. And so Lugosi may not have clearly heard the sound effect to know his cue.

Regardless, the moment is very awkward, and the problems mount when Brent tries to manacle

Lugosi before walling him up. The prop manacles do not properly lock around Lugosi's wrists, particularly his right wrist, which is closest to the camera. Here it seems that unlocked manacles are constraining the general. But Lugosi can hardly be blamed for such prop failures, even if they detract greatly from the dramatic impact of the conclusion.

Nor can Lugosi be blamed for one of the episode's other major blunders, something that had nothing to do with the writing or the acting. When the general is first introduced, the cameraman seems as if he wishes to pan to another character, the count's wife. But at the last minute he swish pans right to catch Lugosi in the frame. It destroys his visual introduction.

Unfortunately, these are not the only problems that occurred during the live broadcast. The episode had only four sets (five, counting Rex Marshall's Auto-Lite commercials), one of which was a series of castle steps. To give the illusion of the count and general descending deep into the catacombs, Brent and Romney walk down what are very obviously the same steps on five occasions. After completing his walk down them, Brent – whose character is carrying a lantern – raced offscreen to get back into position to walk down them again. He accidentally shines his light onto the set while Lugosi is still there. It is as if Brent is momentarily following Lugosi, not the other way around as the story would have us believe.

The staircase has other problems as well. Painted backdrops hang to suggest a winding stone wall. Because they are usually in fairly sharp focus, viewers can easily see that they are nothing more than paintings. That might be acceptable in early television, just as it was in the days of early cinema. But when Lugosi and Brent move past these backdrops, the "stones" on them billow like curtains.

And, when Lugosi and Brent stand up after sitting on the steps, it is aurally clear that one of them has accidentally knocked over an offscreen bottle of wine at their feet. Both of them have left wine bottles on the steps, so it is difficult to determine which actor knocked it over. Here again is an example of the kind of problem that could so easily occur on live television, and it is something of a testament to both Lugosi and Brent that they do not show a visible reaction to it.

Shortly before being walled up alive on *Suspense*. Here it is obvious that the prop manacle has not clasped around Lugosi's wrist.

Suspense apparently became Lugosi's only performance in an extended dramatic story on television, as opposed, say, to all of the many variety show sketches in which he appeared. The key reason was not one bad review in *The Billboard*. No, Lugosi's problem in conquering the land of television was larger than a single bad review, even though it could hardly have helped.

For Lugosi, television increasingly began to share a great deal in common with movie theatres of the late forties. Both forums relied on Lugosi with some regularity, but neither actually needed to hire or pay the actor. The movie theatres relied on reissues of Lugosi horror films, and, by 1949, some of those same movies began turning up on TV with increasing frequency, a trend that continued in 1950 and beyond.

As early as 1941, NBC television bought the rights to some Monogram films of the late thirties, the network realizing that the major Hollywood studios had no interest in allowing their movies to be broadcast.[39] By the end of the forties, Lugosi B-movies made their television debuts.

In 1949, for example, World Wide Pictures' *The Death Kiss* (1933) and PRC's *The Devil Bat* (1941) hit the airwaves.[40] The following year, *White Zombie* (United Artists, 1932), *Chandu on the Magic Island* (Principal, 1935), *Phantom Ship* (Guaranteed, 1936), *Shadow of Chinatown* (Victory, 1936). *The Corpse Vanishes* (Monogram, 1942), and *The Ape Man* (Monogram, 1943) played on various television stations.[41] The trend continued for years thereafter, including in the early months of 1951, during which some of the same films – and others like *Mysterious Mr. Wong* (Monogram, 1935) and *Return of the Ape Man* (Monogram, 1944) – illuminated on television sets across the United States.[42]

And so on many occasions, Lugosi was simultaneously on television and not on television. For him, the Great Unknown was something he came to understand quite well. It was a new entertainment country, and one to which he could not finally immigrate, short of projections of his old screen self.

(Endnotes)

1. Schutz, George. "Television, the Great Unknown." *Motion Picture Herald* 9 Apr. 1949.
2. "Critics Discuss Video's Effect on Films." *Film Daily* 9 Aug. 1948.
3. Ibid.
4. Ibid.
5. "Sees Video Killing B's." *Motion Picture Herald* 26 Mar. 1949.
6. Sconce, Jeffrey. *Haunted Media* (Durham, NC: Duke University Press, 2000).
7. "Spa Theatre Stars to Shine in Television." *The Saratogian* (Saratoga Springs, NY) 7 Aug. 1947.
8. Lebow, Guy. *Are We on the Air! The Hilarious, Scandalous Confessions of a TV Pioneer* (New York: SPI Books, 1992).
9. "Television." *Brooklyn Eagle* 7 June 1950.
10. Television." *Brooklyn Eagle* 3 Jan. 1951. It is possible that Lugosi did not actually appear on this program, unless it was pre-recorded. That same day, newspapers reported that he was ill.
11. "On Television." *New York Times* 28 Dec. 1950.
12. "Television." *Brooklyn Eagle* 1 June 1950.
13. Sullivan, Ed. "Little Old New York." *The Morning Herald* (Uniontown, PA) 7 June 1950.
14. *Daily Variety* 9 Aug. 1948.
15. "ABC Signs Ozzie and Harriet in $1,000,000 Deal." *Chicago Tribune* 23 July 1949.
16. *Daily Variety* 14 July 1949.
17. Ibid.
18. *Daily Variety* 29 July 1949; *The Billboard* 6 Aug. 1949.
19. Hamilton, George. "It's All New York." *Valley Morning Star* (Harlingen, TX) 14 Jan. 1950.
20. Vernon, Terry. "Tele-Vues." *Long Beach Independent* (Long Beach, CA) 3 Feb. 3, 1950.
21. *Washington Post* 27 Jan. 1950.
22. "On Television." *New York Times* 21 May 1950.
23. "Starlit Time." *The Billboard* 23 Apr. 1950.
24. These dates appear in an office memo from Robert Q. Lewis to I. S. Baker dated November 29, 1950. [Available in the Robert Q. Lewis collection at the American Radio Archives at the Thousand Oaks Library in California.]
25. "Television." *Brooklyn Eagle* 24 Dec. 1950.
26. *Robert Q. Lewis Show*. Script dated 24 Dec. 1950. [Available in the Robert Q. Lewis collection in the American Radio Archives at the Thousand Oaks Library in California.]
27. "Television." *Syracuse Herald-Journal* (Syracuse, NY) 2 Oct. 1950.
28. Winchell, Paul. *Winch: The Autobiography of Paul Winchell* (Authorhouse, 2004).
29. "Tele Follow-up Comment." *Variety* 4 Oct. 1949.
30. "Texaco Star Theatre." *The Billboard* 8 Oct. 1949.
31. "Tougher to Scare People!" *Trenton Evening Times* 21 Dec. 1950.
32. Mention of the *Bela Lugosi Show* appears as one of Lugosi's credits in the *Player's Directory Bulletin* for October 1948.
33. See Chapter Five for more details on the Elwell-produced live show that Lugosi was to do with Ann Thomas.
34. "King of Horror Just Tired Businessman to Interviewer." *Rockford Morning Star* (Rockford, IL) 15 Nov. 1947.
35. "Television." *Brooklyn Eagle* 18 Sept. 1950.
36. In addition to the programs discussed in this chapter's main text, it is possible that Lugosi appeared on yet another TV horror show. In an interview with *Starlog* (Oct. 2004), actor Joseph Campanella recalled: "I actually did the live TV show *Suspense* with the real Bela Lugosi! The poor man was dying and did die shortly afterward. They gave him the job so he could make some money. He played the same role he always did, the heavy – but not a vampire. In that episode, Bela ran this lighthouse and I was a young reporter. He had to chase me up the lighthouse, and the poor man was so exhausted and tired."
    Campanella's description is intriguing, in part because elements of it seem similar to the *Suspense* broadcast of *A Cask of Amontillado* (a "young reporter" versus a military investigator; "lighthouse" steps versus the castle steps). But Campanella

did not appear in *A Cask of Amontillado*. And it seems clear that Lugosi did not make a second appearance on the *Suspense* TV show. Campanella's memory seems to be in error, at least to a degree. Perhaps the two actors appeared together on some other, non-*Suspense* TV show.

37   Franken, Jerry. "*Suspense*." *The Billboard* 22 Oct. 1949.

38   Weaver, Tom. "Ray Walston." In *I Was a Monster Movie Maker* (Jefferson, NC: McFarland).

39   "NBC Buys 4-Year-Old Monogram Features for Telecast Programs." *Motion Picture Herald* 29 Nov. 1941.

40   On December 8, 1949, WBAD in New York broadcast *The Death Kiss* ("Programs on the Air." *New York Times* 8 Dec. 1949: 66). *The Devil Bat* was broadcast over WPIX on August 14, 1949 ("On Television." *New York Times* 14 Aug. 1949: X8), and again over WABD on November 17, 1949 ("Programs on the Air." *New York Times* 17 Nov. 1949: 58).

41   *White Zombie* was broadcast over WJZ on September 11, 1950, hosted by Frank Albertson, as noted in the *New York Times* 11 Sept. 1950). *Chandu on the Magic Island* was broadcast by KTLA on July 9, 1950 (Vernon, Terry. "Tele-Vues." *Long Beach Independent* 9 July 1950). *Phantom Ship* was broadcast over WOR on October 11, 1950 ("On Television." *New York Times* 11 Oct. 1950); on September 28, 1950, KTTV in Los Angeles also broadcast the film ("Thursday Television." *Los Angeles Times* 28 Sept. 1950). The feature-version of *Shadow of Chinatown* (it had originally been a serial) was broadcast over WPIX on July 7, 1950 ("On Television." *New York Times* 7 July 1950). *The Corpse Vanishes* was broadcast over WABD on June 7, 1950 ("On Television." *New York Times* 7 June 1950), and *The Ape Man* was seen in Los Angeles over KTLA on August 16, 1950 ("Television This Week." *Los Angeles Times* 13 Aug. 1950). [*Chandu on the Magic Isle* was a feature cut from part of a 1934 serial. *Phantom Ship* was originally titled *The Mystery of the Mary Celeste* and released in England in 1935.]

42   Audiences saw *Mysterious Mr. Wong* on March 6, 1951 on New York's WPIX ("On Television." *New York Times* 6 Mar. 1951). TV listings in the *Bridgeport Telegram* (23 Apr. 1951) report that *Return of the Ape Man* (1944) would be broadcast on April 26, 1951.

With two unknown performers, Lugosi strikes a pose similar to what he would do at many live appearances.

Chapter 14

SPIDER WEB MACHINES

Leonard "Lenny" Litman had good reason to be frantic on that midwinter day in February of 1950. At the last minute, he was desperately trying to find some props for Bela Lugosi's show at his Copa Club in downtown Pittsburgh, Pennsylvania.[1] Litman had already lined up local women to pose as "atmosphere zombies" behind Lugosi's nightclub act, but he knew that vultures and some spider webs would add the finishing touches.[2]

No doubt Litman was keenly aware of the current state of show business. In addition to the decline in movie attendance, live entertainment was also suffering. Several reasons may have been to blame, but by 1950, one of them was television. At any rate, nightclub owners had to develop fresh approaches and gimmicks to lure people out of their homes.

Born in 1914 to Eastern European immigrants, Litman had always been a showbiz survivor. He began his career as a writer, covering sports and entertainment for various newspapers in the Pittsburgh area. His story on Hoot Gibson resulted in the cowboy actor hiring him to be his promoter and press agent. After several years on the west coast, Litman eventually returned to Pittsburgh and purchased a jazz club with his brothers. In 1948, he bought the Villa Madrid Club and renamed it the Copa.[3]

Located at 818 Liberty Avenue, the Copa was directly across the street from its main competition, the Carousel Club. Officially the Copa seated 287, but occasionally Litman sneaked in extra chairs for the big acts he hired. And some of them were very big indeed, ranging from Rudy Vallee and Duke Ellington to Henny Youngman and Lili St. Cyr.[4] For Lugosi, Litman scheduled three shows nightly for six nights, as well as a Saturday afternoon matinee. That meant the possibility of 5,500 people paying to see Lugosi in less than a week's time.

Personal appearances had long been a component of Lugosi's career, whether it was taking onstage bows at film screenings or appearing side by side with city mayors and other politicians. To see Bela Lugosi in person, to see Dracula in person: here was something that thousands, perhaps millions of moviegoers in the years immediately following World War II would have wanted. And now it was more possible than ever before, with Lugosi regularly working outside of Hollywood.

Some of his alleged personal appearances may have actually been little more than publicity inventions. For example, according to the pressbook for the film *Scared to Death* (1947), Lugosi was:

> … asked by the owner of a newly discovered Indian burial ground at Paradise Cove near the famous movie beach colony of Malibu to officiate at the exhumation of many Indian skeletons. Lugosi, whose many roles in horror films seemed to fit him for this real life role, will assist the

Gary D. Rhodes | Bill Kaffenberger

From the *Pittsburgh Post-Gazette* of February 13, 1950.

students of anthropology at Santa Monica and Hollywood High Schools in their work of exhuming the centuries old Indian skeletons.

In real life Lugosi is a mild mannered man and has long shown an interest in the historical background of early America. He readily agreed to take part in the studies made available through the discovery of the Paradise Cove burial ground when requested to do so by the owner, a former motion picture theatre owner.[5]

No other information has surfaced on Lugosi's participation in this event, which may be another indication that it didn't happen.

But Lugosi did make an array of personal appearances after the war, ranging from an impromptu act with Joey Faye at the Casino in Boston in 1947 to the street fairs of New Hope, Pennsylvania in 1947 and Norwich, Connecticut in 1948.[6] Some of these appearances were informal, but still received notice in the press.

And some of these informal appearances meant good publicity. For example, in 1947, Lugosi joined Robert L. Ripley in Albany, New York aboard a Chinese junk, the *Mon Lei*. On August 8, Ripley gave his radio broadcast from the ship and held a press reception for youth reporters from the local *Albany Times-Union*. At 4:30PM, Lugosi — who was then appearing in *Arsenic and Old Lace* at Saratoga Springs — joined Ripley at a cocktail party.[7] The duo traded "believe-it-or-not" stories, with one newspaper joking that Lugosi knew some "oddities of his own – a few items communicated to him from 'another world.'"[8]

The following year, on November 4, 1948, the Lugosis were guests of honor at a buffet supper party sponsored by the Southside American Legion in Binghamton, New York.[9] Here again was a chance to sign autographs, to get free publicity, and to be associated with an important cause. Only eleven days later, Lugosi appeared at the *Night of Stars* event at Madison Square Garden in New York City. It was a special event dedicated to the new state of Israel and given in support of the United Jewish Appeal of Greater New York. Others on the bill included John Garfield, Pat O'Brien, Jane Powell, Peter Lorre, and — in what likely became his final appearance with Lugosi — Boris Karloff.[10]

On April 21, 1950, Lugosi was the "Ghost of Honor" in New York City at the annual meeting of the Mystery Writers of America. The menu included such aptly-named foods as "witches' broth soup," "bared breast of duck euthanasia," and, for dessert, "crème de la crime".[11] The evening included the presentations of annual awards (the "Edgars," named after Poe) and a stage show. Attendees urged Lugosi to give a speech, but he politely declined, asking rhetorically, "[How can] a sweet family man, a henpecked husband like me, stand up in front of these writers?"[12]

The following month, Lugosi made a similar appearance as Guest of Honor as the Gamut Club. The dinner occurred at the Old Garden in New York City on May 24, 1950. It was the club's final event of the season. Among those present were President Essex Dane and Vice-President Grant Mitchell.[13] Lugosi's attendance made the pages of the *New York Times*, and here again it's easy to imagine that he appreciated the attention.

Then, in 1951, Lugosi appeared at the fifth annual National Photographic Show in New York. Sponsored by the Photographic Manufacturers and Distributors Association, the show ran from February 22 to February 25, with other guests including Basil Rathbone, Jinx Falkenburg, Tex McCrary, Bert Lytell, Jane Pickens and Robert Merrill. In earlier years, the show focused on education, but by 1951, the emphasis had changed to entertainment. One sponsor, the DeJur-Amsco company, featured a daily night club style program.[14] Pavelle Color Laboratories (in conjunction with WCBS-TV), offered color television presentations of each day's activities.[15]

All of these various events meant publicity, a valuable commodity, particularly after the war, but many of them did not pay. Lugosi knew that he needed to monetize his live appearances, and he may have been the very person who developed the answer. In the summer of 1947, he told a journalist something that he said on numerous occasions: the old style of horror was no longer having the same effect on audiences. Lugosi explained that he still had to play Dracula seriously, or else it would become "burlesque." As soon as he made that remark, Lugosi added, "Actually, I think it might be a good idea to rewrite it as burlesque – the possibilities are infinite and it would be quite amusing."[16] Following from that basic idea, Don Marlowe tried to find bookings.

Lugosi's first paid nightclub appearance came at Tony's Chi Chi Club in Salt Lake City, where Marlowe booked him for May 17 through May 22, 1948. The actor headlined a show that also included a "band and other entertainment."[17] Advertisements recycled the image and font style from Marlowe's posters for *The Tell-Tale Heart* of 1947. One of them also featured Walter Winchell's quotation, "The most exciting performance I have ever witnessed. My spine tingled."

During his visit, Lugosi stayed at the Hotel

From the *Salt Lake Telegram* of May 21, 1948.

Gary D. Rhodes | Bill Kaffenberger

Utah.[18] Interviewed by the *Salt Lake Tribune*, he admitted that he had no great love for the Dracula character. The journalist then told readers that Lugosi was "extremely distinguished looking and hides his villanous traits beautifully."[19] Unfortunately, the Salt Lake press gave little indication of the contents of Lugosi's act, which makes it difficult to know whether it included a dramatic scene from *Dracula*, a horror-comedy routine, or – perhaps most likely – both.[20]

For his second nightclub appearance, Lugosi played the Gray Wolf Tavern of Masury, Ohio.[21] At first glance, the Gray Wolf seems to be an odd choice of venue, particularly given that it was located in a small town. But under scrutiny, the booking may have made good sense for everyone involved. Masury is centrally located between Cleveland, Youngstown, Akron, Erie, and Pittsburgh, an easy drive from each, and all of them had sizeable populations of Eastern European immigrants.

And the Gray Wolf was a large nightclub, not a small town bar. Owner Pete Myers Jr., whose own parents were Eastern European immigrants, knew that Lugosi could be a major draw.[22] The actor opened on September 20, 1948, booked for one week with two shows nightly, at 11PM and 1:15AM. That very week, a nearby theatre was playing *Abbott and Costello Meet Frankenstein* (1948). A review in the *Youngstown Vindicator* claimed:

> Bela Lugosi's appearance at Gray Wolf Tavern this week is a hair-raiser. His entertainment is quite a novelty for area niteries... you will enjoy his show... and he has some all-star acts to round out an all-around "good entertainment" program.[23]

As with the Salt Lake appearance, it is difficult to determine exactly what comprised Lugosi's show, and whether it was dramatic, comedic, or a bit of both. Mention of the other acts gives the impression it wasn't all that different from a vaudeville bill.

Regardless, the act came to an early and unexpected end when Lugosi failed to appear at the club on September 23. A disclaimer appeared in a Gray Wolf Tavern advertisement published that same day:

> We wish to apologize for not having 'Bela Lugosi' as advertised. This was due to no fault of ours. We had a contract for his appearance, but this contract was violated.[24]

No further explanation was given. Lugosi was due in Atlantic City for a vaudeville show on Saturday, September 25, 1948, and would have needed time to travel, but whether that was

From the *New Castle News* of September 20, 1948.

From the *Youngstown Vindicator* of September 20, 1948.

Lugosi at an unknown live appearance, likely in the late forties. (Courtesy of David Wentink)

the cause of his premature departure is unknown. Perhaps Lugosi was displeased with the Gray Wolf. After all, it was known for attracting seedy characters searching for poker, liquor, and women. According to one account, the management even had men stationed on the roof with guns at the ready in case trouble broke out.[25]

At any rate, nearly a year and a half later, Lenny Litman was looking for those vultures and a spider web machine. Whether or not he had heard about Lugosi's apparent contract violation at the Gray Wolf is unknown, but Litman booked the actor for his Copa Club from February 13 to 18, 1950. That very week, Dorothy Kilgallen's column announced that, "Bela Lugosi, the original celluloid bogeyman, is currently doing his Dracula act in night clubs. (That ought to kill the bar business!)."[26]

The Pittsburgh press wrongly claimed that the Copa was Lugosi's first night club show, but correctly indicated that he was interested in doing more of the same. Lugosi told one interviewer in the city, "I get a kick out of it, because people are not really scared."[27] Instead, his nightclub act blended "humor and horror."

Asked about the show many years later, Lenny Litman's widow Rosslyn remembered it well:

> By that time, we had been open two years, and every once in a while because of Leonard's experience he liked to play what we called 'freaks.' And Bela Lugosi was a freak!

We went to New York about once a month, and the agents there pushed the acts, so that's how the Lugosi show came about. Someone there pushed him.

Lugosi was a very quiet man, he did what he did, and he got paid

From the *Pittsburgh Post-Gazette* of February 17, 1950.

Gary D. Rhodes | Bill Kaffenberger

Another pose of Lugosi at the same unknown live appearance, likely in the late forties. (Courtesy of David Wentink)

on Saturday. His wife was a tall, thin woman, but she didn't talk very much. They were both quiet. He wouldn't stay in a hotel downtown, so we found a place for him in Braddock, and there were decent hotels at the time.

[In his act], he did more or less things from the movie script, recitations. He came out in full costume like in the movie. He did little things that were easy, little side remarks and things like that. 'I'm not really a scary guy,' that type of thing. He did not actually have a comic routine.

Though Lugosi's sketch was already written, Litman recalled that her husband staged the show and costumed the chorus girls as "zombies."[28]

A review published in the *Pittsburgh Post-Gazette* offers further insight into the act: "[Lugosi] does the famous scenes from *Dracula*, and to give the room the right atmosphere, Lenny Litman has decorated the Copa with bats, spider webs, coffins and all the other props out of Dracula's Castle right down to the zombies."[29] The *Pittsburgh Sun-Telegraph* added, "Lugosi will do scenes from the stage and screen versions of [*Dracula*]."[30] *The Billboard* published some information on the show as well: "Bela Lugosi broke in his new nightclub act at The Copa. He used comedienne Tiny Sinclair in his act and after his *Dracula* the two worked to good results in a nine-minute comedy stint."[31]

Fortunately, an entertainment column in the *Pittsburgh Post-Gazette* preserved other details about Lugosi's visit to the city:

Comic Bobby Fife's pretty wife [Mary Lou] is one of the atmosphere zombies in the Bela Lugosi show at the Copa.[32]

Bela Lugosi carries his own bottled drinking water with him wherever he goes. Brought gallons of the stuff here with him.[33]

A third photograph from the same uknown live appearance, likely in the late forties. (Courtesy of David Wentink)

> Bela Lugosi, looking more dude than Dracula in his camel's hair coat and cap to match, standing outside the Copa before show time signing autograph books.[34]

> Tiny Sinclair keeps right up with the news. She's working with Bela Lugosi this week and has one line which goes: 'Don't kill me Count Dracula.' The other night she got howls by adding: 'I can't afford the pallbearers.'[35]

The fact that the Pittsburgh press so closely followed Lugosi's appearance is not only a testament to their fascination with him, but also to the fact that the Copa was the city's premier nightclub.

To help publicize his show, Lugosi gave an interview to Jane Andre at radio station WWSW; Andre also interviewed singer Mindy Carson, who was headlining at the Carousel Club that week.[36] Their competing shows provided more entertainment news for the local press:

> Dracula flapped into town yesterday and skittered up and down Pittsburgh streets – but he didn't scare anyone at all. Bela Lugosi, the Batman, here for a week's horror-klatsch at the Copa, couldn't even scare meltin' Mindy Carson, syrup-voiced sweetie who'll be offering 'Candy and Cake' to the customers right across Liberty Avenue at the Carousel. Well-protected

From the *Pittsburgh Post-Gazette* of February 13, 1950.

Gary D. Rhodes | Bill Kaffenberger

"Dracula Makes Vampire Pass at Mindy [Carson]," as the *Pittsburgh Post-Gazette* of February 13, 1950 claimed.

by an entourage of six men, Miss Carson allowed Mr. Lugosi to call on her in her suite at Hotel William Penn. He clawed up his hand, lowered his eyebrows and glowered. Miss Carson laughed, then burst briefly into song as proof that Mr. Lugosi can't do away so easily with the competition from across the street.

... Anyway, it was a good try by the veteran vampire, and he was just as pleased as anyone that Miss Carson, first magnitude young singing star, escaped undimmed. He tried again, making a claw at the elevator girl in the William Penn, but she only said, 'You can't scare me, I've seen too many of your pictures.' He got some attention in the lobby and walking the streets, but not because he scared anyone. People just noticed the familiar face of the handsome man. He's over six feet tall and straight, and yesterday he wore a tan belted polo coat and cap to match.

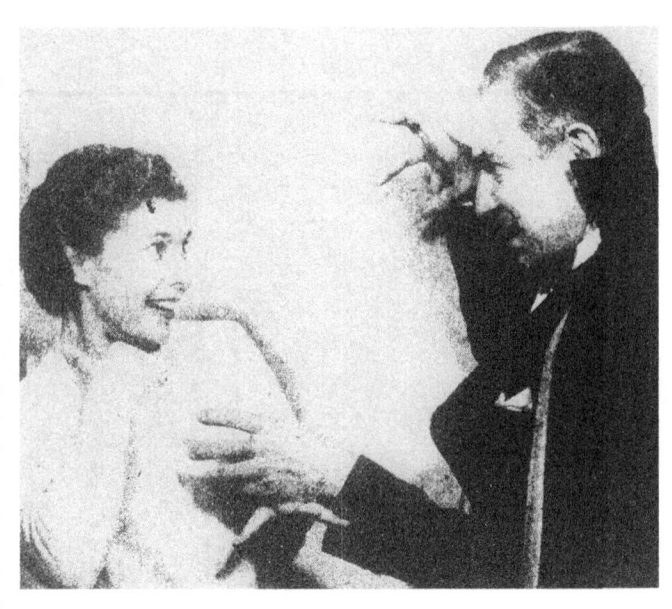

Miss Carson said it wouldn't make any difference at all in her singing to have Mr. Lugosi set up shop across the street from her. All she knows is the two places are going to be decked out differently this week. There'll be no cobwebs or coffins on the stage at the Carousel, the way Lennie [sic] Litman has those props, peopled with assorted zombies, set up in the Copa. Mr. Lugosi has been making a good thing out of scaring people for some 23 years — a year longer than Miss Carson has been kicking around this planet....[37]

The gimmick of playing Lugosi and Carson off one another worked well, as did their radio interviews, which initiated a regular feature of Andre's program.[38]

On February 28, 1950, columnist Dorothy Kilgallen wrote about Lugosi once again, claiming that he was "coming to New York with his *Dracula* nightclub act."[39] However, no details have surfaced on any other Lugosi nightclub appearances, and so Kilgallen's comment may have reflected nothing more than the actor's hope for bookings that didn't materialize.

Indeed, Pittsburgh and the Copa could have brought an end to his efforts to translate personal appearances into a salary. As Rosslyn Litman said, "After meeting him, I realized that Hollywood broke Bela Lugosi's heart. This was a very sensitive man, and he loved the fact that he was very good at what he did. The fact there was no market for it any more was very hard."[40]

(Endnotes)

1   *Pittsburgh Post-Gazette* 6 Feb. 1950.
2   *Pittsburgh Post-Gazette* 15 Feb. 1950.
3   Rawson, Christopher. "Leonard Litman, One of the Brightest Bulbs in Area Entertainment, Night Life." *Pittsbugh Post-Gazette*.com. 2 Aug. 2002. Available at: http:// www.post-gazette.com/obituaries/20020802litman5.asp. Accessed 11 Dec. 2011.

4 "Pittsburgh Music History, Managers and Promoters, Lenny Litman." 30 July 2011. Available at: https://pittsburghmusichistory/pittsburgh-music-story/managers-and-promoters/lenny-litman. Accessed 11 Dec. 2012.
5 *Scared to Death* pressbook. Screen Guild Productions, 1947.
6 For a discussion of the Casino appearance in Boston, see Chapter 3. With regard to the street fairs, see Chapters 4 (New Hope) and Chapter 7 (Norwich).
7 Leahy, Jack. "Planes and Yachts Greet Ripley Today as City's Sirens Herald Welcome." *Albany Times-Union* (Albany, NY) 8 Aug. 1947.
8 "Shiver-Giver to Trade 'Rip' Tales." *Albany Times-Union* 7 Aug. 1947.
9 *Binghamton Press* (Binghamton, NY) 6 Nov. 1948.
10 *Brooklyn Daily Eagle* 29 Oct. 1948.
11 Creagh, Ed. "No Bela Laugh as Writers Spotlight Fearsome Lugosi." *Spokane Daily Chronicle* (Spokane, WA) 21 Apr. 1950.
12 Ibid.
13 *New York Times* 23 May 1950.
14 Ibid.
15 Deschin, Jacob. "National Show, Many Staged Attractions Planned at Armory." *New York Times* 18 Feb. 1951.
16 Hughes, Elinor. "Bela Lugosi Playing First Year in Summer Stock." *Boston Herald* 24 July 1947.
17 Advertisement. *Salt Lake Tribune* 8 May 1948.
18 Lugosi, Bela. Note to Arthur Howard. 21 May 1948. [Lugosi's note mentions the Hotel Utah as the site of his meeting with Howard.]
19 *Salt Lake Tribune* 18 May 1948.
20 This comment is based on a search of the *Salt Lake Tribune*, the *Salt Lake Telegram*, and the *Desert News* (Salt Lake, UT).
21 *New Castle News* (New Castle, PA) 30 Sept. 1948.
22 "Pete Meyers, Jr." 22 July 2010. Available at: http://www.vindy.com/news/tributes/2010/jun/24/pete-meyers-j/guestbook/. Accessed 30 July 2011.
23 Auble, John, Jr. "Bright Lights." *Youngstown Vindicator* (Youngstown, OH) 23 Sept. 1948.
24 Advertisement. *Youngstown Vindicator* 23 Sept. 1948.
25 Mercer County Genealogy Society. Email to Gary D. Rhodes. 17 Nov. 2011.
26 Kilgallen, Dorothy. "Voice of Broadway." *Trenton Evening Times* (Trenton, NJ) 15 Feb. 1950.
27 *Pittsburgh Post-Gazette* 13 Feb. 1950.
28 Rhodes, Gary D. Interview with Rosslyn Litman. 5 Nov. 2011.
29 *Pittsburgh Post-Gazette* 13 Feb. 1950.
30 Mendlowitz, Leonard. "Mystery Shows in Two Clubs." *Pittsburgh Sun-Telegraph* 12 Feb. 1950.
31 "In Short." *The Billboard* 11 Mar. 1950.
32 Cohen, Harold V. "The Drama Desk." *Pittsburgh Post-Gazette* 15 Feb. 1950.
33 Cohen, Harold V. "The Drama Desk." *Pittsburgh Post-Gazette* 18 Feb. 1950.
34 Ibid.
35 Ibid.
36 "Vox Jox." *The Billboard* 25 Mar. 1950.
37 *Pittsburgh Post-Gazette* 13 Feb. 1950.
38 "Vox Jox."
39 Kilgallen, Dorothy. "Dorothy Kilgallen." *Lowell Sun* (Lowell, MA) 28 Feb. 1950.
40 Rhodes, interview with Litman.

Lugosi in a publicity portrait circulated during the late forties.

Chapter 15
FELLOW TRAVELERS

It followed scenes depicting Nazis and the League of Nations and a Polish synagogue. It followed *The Dead City*, an overture composed and conducted by Erich Wolfgang Korngold. And it followed sequences entitled *The Trial* and *Concentration Camp*. In some ways, it was as if the entire play was building towards *Hospital at Vienna*, a scene featuring Bela Lugosi as "Dr. Cohan."

Paul Gordon's elaborate production of William A. Drake's play *That We May Live* premiered on December 17, 1946 at the 6,442-seat Shrine Auditorium in Los Angeles. The first night sold out rapidly, with many would-be theatregoers left to wait until the next evening to see the second and final performance of a show staged in support of the Palestinian Emergency Fund.

Daily Variety told readers that the "dramatic pitch" of the show was "not too forceful"; some of its effect was lost due to "uneven conception."[1] Surviving copies of the script – which reveal that an Etienne ballet occurred in between the music and dramatic scenes – suggests how true that might have been. Broken up by various interludes, *That We May Live* attempted to tell the story of Mendel Singer, a Jewish teacher in Poland who tries to flee from the Nazis and find a home in Palestine.

The trade also complained that the narration was "disjointed," which may have been the result of Drake's decision to use multiple narrators, male and female. Nevertheless, some of their dialogue is quite compelling, at least as written on paper. One announces: "I haunt the empty ghettos of Hungary and Romania. I stalk the lonely graveyard that once was Europe." Another declares, "My name is the name of the Jewish Dead; therefore, my name is Legion." Later, a female voice proclaims: "Thy dead shall live... They shall arise!"[2]

Unlike newspaper advertisements that gave him sixth billing, Lugosi's name appeared third on the playbill, just under Jan Kiepura and Marta Eggerth and just above Howard da Silva. The playbill incorrectly spelled his name as "Bella," and likely his character name was really meant to be "Cohen," rather than "Cohan." Indeed, the Palestinian Emergency Fund was working in support of a Jewish state in the Middle East.

Overall, *Daily Variety* dismissed the production as a "flabby offering" even if it was a "noble one." Whatever the actual merits of *That We May Live*, Lugosi clearly believed in the cause. Some months later, *Daily Variety* published a nonfiction letter entitled *A Call to Action*, which also lobbied for a Jewish state. Lugosi was one of the 236 signatories, with others including a number of his old coworkers: Ralph Bellamy, Jean Hersholt, Victor Jory, Sol Lesser, Arthur Lubin, and Jean Parker.[3]

Lugosi relied on his acting ability to promote political causes on numerous other occasions, including in November 1947, when he appeared at the Hunter College Auditorium in New York City in

Photo of Lugosi from a Hungarian publication, taken during the formative years of his political ideology.

a show called *Continental Varieties*. Others on the bill included actress Ella Flesch, opera singer Deszö Ernster, pianist Miklos Schwalb, and dance impresario Paul Szilard. In this case, the performers raised money on behalf of "needy Budapest actors and artists" who were affected by the war.[4]

Some of Lugosi's causes were quite heroic, just as some of his film roles represented the real-life villains whom he despised. For example, he played Nazis in *Black Dragons* (1942) and *Ghosts on the Loose* (1943). In both cases, his characters fail in their quest to undermine America, something that audiences appreciated both when they saw the films on their original releases and when theatres screened them again in the late forties.

Of all of the Lugosi films reissued in the late forties, none drew more attention than *Ninotchka*, a 1939 MGM film that starred Greta Garbo and Melvyn Douglas. In fact, while New York critics had a general policy of not reviewing film reissues, John Maynard of the *Journal-American* broke with that tradition to critique *Ninotchka* in 1947.[5]

One reason was that Maynard and many others saw *Ninotchka* as particularly relevant in the post-war era. The storyline tackles Communism in a sophisticated and lighthearted manner. But in it, Lugosi played a serious role as a Communist official, appearing in a scene with Garbo that makes no effort to inspire laughter. And by 1947, his character may have seemed as villainous to some audiences as the Nazis he had once portrayed.

Unfortunately for Lugosi, there were at least a few persons in post-war America who believed he really *was* a Communist villain, not because of his appearance in *Ninotchka*, but instead because of his personal politics. This leads to the inevitable question as to how his personal views and political activism may or may not have affected his career, particularly given such high-profile cases as the "Hollywood Ten."

During Lugosi's life in Hungary, it does seem clear that he was a Communist, certainly as of the autumn of 1918. By the end of that year, he was one of nine core members of a "National Union of Theatre Employees." Then, within ten days of Béla Kun's Communist government taking power in Hungary, Lugosi was asked to be a member of the new government, charged with the "Communization" of the country's theatres.[6] But Kun abdicated after only 133 days, with Miklós Horthy's right wing conservative government seizing power. While Horthy's brigands spread "White Terror" throughout Budapest, Lugosi left the country. Had Lugosi remained, he would likely have faced imprisonment or even the possibility of being hanged.

Lugosi's published writing of the era reveals him to be an idealist, sharing a philosophy that many held in Europe following the end of World War I. Having fought in the war, Lugosi realized firsthand

Lugosi's application to become a member of the Screen Actors Guild.

the kind of devastation that prior governments had wrought. He likely viewed Communism as the road to a better life for his homeland and, by extension, himself.

Once settled in America, however, Lugosi was intelligent enough to obscure his connection to Kun's regime. He was aware of the Red Scare that spread across America after the Russian revolution of 1917, as well as the kind of general xenophobia that would lead to the executions of Sacco and Vanzetti. And so Lugosi regularly rewrote his past, often maintaining that his governmental ties had occurred during Count Mihály (Michael) Károlyi's regime, a brief government that preceded Kun's. Lugosi truly had been and would always remain a Károlyi supporter, but he cleverly used that fact to distance himself from Kun, so much so that, by 1950, he falsely claimed that he had been a "political refugee fleeing from the Reds."[7]

During the first two decades of his life in America, Lugosi avoided any active role in politics, a choice probably based on his negative experience in Hungary. He proudly became an American citizen in 1931, with one fan magazine declaring that, "Bela Lugosi of Lugos [Hungary] has become Lugosi of America — with a knowledge of American history and laws that would quite surprise the average native."[8]

Very quickly he found value in the protections afforded by his citizenship. In 1932, the US Congress considered placing a ban on "foreign" actors appearing in American-made films. Lugosi's name ap-

> If you are interested in the work of the
> **HUNGARIAN AMERICAN COUNCIL for DEMOCRACY**
> Come to the Meeting March 18, 1944, at 8:00 P. M.
> Redman Hall, San Francisco
>
> International Pres.   National Pres.   Local Pres.
> **COUNT MIHALY KAROLY**   **BELA LUGOSI**   **M. SIBAK**

Publicity for an HACD event of 1944.

peared in a lengthy list of "outstanding" Hollywood stars in jeopardy, others including Boris Karloff, Greta Garbo, Marlene Dietrich, and Charlie Chaplin.[9] In the end, nothing came of that Congressional effort. But even if it had succeeded, Lugosi would probably not have faced any real problems. After all, he was legally an American.

Lugosi did support a labor union during the Great Depression. He was one of the earliest members of the Screen Actors Guild, joining in July 1933 and becoming Member Number 28. He successfully ran for membership on SAG's Advisory Board in 1934, and he lobbied strongly for the better treatment of freelance actors in Hollywood, a situation in which he would find himself more than once, including in the post-World War II era.[10]

It would not be until 1940 that Lugosi became actively involved in American politics, becoming the key signatory on a letter to US Representative Martin Dies' House Committee on Un-American Activities (HUAC). The letter pledged the support of various Hungarian-American groups to the US government and made clear that they had no sympathy for the Horthy regime, which was not only still in power in Hungary, but which had also aligned itself with the Axis Powers.[11]

The situation was not an easy one for thousands of Hungarian-Americans who supported their homeland, but who disdained the Nazis. After all, some Hungarian-American organizations were quite conservative, while others were quite liberal. And even then, factions existed in both of those two categories, with infighting being common.[12] It was into this dynamic that Lugosi became increasingly vocal in November 1942, when he openly praised a United Nations effort on behalf of Hungary, as well as in the Spring of 1943, when he contributed a series of articles to the leftist publication *Magyar Jovo*.[13]

Of all of the Hungarian-American organizations, one of the most notable during World War II became the Hungarian-American Council for Democracy (HACD), its very name suggesting a patriotic and pro-American stance. The HACD emerged in Chicago in 1942 out of two prior groups, but did not hold its first convention until June 1943. At that time, Bela Lugosi became its first national President, having competed for the position with artist László Moholy-Nagy.[14] At Lugosi's urging, the HACD named Count Mihály Károlyi as its "honorary president."[15]

It is difficult to determine the HACD's membership numbers; they may have been quite small. However, it is clear that the organization developed chapters in a number of cities, including Los Angeles, where Melchior Lengyel, author of *Ninotchka* (1939), served as branch president. One of that branch's two vice-presidents was Stephen Arch, Bela Lugosi's father-in-law.[16]

Though Dr. Mózes (Moses) Simon served as the Executive Secretary and oversaw the HACD's daily operations, there can be no doubt that Lugosi was heavily involved in the organization. He was not simply a figurehead, as his correspondence during the period clearly reveals. And he assumed his role with great interest, appearing at various live events. He rallied against Miklós Horthy and for the plight of Jews in Hungary, worthwhile causes that were certainly not anti-American. Quite the contrary.[17]

On May 4, 1944, Lugosi gave an interview to Santiago Grevi on the Brooklyn-based radio show *Voice of Fighting Spain*, which was affiliated with the Institute for International Democracy (an organization later suspected of having Communist ties), and with the Citizens Victory Committee for Harry Bridges (a support group for the noted Communist who was threatened with deportation). A newspaper column promised that Lugosi would not "crawl up the walls … like Dracula," but did not describe what topics he would actually discuss.[18] It seems likely that he was asked to appear in his capacity as President of the HACD. Promoting their ideals to the general public was an important component of his position.

Lugosi also maintained regular touch with key figures in the anti-Horthy cause, including Count Károlyi. For example, in June 1943, Károlyi wrote to Lugosi a "highly confidential" letter in the Hungarian language, but one that contains nothing subversive or questionable. Rather, he told Lugosi:

> Our movement's main difficulty is funds. We are in a very difficult financial situation. Would there be a possibility of some fundraising? In these very crucial times we cannot be left without money. We cannot even publish a book. There are so many rich Hungarians in the US. They should be able to donate something. Your recent influential propaganda might be able to get to them.

This HACD letter written by Mózes Simon exemplifies the work that the organization tried to undertake.

> … I would very much appreciate if you could make it clear in your propaganda that there is nothing more dangerous for Hungary's future than, a so-called peaceful solution [meaning an "acceptance of the Horthy system"]. That is why I am a supporter of a firm action. One has to be courageous and suffer the consequences of an aggressive resistance. Everyone who accepts this and takes on the fight is making a sacrifice for a better future in Hungary.

> … It is not enough proof that we have sided with the Allied Forces; we have to prove that we are

STANDARD FORM NO. 64

Office Memorandum · UNITED STATES GOVERNMENT

TO: J. Edgar Hoover, Director
Federal Bureau of Investigation

FROM: ~~[redacted]~~

SUBJECT: Immigration and Naturalization Service
Deportable Aliens

56204/104
DATE: September 21, 1948

Supplementing my memorandum to you of August 13, 1948, relative to the above-named subject and file number, you are advised that this Service has under investigation the case of the following-named naturalized citizen whose naturalization may be subject to cancellation or revocation:

NAME: BELA LUGOSI

LAST KNOWN RESIDENCE: To be obtained by local Federal Bureau of Investigation office from local Immigration and Naturalization Service office.

CENTRAL OFFICE FILE NO: C-3448726

DISTRICT OFFICE FILE NO: 246-P-33491 – Los Angeles, California

F.B.I. FILE NO: Unknown

STATUS OF CASE: Investigation pending

RECORDED - 99

From the FBI's file on Bela Lugosi

completely detached from the Germans and the only way to do that is by Caesarean section.[19]

While Károlyi was clearly trying to position himself as the leader of the anti-Horthy forces, his communication indicates a dedication to defeating the Axis Powers and a sincere belief (or at least the hope) that Lugosi could help.

All that said, Lugosi failed in two of his key HACD objectives. The HACD could not persuade the State Department to issue a visa for Count Károlyi to visit to the United States.[20] He was also unable to lobby other key Hungarian-American organizations to join forces with the HACD. For example, in July 1943, Lugosi proved unsuccessful in his attempt to join forces with the conservative Professor Oscar Jászi:

> … we are determined to help and make all anti-Nazi, anti-Hitler and anti-Horthy supporters stronger and start building a democratic Hungary. This, respected Professor, cannot be achieved with isolation and meetings behind closed doors. It can be achieved with communicating with the masses and organizing marches.
>
> If, dear Professor, you do not know many of the council members it does not necessarily mean that their honesty and determination should be questioned. I believe we should find a way for you and the DMASZ [The American Hungarian Democratic Association Committee] to meet our council members and help any new members so that all Hungarian-Americans would be guided under the same democratic agenda.
>
> I believe that the unification of the Council and the DMASZ would help us achieve a united popular front and balance in which the DMASZ would definitely not lose anything. You would bring an excellent intellectual force, and we, in return, could line up the democratic masses you otherwise could not reach. We would definitely become stronger in this union and you would cease to be a minority group and become a joint leader of masses who would follow your leadership.[21]

Count Károlyi had asked Lugosi to bring the various factions together, and the fact Lugosi followed through on the suggestion indicates that he was hardly tethered to any narrow agenda. After all, Jászi was quite conservative, but Lugosi was quite ready to work with him on a "democratic agenda."

Indeed, Lugosi's motives in all of his surviving correspondence and writing reveal a man who was loyal to the United States and who was undertaking a sincere effort to rid his homeland of Miklós Horthy. Though he remained very definitely left wing in his political outlook, he was not particularly strident or doctrinaire. Furthermore, even in "confidential" letters written in Hungarian, Lugosi promoted democratic values, not Communism.

However, that may not have always been true of some HACD members. Mózes Simon's possible Communist affiliations meant that the US government began watching both the organization and Lugosi. For example, the Office of Strategic Services (OSS), the forerunner of the CIA, kept a file on the HACD, which became known in intelligence circles as the "Dracula Council."

The OSS heard allegations that Lugosi had "openly" been a member of the Communist party in Hungary, but came to the conclusion that he had been "politically inactive" in America until assuming leadership of the HACD in 1943. They also knew he was in touch with Károlyi and seem to have monitored their correspondence. However, the OSS was much more concerned with other HACD members like Simon.[22] And so their investigation of Lugosi yielded nothing damning.

The HACD — with Mózes Simon still in charge of day-to-day operations — continued its efforts during most of 1946. Lugosi's name remained on its letterhead, though that may have been little more than the continued use of old stationery.[23] Lugosi claimed to have left the organization in March 1945, though his actual date of departure remains in dispute, as he does seem to have been involved until July 1945. He also said that he asked the FBI investigate the HACD at some point in 1945, which is in fact

Lugosi in the late forties.

possible, though no evidence has yet surfaced to substantiate that claim.

What is certain is that, shortly after Lugosi became president of the HACD, two different informants told the FBI that he had been a Communist in Hungary. But the FBI did not conduct a formal investigation because they learned that Lugosi had never been a member of the Communist Party in America. By contrast, he was a registered Democrat and an avowed supporter of President Franklin D. Roosevelt.

That hardly kept J. Edgar Hoover from signing a letter to the Los Angeles FBI field office the following year in which he asked for assistance "in conducting an investigation concerning [Lugosi's] activities."[24] But once again, the inquiry found nothing of substance, as can be noted in a 1947 communication from the FBI to the Immigration and Naturalization Service, which was then considering the revocation of Lugosi's citizenship based upon allegations that he was a "Hungarian Communist."[25]

After a search of their records, the FBI was unable to tell Immigration anything other than a few brief and unsubstantiated allegations. They noted that Lugosi was head of the HACD, a possible Communist-front organization, adding that his father-in-law was involved in similar activities. The FBI referred to his 1943 articles in *Magyar Jovo*, and the fact he had signed a petition to prevent the deportation of Harry Bridges. The FBI also mentioned allegations that Lugosi had been a member of the Communist Party in Hungary. That was really it, save for a comment from an informant who alleged that Lugosi was "intoxicated most of the time."[8]

But this raw data meant little. Quite a few persons had supported Bridges' right to remain in the United States, and Lugosi's articles for *Magyar Jovo* were not Communist propaganda. And so three years after J. Edgar Hoover's initial decision to investigate Lugosi, nothing particularly problematic had surfaced. There was no evidence of anything. In fact, it was the lack of evidence that became compelling. As the FBI had learned when they first turned their attentions to Lugosi, he had never been a member of the Communist Party in America, nor had he actively supported it.

After closing their investigation due to "insufficient evidence," Immigration and Naturalization returned to the topic of Lugosi in September 1948, contacting J. Edgar Hoover once again. The timing of their renewed interest did not occur by mistake. On September 21, 1948, the very day that they wrote to the FBI, the US Civil Service Commission issued a press release citing the HACD as having been a "subversive" organization. Again, though, nothing damning surfaced. There was no new evidence on Lugosi whatsoever. By contrast, it seems that Mózes Simon — who had left America for Hungary sometime in late 1946 or shortly thereafter — was the one with a questionable history. After returning to Budapest, Simon received an important position in the Communist government, but for reasons unknown he was eventually imprisoned. More than anyone else, Simon was likely the reason for the HACD's "subversive" label.

Why then would such offices have continued to be interested in Lugosi after years of monitoring him resulted in essentially nothing? The key reason was his fame. The simple reality was that the FBI (and the Immigration and Naturalization Service) kept files on many other entertainers and film stars, some of whom they watched far more closely than Lugosi. For example, Peter Lorre's FBI file was much more extensive than Lugosi's. And the FBI kept files on some other persons associated with the horror film as well, including Vincent Price and Val Lewton.

FBI investigations during the post-war period were routine, particularly when allegations against people surfaced, even if those allegations were unfounded and/or put forward by their enemies. For example, in April of 1946, columnist George E. Sokolsky noted that someone in the US government recommended that the American Hungarian Relief organization join forces with the HACD in order to provide aid to Hungarians abroad. Sokolsky believed that such advice was terrible, as it was an effort to force Hungarians to work with those that they perceived "to be Communists or who they fear have Communist associations."[26]

Lugosi's worst moment probably came at a 1949 hearing of the Senate Subcommittee on Immigration and Naturalization, when undercover FBI agent John J. Huber named Lugosi as having contributed services to the "Communist front."[27] The Reverend Steven E. Balogh identified him as a member of the "Communist movement," as did Paul Nadanyi.[28] And the Reverend George E. K. Borshy gave similar testimony, speaking about Lugosi in particularly negative terms.[29]

Borshy, who didn't actually know Lugosi, was the most damning of the group; he even read from an article in a Hungarian Catholic church weekly:

> Thus the chairman of the so-called Hungarian-American Democratic Council, Dracula Lugosi is proven by a Budapest paper that he is not democratic but extreme leftist, that is, Communist–as we always knew it.[30]

The article's complete text was entered into the Senate Subcommittee record as "Borshy Exhibit 3."[31]

Perhaps Borshy and the others believed everything they said and that it was their patriotic duty to inform the Senate of what they knew, even though they knew nothing about Lugosi other than a few unsubstantiated rumors. It is also important to note that much hatred existed between left-wing and right-wing Hungarian activists in America. And in the political climate that existed after World War II, it was quite easy for the former to blacken the names of the latter.[32] After all, the article that Borshy read at the Senate happily (and problematically) conflates being "leftist" with being "Communist."

The national press generally ignored the accusations against Lugosi. In December 1949, the *Chicago Tribune* ran the words of the same John J. Huber who testified before that Senate Subcommittee. He named Lugosi as one of a group of "show people who have been connected with fronts or who have contributed their services to the Communist front."[33] But this kind of negative publicity was extremely rare. It certainly didn't penetrate the mainstream media in any major way.

In the end, the Senate testimony amounted to little more than a few baseless allegations. Reading Borshy's testimony reveals someone who was very quick to use the word "Communist" against any person, organization, or publication with which he did not agree. By contrast, one other person who testified at the same hearings openly praised Lugosi for being a "wonderful man," a description that did not bring any rebuke or question from the Senate Subcommittee.[34]

It is also telling that the Senate Subcommittee never requested that Lugosi appear. Nor did HUAC. It also seems apparent that no one in the film industry made accusations against Lugosi. Outside of Huber, a few conservative Hungarians, and a few unnamed informants (who were likely those very same conservative Hungarians), no one accused Lugosi of anything.

But Lugosi's connection to the HACD was hardly helpful after the organization was labelled subversive. For example, when Lugosi was scheduled to speak at a New Jersey reception in 1950, Congressman C. R. Howell contacted the FBI to determine whether or not Lugosi was himself subversive.[35] The FBI does not seem to have responded in the affirmative.

Lugosi was probably unaware of the degree to which people like Howell or government agencies were keeping tabs on him. Immigration and Naturalization knew that he wrote to Count Károlyi as late as 1949, for example.[36] But Lugosi knew about Borshy, and likely grew tired of their smears. Indeed, he wrote a letter to Laszlo Dienes, editor of the publication *California Hungarians*, dated December 27, 1950:

> I herewith emphatically say–I AM NOT NOW, NOR HAVE I EVER BEEN A MEMBER OF THE COMMUNIST PARTY. I HAVE NEVER ATTENDED ANY COMMUNIST MEETINGS–I HAVE NEVER ENTERTAINED AT ANY COMMUNIST GATHERING–I HAVE NEVER DONATED ONE CENT TO ANY COMMUNIST CAUSE.[37]

Here Lugosi was telling the truth, at least so far as his life in America was concerned. Even if a few HACD members were Red, others were not. Lugosi was not. He had never been a member of the Communist Party in America.

Ballyhoo for a 1949 revival double bill of *Spooks Run Wild* (1941) and *Ghosts on the Loose* (1943) at the Gopher Theatre in Minneapolis.

And so the Immigration and Naturalization Service never revoked Lugosi's citizenship for the same reason that the FBI's file on Lugosi is rather brief. What was the reason? "Insufficient evidence." A few allegations – whether made secretly to the FBI or openly at the US Senate – were not enough to revoke his citizenship. Such allegations might have been enough for the FBI and Immigration to keep files on Lugosi, but for them such data collection was standard practice. They kept files on a large number of stars, including many who were never blacklisted.

Indeed, Bela Lugosi was *not* blacklisted in Hollywood. On that point, there can be absolutely no doubt. His appearance in *Abbott and Costello Meet Frankenstein* (1948) is a key piece of evidence. To consider even the possibility of Lugosi being blacklisted, it would have necessarily followed the production of that major film. But Lugosi being blacklisted in 1949 seems impossible to believe as well, as the William Morris Agency involved Lugosi in an important TV production that year. In fact, William Morris signed Lugosi to a representation contract in November of that year, a decision made *after* Borshy and the others had testified at the Senate Subcommittee. The most famous of all Hollywood agencies would never have done either if there been any real taint to Lugosi's name or if there was any real effort to blacklist him.

So any Hollywood blacklisting would have necessarily occurred after 1949, but that is not possible either, specifically due to Lugosi's work in film and television in the early and mid-1950s. Had he ever been blacklisted, for example, Jack Broder would never have built an entire film around him, *Bela Lugosi Meets a Brooklyn Gorilla* (1952), particularly at a moment when Broder was generating millions of dollars from reissuing old movies. Lugosi would not have appeared on major television programs like *The Red Skelton Show* in June 1954. And, importantly, United Artists would never have allowed Lugosi to be cast in *The Black Sleep* (1956). For those actors who actually were blacklisted, it took *many* years to return to Hollywood filmmaking, if *ever*. They certainly were not costarring in American films as early as 1956. Consider for example Howard da Silva, with whom Lugosi had appeared in *That We May Live*. He was blacklisted, which left him unable to find work in any film until 1962.

By contrast, Bela Lugosi was *never* blacklisted. To suggest that he was makes for a seductively simple and easy explanation for what were complicated career problems, but such an argument crumbles under the slightest scrutiny. Instead, the very same problems that plagued his film career from 1945 to 1947 — meaning a few years prior to the production of *Abbott and Costello Meet Frankenstein* – continued to do so in the years that followed. And the same kinds of problems affected many other persons in Hollywood, including some who had been affiliated with the horror film.

Writing in 1949 about the general slump in movie attendance, columnist Wood Soanes noted:

> It wasn't so long ago, for instance, that the screen writers [sic] seemed chiefly concerned with an attempt to frighten audiences to death.
>
> ... Some of the horror pictures were quite good, to be sure, but it wasn't long before the hack writers were turning them out by the gross and the quality disappeared. Today Karloff is back in New York as a stage and radio actor; Lugosi has disappeared from the scene; Lorre sought relief from his creditors in the bankruptcy court recently; and Chaney is making only infrequent appearances as the Wolf Man or the Dog Faced Boy or such like. The audience for horror pictures has disappeared, sure death for any trend.[38]

The same trend had affected all of the horror film stars, at least to some degree and it was in fact part of the larger problem that Hollywood experienced in the years after 1946.

And so, for reasons that had nothing to do with politics, Lugosi had to continue his quest to find work outside of California, just as so many actors had to do after the end of World War II.

(Endnotes)

1. *Daily Variety* 18 Dec. 1946.
2. Two drafts of the original script and other ephemera (including a playbill) exist in the William A. Drake Papers, ca. 1915-1946, Collection 289 in the UCLA Library Special Collections.
3. *Daily Variety* 17 Mar. 1947.
4. "Opera and Concert Programs of the Week." *New York Times* 9 Nov. 1947.
5. "*Ninotchka* Timely Re-Issue Applauded for Red Ribbing." *Hollywood Reporter* 26 Jan. 1948.
6. "Lugosi Béla Feladata." *Színházi Élet* 30 Mar. 1919.
7. Upchurch, C. Winn. "Lugosi Assails Crime Comics, Radio Dramas." *The Independent* (St. Petersburg, FL) 16 Mar. 1950.
8. Sinclair, John. "Master of Horrors!" *Screenland* (Jan. 1932).
9. "Hollywood Panic Stricken at Possibility of Congress Placing Ban on Foreign Stars." *Sheboygan Press* (Sheboygan, WI) 29 Feb. 1932.
10. See, for example: Thompson, Kenneth, SAG Executive Secretary. Letter to Bela Lugosi. 17 Mar. 1938.
11. "Dies Called Publicity Seeker in Oral Blast by Dickstein." *Los Angeles Times* 29 Nov. 1940.
12. See, for example: Várdy, Steven Béla. "Hungarian Americans during World War II: Their Role in Defending Hungary's Interests." *Ideology, Politics and Diplomacy in East Central Europe*. Ed. by M. B. B. Biskupski (Rochester, NY: Univ. of Rochester Press, 2003).
13. "International Group Maps Germany Future." *Los Angeles Times* 26 Nov. 1942.
14. Lyons, Leonard. "Heard in New York." *Dallas Morning News* 9 July 1943.
15. Dreisziger, N. F. "Emigré Artists and Wartime Politics, 1939-1945." *Hungarian Studies Review* 1-2 (Spring-Fall, 1995).
16. "Hungarian Council Unit Formed Here." *Los Angeles Times* 20 Dec. 1943.
17. For an extensive account of the HACD's history, see Gary D. Rhodes' *Bela Lugosi: Dreams and Nightmares* (Narberth, PA: Collectables, 2007).
18. Juengst, William. "Radio." *Brooklyn Eagle* 4 May 1944.
19. Károlyi, Count Míhaly. Letter to Bela Lugosi. 25 June 1943.
20. Dreisziger, "Emigré Artists and Wartime Politics, 1939-1945."
21. Lugosi, Bela. Letter to Professor Oscar Jászi. 21 July 1943.
22. For an extensive account of these OSS files, see *Ibid*.
23. A letter from Mózes Simon to Alfred A. Knopf, Inc. exists at the Harry Ransom Center at the University of Texas at Austin. Dated 31 Oct. 1946, Simon wrote it on HACD stationery that featured Lugosi's name as President.
24. Hoover, J. Edgar. Letter to the Special Agent in Charge, FBI Field Office of Los Angeles. 5 Sept. 1944. [A copy of this letter is reprinted in Rhodes' *Bela Lugosi: Dreams and Nightmares*.]

25 FBI response to the Immigration and Naturalization Service, dated 2 Dec. 1947.
26 Sokolsky, George E. "These Days." *Kingston Daily Freeman* (Kingston, NY) 2 Apr. 1946.
27 *Communist Activities Among Aliens and National Groups. Hearings before the Subcommittee on Immigration and Naturalization of the Committee on the "Judiciary of the United States Senate. Eighty-First Congress. First Session on S.1832, a Bill to Amend the Immigration Act of 16 Oct. 1918, as Amended*. Washington: Government Printing Office, 1950.
28 *Ibid.*
29 *Ibid.*
30 *Ibid.* [The article was printed in the 28 Jan. 1949 issue of the *Magyarok Varsarnapja*; the Budapest article to which it referred was published in the December issue of the *Budapest Kisujag*.]
31 *Ibid.*
32 Várdy, "Hungarian Americans During World War II."
33 Moore, William. "Tells How Reds Used Girls to Lure GIs in War." *Chicago Daily Tribune* 21 Dec. 1949.
34 *Ibid.*
35 Belmont, A. H. Office Memorandum to Mr. Ladd. 20 Dec. 1950. [Contained in Lugosi's FBI file. In response to Congressman Howell, the FBI stated that, given the confidential nature of their files, they were unable to furnish him with any information.]
36 Bela Lugosi file, US Immigration and Naturalization Service.
37 Qtd. in Robert Cremer's *Lugosi: The Man Behind the Cape* (New York: Henry Regnery, 1976). [The Hungarian name of *California Hungarians* was the *Californiai Magyarság*.]
38 Soanes, Wood. "Soanes' Curtain Calls." *Oakland Tribune* 10 July 1949.

Lugosi as Dracula in the late forties. (Courtesy of George R. Snell)

Chapter 16

DRACULA'S END

Summer came early for Bela Lugosi in 1950. Two wealthy, young siblings in St. Petersburg, Florida had recently formed a new straw hat company. The brother wanted to be a producer and director; the sister dreamed of becoming a publicist. Though they don't seem to have known much about the theatre, they planned a fourteen-week season of winter stock, booking a number of notable plays and stars, including the venerable Edward Everett Horton in his warhorse *Springtime for Henry*.[1]

The St. Petersburg Players inaugurated their season shortly after the New Year, operating a company of actors who were cast almost entirely out of New York. Local talent appeared in only very minor roles. Though the brother-and-sister team may have had money, they held it close to their hearts. The plays were staged at the South Side Junior High auditorium, and no professional photographer was hired to snap pictures.

Constance Kelly, one member of the company, later recalled, "Little did we know, those of us from New York, that these people didn't know a thing. They were so unequipped to be producers. The young man was going to be a producer and director, and his sister was arrogant, a tough, know-it-all cookie. Anyhow ... there was no real decent housing provided. They had arranged for us to be in an old building that had been abandoned by the army. There was like one bed in it. According to our equity contracts, we could either have them supply housing, or we would go out and find our own. We said, 'Just pay up!'"[2]

The St. Petersburg Players ended their season with *Dracula–The Vampire Play*, starring Lugosi in the title role. While the William Morris Agency was handling Lugosi's film career, Don Marlowe was apparently still acting as Lugosi's manager in late 1949 and early 1950, and so he probably made the arrangements in coordination with a theatrical representative of the Lyman Brown variety.

At any rate, this was the first time that Lugosi appeared in the full-length play since the summer of 1948. Opening night was Monday, March 20, 1950. The show ran through Saturday, March 25, with performances staged each evening, as well as matinees on Wednesday and Saturday. Advertisements promoted *Dracula* as "the most thrilling mystery play ever written."

Lugosi and his wife Lillian — who were living in Greenwich Village at the time — drove to Florida, arriving several days before the play opened. The two stayed at the Tides Hotel, a large resort at Redington Beach. The brother-and-sister team probably selected the hotel, as they had earlier booked the same lodging for Edward Everett Horton. Despite his early arrival, Lugosi did only one rehearsal with the cast, though he watched his co-actors run through the play using a Dracula stand-in.[3]

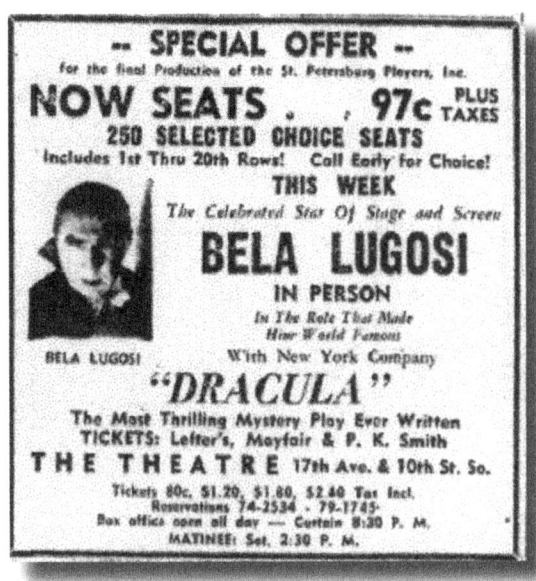

A local journalist interviewed Lugosi, finding him "modestly dressed" in "white sport shoes and sporting a bow tie." Speaking of his role as Dracula, Lugosi told the journalist that he wore no special makeup. "I just mug the part," he said, adding that he didn't really think of his screen performances as horror roles. "I just make funny faces," he said.[4] With regard to the fact that he was not under contract to any studio, Lugosi tried to make the situation sound as good as he could, claiming that freelancing allowed him to select his own roles.

The St. Petersburg *Independent* noted that Lillian was Lugosi's manager, though cast member Fred Scollay (who played Butterworth) remembered that someone had arrived ahead of the Lugosis acting in much the same capacity. That person may well have been Don Marlowe.[5] At any rate, Lillian became crucial to this version of the play, particularly after Lugosi grew concerned about the producers.

As Constance Kelly (who played Miss Wells, the maid) recalled, "The ineptitude of the producers. They had money to spend, but didn't know what to do. Lugosi's wife *did* know, though. She knew about everything in *Dracula*, including the sound effects, which are so important in the play. She took over and directed all the sound and everything. She knew we didn't have anybody competent. The actors knew, but we weren't about lift a finger to help these people."[6]

From the *St. Petersburg Times* of March 23, 1950.

Though Lugosi had little confidence in the producers, he enjoyed working with the cast. Fred Scollay recalled that Lugosi:

> ... was a funny guy, with a good sense of humor. He very seldom got moved or upset, until he got on stage and then he became an animal, playing *Dracula* to perfection. He was very serious about *Dracula*. That was his livelihood; there was no fooling around with that.
>
> I had this guy with me, a dear friend named Bob Blair who had been a sea captain. He knew nothing of show business, but when he heard I was heading to Florida, he said 'I'll go with you.' He and I built the sets for *Dracula* and that was how he got to

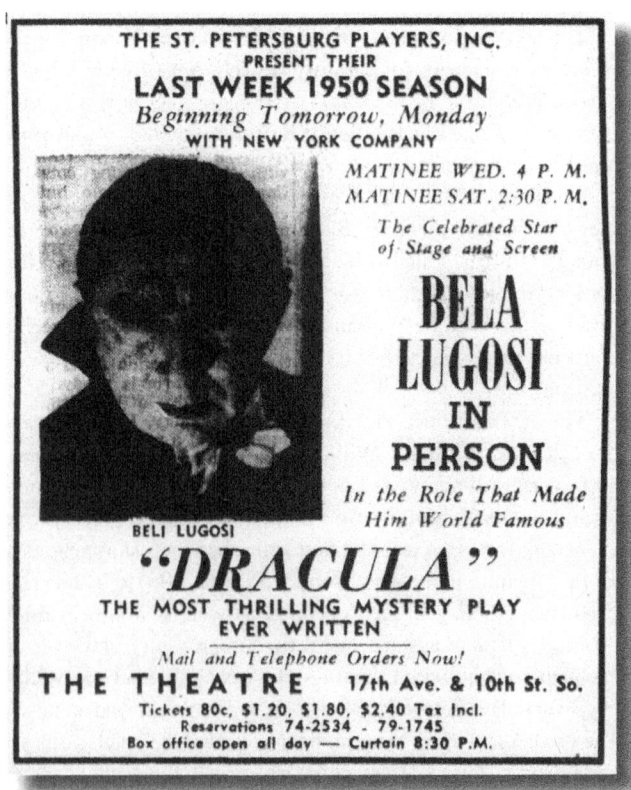

From the *St. Petersburg Times* of March 19, 1950.

know Bela, who practically adopted him. I can still hear Bela saying, 'Where's Bobby?' or 'Can you do this for me, Bobby?' Bob was like a major domo to Lugosi, who really took a shine to him.[7]

According to Scollay, his friend Bob – as well as the entire cast and crew – "respected" Lugosi a great deal.

Scollay also noticed that Lugosi was at times glassy-eyed. He attributed it to drug use, which he thought was likely the reason why Lugosi retired shortly after the performances ended. "You'd speak to him, and then he would drift off every once in awhile. But it never interfered with his work." By contrast, Constance Kelly never had any inkling of Lugosi's drug use, to the extent that she was "shocked" to learn of it in later years. Instead, she mainly recalled that "Lugosi used to try to paw me in the wings, and I'd feel his hand creeping above my waist, and I'd elbow him."[8]

Whatever the exact nature of Lugosi's health, he did attend a cast party, indulging in some conversation and one drink before leaving.[9] More notably, at least in terms of publicity, the Lugosis were Guests of Honor at a "meet and greet" hosted at the Tramor Cafeteria's Fourth Street South location on March 23, 1950; the venue featured etched glass, a sweeping staircase, and a light fixture shaped like a star, all underneath a ceiling painted to resemble a blue sky. A newspaper advertisement promised readers the chance to meet the Lugosis in person.

From the *St. Petersburg Times* of March 23, 1950.

Harry Haige – the son of one of the four brothers who started the restaurant – recalled meeting Lugosi that day:

I remember at age ten being introduced to Bela Lugosi … in the dining room by my father, Enar… Mr. Lugosi graciously gave me his autograph upon request… Lugosi probably dined more than once at the Tramor.

I recall his party was seated on the main level and he was 'holding court' as it were.[10]

While the Lugosis likely dined at the Tramor several times that week, they also ate at the Coral Dining Room of the La Playa Hotel in Redington Beach, where Lugosi personally visited the kitchen in order to thank the chefs.[11]

As for the production of *Dracula*, one critic wrote that the audience, which included several hundred children, "gasped, screamed, and applauded in a manner their inhibited elders have long abandoned."[12] Another reviewer noticed much the same, writing:

Lugosi faced an almost full house last night. Half the audience were youngsters 10 to 16 years of age and they received the thriller with wild enthusiasm and did not overlook a line. They were silent when the curtain was up, thoroughly absorbed in the drama that was presented and the star of stage and screen could not have asked for a better or more attentive audience.

… Lugosi is, of course, the star and is the central figure of the play. But he needs good support and

Lugosi in a meeting about the summer stock version of *Dracula* in Vermont. To his left is Eliot Duvey, and to his right are Lillian Lugosi and Henry Fairbanks, the latter being the man who started the Saint Michael's Playhouse. (Courtesy of the Saint Michael's Playhouse Collection, Saint Michael's College Archives, Saint Michael's College, Colchester, Vermont)

got it from a good cast. The mysterious background was well built up in the first act before Lugosi appears and the scene was well set for his appearance. The best tribute that could be paid the performance was the tense silence that prevailed through the play.[13]

The reviewer concluded his positive review by advising readers that "*Dracula* is well worth seeing."

Fortunately, no critics attended the matinee performances, as the first one encountered serious problems. Constance Kelly remembered:

There was the big scene where Dracula suddenly appears. Lucy is lying on the sofa, and the audience is supposed to scream when Dracula appears, then he leans over to bite her, and the curtain comes down.

The set was black and dark, and light would come on when he would jump up. To do that, Lugosi would crawl from backstage into the fireplace, on the back of the set, he would crawl down to the sofa, then when the light came on, he would stand up and everyone would scream.

Florida is very bright in the summer, very light, and there were lots of windows in the auditorium, so when Lugosi made his dramatic appearance at one performance, they didn't have blinds pulled. So there he was crawling across the stage, and the audience knew exactly what he was doing, and there was Dracula crawling… it was a long crawl, and they started tittering, and the laughter got louder and louder, and soon everyone was convulsed. We were too, backstage, the actors.

Well, poor Bela leapt up and the audience screamed with laughter, and the light came on, and the audience applauded, and they finished the scene.

But poor Bela, he took it so seriously, the part, that it was so very sad. He really wanted to do the best he could. He was so humiliated. I saw him backstage wiping tears from his eyes. …then we were all ashamed because we had laughed.[14]

Recalling that the "show did go on," Kelly added that Lugosi "rallied" and finished the rest of the week. But Lugosi's winter stock appearance in the early spring of 1950 was the lowest ebb of his straw hat career.

By June, the summer stock season of 1950 was underway, though it was not in "full bloom" until July 1.[15] Writing in the *New York Times*, Richard Aldrich, manager of two different summer stock theatres, told readers, "The star system, for all its supposed failings, has been instrumental in bringing summer theatre interest to its present level."[16] Whatever anyone believed about the use of stars, they continued to be as great a presence as ever, their names that year ranging from Jean Parker and Lillian Gish to Basil Rathbone and Brian Aherne.[17]

From the *Burlington Free Press* of July 3, 1950.

Even more than stars, the key issue for 1950 became the "exorbitant" royalties that summer theatres had to pay in order to produce recent Broadway hits.[18] One of the most costly to stage was *Harvey*, the play in which Lugosi

Lugosi flanked by two usherettes during the run of *Dracula* in St. Petersburg.

Lugosi at a reception held at the library of Saint Michael's College.

had hoped to star.[19] Nevertheless, *Harvey*'s popularity with audiences caused at least 24 summer stock managers to stage it that season. Rather than use Lugosi, the theatre managers booked such actors as Stuart Erwin and Bert Wheeler.[20]

And so Lugosi returned once again to *Dracula*, this time at the St. Michael's Playhouse in Winooski Park, Vermont, only miles from Burlington. St. Michael's College operated the Playhouse, a 480-seat theatre located right on campus. Executive Director Henry G. Fairbanks, then a young professor at the college, had limited funds for stars, hiring only three that summer: Lugosi, Ethel Barrymore Colt, and Marian Seldes.[21]

Even at that, Fairbanks had to sign Lugosi at a cheaper price than the actor's usual rate. He was successful, persuading Lugosi to agree to $500 for the week. When Fairbanks communicated that result to Father Gerald E. Dupont, President of St. Michael's, he implied that he had dealt directly with Lugosi:

> Just completed arrangements over the phone for the 'opener.' It gives us a *name* and a mystery thriller to add balance as well as drawing power to the season. Lugosi is beyond our maximum offer, but I persuaded him to accept on our terms, by agreeing to find quarters for his wife and son (age 12) during his residence on campus (June 27-July 8).[22]

Lugosi's contract included those very terms, with the Lugosi family receiving "free room and board" for the week. Lugosi also received an additional check for $23.63 in travel reimburse-

(Courtesy of Saint Michael's Playhouse Collection, Saint Michael's College Archives, Saint Michael's College, Colchester, Vermont)

ST. MICHAEL'S COLLEGE
WINOOSKI PARK, VERMONT

HENRY G. FAIRBANKS, *Executive Director*

presents

"DRACULA"

July 4-8, 1950

STARRING

BELA LUGOSI

STAGED BY ELIOT DUVEY

SETTINGS BY MATT HORNER   COSTUMES BY DEBORAH CARROLL

Next Week
"ARSENIC AND OLD LACE"

Gary D. Rhodes | Bill Kaffenberger

ment, the standard amount that St. Michael's paid to performers that summer.[23]

Eliot Duvey, formerly of the Boston Tributary Theatre, was the company's stage director. In addition to Lugosi, the cast featured Robin Ladd as Lucy Seward. Ladd, the daughter of an army colonel, had acted at St. Michael's the previous summer, and, before that, at the Boston Tributary Theatre, where she apparently met Duvey.[24] Ladd's father died only a couple of weeks before rehearsals began, with her mother traveling to St. Michael's to spend time with her. Other resident players in the *Dracula* cast included George Pillette (as Jonathan Harker), Harry Coble (as Van Helsing), and Matt Horner (as Renfield). Horner also designed the sets.[25]

Dracula opened the Playhouse's summer season, playing from Tuesday, July 4 to Saturday, July 8. The company gave performances each evening at 8:30PM, but did not stage matinees, a factor that may have helped convince Lugosi to take a lower rate than his more usual $750.[26] Though Lugosi traveled with Lillian, his son remained in California that summer.

Financial paperwork on the production of *Dracula* at Saint Michael's Playhouse. (Courtesy of Saint Michael's Playhouse Collection, Saint Michael's College Archives, Saint Michael's College, Colchester, Vermont)

The local press covered Lugosi's appearance at an equity reception for the play, with one photo caption noting that he compared "his charms with those of two Burlington girls."[27] The *Burlington Free Press* also gave much space to actress Helen Kelly, who appeared in the play as Miss Wells, the maid. While the role was not as central as Harker or Van Helsing, it was Kelly's background that appealed to the newspaper. In addition to her acting career, Kelly was an author and director, as well as a faculty member at Mercyhurst College in Erie, Pennsylvania.[28]

Reviewing the play for the *Burlington Free Press*, Milton Slater was generally impressed:

> Although the vehicle may creak a little around the joints and may be suffering a trifle from hardening of the first act, it is still a whopping good thriller.
>
> ... [The play's philosophical meaning] is almost eclipsed by the Lugosi personality itself, which embodies a quality of unreality, an animalistic ferociousness, and a fluidity of motion which is arresting.

Intoning his lines in meticulous fashion, Mr. Lugosi's rich voice is sent scattering from a mobile face which contorts in such variety guaranteed to raise the hackles.

The actor, although bulking large, moves with cat-like grace and manipulates his cape in the second act in a way which would put Sidney Franklin, the bull-fighter, to blame.[29]

Like Jayne Altobell (who later remarked on the same attribute after seeing Lugosi in Litchfield in 1947), Slater was impressed by Lugosi's use of his cape, a technique that he apparently employed on the stage more than in his films.

In the end, the St. Michael's Playhouse *Dracula* was the only version of that play staged at a major summer theatre in 1950. It is difficult to know why, particularly in an environment when more recent Broadway hits commanded such high royalty payments. Perhaps the industry publicity over the Phipps Playhouse version of 1948 continued to make some producers leery of it. At any rate, the St. Michael's run of *Dracula* was a success, generating a net profit of $1,295.85. It was their second most profitable play that summer.[30]

As *Dracula* finished its run at St. Michael's, rehearsals began for the company's next production, *Arsenic and Old Lace*. However, Lugosi did not appear in it. Instead, director Eliot Duvey played Jona-

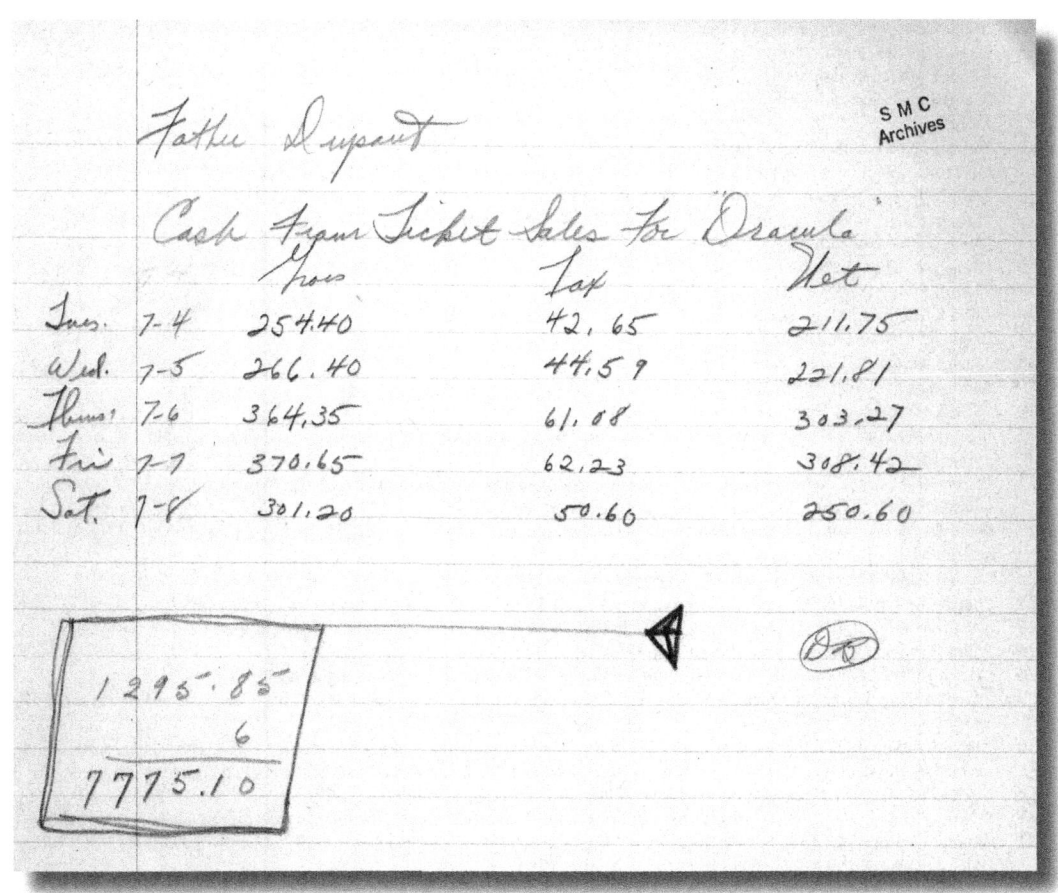

Notes on the ticket sales for the Saint Michael's Playhouse production of *Dracula*. (Courtesy of Saint Michael's Playhouse Collection, Saint Michael's College Archives, Saint Michael's College, Colchester, Vermont)

than Brewster, with Robin Ladd shifting from the role of Lucy Seward to Elaine Harper.[31]

During July and August, *Arsenic and Old Lace* appeared at a number of other stock theatres: The Mill Stream Playhouse in Sea Girt, New Jersey; the Auditorium in Luray, Virginia; the Deertrees Theatre in Harrison, Maine; the Playhouse in Duxbury, Massachusetts; the Duke's Oak Theatre in Cooperstown, New York.[32] Lugosi appeared in none of those productions either. Nor did he appear at the Watkins Glen Summer Theatre in New York, which had announced in the spring that he would star in their version of *Dracula*; in the end, they didn't stage *Dracula* with or without him.[33]

Instead, Lugosi's summer became dominated by a new play, *The Devil Also Dreams*, and with it, a final chance at Broadway. As a result, he probably didn't care about those other versions of *Arsenic and Old Lace*. And he probably gave little thought to the St. Michael's Playhouse when he left Vermont. He could scarcely have known that it be would the last time he would ever appear in the full-length version of *Dracula* on American soil.

(Endnotes)

1. Rhodes, Gary D. Interview with Constance Kelly. 5 Sept. 2009.
2. *Ibid.*
3. Rhodes, Gary D. Interview with Fred Scollay. 27 Aug. 2009.
4. Upchurch, C. Winn. "Lugosi Assails Crime Comics, Radio Dramas." *The Independent* (St. Petersburg, FL) 16 Mar. 1950.
5. Rhodes, interview with Scollay.
6. Rhodes, interview with Kelly.
7. Rhodes, interview with Scollay.
8. Rhodes, interview with Kelly.
9. *Ibid.*
10. Haige, Harry. Emails to Bill Kaffenberger. 29 Aug. 2011 and 31 Aug. 2011.
11. Oberlander, Wally. "On the Surf Side." *The Evening Independent* (St. Petersburg, FL) 24 Mar. 1950.
12. Bunin, Norman. "Screams, Applause Greet Lugosi in Role of Dracula." *St. Petersburg Times* 22 Mar. 1950.
13. "Lugosi Suave, Smooth in Famous Melodrama." *The Evening Independent* 21 Mar. 1950.
14. Rhodes, interview with Kelly.
15. Bamberger, Theron. "Summer Theatres." *New York Times* 18 June 1950; "Summer Theatres Await First Night." *New York Times* 15 May 1950.
16. Aldrich, Richard. "Straw Hat Theatres." *New York Times* 2 July 1950.
17. Bamberger, "Summer Theatres."
18. "Rustic Managers Elect." *New York Times* 28 Apr. 1950.
19. Bamberger, "Summer Theatres."
20. "Schedules Along the Straw Hat Circuit." *New York Times* 18 June 1950.
21. In addition to their six major plays in the summer of 1950, the St. Michael's Playhouse offered three more plays featuring their apprentices.
22. Fairbanks, Henry G. Letter to Father Dupont. Undated. Available in the Saint Michael's Playhouse Collection, Saint Michael's College Archives at Saint Michael's College in Colchester, Vermont.
23. Handwritten note dated 21 June 1950. Available in the Saint Michael's Playhouse Collection, Saint Michael's College Archives at Saint Michael's College in Colchester, Vermont.
24. "Robin Ladd Plays Opposite Lugosi." *Springfield Union* 24 June 1950.
25. "Playhouse Opens Tonight at 8:30, Starring Lugosi." *Burlington Free Press* (Burlington, VT) 4 July 1950.
26. See, for example: "Bela Lugosi Stars at St. Michael's." *Springfield Union* (Springfield, MA) 30 June 1950.
27. Photo Caption. *Burlington Free Press* 1 July 1950.
28. "Helen Kelly Making Bow at Playhouse with Bela Lugosi." *Burlington Free Press* 3 July 1950.
29. Slater, Milton. "Patrons of Opening Week at Playhouse Icily Thrilled; Mr. Lugosi Sees to That." *Burlington Free Press* 6 July 1950.
30. "Memorandum on Summer Theatre." 10 July 1950; "Memorandum on Summer Theatre." 14 Aug. 1950; Handwritten and untitled figures detailing net profits of summer plays. Undated. Available in the Saint Michael's Playhouse Collection, Saint Michael's College Archives at Saint Michael's College in Colchester, Vermont.
31. "Duvey to be Brewster in Playhouse's Next Offering, *Arsenic and Old Lace*." *Burlington Free Press* 7 July 1950.
32. "Along the Straw Hat Trail." *New York Times* 25 June 1950; "Along the Straw Hat Trail." *New York Times* 23 July 1950; "Along the Straw Hat Trail." *New York Times* 20 Aug. 1950.
33. "Summer Theatre Will Open 3rd Season at Watkins Glen July 3." *The Evening Leader* (Corning, NY) 11 Apr. 1950.

Chapter 17

THE DEVIL ALSO DREAMS

During the production of *Scared to Death* (1947), the press reported that Bela Lugosi was hard at work on his autobiography, to the extent that he was jotting down his memories in between shooting scenes for the film.[1] He must have given up on the project at some stage, as it was never published. But Lugosi remained a student of his own life, as much as he was a student of subjects like philosophy and history. That meant keeping extensive scrapbooks, clippings, and photos.

Lugosi's interest in his own career extended to the stories he shared with others during the late forties. He routinely told journalists about his early days as an actor, years before America, and before Dracula. He was classically trained, he always said, and he had portrayed all of the great character roles on the Hungarian stage. Then came Hollywood and typecasting, and so he suffered as the man of horror, or at least as one of the men of horror, given competition from the likes of Boris Karloff.

His memories of the past – however vivid and present they may have been – could not overshadow the ongoing need to work and to make money, but they also shaped his plans to break free of the horror genre. So many of the projects he tried to initiate himself had come to nothing, and the rare attempts made by others – such as the ill-fated play *Three Indelicate Ladies* in 1947 – had not allowed him to escape Dracula, who was as much his traveling companion in the late forties as his wife Lillian. But that did not keep Lugosi from remaining optimistic, even as the decade came to an end.

On May 12, 1950, the *New York Herald-Tribune* announced that the "managerial team" of longtime Broadway producer H. Clay Blaney (a member of one of America's oldest theatrical families) and C. Peter Jaeger (a television producer) would stage their first joint production: *The Devil Also Dreams*. Authored by songwriter and playwright Fritz Rotter and Rose Simon Kohn (under her pen name Elissa Rohn), the play was originally titled *The Devil Can Also Dream*. Two years earlier, when Robert McCahon had considered producing it, the play was known as *Really, Mr. Quill*.[2]

Set in Buckinghamshire, England in the 1890s, *The Devil Also Dreams* revolves around the aging and scheming writer Aloysius Quill, who discovers a brilliant young playwright in Bernard Perkins. Quill lures Perkins to his country home and tries to pass him off on his mistress, Effie Verrecka, so that he can plagiarize Perkins' new drama, *This Way to Your Coffin*. To pull off his plan, Quill intends to murder Perkins with the help of his major domo, Alexander Martin Petofy, a Hungarian actor-turned-butler. But Perkins learns about Quill's plot shortly before a "twist" ending. The tale blended elements of comedy, drama, and suspense, something that resulted in a lack of clear generic identification.

By mid-May 1950, Blaney and Jaeger announced that Francis L. Sullivan, who had appeared in

Cast biographies as printed in theatre programs for *The Devil Also Dreams* (1950).

such films as *Oliver Twist* (1948), would play the role of Quill. Angela Lansbury was named as a possible actress for the planned "all-star cast." The two producers also told the press that Reginald Denham – of *The Two Mrs. Carrolls* and *Ladies in Retirement* fame – would direct the show. Denham had only recently recovered from being hit by an automobile.[3]

With rehearsals set to begin on July 1, 1950, Blaney and Jaeger quickly tried to attach other actors to the project. By May 22, the *New York Times* noted that the duo "sought" Bela Lugosi (for the role of Petofy) and Richard Waring (for the role of Perkins).[4] Like Lugosi, Waring appeared in summer stock in 1950, starring in *What Every Woman Knows* at Gloucester, Massachusetts in late June.[5]

As of June 6, the *New York Herald-Tribune* published an account of Lugosi's desire "to escape from the rut of horror into which motion pictures have plunged him." He was "considering" appearing in the summer try-out of *The Devil Also Dreams*, but apparently had not yet signed a contract. Nor had Blaney and Jaeger signed a female lead, as the same article claimed that both Angela Lansbury and Alexis Smith were being "mentioned" for the role of Effie.[6]

A little more than a week later, another press account claimed that Sullivan, Waring, and Lugosi would definitely appear in the play.[7] Then, at some point prior to June 20, Blaney and Jaeger cast Claire Luce as Effie; Luce had earlier portrayed Curley's wife in the 1937-38 Broadway version of Steinbeck's *Of Mice and Men*.[8] Only the fifth and final role remained, the small part of Dr. Woodruff, who makes his first entrance near the end of the play. By July 6, the *New York Times* announced the cast was complete, with Oswald Marshall agreeing to portray Woodruff. By that time, Fritz Rotter and Elissa Rohn had arrived in New York from Los Angeles; Francis L. Sullivan had also made his way to New York on the heels of a trip to England in June.[9]

Lugosi, still living in New York when he signed the contract, was no doubt elated to appear in the show. By mid-1950, he was increasingly relying on Bertha Klausner, a New York literary agent, to act as his key representative. She replaced Don Marlowe in that regard, and she was likely the person who dealt with Blaney and Jaeger.[10] At any rate, during the production, Lugosi would travel with wife Lillian behind the wheel of their convertible coupe. And *The Devil Also Dreams* was bound for Broadway, where Lugosi had not worked since 1933.

His character, the Hungarian actor-turned-butler Petofy, was a departure from all things horrific. Though it was a relatively small part, it was perfect for him. To an extent, Petofy represented an biographical sketch of Lugosi. A former actor, the Hungarian butler represents the "Other" in a foreign land where he lives and works. He holds tightly onto his stage traditions, to the extent that every household chore requires a careful theatrical performance, even when he dusts the mantelpiece.[11]

Petofy cannot forget that he once played Hamlet, that he once had the privilege of speaking the immortal phrase "To be or not to be" in front of an appreciative audience.[12] He even goes so far as to suggest that Shakespeare sounds better in Hungarian, quoting a passage in his native language. But those days are over, except in Petofy's mind, where the past is always present.

Rounding out the key personnel on the play were Lester Al Smith, who acted as General Manager of the company, H. Clay Blaney, Jr., who was an assistant to his father, and – as Technical Advisor – Leonard Altobell. Altobell and Lugosi knew each other well from the 1947 and 1949 seasons at the Litchfield Summer Theatre.

Rehearsals for *The Devil Also Dreams*, which had already been rescheduled to begin on July 6, 1950, were briefly delayed while Blaney and Jaeger plotted their strategy. The two decided to use summer stock theatres as a way to launch the play, originally considering a seven-week tour that would have included such towns as Ivoryton. From there, they planned a Broadway opening in late September.[13] But that schedule changed, as they were only able to make agreements with three American summer stock theatres and a trio of Canadian theatres.

At summer stock theatres, *The Devil Also Dreams* represented what was known as a package show, its cast and key personnel traveling with it. The given summer theatre supplied the venue and only a small number of employees, such as carpenters to assemble set pieces that usually toured with the show. The fact that such plays did not rely on resident companies made them the bane of many summer stock employees. In June 1950, William Miles, a producer at the Berkshire Playhouse in Massachusetts, condemned package shows as the "Frankenstein of the summer theatre."[14]

On July 24, 1950, *The Devil Also Dreams* made its world premiere at the Somerset Summer Theatre in Fall River, Massachusetts. The show played six evening performances and two matinees. Publicity for the Somerset dubbed it "America's most beautiful summer theatre."[15] Among its more distinctive features was the fact that air conditioning could not be used during performances, as noise from it made it difficult for actors to hear each other. Backstage lavatories also had to be avoided during the shows, as the flushing sounds could be heard throughout the audience.[16]

Just before the opening, the *Providence Journal* reported, "Top theatre, motion picture and television executives are gathering

Advertisement promoting the play's premiere performance.

Gary D. Rhodes | Bill Kaffenberger

The Devil Also Dreams cast. From left to right are Francis L. Sullivan, Claire Luce, Lugosi, and Richard Waring.

in the Spindle City for attendance tomorrow night at the world premiere of *The Devil Also Dreams*." The newspaper added, "Whether it will be good enough to graduate from summer stock into Hollywood, Broadway, or TV network studios will depend upon how a house full of scouts receive tomorrow night's opening performance."[17] Those scouts included Saul Lancourt (owner of the Forty-Eighth Street Theatre in New York), Blake Johnson (a producer at the summer theatre in Beverly, Massachusetts), and Miriam Howell (a representative at a New York booking agency).[18] George Clark was also "on hand to observe [the] TV possibilities of Lugosi and Sullivan."[19]

Reviewing the show, the *Fall River Herald News* praised the sets and Sullivan's acting, but hardly mentioned Lugosi.[20] Another review believed the play "may well be the most interesting … that has come our way during this summer season," but added that the opening performance was "so ragged, timing so bad, and pace sometimes so slow that it is difficult to judge properly this new venture." Its acting was "uneven," and while Lugosi revealed "a hitherto unsuspected talent for comedy … a good part of his dialogue is drowned by his thick accent." The verdict: *The Devil Also Dreams* was "not quite good enough" and required "a tremendous amount of rewriting."[21]

A critic from *Variety* was also present on opening night. The published review, which ignored Lugosi, was hardly an endorsement:

OPENING TONIGHT
Famous Artists
COUNTRY PLAYHOUSE
At E. Rochester Presents

★ CLARA LUCE ★ BELA LUGOSI
★ RICHARD WARING
★ FRANCIS L. SULLIVAN

In Person—IN

"The Devil Also Dreams"
July 31 thru Aug. 5—Mats. Wed., Sat., 2:30 P. M.

Tickets Now On Sale
In Rochester—Knopf's Store, Seneca Hotel—BAker 7477.
In E. Rochester—Playhouse, E. Rochester High School—E. Roch. 590.
E. Roch. 581. Mail Orders filled promptly. Address to Country Playhouse,
E. Rochester.

SPONSORED BY E. ROCHESTER FIRE DEPT.

Coming Aug. 7
★ HELMUT DANTINE ★ BEATRICE PEARSON
in
"ARMS and the MAN"

From the *Rochester Democrat and Chronicle* of July 31, 1950.

Though the comedy-melodrama tag is a misnomer, this piece is well written and contains a tricky psychological element which might be better exploited. Present billing has a tendency toward greater expectation on the part of the viewer. When it doesn't materialize, despite the cleverness of the fairly simple plot and the suspense it generates, there is a letdown.

… Considerable skill is evident in the handling of lines and direction. … Clay Watson's set is excellent and Reginald Denham's direction is expressive.[22]

Summing up the play's strengths and weaknesses, *Variety*'s critic damned it with a single phrase: "doubtful Broadway material."

From Fall River, *The Devil Also Dreams* company journeyed some four hundred miles to its next destination. As a teenager, H. C. Blaney III traveled with his father and grandfather during the entire tour. He later recalled:

> My dad hired a driver with a Cadillac to transport most of the small cast and my Dad, my mom and myself. But Bela had a lovely large white convertible that his wife drove … sometimes they would follow us on the road and we would stop from time to time to look at the countryside or take lunch. One trip was through the Finger Lakes. He was delightful and friendly to everyone, and had a great sense humor.
>
> Another time Bela sided with me on sitting up front in the car to see the countryside while one of the main characters in the play and very large and inflated man indeed also wanted to be front with the driver. Bela sided with me and his booming voice and personality won that day a place in front for a very silly boy.[23]

Blaney also remembered that Lugosi praised him to his father.

The Famous Artists Country Playhouse of East Rochester

PAUL CRABTREE
MANAGING DIRECTOR
PRESENTS

H. Clay Blaney and C. Peter Jaeger's Production

Claire **LUCE**   Francis L. **SULLIVAN**
Bela **LUGOSI**   Richard **WARING**

IN

"THE DEVIL ALSO DREAMS"

July 31, August 1, 2, 3, 4, 5 — Season of 1950

From the East Rochester theatre program.

Gary D. Rhodes | Bill Kaffenberger

From the *Syracuse Herald-Journal* of August 7, 1950.

Originally, Jaeger and the eldest Blaney intended to stage *The Devil Also Dreams* at the Lake Whalom Playhouse in Fitchburg for the week of July 30, 1950, but the final choice became the Famous Artists Country Playhouse of East Rochester. Paul Crabtree, its managing director, had been one of those persons who attended the Somerset premiere.[24] The East Rochester run lasted from July 31 to August 5.[25] While there, the Lugosis stayed at the Green Lantern Inn.

Not surprisingly, publicity for opening night drew attention to Claire Luce, whose parents lived in Rochester; years earlier, she had studied dance in the city.[26] As for *The Devil Also Dreams*, critic Ham Allen said that it was "plodding in spots, but interesting enough to keep a perspiring audience intent on the dialogue. The Devil and his five cohorts won rounds of appreciative applause at the final curtain." Allen added that, "Most of the applause probably was for the cohorts."[27] Another review spoke of some minor concerns, but lauded the performances, including Lugosi's, which was "clever and amusing."[28]

DISTINGUISHED COMPANY. Francis L. Sullivan, Claire Luce, Elissa Rohn and Bela Lugosi as they arrived in Fayetteville yesterday for the opening of "The Devil Also Dreams" tonight at the Country Playhouse.

Working at the theatre for the whole of the 1950 summer season was apprentice Michael Ambrosino. He later recalled:

> The show came through with full cast and everything, but we built the sets, which were already designed.
>
> The Famous Artists Country Playhouse rented a high school to stage the plays, which worked out well, because there was a wood shop in the building. And the auditorium only seated 500 to 700 people, so if you didn't sell that many tickets, it didn't look like the world was coming to an end.
>
> The real issue was getting people to come to East Rochester. That was difficult, because at the time, it was seen as very downmarket. East Rochester was the blue-collar suburb.[29]

Ambrosino also noted that the East Rochester location was one of three Famous Artists Country Playhouses, with one of the other two located in Watkins Glen, New York.

The third Famous Artists Country Playhouse was

Advertisement for the play's appearance in Fayetteville, New York.

Francis L. Sullivan, Claire Luce, and Lugosi during the Toronto run of *The Devil Also Dreams*.

in Fayetteville, New York, which became the company's next destination. Lugosi had appeared in a stock performance of *Arsenic and Old Lace* at the same venue in 1949. In advance of the show's opening, one journalist extolled the virtues of the cast and their attire:

> The summer theatre tradition, especially among the younger thespians, runs to blue jeans and sweat shirts, so when Claire Luce appeared, complete with long blonde hair, black dress, floating scarf, arranged a la turban, and smoked her cigarette in a long red holder, it was a change, at any rate.

> These jolly people ... looked at each other and smiled secretively when asked about *The Devil Also Dreams*. Apparently they like it, but they are too experienced in the unpredictable fortunes of the theatre to wax enthusiastic about a budding production... '

> 'It has suspens-s-se,' hisses Lugosi. ... Bela Lugosi was very busy making a fuss over the host at the Fayetteville Inn, where he said he had the time of his eventful life last summer ... along with his pal, Paul Lukas. The visiting stars will stay there this summer. Bela kisses your hand and begs you to come backstage to see him ... and you know he wouldn't recognize you if he fell over you within the next 10 minutes. A very nice guy....[30]

As for the play, newspapers noted that it would run from August 7 to 12, 1950, with performances on each of those evenings and at matinees on Wednesday and Saturday. In advance of opening night, Fritz

Bela Lugosi

Lugosi during the play's run in Canada.

Rotter and Elissa Rohn "planed in from Los Angeles" to do some rewrites.[31]

Two critics from Syracuse gave generally positive reviews of the play, which might indicate that the pacing had improved after the Fall River and East Rochester engagements. In the *Post-Standard*, Thola Nett Tabor wrote, "One by one, and as a fine complete cast, the four stars ... received plaudits last night...."[32] She praised all of them for their "excellently portrayed" performances.[33]

The *Syracuse Herald-Journal* offered similar opinions on the play and also witnessed the positive audience response:

> If audience reaction is of any value, the new play... has more than a good chance of making the grade. Response to witty and pointed dialogue was quick, and the welcome to the cast was enthusiastic ... [It] is an actor's play. It is intimately concerned with playwrights, a beautiful actress and a broken down Hungarian actor... the writers have constructed a play of suspense and emotional conflict which builds to a melodramatic climax, complete with poison cup and retribution. They have a fine second act, with all the characters clearly defined. The third act lets down pretty badly, which is a great disappointment, and should be possible of correction ... Bela Lugosi is interesting in a sort of comic relief role, which he plays with relish ... It is an interesting play, in the hands of a competent cast, which still needs some work.[34]

From the rather austere program to the play's appearance in Montreal.

Such reviews, while underscoring the fact that the play had problems, may have restored the company's hopes that they could still reach Broadway.

At any rate, after Fayetteville, the company journeyed some 250 miles to Toronto, where they staged *The Devil Also Dreams* at the Royal Alexandria Theatre from August 14 to 19, 1950. Ads promoted not only the play, but also the fact that the theatre was air-conditioned.[35] One article in the *Toronto Star* claimed that it was a "surprise" to see the theatre booking a "single show smack in the middle of the summer season," but that "according to reports" the play was "too good a bet to pass up."[36] And so in this case *The Devil Also Dreams* was playing a different kind of venue, one that wasn't a straw hat theatre.

Critic Jack Karr of the *Toronto Star* was relatively impressed, telling readers the play had:

... several things to recommend it. It has an interesting premise, a fine flow of rhetoric, and a cast that could scarcely be improved upon. Yet for a piece of theatre that gets billed as a 'comedy melodrama,' it only occasionally belongs in either of those categories. Perhaps it's better described as a psychological thriller ... but even that is open to argument.

But Karr also argued that the script was a problem. "The main trouble here," he added, "seems to be that Rotter and Miss Rohn have had difficulty in getting to the point, in providing a suitable buildup to the brief climactic moment in the third act.[37]

Other local papers lauded Lugosi's performance, giving him more praise than he had received in previous cities. The *Toronto Gazette* said that he was "delightfully out of his conventional character. ... This in itself will make the play worth seeing for many."[38] The *Toronto Globe and Mail* echoed that sentiment, telling readers he was "sometimes amusing and occasionally ridiculous," placing blame for the latter on problems with the script.[39]

In some respects, the Toronto newspaper reviews give the impression that the play had improved, and in at least a few respects – such as the actors' familiarity with their roles and with one another – that was likely true. But other problems remained, as a critic for *The Billboard* noticed in Toronto. With the exception of Claire Luce's portrayal, he praised all of the acting, referring to Lugois's performance as "deft." But he disparaged the play, advising the producers that, "considerable rewriting is in order ... before it can open on Broadway." He added:

At times there comes a glimmer of hope that the play is not as bad as it seems. The dialog occasionally breaks out to provide enough strength for the devil to carry his dream to Broadway. But a brave quintet of actors struggle through what must be a bad dream for them.[40]

That wasn't all. For this critic, even the play's vaunted twist ending was "ineffectual."

And so, at a crucial moment, a major industry trade publication lambasted *The Devil Also Dreams*, thus following in the footsteps of *Variety*, which had already done the same one month earlier. Then came the Toronto theatre manager's report. The play had grossed only a "mild" $6,200 for the week.[41] As a result, Fritz Rotter and Elissa Rohn traveled to Toronto to rework various aspects of the script.

The result meant a play that was twenty minutes shorter and sported a new ending. Moreover, *Variety* mentioned two of the leads would be recast before pending performances in Boston and Philadelphia that would precede the Broadway opening.[42] There is no indication that Lugosi was one of those two leads; it seems highly doubtful he was, given his strong notices and the fact that the role (at least as originally written) required an actor who could speak Hungarian.

At any rate, before returning to America, *The Devil Also Dreams* had to move on to two more scheduled venues in Canada. The company traveled over 250 miles to Ottawa's Capitol Theatre, where they gave only one performance, on the night of August 21, 1950. Newspaper publicity in the city optimistically claimed that the play was bound for Manhattan's Booth Theatre.[43]

A review in the *Ottawa Citizen* suggested that most of *The Devil Also Dreams*' "meat" was "packed into the last act," a comment that likely reflects the rewriting that occurred in Toronto. The critic reserved her greatest praise for Lugosi, noting that he was a "tremendous drawing card and did not fail his audience. His role ... was extremely difficult, but he delighted the audience with his characterization." Nevertheless, she bemoaned the fact that some of his lines "were lost before they crossed the footlights."[44]

While the stop at the Capitol became the briefest on the play's journey, Lugosi did take the time to grant an interview to the *Ottawa Journal*. "Having threatened people for the last 23 years," he said. "I'm having the best time of my life making people laugh."[45] Lillian added that her husband was initially surprised by the sound of audience laughter, but quickly got used to it, so much so that if he didn't

Lugosi clowning while on tour in *The Devil Also Dreams*.

receive it after a given line of dialogue, his face shifted into the "scary expression that made him tops among the nastiness boys."[46]

And so Lugosi was generally happy, even as the show's backers must have been increasingly worried about their prospects. Another member of the troupe having fun was H. C. Blaney III, who had much fun joking around with Lugosi:

> I played a trick backstage on Bela and Dick Waring during one show in which my job was to take a piece of bread that was put into the fireplace to toast and put a dark toasted slice on the tip of the poker to show that it was done. But instead I kept leaving the while bread as is. This resulted in them ad libbing and me putting the bread back again ... until I relented and put on the toast. Bela who was on stage could not help but laugh and later we had great fun with this little change in the script! (My Dad was not happy!)
>
> Lugosi was very generous to all ... and a great trooper. We never had any problems with him at all – he was the most normal and kind hearted person of the whole cast and staff of that play.

Lugosi's affinity for the youngest Blaney may have stemmed in part from the fact that he had to spend so much time away from his own son.

From Ottawa, the company quickly moved over 100 miles to His Majesty's Theatre in Montreal, where they would stage *The Devil Also Dreams* from August 22 to August 26, 1950. In addition to five evening shows, the theatre presented matinee performances on Wednesday and Saturday. The *Montreal Star* commended Lugosi, as did the *Montreal Herald*, though the latter believed his "splendid technique" was "going to waste on what only he saved from a walk-on."[47]

Lugosi also impressed the *Montreal Gazette*, which told readers that his presence alone would "make the play worth seeing for many."[48] But the *Gazette*'s critic was less impressed with the play, claiming, "There was a certain feeling all the way through that dialogue and situation were improvised. Often the situations were brilliantly taken. Sometimes we felt a labored effort to make it all go."[49] Here the rewriting could have been the source of new troubles, with the play now suffering from actors adjusting to different scenes and dialogue.

According to *Variety*, the seven performances in Montreal generated "only about $4,500," with the blame going to a combination of "mixed reviews and hot weather."[50] Similar to what had been said in Ottawa, the Montreal press announced that *The Devil Also Dreams* was destined for the Booth Theatre in New York. But at that point, such talk was little more than publicity.

There would be no recasting, and there would be no more rewriting. No Boston and no Philadelphia. And no Broadway, not in September or any other month. Dubious reviews and disappointing grosses had taken their toll. By September 1, 1950, the *New York Daily News* announced that Francis L. Sullivan and Claire Luce were in New York "looking for new vehicles."[51] Lugosi would have had to do the same.

As a student of history, Lugosi enjoyed revisiting the past. As the summer of 1950 came to an end, he could look back to a play that meant a great deal to him, not only financially, but also artistically. After all, *The Devil Also Dreams* had given him an opportunity that was far more significant than *Three Indelicate Ladies* and *No Traveler Returns*.

Indeed, it was something more vital than any play had given him since at least the 1920s. And it was far more satisfying than just sharing old stories with journalists. Thanks to *The Devil Also Dreams*, Lugosi was actually able relive his days in the Hungarian theatre. His role granted him a final chance to deliver Shakespearean dialogue onstage in his native language. Such moments must have been among the happiest that he experienced after becoming a Hollywood exile.

(Endnotes)

1. Crocker, Harry. "Behind the Makeup." *Los Angeles Times* 2 May 1946.
2. Zolotow, Sam. "*The Liar* Closing Untrue; It Stays." *New York Times* 22 May 1950.
3. *Ibid.*
4. *Ibid.*
5. "Along the Straw Hat Trail." *New York Times* 25 June 1950.
6. "Lugosi Wants to Reform." *New York Herald-Tribune* 8 June 1950.
7. "Play Readied by Film Duo." *Los Angeles Times* 14 June 1950.
8. "Premiere Tonight of *Julius Caesar.*" *New York Times* 20 June 1950.
9. "Oswald Marshall Signed." *New York Times* 6 July 1950.
10. In the *Players Directory Bulletin* for August 1950, Lugosi named Klausner as his representative. Given that such information was likely supplied days or weeks in advance of that date, Klausner may well have been acting as his agent when he was offered the role in *The Devil Also Dreams.*
11. "World Premiere Presented of *The Devil Also Dreams.*" *Fall River Herald News* 25 July 1950.
12. Archer, Thomas. "Sullivan Stars at His Majesty's, British star here in *Devil Also Dreams.*" *Montreal Gazette* 23 Aug. 1950.
13. "Premiere Tonight of *Julius Caesar.*"
14. Miles, William. "The Frankenstein of Summer Stock." *Theatre Arts* June 1950.
15. "*Streetcar* to Run on Subway Circuit." *New York Times* 12 June 1950.
16. Campbell, Alan. Email to Gary D. Rhodes. 30 Oct. 2011.
17. "New Play Draws Top Executives." *Providence Journal* 23 July 1950.
18. *Ibid.*
19. *Ibid.*
20. "World Premiere Presented of *The Devil Also Dreams,*" *Fall River Herald News.*
21. E. J. D. "*The Devil Also Dreams* Accorded Ragged Premiere." 2 Aug. 1950. [Publication title unknown; clipping in the Billy Rose Theatre Collection of the New York Public Library for the Performing Arts."]
22. Malo. "*The Devil Also Dreams.*" *Variety* 2 Aug. 1950.
23. Blaney, H. C., III. Email to Gary D. Rhodes. 28 Apr. 2012.
24. "New Play Draws Top Executives."
25. *The Devil Also Dreams.* Program. East Rochester, NY: The Famous Artists Country Playhouse, 1950.
26. See, for example: "Broadway-Bound Play Opens at Insistence of Claire Luce." *Rochester Democrat and Chronicle* (Rochester, NY) 30 July 1950.
27. Allen, Ham. 4 Aug. 1950. [Clipping available at the Billy Rose Collection of the New York Public Library for the Performing Arts].
28. David, George L. "Excellent Cast Offers New Play on East Rochester's Stage." *Rochester Democrat and Chronicle* 4 Aug. 1950.
29. Rhodes, Gary D. Interview with Michael Ambrosino. 26 Oct. 2011.
30. "Four Stars in F'ville for *The Devil Also Dreams,*" *Syracuse Herald-Journal* (Syracuse, NY) 7 Aug. 1950.
31. Baldwin, Ellis K. "What Happens When a Famous Dramatist Runs Out of Plots? Fayetteville Players Try Out Chiller with Eye to Broadway." *Utica Observer Dispatch* (Utica, NY) 10 Aug. 1950.
32. "Actors, One by One, Greeted in Preview of Broadway Play." *Syracuse Post-Standard* (Syracuse, NY) 8 Aug. 8, 1950
33. *Ibid.*
34. M. L. T. "*Devil Also Dreams* Pleases First Night Audience." *Syracuse Herald-Journal* 8 Aug. 1950.
35. Advertisement. *Toronto Star* 29 July 1950.
36. *Toronto Star* 1 Aug. 1950.
37. Karr, Jack. "Showplace." *Toronto Star* 15 Aug. 1950.
38. Archer, Thomas. *Toronto Gazette* 15 Aug. 1950.
39. Barris, Alex. *Toronto Globe and Mail* 15 Aug. 1950.
40. Allen, Harry Jr. "*The Devil Also Dreams.*" *The Billboard* 2 Sept. 1950.
41. "*Dreams* $6,200, Toronto; To Layoff for Recasting." *Variety* 23 Aug. 1950.
42. *Ibid.*
43. "Include Ottawa in Summer Tour." *Ottawa Citizen* 2 Aug. 1950.
44. DeProse, Molly. "Splendid Acting Marks *The Devil Also Dreams.*" *Ottawa Citizen* 22 Aug. 1950.
45. "Bela Balks at Blood, Lives for Laughs." *Ottawa Journal* 21 Aug. 1950.
46. *Ibid.*
47. *Montreal Herald* 23 Aug. 1950. [Contained in the Claire Luce Scrapbook, available at the Billy Rose Collection of the New York Public Library for the Performing Arts].
48. *Montreal Daily Star* 23 Aug. 1950. [Contained in the Claire Luce Scrapbook, available at the Billy Rose Collection of the New York Public Library for the Performing Arts]; "Sullivan Stars at his Majesty's, British Star Here in *Devil Also Dreams.*" *Montreal Gazette* 23 Aug. 1950.
49. *Ibid.*
50. "*Dreams*, $4,500, Montreal." *Variety* 30 Aug. 1950.
51. Walker, Danton. "Broadway." *New York Daily News* 1 Sept. 1950. [Contained in the Claire Luce Scrapbook, available at the Billy Rose Collection of the New York Public Library for the Performing Arts].

Advertisement promoting Lugosi's first spook show.

Chapter 18

LUGOSI AND THE BLOODY GUILLOTINE

In November of 1950, columnist Earl Wilson announced that Bela Lugosi was going into the soda business, endorsing a new product called "Dracola."[1] Given that the soda never appeared on the market, it is difficult to tell whether Wilson's comment refers to a potential business deal or whether it was nothing more than an example of dry humor. Either way, it serves as a reminder of the fact that Lugosi was in need of income during the autumn of 1950.

Bertha Klausner continued her effort to arrange new projects for the actor, who had gone over two years without a film role. Hopes for a return to Broadway ended in the summer of 1950 when *The Devil Also Dreams* closed. Radio, television, vaudeville, and nightclubs provided some work that year, but not enough. And of course by the time that Wilson's column appeared in print, the summer stock season was but a fading memory.

Lugosi needed to find a way to monetize his own image, his own brand, even if the end result was something different than Dracola. Many people profited from Lugosi's image after World War II, including at least one organization that Lugosi endorsed. In 1946, he allowed the Motion Picture Relief Fund the right to use his likeness as part of a collectible set of stamps that would be sold to fans and thus raise money for a good cause.[2]

Of course Lugosi's likeness on the stamp was not the way he would have pictured himself, meaning the leading man of Hungarian theatre. Nor did it arise out of the ashes of ill-fated plays like *Three Indelicate Ladies* or *The Devil Also Dreams*. No, Lugosi's image was what it had been since 1931: Bela "Dracula" Lugosi, the horror man of the movies.

It may well have been Lugosi, rather than Bertha Klausner, who realized that there was a particular entertainment forum in which his Dracula brand had a bankable meaning: the American spook show. Such shows crisscrossed America, playing the stages of movie theatres in large cities and small towns. They reached their peak of popularity during the late forties and early fifties, with such acts as *Dr. Neff's Madhouse of Mystery* and *Dr. Silkini's Asylum of Horrors* being among the most popular.[3]

Describing the history of these spook shows, theatre scholar Beth Kattleman noted that they:

> ... showcased monsters from popular horror films and featured horrific illusions such as decapitations, immolations, and buzz saw effects. While the content of the ghost shows varied widely from presenter to presenter, they were all similar in that they were usually part of a double-bill with a film, each featured some traditional stage magic, and, most importantly, each built to a climax containing a blackout sequence in which luminous apparitions appeared throughout the theatre.
>
> ...magicians were able to capitalize on the public's interest in ... horror films to create shows that

Gary D. Rhodes | Bill Kaffenberger

From the *San Diego Union* of February 7, 1947.

could be sold to theatres and movie houses at a time when new film entertainments were supplanting many genres of live performance.[4]

Not surprisingly, spook shows of the forties and fifties regularly screened old Lugosi films – particularly his B-movies, yet another way in which he could be simultaneously present and absent from the entertainment business of the era.

The combination of horror and magic surfaced repeatedly during Lugosi's film career, most notably in his connection to the popular radio character Chandu. In the 1932 film *Chandu the Magician*, Lugosi played Roxor, the title character's arch nemesis. Two years later, in a fascinating turn of events, Lugosi assumed the role of Chandu himself, playing the heroic magician in the serial *The Return of Chandu* (1934).

Then, in 1941, Lugosi appeared in the horror-comedy *Spooks Run Wild*. For the bulk of the film, the East Side Kids believe Lugosi's character is a maniacal killer on the loose in a small town, but a plot twist reveals him to be nothing more than a harmless magician named Nardo. Once the real culprit is apprehended, Nardo stages his "famous disappearing cabinet" act for the very folks who thought he was a murderer.

But these film roles were not the reasons why Lugosi considered the spook show idea as a way to maximize his own brand during the second half of 1950. Instead, Lugosi – or whoever thought of devising a new Lugosi spook show – likely recalled the actor's association with previous spook shows. For example, in 1941, Lugosi headlined *One Night of Horror* at Chicago's 3,127-seat Oriental Theatre. Paired with the Lugosi film *Invisible Ghost* (1941), the program was as much of a vaudeville bill as a spook show, with several other acts appearing in between Lugosi's trio of horror sketches.[5]

The following week, Lugosi and the rest of the troupe – except for comedienne Diane Moore, who was replaced by Sam Bramson ("Frankenstein's Successor") – appeared at the 1,800-seat Palace Theatre in Fort Wayne, Indiana, the next stop on what was intended to be a multi-city tour. By that time, someone – perhaps producer Irving Yates – had retitled the show, advertising it as "Bela 'Dracula'

Lugosi in *Mirth and Horror*."⁶ However, a "sudden attack of indigestion" meant that Lugosi sought a doctor's care and appeared at only some of his scheduled performances in Fort Wayne.⁷

Shortly thereafter, *Variety* told readers: "Bela Lugosi's illness resulted in the foldup of the 'Horror Show', produced by Irving Yates, after its date at The Palace, Ft. Wayne, early last week. Lugosi returned to the Coast."⁸ Here is an early example of Lugosi using – perhaps quite legitimately, of course – illness as the reason to end a tour, something that would happen on numerous occasions during his career.

Six years later, in early 1947. Irving Yates produced another Lugosi spook show. *A Nightmare of Horror* opened at San Diego's 1,952-seat Orpheum Theatre on February 7, playing for two days only, with both performances scheduled "at the stroke of 12 midnight."⁹ Advertisements referred to Lugosi as "Dracula, the Batman," with "Frankenstein the Mad Monster" taking second billing. Advance publicity promised that "'Dracula' will turn into a bat and that he will hold a fiesta with 'Frankenstein' up and down the aisles of the theatre." The same newspaper article added that the show would be "filled with thrills, moans, groans, screams, and hair-raising scenes."¹⁰ Some of those hair-raising scenes came thanks to a screening of *Voodoo Man*, a 1944 Lugosi film.

When discussing the show, *Variety* noted that Irving Yates was "agenting the layout" at $7,500 per week, which may be a reason it played only two days at the Orpheum.¹¹ At any rate, the trade added that Lugosi would perform only one show per day, each to be scheduled at midnight, during a "trek of personals in film houses." But *A Nightmare of Horror* does not seem to have made it to another theatre that year, likely due to Lugosi's contractual involvement with the play *Three Indelicate Ladies*. One week later, on February 19, *Variety* noted that the actor was on his way from Los Angeles to New York, leaving *A Nightmare of Horror* behind him.¹²

Later that same year, after *Three Indelicate Ladies* closed abruptly and no film work appeared, Lugosi returned to the spook show, but this time he joined an established production, *Dr. Bill Neff's Madhouse of Mystery*. Neff was a talented magician, and by the late forties *The Madhouse of Mystery* was famous. As McCarl Roberts, who staged spook shows himself, once recalled:

> ... there was one outstanding production in a category by

From the *Newark Evening News* of December 17, 1947.

Gary D. Rhodes | Bill Kaffenberger

289

Lugosi and Bill Neff. (Courtesy of Willian V. Rauscher)

itself. *Dr. Neff and His Madhouse of Mystery* was a full stage show with big illusions, special scenery, and many assistants. There were always a few comedy spots, but the main theme of Neff's show was the macabre, the supernatural, the world of spirits. This was the most elaborate ghost show that ever crowded movie houses across the country, and was a superior production in every sense of the word.[13]

Though the content of Neff's show varied over the years, each performance always ended with "The Blackout," during which all of the theatre's lights were turned off. Dozens of "ghosts" soared over the screaming audience. Then the sound of a gunshot filled the auditorium, at which time the house lights returned. Neff offered his closing line, bidding the audience "Pleasant Nightmares," before exiting the stage so that a horror film could be screened.[14]

It is difficult to determine exactly how Lugosi joined the *Madhouse of Mystery*, though he was booked through the Edward Sherman Agency, likely with Don Marlowe acting as his manager. On the heels of the brief *Tell-Tale Heart* tour, which ended on December 3, 1947, if not even a little earlier, Lugosi was available for other work. By Christmas Day of that year, for example, he began his one-week stand at Baltimore's Hippodrome with Robert Alda.

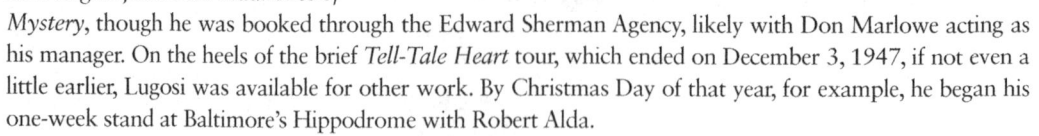

Between those two other shows, Lugosi worked with Neff at the 2,037-seat Adams Theatre in Newark, New Jersey for the week starting December 18, 1947. The show closed on December 24, which meant that the Lugosis must have experienced a tiring Christmas Eve drive to reach Baltimore some 175 miles away.

Advance publicity gave Lugosi a "co-starring" credit with Neff, adding that the *Madhouse of Mystery* would offer:

> … a program of illusions, spirit séances, and spooks on the rampage. Neff's 'Suttee' or the burning of a woman and her return as a ghost; his 'Glamour Ghouls,' and his latest discovery, 'The Atomic Ghost', are featured in the revue.[15]

Curiously, the chosen film for the week was not a Lugosi movie, but instead *Revolt of the Zombies*

(1936). That said, when the Lugosi-Neff show opened, the nearby RKO Proctor's in Newark screened Lugosi in *Son of Frankenstein* (1939) on a double bill with *Bride of Frankenstein* (1935).[16]

For the *Madhouse of Mystery*, Lugosi did what he had done so many times before in various live appearances: he re-enacted a scene from *Dracula*, this time under a "scary green spotlight."[17] By way of an introduction, Neff asked Lugosi some questions at the microphone. Apparently Lugosi had limited time onstage, though he did raise his cape and walked towards the audience right before "The Blackout," thus adding to its build-up and its potential to inspire fear.[18]

A review in the *Newark Evening News* praised the show, claiming the Lugosi "Blackout" was appropriately "gruesome":

> The program yesterday turned out to be better than merely [a] competent magician show, compete with disappearing girls (who are too pretty to vanish like that!), tricks with lengths of cloth, mystifying cabinets, and a vast amount of similar truck.
>
> Some of the stunts are really baffling. ... One is a damsel who is suddenly suspended in the air, her only prop being a rather frail looking broom. In another, a damsel pops out of a large trunk and Dr. Neff pops in, behind a curtain, naturally, and all in a trice. The whole thing leaves one bemused and outwardly cynical – but inwardly in a state of confusion.[19]

Overall, the critic believed it was a great show for the "kiddies," provided they had "strong nerves." Reporting on the Newark show, *The Sphinx* – a publication for magicians – offered the following anecdote:

> ... the program had just come to the presentation of the Spirit Cabinet. The youngsters who come on the stage at this time usually get pretty nervous and jittery and are apt to run all around the stage and even right off the stage. At this show, one funny kid really got scared and bolted out of the spook cabinet and into the wings. Around a piece of scenery he came face to face with Lugosi, as Dracula.
>
> Then the boy's fright doubled; he reversed his running, let out a yell, jumped off the stage, ran down the aisle and out of the theatre. The boy's fright was so genuine that the audience was in hysterics.
>
> Lugosi was in the wings merely because he likes to watch the show. Neither Neff nor the audience knew what had so frightened the boy.[20]

Perhaps Lugosi did enjoy watching the show. Regardless, it seems likely that he would have needed to be in the wings

Lugosi onstage with Bill Neff.
(Courtesy of Willian V. Rauscher)

From the *Newark Evening News* of December 18, 1947.

because he was a cast member.

Neff's own memories of Lugosi were hardly kind, at least as later reported by two of his colleagues. One performer has said that Neff complained about Lugosi's use of narcotics, with Neff adding that he was scared that the drug-addled Lugosi might fall off the stage. To keep that from happening, Neff allegedly said that he purchased a large throne-like chair in which Lugosi could sit onstage, with the magician strapping him into it.[21]

Charles Windley, who became Neff's manager in 1962, also recalled Neff's memories of Lugosi. To Windley, Neff complained that Lugosi was simply too difficult to keep in the show.[22] Such memories imply that Lugosi made numerous appearances with the *Madhouse of Mystery*, though that seems quite unlikely for several reasons, in large measure because of the actor's schedule. And then there is the fact that articles about Neff from 1948 as published in both *The Sphinx* and *Tops Magazine* refer only to the 1947 Newark appearance.[23] Rather than Neff not keeping Lugosi in his show, it seems clear from Lugosi's own schedule – a vaudeville show already booked in Baltimore and, in January 1948, a signed contract for *Abbott and Costello Meet Frankenstein* – that the actor had other obligations and priorities than the *Madhouse of Mystery*.

Possibly the Neff-Lugosi connection has been overstated given that Neff often screened old Lugosi films in conjunction with his show. Rumors also persist that Lugosi appeared in a trailer promoting the *Madhouse of Mystery*, another reason that their association might seem more substantial than it was. No trailer has ever surfaced, but it's possible that if it in fact existed, it may well have featured clips from a Lugosi movie or still photos of the actor, rather than unique Lugosi footage shot specifically for it.

Regardless, other memories of Lugosi from the same time period do not necessarily seem to support what Neff told his friends. It is true that on December 3, 1947, the press reported that Lugosi's "illness"

OPPOSITE: Poster promoting the second version of *A Nightmare of Horror*, which was apparently staged sometime during the first several months of 1949.
(Courtesy of Bob Burns)

292 NO TRAVELER RETURNS | The Lost Years of Bela Lugosi

AT THE STROKE OF 12
— MIDNIGHT —
FRIDAY and SATURDAY
STAGE
BELA LUGOSI IN PERSON
"DRACULA"
THE BATMAN
Presents
A NIGHTMARE OF HORROR
featuring
STAGE
FRANKENSTEIN
THE MAD MONSTER
IN PERSON
SCREEN 1ST SHOWING
UNIVERSAL INTERNATIONAL presents
BUD ABBOTT & LOU COSTELLO
meet FRANKENSTEIN
TICKETS ON SALE AT BOX OFFICE NOW!
ALL SEATS $1.10 TAX INCL.
ORPHEUM
5th AT B ST. ★ PHONE F. 5262

19 RKO's to Give Bela Lugosi Shows

Bela Lugosi, "Mr. Horror" himself, bring his Horror and Magic stage and screen show to 18 RKO theatres all over town during the next month and starting tonight at the Yonkers Theatre. The show features 13 scenes of mystery and magic, and a full length screen thriller, "They Creep in the Dark," also starring Bela Lugosi.

The balance of the Bela Lugosi entertainment schedule: RKO New Rochelle, tomorrow midnight; Alden, New Year's Day at three showings; Alhambra, Wednesday midnight; Albee Friday midnight, Jan. 5; Richmond Hill, Saturday midnight, Jan. 6; Strand, Far Rockaway, Monday at 8:30 p.m., Jan. 8; Jefferson, Wednesday, at 8:30 p.m., Jan. 10; 125th St., Jan. 11; Newark, Jan. 12; Dyker, Jan. 13; Fordham, Jan. 19; Franklin, Jan. 20; 86th St., Jan. 23; Regent, Jan. 25; Kenmore, Jan. 26; Mt. Vernon, Jan. 27; Orpheum, Jan. 29; Bushwick, Jan. 30.

---

brought an end to the *Tell-Tale Heart* tour. It might be possible that such an illness was due to drug usage of the type that Neff described. However, that seems somewhat unlikely given the fact that, immediately after the Neff show ended, Lugosi appeared in vaudeville in Baltimore with no difficulties. Instead, Neff's comments could have resulted from other factors, such as the very real possibility that the two men simply did not get along with one another.

Lugosi's brief ties to Neff hardly brought an end to his spook show career. A little over a year later, Lugosi seems to have appeared in a new incarnation of *A Nightmare of Horror*. A surviving poster reused the same artwork from the 1947 version of the show, but with one exception: instead of screening *Voodoo Man* (1944), the show concluded with *Abbott and Costello Meet Frankenstein* (1948). Famed horror film collector Bob Burns attended the show in Los Angeles:

> It only played the two nights. Friday and Saturday. What I can't remember is the year. It was either 1948 or 1949.
>
> The show was pretty simple. It only lasted about an hour. It started off as most Spook Shows of the period. The host was some local magician. He did tricks like escaping from a locked up trunk and other illusions like that. The last twenty minutes were when Bela and Glenn [Strange, who had appeared as the Monster in *Abbott and Costello Meet Frankenstein*] did their bit at the 'stroke of midnight.' The magician talked to the audience and said something like, 'Now it's the stroke of midnight, and we have special guests that will come on this stage direct from Europe. The lights on the stage got very dim and the magician threw his hands outward and a big flash and smoke suddenly hits the stage.
>
> When the smoke cleared Bela was standing there dressed as Dracula. The magician then said. 'I present Dracula, the vam-

From the *Trenton Evening Times* of December 19, 1950.

Window card promoting the premiere performance of Lugosi's *Horror and Magic Stage Show*.

Gary D. Rhodes | Bill Kaffenberger

pire.' The magician quickly exited the stage, and the audience broke into clapping and yelling. You could tell that Bela was pleased. He looked over the audience and with his hands out said, 'Come to me. I command you come to me.' The house lights slowly came up, and down the aisle came Glenn Strange as the Frankenstein Monster. The people really screamed.

He got to the stage and looked out at he audience, and then the magician reappeared. Then a guillotine was visible. They proceeded to have an Ygor-type guy grab a girl – maybe a plant – from the audience. After she got on stage, Bela directed the Monster to grab her, put a black hood over her, and then put her head into the guillotine. The magician pulls the rope and down comes the sharp blade and cuts the girl's head off and it falls into a basket.

The Monster grabbed the severed head out of the basket and tossed it out into audience. That caused screams aplenty. The person who caught the head then realized that it was actually a head of cabbage.[24]

From the *Trenton Evening Times* of December 26, 1950.

Burns concluded by remembering that, "the audience seemed totally thrilled. I know I was."

Years after the show, Burns befriended Glenn Strange, who gave Burns a poster for the show, which – as the theatre's street address reveals – was from its appearance at San Diego's Orpheum. Given that Burns saw the show in Los Angeles, the show seems to have played at least two cities. However, Strange told Burns that Lugosi did not want to travel all over the United States, and so this incarnation of *A Nightmare of Horror* was nearly as brief as the 1947 version.[25]

On the one hand, Burns' memories and his poster likely solve the longstanding rumors that Lugosi made personal appearances with the film *Abbott and Costello Meet Frankenstein*. The actor did not attend that film's premiere, and no evidence in film trade publications or newspapers has surfaced to suggest that he attended other screenings of it. The fact that *A Nightmare of Horror* utilized both a print of the film and actor Glenn Strange in person suggest that it is the source of these rumors.

On the other hand, there remains

Mayor Connolly Gives Lugosi Key to City

From the *Trenton Evening Times* of December 21, 1950.

Bela Lugosi Ill, RKO Tour Off

Bela Lugosi, who has defied vampires, ghosts, monsters and all the death-dealing creatures of stage and screen, has been laid low by a tiny bug—commonly known as Virus X.

Because of this the RKO theatres' dates set for Lugosi's personal appearances have been canceled. As soon as he recovers, he will resume his RKO tour with his new in-person horror and magic show.

the mystery of when Burns and others saw this version of *A Nightmare of Horror*. Obviously, it had to have been staged after the release of *Abbott and Costello Meet Frankenstein*. That film did not premiere in the Los Angeles area until July 24 1948, when it opened at five first-run theatres and was then held-over at the same for a second week.[26] It then moved onto some other area first-run theatres in Los Angeles in August before moving onto smaller venues in the autumn.

During the classical Hollywood period, agreements between the studios and exhibitors were founded on two key issues: clearance and zoning. Clearance was the interval of time between the end of the screening of a given film at one theatre and the beginning of its run at another, while zoning denoted a geographical area of given boundaries.[27] The issue was serious enough that zoning boards for film screenings existed across the country. For thirty years, Universal had followed clearance and zoning protocols. It is true that the new Universal-International was considering slashing clearance in the autumn of 1948, but even if they did proceed to do so, it would have not affected the first run of *Abbott and Costello Meet Frankenstein*. Contracts with theatres in Los Angeles and elsewhere predated any changes that U-I was considering to clearance agreements.[28]

Given that *A Nightmare of Horror* was using *Abbott and Costello Meet Frankenstein* as part of a self-contained show, rather than the film being scheduled as part of a theatrical run at a given venue, it is extremely unlikely that the show occurred during the second half of 1948 when the film was still in general release at Los Angeles theatres. Clearance and zoning would likely have prohibited that from occurring, as those theatres would have rightly viewed the spook show screenings as unfair competition. As a result, it is highly probable that the second version of *A Nightmare of Horror* occurred during the first half of 1949. Another reason to suggest that time frame is Lugosi's own schedule: he was living in California for the first several months of that year.

Lugosi's most sustained association with a spook show came near the end of 1950, that year in which he was searching for a new way to profit from his own brand. *The Bela Lugosi Horror and Magic Stage Show* became a fasci-

Montage used to publicize Lugosi's *Horror and Magic Stage Show*.

Gary D. Rhodes | Bill Kaffenberger

Window card publicizing Lugosi's *Horror and Magic Stage Show* at the 1,771-seat RKO Regent in Manhattan.

Photograph taken of Lugosi at his Horror and Magic Stage Show, *venue unknown.*

nating and somewhat misunderstood aspect of his post-war career. What became a journey lasting over three months was first chronicled in *Variety* in early December 1950:

> In an effort to bolster dwindling biz pre-Christmas, several major film theater circuits along the Atlantic seaboard are booking Bela Lugosi's Horror Show as a special stage attraction. Film menace has patterned his show somewhat along lines of Dr. Neff's spook display and Asylum of Horrors.
>
> However, a new departure is that the Lugosi show has been booked to play starting at 8:30 p.m. whereas previous such units have been staged at midnight.

Both RKO and Warner circuits have already set dates for the Lugosi Show with initial playdate scheduled soon for the Capitol in Trenton, NJ. It is going into a number of Westchester and Brooklyn RKO houses.[29]

Variety added that the show "claimed" to have the backing of famed producer Mike Todd. Todd's name was never mentioned again, which suggests that he may have dropped out of the production, or that – given *Variety*'s skeptical tone — he was never even involved to begin with.

On December 23, 1950, *The Billboard* offered further details on the pending show, reporting that a:

> … package headed by Bela Lugosi will start a series of one and two nighters, in and around New York, beginning December 26 and running to December 31. The unit, produced and booked

Gary D. Rhodes | Bill Kaffenberger

From the *Springfield Union* of February 10, 1951.

by Dave Dietz, will include a magician, six girls, four boys and a gorilla. Included will be a Lugosi flicker to run about 60 minutes. The stage show will run less than an hour. Package is being sold at a base rate of 50 – 50, tho every house will be dickered with differently. Dates so far set include RKO, Paramount and Skouras houses, starting at the RKO Capitol, Trenton, NJ. All shows will be scaled at $1 flat.[30]

The article also claimed that a week at the Baltimore Hippodrome would likely follow a lengthy series of "one and two nighters."

The original schedule had the *Bela Lugosi Horror and Magic Stage Show* premiering on December 26, 1951 and running just over five weeks to January 30, 1951. During that time, it was set to play nineteen RKO theatres in New York and New Jersey.[31] Advertisements promised a show that featured "13 Breath-Taking Scenes to Hold You Spellbound!" and "A Carload of Scenery!" In terms of its content, one newspaper claimed:

> Lugosi will 'come to life' from his coffin, and other acts include the Beauty and the Monster, ghosts, goblins, imps of darkness that fly through the air, vampire maidens, voodoo magic, the bloody guillotine, and the Bat man and the Monster in a death struggle.[32]

Here the act sounds similar to at least one of Lugosi's prior spook shows. The use of the Frankenstein Monster and the "bloody guillotine" recall the version of *A Nightmare of Horror* show that Bob Burns saw.

In addition to Lugosi, the act featured his friend Charles Stanley, who sometimes worked as a comedian. For the Lugosi show, Stanley donned a gorilla outfit, with their routine echoing elements of a film that was screened on the same bill: *The Ape Man* (1943, under the title *They Creep in the Dark*). As for the "six girls" and "four boys" who appeared in the show, their identities are regrettably unknown.

The magician in the *Bela Lugosi Horror and Magic Stage Show* was Yen Soo Kim, generally known onstage as "Kuma," but referred to in the Lugosi advertisements as "Chu Chang." Born in 1884, Yen Soo Kim became famous for his "Kuma Tubes"

From the *Hartford Times* of February 9, 1951.

trick in which he produced a brass bowl from a thin cylinder. As magician Charles Windley once recalled, "I understand it was a hell of an act, but it was his personality that sold it, not the prop itself."[33]

Yen Soo Kim once remembered working in a spook show with Lugosi, but he incorrectly noted the date as being 1952. He wrote:

> ... I performed all the magic. He closed the show by getting out of the coffin, forcing me to cut off a girl's head, and then a large gorilla and I, and Lugosi, played football with the head, until he climbed back into the coffin.[34]

He concluded his memory by stating the show provided "an interesting season," which underscores the fact he had to have been recalling late 1950 and early 1951, rather than 1952, a year in which Lugosi did not star in any known spook show, and certainly not for the duration of a "season."

The key memory of the *Bela Lugosi Horror and Magic Stage Show* from the standpoint of a viewer comes from film historian William K. Everson. He wrote that – contrary to general spook show practice – theatres screened the film first, prior to Lugosi's stage performance. Everson also said the:

> ... sketch hardly seemed to be written at all and consisted of Lugosi playing around in a laboratory with a giant gorilla and a manacled girl. The poor quality of the film had done nothing to give Lugosi an audience build-up. And in this era before the horror film had 'comeback,' the kids in the audience knew nothing of the serious work that Lugosi had done, so reception to the act was noisy and seldom respectful.

> Lugosi knew it was a wretched act, and hated doing it, but at the time it was his only income. In his performance, he gave the act far more than it deserved – but no matter whether it was well or badly received, he was always embarrassed when he left the theatre.

> Once, accidentally, the embarrassment spread to Alex Gordon, too. Alex seemed short when standing side-by-side with the towering Lugosi, and the audience, thinking that he had played the grotesque ape in the act, shouted their farewells to 'Ygor!'[35]

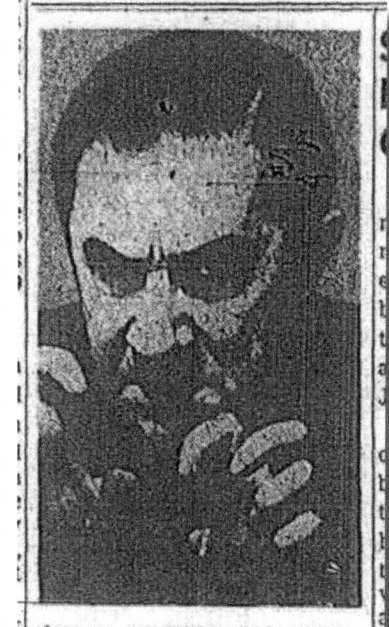

It is difficult to determine whether Everson saw the show once, or perhaps two or three times, given his anecdote about Alex Gordon. While Everson's memories are crucial to understanding the *Bela Lugosi Horror and Magic Stage Show*, they have all-too-often served as the only perspective on a lengthy series of performances that had better moments.

To augment Everson's memory with other information necessitates an investigation of the show's history, which became a three-month odyssey, not a five-week tour as originally planned. Prior to its premiere performance at the RKO Capitol Theatre in Trenton, exhibitor Henry Scholl described the *Bela Lugosi Horror and Magic Stage Show* to the press, telling them it was one of the most elaborate of its kind. "This is a big production," he said.[36] And it was a big production for a big theatre, as the Capitol seated 1,878.

Given that it was a new act, Lugosi and Lillian arrived in Trenton on December 21, 1950 for several days of rehearsals. Speaking to the *Trenton Times*, Lugosi reiterated his belief that it was becoming

BELA LUGOSI, "Mr. Horror" himself, brings his mystery and horror show to the stages of RKO Bushwick Theater, at 8:30 p.m. on Feb. 13, and RKO Greenpoint Theater, at 8:30 on Feb. 15.

From the *Brooklyn Eagle* of February 9, 1951.

"tougher to scare people."[37] Nevertheless, he was treated with great respect in the city, a far cry from the "wretched" situation that Everson witnessed. For example, Lugosi visited the City Clerk's office where he delighted workers, even speaking to one of them in Hungarian. The encounter came as a result of Mayor Connolly presenting Lugosi with the key to the city.[38]

Lugosi was also a special attraction at the "Trenton Times Annual Carrier Boys Yule Party," at which 500 newspaper carriers marched to the Capitol Theatre. Lugosi appeared in Santa Claus garb. He greeted all of the young men, who then received candy treats and free admission to a double feature of *Dark City* (1950) with Charlton Heston and *Train to Tombstone* (1950) with Don Barry. A photograph of the event depicts a beaming Lugosi surrounded by a large number of happy newsboys: hardly an embarrassing image.

As for the *Bela Lugosi Horror and Magic Stage Show*, a brief notice in *The Billboard* indicates that its opening night was a success. "Lugosi Spook Show Opens to Standees TRENTON, N.J., Dec. 30. – The Bela Lugosi package preemed at the RKO Capitol here Tuesday night (26) and drew over 2,000 for a midnight showing despite a heavy snowfall."[39] A crowd of 2,000 required "standees," as the Capitol seated only 1,878.

From Trenton, the Lugosi company traveled to Yonkers, staging the show at the RKO Proctor's Palace on December 28; the theatre seated 2,060.[40] The following night, the company appeared at the RKO Proctor's in New Rochelle; that theatre seated 2,688.[41] And then, on New Year's Day 1951, they played three shows at the RKO Alden in Jamaica, New York, which seated 1,888. Like the others, it was not a large venue, but it was also not a small "neighborhood house." At the time, these were respectable theatres.

It was after the Alden shows that tour plans had to change. By January 3, 1951, in a replay of a scenario that had occurred more than once before, Bela Lugosi became ill with either a bad cold or flu. The *New York Post* called it "a tiny bug – commonly known as Virus X."[42] But it may have been something more than a tiny bug, as over three weeks of shows had to be cancelled.

The *Bela Lugosi Horror and Magic Stage Show* returned to theatres on January 27, 1951, playing the RKO Dyker in Brooklyn. By that time, a few of the missed dates had been rescheduled and a number of new theatres had been booked, and not just RKO theatres. The revised tour continued into March, with its appearances covering much more geography than the original schedule, which had focused mainly on the New York City area.

For example, the *Bela Lugosi Horror and Magic Stage Show* played the 3,064-seat Warner's State Theatre in Hartford, Connecticut on February 10, 1951, just one day before Frank Sinatra appeared at the same venue. Like the Trenton premiere, the Hartford show seems to have gone very well, a far cry from the show(s) that Everson saw in the New York City area.

While in Hartford, the Lugosis stayed at the Bond Hotel, with the actor granting an interview to a reporter from the *Hartford Courant*. She wrote:

> Bela Lugosi, at the State Theater for just today, created a reputation in films by scaring people to death. As a vampire.

From the *Brooklyn Eagle* of February 24, 1951.

302　NO TRAVELER RETURNS ｜ The Lost Years of Bela Lugosi

As the half-human, half-beast character, he was the scare-crow in films which held people to their seats and made them scream with fright.

... Now people are not scared at imaginary things. We have real scares (A Bomb, etc.) to worry about. Dracula is apple-pie alongside the machinations of the Communists. ...When he walks about the lobby of The Bond, I bet no one runs.

He is an amiable looking man with dignity and years. Intelligence is written all over him. But gee, he may suddenly, when we are sitting there, spring up and point one of those long, lean fingers at me and scare me out of the place. I had better make no predictions. Actors sometimes fall back into their film roles. From habit, as much as from anything else. Maybe I will just drop in at the opening show today at the State Theatre and call it a day."[43]

Her description seems to have been informed by Lugosi's regular refrain that scaring audiences was not as easy as it used to be.

Lugosi's performance in Hartford went quite well. Magician Jean L. Casey (known onstage as Professor J. Stonehurst) told the press that he "caught Bela Lugosi's horror show at the State Theatre, Hartford, Conn., and found it an excellent presentation by a master showman...."[44] And *Hartford Courant* writer M.O.S. offered the following positive critique:

Frank Sinatra is at the State Theatre today for just this day. But yesterday Bela Lugosi was at the theatre. His stay was only for one day. Maybe everyone in town was at the theatre, so staying over would have been unnecessary. That was the way it seemed anyway. He rewarded his fan following with a performance as scary as any he has given in films. All the famous film tricks of lights and shadows, noise and screams. Even to the costume. The bat man. The Vampire King who knows all the angles of scaring the daylights out of people. Apparently though, that was what the audience went for. It got what it expected, breath-taking surprises.

From the *Camden Courier-Post* of March 12, 1951.

Other acts surrounded him. An excellent magic act done in the old time vaudeville manner with all the fanfare that used to go with magic. Oriental costuming, background and what have you. Tricks which proved the mind is a lot faster than the eye... The show was a real all-out vaudeville bill of the old-time vaudeville houses. A good buildup prelude to Frank Sinatra's arrival... Saturday's bill being like a good dinner of meat and potatoes....[45]

Snow, rain, and chilling temperatures adversely affected attendance and grosses at Hartford-area theatres during the week that Lugosi and Sinatra appeared onstage, but grosses for both shows were the highest reported in the city.[46]

By mid-February, *Variety* reported that, "Bela Lugosi ... has a horror unit that's touring the smaller houses. Business is reported good."[47] Here the mention of smaller theatres likely refers to such bookings as the Warner's Regent in Paterson, New Jersey on February 9.[48] Increasingly, despite the announcements made in December, the Lugosi company gave shows at midnight and sometimes offered three shows in a single day.

That said, the *Bela Lugosi Horror and Magic Stage Show* may also have grown more elaborate during the course of the tour. On March 5, the show appeared at the 2,560-seat Skouras Astoria Theatre in Astoria on Long Island, New York; it then played the 1,821-seat Skouras Boulevard Theatre in Jackson Heights on Long Island.[49] One advertisement claimed that Lugosi would appear "with a troupe of 50 people," which if true would be quite a few more performers than originally announced.

On the other hand, it seems quite possible that the *Horror and Magic Stage Show* was scaled back for at least some of its final bookings in March of 1951. That was certainly true when Lugosi brought the act to the 1,620-seat Skouras Jamaica Theatre in Queens. At the age of 15, Paul Noble – who later worked for WNEW-TV in New York, where his many duties included scheduling films for their show *Creature Features* – attended the Jamaica show with a group of his friends. On that occasion, Lugosi's act was sandwiched between *The Ape Man* (1943) and *The Devil Bat* (1940). Noble remembered that:

> The Skouras Jamaica was an old-time vaudeville theatre that had been modernized, and we were curious how it looked. So we said 'Let's go see him. Let's go see what Bela Lugosi looks like.' We weren't sure why he would be doing a show like this [in a neighborhood theatre]. We had not heard that he was doing an entire tour. ... The theatre was right next to the elevated subway and there was no façade visible. You could hear the noise inside the theatre when the trains came through!
>
> [In the act], a Chinese magician came out and did tricks, including sawing a woman in half. When the magician was done, the curtains slowly opened to reveal a coffin bathed in purple and green lighting. The coffin lid opened with a creaking sound piped in [over the sound system]. Bela Lugosi sat up in the coffin. This was repeated three times, the magician, then Bela, and that was the extent of the show, [which] lasted 35 to 40 minutes.
>
> Lugosi recited lines from his movies, like 'Listen to them, the children of the night' and 'I never drink wine.' You know, the ones always used by the impersonators. We were raised on Lugosi's grade B movies like the ones from Monogram and PRC through all the reissues. [At that time], we were not familiar with his classic films except for *Dracula* (1931) and weren't aware that he was classically trained in the theatre, so we thought the show was tacky.[50]

Noble did not recall any other performers in the act, including anyone in a gorilla costume.

Here might well be the key reason why a few memories of the show seem to be at odds with at least some reviews. The act was not always the same. Depending on the stage of the tour, as well as perhaps how much money a given theatre chain offered, the contents of the *Horror and Magic Stage Show* varied. Sometimes the show sported a larger cast and perhaps a longer running time that featured more elaborate stage action and props; in other cases, such as the performance Noble witnessed, it was more compact, featuring fewer persons and less stage action.

The final performance seems to have occurred at the stroke of midnight at the 2,213-seat RKO Stanley in Camden, New Jersey on March 17, 1951. The show followed notable performances at RKO theatres in such cities as Newark and a return visit to Brooklyn.[51] Whether these RKO appearances were as austere as the Skouras show at the Jamaica Theatre is unknown. At any rate, by that time, the *Bela Lugosi Horror and Magic Stage Show* had appeared at 22 venues, if not more.

During its run, the show certainly appeared at some prominent theatres in front of very receptive audiences. William K. Everson's oft-repeated anecdote is an important part of the story, but it alone does not reveal the complexities of a tour that may have faced some disrespectful teenagers, but that also found Lugosi accepting the key to the city of Trenton. No doubt Lugosi would have preferred work in film, radio, television, or legitimate theatre to this spook show, but – that said – the tour was not nearly as humiliating as previous histories have suggested. In fact, at times it seems to have been quite the opposite.

And so, at long last, Lugosi had finally made a lengthy spook show tour. When its curtain closed, so did his "lost years." What followed next would take him far from American soil, ushering him firmly into the 1950s: a period quite different from the late forties, a period of fewer career opportunities and much greater personal hardship.

(Endnotes)

1. Wilson, Earl. "It Happened Last Night." *Uniontown Morning Herald* (Uniontown, PA) 13 Nov. 1950.
2. The Motion Picture Relief Fund received Lugosi's signed authorization on 6 Sept. 1946. The stamp was issued in 1947.
3. Kattelman, Beth A. "Magic, Monsters, and Movies: America's Midnight Ghost Shows." *Theater Journal* 62:1 (2010).
4. *Ibid.*
5. "*One Night of Horror.*" *The Billboard* 10 May 1941.
6. Advertisement. *Fort Wayne Journal-Gazette* (Fort Wayne, IN) 10 May 1941.
7. "Bela Lugosi Suffers Indigestion Attack Before Show Friday." *Fort Wayne Journal-Gazette* 10 May 1941.
8. *Variety* 21 May 1941.
9. Advertisement. *San Diego Union* 7 Feb. 1947.
10. "Orpheum Spook Show Full of Chills, Thrills." *The Tribune-Sun* (San Diego, CA) 7 Feb. 1947.
11. "Spook in Person." *Variety* 22 Jan. 1947.
12. See Chapter 3 for an extended discussion of *Three Indelicate Ladies*.
13. Roberts, McCarl. "Foreword." In William V. Rauscher's *Pleasant Nightmares: Dr. Neff and His Madhouse of Mystery*. (New Jersey: S. S. Adams, 2008).
14. Rauscher, *Pleasant Nightmares*.
15. "Mystery Revue." *Newark Evening News* (Newark, NJ) 16 Dec. 1947.
16. Advertisement. *Newark Evening News* 21 Dec. 1947.
17. *Newark Star-Ledger* (Newark, NJ) 19 Dec. 1947.
18. Rauscher, *Pleasant Nightmares*.
19. "Magic Stuff." *Newark Evening News* 19 Dec. 1947.
20. "Rabbit Eggs." *The Sphinx* (February 1948).
21. Rauscher, *Pleasant Nightmares*.
22. *Ibid.*
23. "Rabbit Eggs"; Untitled. *Tops Magazine* (February 1948).
24. Burns, Bob. Email to Gary D. Rhodes. 11 Nov. 2011.
25. *Ibid.*
26. These theatres were the United Artists at 9th and Broadway, the Fox Ritz on Wilshire, the Iris on Hollywood Boulevard, the Guild on Hollywood Boulevard, and the Studio City on Ventura at Laurel.
27. Ricketson, Frank H., Jr. *The Management of Motion Picture Theatres* (New York: McGraw-Hill, 1938).
28. "Universal to Slash Clearance." *Film Daily* 27 Sept. 1948.
29. "Lugosi's Horror Show Set to Hypo Nabe Biz." *Variety* 6 Dec. 1950.
30. *The Billboard* 23 Dec. 1950.
31. "19 RKO's to Give Bela Lugosi Shows." *New York Post* 28 Dec. 1950.
32. "Lugosi in Person Tomorrow Night." *Newark News* 29 Feb. 1951.
33. Windley, Charles "Chuck." Email to Gary D. Rhodes. 21 Feb. 2006.
34. "Kuma and the Kuma Tubes, as Related to Ray Muse by Yen Soo Kim (Kuma)." *Genii* (Sept. 1955).
35. Everson, William K. "The Last Days of Lugosi." *Castle of Frankenstein* (Apr. 1966).
36. "Lugosi in Horror, Magic Show at Capitol." *Trenton Evening Times* (Trenton, NJ) 18 Dec. 1950.
37. "Tougher to Scare People! That's What Bela Lugosi Finds, Declaring 'Art Of Blood Chilling' Has Changed – Visits Mayor Connolly." *Trenton Evening Times* 21 Dec. 1950.
38. *Ibid.*
39. *The Billboard* 6 Jan. 1951.
40. Advertisement. *Yonkers Herald-Statesman* (Yonkers, NY) 28 Dec. 1950.
41. Advertisement. *New Rochelle Standard-Star* (New Rochelle, NY) 29 Dec. 1950.
42. "Bela Lugosi Ill, RKO Tour Off." *New York Post* 3 Jan. 1950.
43. Stafford, M. Oakley. "Informing You." *Hartford Courant* (Hartford, CT) 10 Feb. 1951.
44. *The Billboard* 17 Mar. 1951.
45. "Frightening Show Given At State By Bela Lugosi." *Hartford Courant* 11 Feb. 1951.
46. *Boxoffice* 17 Feb. 1951.
47. *Variety* 14 Feb. 1951.
48. Advertisement. *Paterson Morning Call* (Paterson, NJ) 8 Feb. 1951; Advertisement. *Paterson Morning Call* 9 Feb. 1951.
49. Advertisement. *Long Island Star-Journal* (Long Island City, NY) 5 Mar. 1951.
50. Kaffenberger, Bill. Interview with Paul Noble. 28 May 2012.
51. Advertisement. *Camden Courier-Post* (Camden, NJ) 15 Mar. 1951.

Lugosi on a publicity tour for *The Black Sleep* (1956). Here he is seated to the right of John Carradine. Lon Chaney Jr. (left) and Tor Johnson (right) look over their shoulders. (Courtesy of the Bancroft Library, University of California, Berkeley)

306   NO TRAVELER RETURNS | The Lost Years of Bela Lugosi

Chapter 19

FAREWELL

"Lofty timbers. The walls around are bare, echoing to our laughter as though the dead were there.

Quaff a cup to the dead already. Hurrah for the next who dies!"

– Lucy (Frances Dade) in *Dracula* (1931)

On November 30, 1950, Erskine Johnson's Hollywood column advised readers that the "screen's newest merchant of menace, *The Thing*, will send the Frankenstein Monster, Bela Lugosi, the Bat Man, and other movie spook men running for air-raid shelters."[1] Directed by Howard Hawks, *The Thing from Another World* (1951) is an important example of the kind of horror movie that came to dominate the fifties, one that relied on science fiction and visitors from outer space.

The very same day that Johnson's column was published, Bela Lugosi requested a withdrawal card from the Screen Actors Guild. He had not worked on a film set in 1947, 1949, or 1950, and he had no pending offers of film work in Hollywood in 1951. At first, it would seem that his request was the culmination of so many months and months without film work.

But that was not the reason why Lugosi stopped paying his SAG dues. Instead, he knew that he would soon be working in another country, perhaps for many months. Richard and Alex Gordon, who had befriended Lugosi in 1948, suggested that Lugosi should star in *Dracula–The Vampire Play* in England. As Richard Gordon later remembered, the two brothers hoped that:

> … a successful production in London's West End would lead to an offer to bring it to Broadway. Unfortunately, London managements were … uninterested, but finally we arranged with a British management to put the show on the road in England with the idea that a successful tour of the Provinces would lead to a London production.[2]

The idea likely appealed to Lugosi, who had nearly made a tour of England in *Dracula* in 1948.

By October 1950, discussions of the British tour were well underway.[3] Bertha Klausner acted as Lugosi's agent in the matter, in charge of all negotiations on his behalf. During the autumn of that year, Klausner was already working with Mary Vignoles, an administrator at Associated Playwrights & Composers Limited of London, on a version of the play *Lili Marlene*.[4] On October 28, Vignoles responded to Klausner's request to find backers in London who could stage *Dracula*.

Only days earlier, Vignoles had dined with Williams and Woolley, two London theatrical agents who expressed interest in staging *Dracula* as a "short tour and West End" production. Initially communicating through Vignoles, Williams and Woolley approached Klausner for "full particulars."[5] Klausner

Lugosi's application for a withdrawal card from the Screen Actors Guild.

informed them that Lugosi would be available from June 1 to October 1, 1951, and that he wanted ten percent of the gross, with a $1,000-a-week minimum.[6]

Within a few weeks, Klausner began working directly with Williams and Woolley. On November 30, 1950, Michael Williams wrote to her that they had been able to locate "a first-class management" for the show, "subject to all terms being of mutual satisfaction."[7] One of those points had to do with *which* version of the play would be used. Klausner had already told them that Lugosi needed to use "a version of his own." That caused Williams to become concerned about royalties on what seemed to be a variant of the Hamilton Deane-John L. Balderston play.

More importantly, Williams told Klausner that the backers believed Lugosi's financial demands were too high. His counter offer proposed that Lugosi would make 15% of the weekly gross, minus entertainment tax deducted at source, with a minimum guarantee of £200 British Pounds Sterling per week. Lastly, there remained the matter of agency fees, as the resulting production would find Lugosi represented by Klausner in America and Mary Vignoles and Michael Williams in London, a potentially complicated situation, but hardly the first time that Lugosi's management would involve several persons.

By December 12, 1950, Klausner accepted Williams' payment terms on Lugosi's behalf, but she also offered to drop his weekly take to 13% of the gross if his round trip transportation from New York to London could be covered. Klausner also explained to Williams that Lugosi needed to use the Broadway version of the play, on which royalties would have to be paid.[8] Here it seems that Lugosi did wish to use the Deane-Balderston play, but with perhaps a few minor modifications that suited his particular needs.

On December 18, Williams sent Klausner an urgent telegram, informing her that the backers would "require Lugosi" to "open March 1951 or nearest date."[9] By January 5, 1951, Vignoles sent Klausner a letter requesting the same. She added:

> I was talking to our Chairman, Mr. Cutter, about the production, and he said undoubtedly this play will have to be produced exactly as Mr. Lugosi wishes, and according to his master script, and if it is his wish that we do it for him, we will be pleased if you make this suggestion to the Williams and Woolley office direct. It would certainly relieve Mr. Lugosi of any worry apart from playing his part.[10]

Here again the complications of the management team are apparent, with one London representative (who was increasingly involved in the actual production) asking an American agent to communicate with another London representative.

Klausner informed Lugosi of her progress on January 10, 1951, underscoring the need for the actor to be in England in "early spring."[11] She must have already realized that such a timeframe was problematic, as she sent a letter to Michael Williams on the same day reiterating Lugosi's desire for a June opening. In fact, she repeated the same request in another letter to Williams as well.[12] Lugosi's desire to postpone the start of the play may have been due in part to his illness as reported in the press on

January 3, which necessitated changes to his spook show schedule.

However, Lugosi (through Klausner) had proposed the June start date *prior* to that illness, so he may have had good reason to believe that other – and potentially better – work was to be had in America that spring. After all, by requesting a June 1951 opening, he was perfectly willing to forego the summer stock circuit that year, even though it had been core to his career in the summers of 1947, 1948, 1949, and 1950. No doubt he wanted to undertake the British tour, but something was keeping his attentions focused in America until June. If nothing else, his desire to delay the journey suggests that he was hardly desperate to get on a London payroll.

In the end, however, Lugosi relented. Lillian packed their clothes at their New York apartment at 200 West 54th Street. The Lugosis then left for England aboard the *Mauritania*, traveling further and further from their son. They arrived in London on April 11, 1951. Soon thereafter, Lillian wrote a letter to Charles Stanley, who had played the gorilla in the *Bela Lugosi Horror and Magic Stage Show*:

> We want to thank you again for coming to see us off and the cable. We had a very rough sea most of time and naturally [became] seasick. We only got out of bed for dinner. It felt good to set foot on solid ground. The press turned out in full force on both the boat in Southampton and the station in London. They made us feel most welcome. We are very happy here and our only wish now is for the success of *Dracula*. With kindest regards, we remain, sincerely your friends, Bela and Lillian Lugosi.[13]

And so whatever reservations Lugosi had about the spring voyage to England, he hoped for a success. If *The Devil Also Dreams* could not reach the Great White Way in 1950, perhaps *Dracula* could make it to the West End in 1951.

But Lugosi and *Dracula* didn't see the West End. All of the weeks and weeks of planning came to naught. Klausner's lengthy negotiations resulted in little more than problems on foreign soil. As Richard Gordon later recalled:

> … the British management had great difficulty in raising the money for the production and was counting so strongly on Bela's name to carry the show that they had skimped horribly on every other aspect of the tour. Sets, costumes, and the supporting cast smacked of 'poverty row' and the disappointment of being surrounded by such amateurish elements crushed Bela's hopes and reduced him to desperation.[14]

In an effort to generate money, Lugosi appeared in his first film in three years, a low-budget British horror-comedy entitled *Mother Riley Meets the Vampire* (1951, aka *Vampire Over London* and *My Son, the Vampire*).

The Lugosis returned to New York on December 11, 1951. Rather than remaining in the city, they rapidly made their way to California. The key reason was to reunite with their son. Another was the fact that *Variety* announced

The envelope that contained Lillian Lugosi's 1951 letter to Charles Stanley from England.

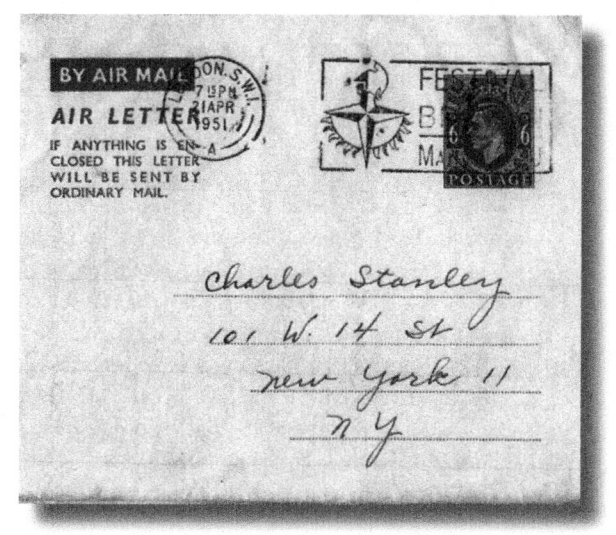

that Lugosi would possibly "star in a half-hour weekly TV series to be filmed in Hollywood. Package, of course, would have a mystery format. While the deal is in its advanced staged, it's understood that the project won't be finalized for contractual reasons until after December 26."[15] But the show, which was to be called *Mysterioso*, did not come to be.

In February 1952, theatrical agent Lyman Brown wrote Lugosi, telling him about an offer to star in *Dracula–The Vampire Play* in Bermuda. The theatre, which had only 400 seats, guaranteed Lugosi $500 a week, as well as room and board. But the producers were unwilling to pay his transportation to and from California.[16]

Lugosi thanked Brown for his time and help, but turned down the Bermuda offer:

> I certainly am enjoying my vacation home with my son – the 8 month job in England certainly took the skids from under me. I never want to go thru a spell like that again. There is a strong chance that I may go over there again for a picture in August or September, but I would only have to spend 4 or 5 weeks.[17]

His letter reveals his true feelings about the British tour, as well as his fear of being trapped in another country in another failed play.

And so Lugosi lived in California for the rest of his life. At that point, he became a different kind of exile. In 1953, Lillian divorced him. Two years later, he publicly admitted he was addicted to drugs and sought a cure. Though he would remarry in 1955, his family life was never the same.[18] Feeding on dreams was increasingly hard to do.

Work became scarce, far more than ever before. Some of this was due to the growing grip that science fiction held on Hollywood, and some of it was due to Lugosi's advancing years. And as before, much of it was also due to Lugosi's ongoing struggle with his own image.

For example, in August 1951 while Lugosi was still in England, an "attractive housewife" named Lillian Laskin in New York reported that:

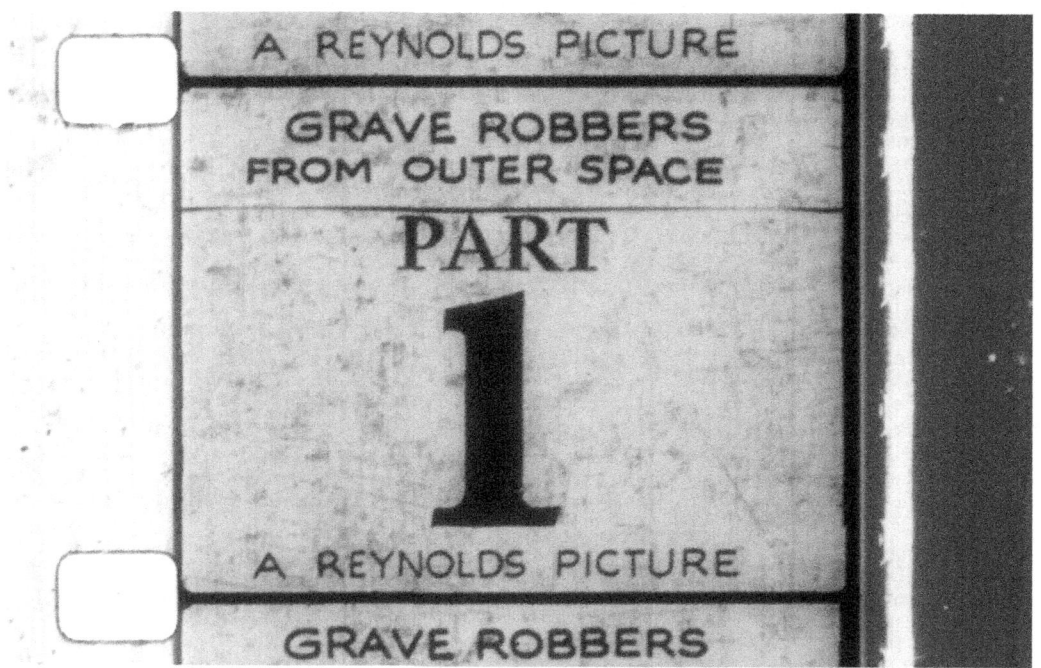

A frame from the leader footage to *Grave Robbers from Outer Space* (1959, aka *Plan 9 from Outer Space*). (Courtesy of Lee Harris)

… her husband was at work Saturday night so she switched on her TV set and settled back to watch actor Lugosi's interpretation of a vampire in an old movie. Mrs. Laskin said she suddenly heard a noise that did not belong, and spotted a man peering through her window.

She let out a blood-curdling yell that almost turned the TV screen's vampire back into Lugosi – and a couple of policemen passing her home nabbed the onlooker.[19]

Laskin's experience was unique, but only in terms of the peeping tom. Old Lugosi films commonly flickered on television screens throughout the fifties, just as they did at movie theatres. A major reissue of *Dracula* (1931) occurred in 1951 and 1952. Audiences once again saw Lugosi descend that aged staircase in Transylvania; they once again heard him speak the dialogue "I am Dracula."

Though Lugosi did guest star on a few television shows and act in a couple of new films, he traversed into stranger and stranger terrain when he became affiliated with the weird world of Edward D. Wood, Jr., who directed the cheapest movies in which Lugosi ever appeared: *Glen or Glenda* (1953), *Bride of the Atom* (1955, aka *Bride of the Monster*), and, posthumously, *Plan 9 from Outer Space* (1959, aka *Grave Robbers from Outer Space*). Never was he further from classical Hollywood film production than when he stepped onto the sets of such Z-grade movies. No traveler returns.

On August 16, 1956, Lugosi moved one last time, from life to death. At the age of 73, on the brink of a divorce from his last wife, Hope Lininger, the actor made his final appearance as Count Dracula. He was laid to rest in one of his famous vampire capes.

(Endnotes)

1 Johnson, Erskine. "In Hollywood." *Statesville Daily Record* (Statesville, NC) 30 Nov. 1950.
2 Gordon, Richard. Letter to Gary D. Rhodes. 20 Aug 1986.

3 Thanks to our rediscovery of Bertha Klausner's papers, this chapter clearly shows that negotiations for Lugosi's *Dracula* tour of Great Britain and Northern Ireland started much earlier than previously believed and, in addition, provides much new detail and insight to the story.
4 Vignoles, Mary. Letter to Bertha Klausner. 21 Oct. 1950. [Available in the Bertha Klausner Papers. University of Wyoming, American Heritage Center. Box 73. Folder 15.]
5 Vignoles, Mary. Letter to Bertha Klausner. 28 Oct. 1950. [Available in the Bertha Klausner Papers. University of Wyoming, American Heritage Center. Box 73. Folder 15.]
6 Klausner, Bertha. Letter to Mary Vignoles. 11 Nov. 1950. [Available in the Bertha Klausner Papers. University of Wyoming, American Heritage Center. Box 73. Folder 15.]
7 Williams, Michael. Letter to Bertha Klausner. 30 Nov. 1950. [Available in the Bertha Klausner Papers. University of Wyoming, American Heritage Center. Box 73. Folder 15.]
8 Klausner, Bertha. Letter to Michael Williams. 12 Dec. 1950. [Available in the Bertha Klausner Papers. University of Wyoming, American Heritage Center. Box 73. Folder 15.]
9 Williams, Michael. Telegram to Bertha Klausner. 18 Dec. 1950. [Available in the Bertha Klausner Papers. University of Wyoming, American Heritage Center. Box 73. Folder 15.]
10 Vignoles, Mary. Letter to Bertha Klausner. 5 Jan. 1951. [Available in the Bertha Klausner Papers. University of Wyoming, American Heritage Center. Box 73. Folder 15.]
11 Klausner, Bertha. Letter to Bela Lugosi. 10 Jan. 1950. [Available in the Bertha Klausner Papers. University of Wyoming, American Heritage Center. Box 73. Folder 15.]
12 Klausner, Bertha. Letter to Michael Williams. 10 Jan. 1950; Klausner, Bertha. Letter to Michael Williams. 13 Jan. 1950. [Available in the Bertha Klausner Papers. University of Wyoming, American Heritage Center. Box 73. Folder 15.]
13 Lugosi, Lillian. Letter to Charles Stanley. 20 Apr. 1951.
14 Gordon, letter to Rhodes.
15 *Variety* 19 Dec. 1951.
16 Brown, Lyman. Letter to Bela Lugosi. 6 Feb. 1952. [Available in the Chamberlain and Lyman Brown Papers, and Undated, Series II: Correspondence, Box 64, Folder F.9 at the New York Public Library/Lincoln Center for the Performing Arts in New York.]
17 Lugosi, Bela. Letter to Lyman Brown. 26 Mar. 1952. [Available in the Chamberlain and Lyman Brown Papers, and Undated, Series II: Correspondence, Box 64, Folder F.9 at the New York Public Library/Lincoln Center for the Performing Arts in New York.]
18 For a thorough investigation of Lugosi's last years, see Gary D. Rhodes' *Bela Lugosi, Dreams and Nightmares* (Narberth, PA: Collectables, 2007).
19 "Woman Out-Performs Television Vampires When Peeper Appears." *Charleston Gazette* (Charleston, WV) 20 Aug. 1951.

Lugosi as Dracula, his regular traveling companion. This rare photo originally appeared in the March 1932 issue of *The Cast*.

A publicity photograph for *Abbott and Costello Meet Frankenstein* (1948) offers one of the most recognizable images of Lugosi from his "lost years."

Afterword

By Bela G. Lugosi

No *Traveler Returns The Lost Years of Bela Lugosi* by Gary D. Rhodes and Bill Kaffenberger was an awakening for me from my limited view of the world during the years 1945-1951. From the time I was six years old in 1944 and in the first grade, until sixth grade, I was living in a military boarding school. I would see Dad on occasion when he would come to the school to view our regular Sunday parades. I would visit with Dad in the home of my grandparents, who lived near the academy which was in Lake Elsinore, California.

I lived with my grandparents and attended public school in Lake Elsinore in the seventh, eighth and ninth grades. When my Mom and Dad returned from abroad, we moved to Los Angeles, California where I graduated from high school and college. Dad and Mom were divorced while I was in high school and Dad died the next year.

My Dad and I did not speak about the lost (to me) years of 1945-1951. In later years, I often wondered why I was put in a boarding school and separated from my parents at such a young age. I am grateful to the authors' research and writing, as it has helped me to understand that in order for my Mom and Dad to make sure I had a stable and safe childhood, they were compelled by their circumstances to provide for my schooling at the military academy while they traveled to make a living wherever Dad's craft took him.

Lugosi at an unknown live appearance in the late forties. (Courtesy of David Wentink)

Appendix

A BELA LUGOSI TIMELINE
1945 to 1951

1945

No Traveler Returns Tour

Monday 2/5 – Friday 2/23: BL begins rehearsals for *No Traveler Returns* at the Mayan Theatre in Los Angeles.

Wednesday 2/14: BL – or someone imitating him, as per the program's gimmick – guest stars on Ken Murray's *Which is Which?* radio show.

Saturday 2/24: *No Traveler Returns* premieres at Lobero Theatre, Santa Barbara, CA with one matinee and one evening performance.

Monday 2/26 – Friday 3/9: *No Traveler Returns* opens at the Curran Theatre in San Francisco, CA.

Saturday 3/10 – Monday 3/12: Down time and then travel to Seattle, WA. Lillian's divorce lawsuit is officially dismissed on March 10, 1945, and she is with him in Seattle.

Monday 3/12: BL and Lillian interviewed by the *Seattle Times* while staying at the Olympic Hotel.

Tuesday 3/13 – Sunday 3/18: *No Traveler Returns* opens at Metropolitan Theatre, Seattle, WA.

Monday 3/19: Play closed early. BL and Lillian return to Los Angeles.

Monday 4/23 – Saturday 5/19: BL signs for vaudeville tour of the Midwest, but it was cancelled for reasons unkown.

Tuesday 5/1: *Zombies on Broadway* released by RKO.

Friday 5/25: *The Body Snatcher* opens in NYC.

Tuesday 7/31: BL guest stars on *County Fair*, a radio show hosted by Jack Bailey.

Saturday 8/4: *The Billboard* announces BL being submitted for theatre vaudeville dates in an act written by Don Marlowe, set to premiere at Loew's State in NYC. This vaudeville tour probably did not occur. If it did happen, it would likely have been in October and/or November.

Saturday 8/18 – Sunday 9/9: *Genius at Work* shoots at RKO with BL in the cast.

Friday 11/30: BL returns to RKO to appear in more footage for *Genius at Work*.

Gary D. Rhodes | Bill Kaffenberger

1946

Monday 3/25 – Friday 4/19: *Scared to Death* (originally titled *Accent on Horror*) is filmed with BL in the cast.

Tuesday 7/16: BL appears on the *Command Performance Show*, Armed Forces Radio Service.

Friday 7/19: *Variety* reports that BL will do personal appearances for *Scared to Death* at the Golden Gate Theatre in San Francisco. These events did not occur given the delayed release of the film.

Saturday 7/20: Musicraft announces a series of eight 12-inch records of horror stories entitled *Mysterioso*, which are to be narrated by BL. This series was never produced.

Sunday 10/20: RKO releases *Genius at Work*.

Tuesday 10/22: BL guest stars on radio on *The Rudy Vallee Show*.

Wednesday 11/6: Screen Guild announces release of Golden Gate Pictures' *Scared to Death*. However, the announcement was premature, as the film would not debut until May 1947.

Tuesday 12/17 – Wednesday 12/18: BL has a featured role in *That We May Live*, a production at the Los Angeles Shrine Auditorium (6,442 seats) staged in support of a Jewish free state.

1947

Friday 2/7 – Saturday 2/8: BL stars in *A Nightmare of Horror*, Orpheum Theatre (1,952 seats), San Diego, CA.

Sunday 2/9: *New York Times* reports that BL has signed to perform in the play *Three Indelicate Ladies*.

Wednesday 2/19: By this time, BL has left Los Angeles for New York City and *Three Indelicate Ladies*.

Friday 2/21: BL arrives in New York City, staying at the Gotham Hotel.

Monday 3/3: *Variety* reports that BL receives a Federal Tax Refund of $571.

Sunday 3/9: Lugosi guest stars on the *Exploring the Unknown* radio show.

Monday 3/10 – Wednesday 4/9: BL in rehearsals for *Three Indelicate Ladies*. It is possible that rehearsals did not start until as late as 3/17.

Monday 3/17: BL signs *A Call to Action*, an open letter in support of Palestine, published in *Variety*.

Wednesday 3/19: BL guest stars on *The Adventures of Ellery Queen* radio show.

Thursday 4/10: BL makes a guest appearance as part of the Governer's and Celebrities Day, New England Modern Homes Show, Boston, MA.

Three Indelicate Ladies Tour

Thursday 4/10 – Saturday 4/12: BL in the premiere of *Three Indelicate Ladies*, Shubert Theatre, New Haven, CT.

Monday 4/14 – Saturday 4/19: BL and *Three Indelicate Ladies*, Wilbur Theatre, Boston, MA.

Monday 4/14: BL guests at a noon luncheon at Dinty Moore's Restaurant follwed by an afternoon appearance at a Red Cross show.

Thursday 4/17: Announcement that BL would lecture at Boston University on Monday 4/17. There is a strong possibility that the event never took place.

Friday 4/18: BL appears in a midnight show with Joey Faye at The Casino, Boston, MA.

Saturday 5/3: Screen Guild officially releases *Scared to Death*.

Sunday 5/18: BL guest stars on the radio show *Quick As A Flash*.

Wednesday 6/25: BL arrives in New Hope, PA for summer stock rehearsals.

Tuesday 7/1 – Saturday 7/5: BL stars in *Arsenic and Old Lace*, Bucks County Playhouse, New Hope, PA.

Thursday 7/3 – Saturday 7/5: BL makes daily personal appearances as part of the "Chamber of Horrors" at the New Hope Street Fair.

Thursday 7/10: *Variety* reviews *Scared to Death*.

Monday 7/14 – Saturday 7/19: BL stars in *Dracula*, John Drew Theatre, East Hampton, Long Island, NY.

Tuesday 7/15: *Variety* reports that *Scared to Death* brought in $25,000 in one week at the Million Dollar Theatre (2,093 seats) in Los Angeles, CA.

Monday 7/21 – Saturday 7/26: BL stars in *Dracula*, Boston Summer Theatre, New England Mutual Hall, Boston, MA.

Monday 7/28 – Saturday 8/2: BL stars in *Dracula*, Cambridge Summer Theatre, Cambridge, MA.

Monday 8/4: BL makes a personal appearance at the Saratoga Springs Racetrack and is interviewed on the *Bill and Fan Show* over Albany, NY's radio station WOKO.

Tuesday 8/5 - Sunday 8/10: BL stars in *Arsenic and Old Lace*, Spa Summer Theatre, Saratoga Springs, NY.

Wednesday 8/6: BL makes what is likely his first television appearance on *Backstage at the Spa Theatre*, WRGB-TV, Schenectady, NY.

Thursday 8/7: BL does another interview on WOKO, this time on the program *Hollywood Soundstage* with Cathy Rice.

Friday 8/8: BL appearance with Robert Ripley aboard the *Mon Lei*.

Monday 8/11: Newspapers announce the pending production of *Brain of Frankenstein* (1948, aka *Abbott and Costello Meet Frankenstein*).

Monday 8/18 – Saturday 8/23: BL stars in *Dracula*, Kenley Deer Lake Theatre, Deer Lake, PA.

Friday 8/22: The *Lock Haven Express* announces that the Kiwanis Club of Lock Haven, PA will bring BL in (tentatively scheduled for October 8) for a one night performance of *Dracula*. There is no evidence that this performance occurred.

Monday 8/25 – Saturday 8/30: BL stars in *Arsenic and Old Lace*, Fairhaven Summer Theatre, Fairhaven, MA.

Tuesday 9/2 – Sunday 9/7: BL stars in *Dracula*, Litchfield Summer Theatre, Litchfield, CT.

Thursday 9/18: BL signs with Don Marlowe Agency. He has already been relying on Marlowe for some months.

Tuesday 9/23: Don Marlowe announces that he is arranging a *Dracula* play revival in London for BL.

Wednesday 10/8: BL writes agent Virginia Doak claiming that financial problems have caused him to sign with Don Marlowe.

Saturday 11/1: *Motion Picture Herald* announces BL will star in a Midwestern tour of *The Tell-Tale Heart* beginning 11/19. That same day, BL signs contract with Don Marlowe for the tour.

Saturday 11/8: The Tom Elwell Agency announces a new Bela Lugosi vaudeville-style "package" available for theatres.

Sunday 11/9: BL appears at the *Continental Varieties* live production in New York.

Friday 11/14: BL and Lillian arrive in Rockford, IL by train to prepare for the *Tell-Tale Heart* premiere.

Sunday 11/16: *Wisconsin State Journal* (Madison, WI) announces BL will appear at the Capitol Theatre on December 13.

Tell-Tale Heart Tour

Wednesday 11/19 – Wednesday 12/23: These dates represent the original planned length of the tour based available newspaper articles and surviving window cards.
Wednesday 11/19 – Thursday 11/20: *Tell-Tale Heart* Premiere, Rockford, IL at the Coronado Theatre (2,556 seats). Two nights of midnight shows. *Dracula* (1931) is on the screen.
Saturday 11/22: *Boxoffice* magazine reports BL in Minneapolis, MN to schedule *Tell-Tale Heart* appearances.
Monday 11/24: BL at the Venetian Theatre (1,935 seats) in Racine, WI. A midnight show that, according to the newspaper advertisement, included "Bela Lugosi Hypnotizes Frankenstein Monster." *One Body Too Many* (1944) is screened.
Thursday 11/27: BL at Geneva Theatre (705 seats) in Lake Geneva, WI. Midnight show. *Ghosts*

Break Loose is the advertised film (likely actually either *Spooks Run Wild* [1941] or *Ghosts on the Loose* [1943]).

Thursday 11/27: BL at Delavan Theatre (405 seats) in Delavan, WI. Midnight show. *Return of the Ape Man* (1944) is on the screen. Delavan is located about a 20 minute drive to the west of Lake Geneva. BL more than likely shuttled between the two towns, with the film being shown first at one theatre with the stage appearance second, and the reverse order at the other theatre.

Wednesday 12/3: BL scheduled to appear at Capitol Theatre (1,383 seats) in Manitowoc, WI, but this might have been cancelled.

Friday 12/5: BL scheduled to appear at Park Theatre (864 seats), Waukeesha, WI. Cancelled due to purported illness.

Monday 12/8: BL scheduled appearance at Vista Theatre (929 seats), Negaunee, MI did not happen.

Saturday 12/13: BL scheduled appearance at Capitol Theatre (2,244 seats), Madison, WI did not occur.

Tuesday 12/23: BL scheduled appearance at Hollywood Theatre (944 seats), Eau Claire, WI did not occur. Originally set for two shows, one at 8 p.m. and one at midnight.

Wed 12/10: *Variety* reports that BL has stopped Midwest barnstorming tour and has signed with Edward Sherman Agency for vaudeville appearances at $1,250 a week. Two first shows scheduled under the deal: the Adams Theatre, Newark, NJ with Dr. Bill Neff, and the Hippodrome, Baltimore, MD with Robert Alda and Gordon MacRae.

Monday 12/15: *Variety* reports BL will sign a contract this week for England *Dracula* revival.

Thursday 12/18 – Wednesday 12/24: BL costars with Dr. Bill Neff and his *Madhouse of Mystery* show, Adams Theatre (2,037 seats), Newark, NJ.

Thursday 12/25 – Tuesday 12/30: BL vaudeville act at Hippodrome Theatre (2,100 seats), Baltimore, MD.

Saturday 12/27: BL appears with Hippodrome cast at the Baltimore Variety Club. Exact date uncertain, but more than likely was either Friday or Saturday of the week.

1948

Tuesday 1/13: *New York Times* reports that BL is signed for *Abbott and Costello Meet Frankenstein*.

Friday 1/16: Contract signing date for *Abbott and Costello Meet Frankenstein*. Don Marlowe signed for BL.

Monday 1/26: *Variety* announces that BL has arrived in LA from NYC and also mentions a potential London *Dracula* play revival.

Monday 2/2: *Variety* announces that BL will star in a *Dracula* revival and in *Harvey*, both for London.

Thursday 2/5 – Saturday 3/20: Universal shoots *Abbott and Costello Meet Frankenstein*, with Thursday 2/12 being BL's first day on the set.

Thursday 2/19: *Variety* reports 20th-Fox has signed BL to a "term contract." BL appears in no films under this contract.

Wednesday 4/14: *Variety* reports that the deals for BL to perform in both *Dracula* and *Harvey* in London have been cancelled.

Saturday 5/1: *The Billboard* announces that the Don Marlowe Agency is joining forces with McConkey Music Corporation, an outfit that specializes in vaudeville one-nighters.

Wednesday 5/5: BL appears on the *Abbott and Costello Show* on radio.

Monday 5/17 – Saturday 5/22: BL nightclub act at Tony's Chi Chi Club in Salt Lake City, UT. BL stays in the Hotel Utah during the engagement. This appears to be his nightclub debut.

Friday 7/2: BL in Denver, CO for *Dracula* play rehearsals. BL and Lillian stay at Denver's Park Lane Hotel.

Thursday 7/8 – Tuesday 7/13: BL stars in *Dracula*, Phipps Auditorium, Denver, CO.

Wednesday 7/14: Having departed Denver for the East Coast, BL, Lillian, and manager Don Marlowe stay overnight in Hastings, NE.

Thursday 7/15: BL, Lillian, and Don Marlowe stay overnight at Hotel Burlington, Burlington, IA. BL was the Guest of Honor at the Philco Dealers Dinner.

Friday 7/16: BL, Lillian, and Don Marlowe stay overnight at the Mansfield-Leland Hotel, Mansfield, OH.

Saturday 7/17: BL and Lillian arrive in Reading, PA for the summer stock season.

Monday 7/19 – Saturday 7/24: BL stars in *Dracula*, Green Hills Theatre, Reading, PA. BL interviewed on WHUM-Radio sometime during the week. BL also made a publicity appearance at a Rotary Club Luncheon, where he gives a speech.

Saturday 7/24: *Abbott and Costello Meet Frankenstein* premieres in Hollywood without BL in attendance.

Monday 8/2 – Saturday 8/7: BL stars in *Dracula* at the Norwich Summer Theatre, Norwich, CT. During the week, BL makes a live appearance at the local Elk's Fair (on Friday 8/6) and also attends a Lion's Club Luncheon where he makes an impromptu speech.

Monday 8/9: The *Pittsburgh Press* announces plans for a Karloff, Lorre, and Lugosi joint stage appearance with clips from their films. Nothing comes of these plans.

Monday 8/9: BL appears on the *Martha Deane Program* on WOR-Radio in New York City.

Monday 8/9 – Saturday 8/14: BL stars in *Arsenic and Old Lace*, Sea Cliff Summer Theatre, Sea Cliff, Long Island, NY.

Wednesday, 8/18: BL appears in special "pre-filmed" *Variety Show* broadcast over KTSL-TV in Los Angeles, CA. BL's participation in this "special" was likely filmed in Los Angeles prior to his departure for the summer stock season.

Friday 8/20 – Thursday 8/26: BL Vaudeville Show, Broadway-Capitol Theatre (3,367 seats), Detroit, MI.

Wednesday 9/1 – Tuesday 9/7: BL Vaudeville Show, Olympia Theatre (2,500 seats), Miami, FL. Four shows a day.

Wednesday 9/1: BL and Lillian were special guests at the Club Bali, Miami, FL.

Friday 9/3: BL interviewed on WIOD Radio, Miami, FL. BL and Lillian were special guests at the Five O'Clock Club, Miami, FL.

Tuesday 9/14: BL and Lillian arrive in Springfield, MA. BL attends a press luncheon.

Thursday 9/16 – Sunday 9/19: BL Vaudeville Show, E. M. Loew's Court Square Theatre (1,730 seats), Springfield, MA. Three shows a day.

Monday 9/20 – Wednesday 9/22: BL nightclub act at Gray Wolf Tavern, Masury, OH. Originally scheduled to run through 9/26. Two shows each evening.

Thursday 9/23: BL night club act receives a brief favorable review in the local Youngstown, OH daily paper. However, BL cuts the engagement short.

Saturday 9/25 – Sunday 9/26: BL Vaudeville Show at the Steel Pier, Atlantic City, NJ. This popular beach and entertainment/amusement complex boasted three "theatres": the Music Hall, the Ocean Hall, and the Steel Pier (Boardwalk). BL's show was booked into the mid-sized Music Hall (2,500 seats) along with Sonny Sparks as MC, Pansy the Horse, The Elgins, Marilyn Frechette and Larry Fotine and His Orchestra.

Monday 10/11: BL Vaudeville Show, Loew's Bedford Theatre (1,866 seats), Brooklyn, NY.

Tuesday 10/12: BL Vaudeville Show, Loew's Triboro Theatre (3,290 seats), Astoria, NY.

Sunday 10/24: BL was second billed to Gene Krupa in a vaudeville show at the Valley Arena Gardens (2,000 seats), Holyoke, MA. One matinee and two evening shows.

Friday 10/29: BL Vaudeville Show, Manhasset Theatre (968 seats), Manhasset, NY.

Thursday 11/4 – Saturday 11/6: BL Vaudeville Show, Binghamton Theatre (1,747 seats), Binghamton, NY. Three shows each day.

Thursday 11/4: BL and Lillian are guests of honor at a buffet supper party sponsored by the Southside American Legion in Binghamton, New York. Event co-sponsored by WMBF-Radio.

Monday 11/15: *Night of Stars*, Madison Square Garden, NYC. BL – along with Boris Karloff, Peter Lorre, and others – appears at this event dedicated to the new state of Israel and in support of the United Jewish Appeal of Greater New York. Performance began at 8:15PM EST.

Monday 11/22: BL appears on *Herb Shriner Time* at 6:30PM EST. on WCBS-Radio, NYC.

Wednesday 11/24: BL Vaudeville Show at Loew's Oriental Theatre (2,731 seats), Brooklyn, NY. Special Thanksgiving Day booking.

Sunday 11/28: BL and Lillian likely begin journey to California on this date. They do not return to the East Coast until June of 1949.

Wednesday 12/1: BL and Lillian stay at the Roundup Lodge in Deming, New Mexico on their way back to California.

1949

January – June: BL enters an extended period of apparently voluntary unemployment, likely in order to reconnect with his wife and son. In addition, during this period he communicates with several agents in New York City attempting to line up a return to Broadway, as well as to line up additional summer stock for the next season. Sometime during this period, BL likely performs in a new incarnation of *A Nightmare of Horror* in San Diego and Los Angeles. Glenn Strange appears live as the Monster, and the show includes screenings of *Abbott and Costello Meet Frankenstein* (1948).

Tuesday 3/15: BL signs a contract with the Charles Beyer Agency. It authorizes Beyer to find BL work in films.

Saturday 4/23: *The Billboard* announces that actor Hampton White will appear in a roadshow version of *Dracula* with BL. The trade also claims the two will appear in a 3-D motion picture together. Neither comes to pass.

Monday 6/27: BL, Lillian and Bela Jr.'s likely departure date from Lake Elsinore to the East Coast for the summer stock season.

Thursday 6/30: BL and family stop for breakfast at a café in Carroll, IA.

Friday 7/1: BL and family spend the night at Cedar Lawn Tourist Camp, a mile west of Warsaw, IN.

Saturday 7/2: BL and family stop for lunch in Cairo, OH.

Sunday 7/3: BL and family stop over in Buffalo, NY.

Monday 7/4: BL and family arrive in the Syracuse, NY area in advance of rehearsals for *Arsenic and Old Lace*.

Tuesday 7/5: BL meets fellow Hungarian actor Paul Lukas and attends a performance of his play at the Famous Artists Country Playhouse.

Saturday 7/9: BL visits a paralyzed war veteran to show his support.

Monday 7/11 – Saturday 7/16: BL stars in *Arsenic and Old Lace* at Famous Artists Country Playhouse, Fayetteville, NY.

Thursday 7/14: *Variety* announces production of a TV series featuring William Morris Agency artists to be called *Surprise Theatre*. BL named as one of the participants.

Tuesday 7/26 – Sunday 7/31: BL stars in *Arsenic and Old Lace*, Lakeside Theatre, Lake Hopatcong, Landing, NJ.

Friday 7/29: *Variety* announces that KNBH TV in Los Angeles will televise William Morris Agency's *Surprise Theatre*, including one episode with Lugosi.

Monday 8/1 – Saturday 8/6: BL stars in *Arsenic and Old Lace* at Litchfield Summer Theatre, Litchfield, CT.

Tuesday 8/9 – Sunday 8/14: BL stars in *Arsenic and Old Lace* at the Ocean Playhouse (aka Ocean Hall) (1,450 seats) on the Steel Pier, Atlantic City, NJ. Peformances were at 9PM EST each evening. While there were no matinees, special extra late performances were offered on Friday and Saturday evenings in addition to the regularly scheduled performances.

Tuesday 8/16 – Sunday 8/21: BL stars in *Arsenic and Old Lace* at Green Hills Theatre, Reading, PA.

Wednesday 8/31: Broadcast date of a 30-minute episode of *Surprise Theatre* over KNBH-TV in LA. This was likely the episode that featured BL.

Friday 9/9: BL Vaudeville Show, Loew's Coney Island Theatre (2,472 seats), Brooklyn, NY.

Saturday 9/10: BL costars with Basil Rathbone on the *Man in the Shadows* episode of *The Tales of Fatima* radio show, NYC.

Friday 9/16 – Sunday 9/18: BL Vaudeville Show, Loew's Melba Theatre (2,156 seats), Brooklyn, NY.

Tuesday 9/20: BL Vaudeville Show, Loew's Triboro Theatre (3,290 seats), Astoria, NY.

Friday 9/23: BL Vaudeville Show, Loew's Bedford Theatre (1,866 seats), Brooklyn, NY.

Thursday 10/6: BL appears on *Art Linkletter's House Party* radio show, NYC.

Tuesday 10/11: BL stars in *A Cask of Amontillado*, an episode of the *Suspense* TV show, NYC.

Friday 10/14: BL's vaudeville show, Loew's Hillside Theatre (2,653 seats), Jamaica, Queen's, NY. Also, BL's nephew Bela Loosz and his wife arrive in Boston from Hungary.

Thursday 10/27: BL with Milton Berle on *Texaco Star Theatre* TV show, NYC.

Thursday 11/10: BL signs long term agreement with the William Morris Agency.

Wednesday 11/16 – Tuesday 11/22: BL vaudeville show, Fox Theatre (5,037 seats), St. Louis, MO.

Wednesday 11/23 – Wednesday 11/30: BL vaudeville show, Orpheum Theatre (1,659 seats), Wichita, KS.

Sunday 12/12: BL appears on the *Crime Does Not Pay* radio show. The show was prerecorded; this date represents its New York City radio premiere.

Although presently unconfirmed, the Lugosis may have returned to California for the Christmas season directly after completion of the Wichita, KS vaudeville show. It seems that BL would have had time for a brief vacation with his son prior to returning to NYC.

1950

Sunday 1/22: BL appears on the *Celebrity Time* TV show, New York City.

Friday 1/27: BL guest stars on the *Versatile Varieties* TV show, New York City.

Sunday 2/12: BL arrives in Pittsburgh, PA in advance of a nightclub show.

Monday 2/13 – Saturday 2/18: BL nightclub act at the Copa Club, Pittsburgh, PA. BL also gives interview on WWSW Radio sometime during the week.

Thursday 3/2 – Friday 3/3: BL Vaudeville Show, Schine's Oswego Theatre (1,805 seats), Oswego, NY. Three shows daily.

Wednesday 3/8: BL vaudeville act at State Theatre (999 seats), Torrington, CT.

Monday 3/13: BL and Lillian leave for St. Petersburg, FL.

Wednesday 3/15: BL and Lillian arrive in the St. Petersburg, FL area to prepare for an upcoming *Dracula* play appearance. They stay at The Tides Hotel. Local press interviews BL.

Thursday 3/16: Press again interviews BL. Rehearsals begin for *Dracula*.

Monday 3/20 – Saturday 3/25: BL stars in *Dracula*, presented by the St. Petersburg Players, Southside Junior High School, St. Petersburg, FL.

Wednesday 3/23: BL and Lillian are Guests of Honor the famous Tramor Cafeteria's Fourth Street South location in St. Petersburg, FL.

Sunday 3/26: BL and Lillian leave for NYC.

Wednesday 3/29 – Thursday 3/30: BL Vaudeville Show, Schine's Geneva Theatre (1,868 seats), Geneva, NY. Three shows daily.

Thursday 4/13 – Saturday 4/15: BL Vaudeville Show, Rialto Theatre (1,400 seats), Amsterdam, NY.

Friday 4/21: BL is "Ghost of Honor" at the Mystery Writers of America dinner in NYC.

Sunday 5/21: BL appears on the *Starlit Time* television show.

Wednesday 5/24: BL is Guest of Honor at Gamut Club Dinner, NYC.

Thursday 6/1: BL appears on the television version of Ed Sullivan's *Little Old New York* at 7:30PM EST on WPIX-TV.

Wednesday 6/7: BL guest stars on *The Bill Slater Show* at 7:30PM EST on WOR-TV. Florence Rinard, Fred Vandeventer and Roger Price are also guests on this 30-minute show.

Tuesday 6/27: BL appears on Allen Funt's *Candid Microphone* radio show, WCBS at 9:30PM EST.

Tuesday 6/27: BL and Lillian arrive at Winooski Park, VT for *Dracula* rehearsals.

Tuesday 7/4 – Saturday 7/8: BL stars in *Dracula* at St. Michael's Playhouse, Winooski Park, VT.

Monday 7/9: Rehearsals begin for *The Devil Also Dreams*.

The Devil Also Dreams Tour

Monday 7/24 – Saturday 7/29: Somerset Theatre, Somerset, MA.
Monday 7/31 – Saturday 8/5: Famous Artists Country Playhouse, Rochester, NY.
Monday 8/7 – Saturday 8/12: Famous Artists Country Playhouse, Fayetteville, NY.
Monday 8/14 – Saturday 8/19: Royal Alexandria Theatre, Toronto, Canada.
Monday 8/21: Capitol Theatre, Ottawa, Canada.
Tuesday 8/22 – Saturday 8/26: His Majesty's Theatre, Montreal, Canada.

Monday 9/18: A new television show entitled *Murder and Bela Lugosi* premieres at 8:30PM EST on WPIX-TV. The nature of BL's contribution or performance is unknown. This program may have been nothing more than the broadcast of an old BL film.

Monday 10/2: BL appears on *The Paul Winchell Show* (aka, *The Paul Winchell-Jerry Mahoney Show*), WNBT-TV, NYC.

Saturday 10/28: Associated Composers and Playwrights Ltd. in England send Bertha Klausner a letter requesting that serious negotiations begin for BL to appear in a tour of *Dracula–The Vampire Play* in Great Britain.

Friday 12/15: BL rehearses and appears in a kinescope for his upcoming appearance on *The Robert Q. Lewis Show*, sponsored by Arnold Bakers, at CBS TV Studio 58 (Town Theatre at 55th Street and 9th Avenue). A rehearsal with the set but no cameras occurred from 4PM to 4:30PM, followed by a full rehearsal with cameras from 4:30PM to 6PM. The kinescope was filmed from 6PM to 6:15PM.

Saturday 12/16: Producer and booking agent Dave Dietz announces the upcoming *Bela Lugosi Horror and Magic Show* for the NYC area. Though it had to change due to BL's reported illness, the original schedule would have taken him to the following locations in 1950:

> **Tuesday 12/26:** RKO Capitol Theatre (1,878 seats), Trenton, NJ; **Thursday 12/28:** RKO Proctor's Palace (2,060 seats), Yonkers, NY; **Friday 12/29:** RKO Proctor's (2,688 seats), New Rochelle, NY.
>
> The original tour also scheduled BL to appear at the following locations in 1951: **Monday 1/1:** RKO Alden (1,888 seats), Jamaica, NY. Three shows; **Wednesday 1/3:** RKO Alhambra (1,332 seats), Harlem, NY; **Friday 1/5:** RKO Albee (3,250 seats), Brooklyn, NY; **Saturday 1/6:** RKO Richmond Hill (2,234 seats), Richmond Hill, NY; **Monday 1/8:** RKO Strand (1,750 seats), Far Rockaway, NY; **Wednesday 1/10:** RKO Jefferson (1,787 seats), New York City, NY; **Thursday 1/11:** RKO Proctor's 125th Street (1,564 seats), Harlem, NY; **Friday 1/12:** RKO Proctor's Palace (2,275 seats), Newark, NJ; **Saturday 1/13:** RKO Dyker (2,142 seats), Brooklyn, NY; **Friday 1/19:** RKO Fordham (2,353 seats), Bronx, NY; **Saturday 1/20:** RKO Franklin (2,937 seats), Bronx, NY; **Wednesday 1/24:** RKO 86th Street (3,131 seats), New York City, NY; **Thursday 1/25:** Warner's Regent (1,949 seats), Paterson, NJ. While it is possible that the Warner's Regent was the intended venue, the published schedule is unclear; the planned venue could have been the RKO Regent (1,771 seats) in Manhattan, NYC, NY as the original tour appeared to be exclusive to RKO Theatres; **Friday 1/26:** RKO Kenmore (3,017 seats), Brooklyn, NY; **Sunday 1/28:** RKO Proctor's (1,879 seats), Mt. Vernon, NY; **Tuesday 1/30:** RKO Bushwick (2,004 seats), Brooklyn, NY.

Monday 12/18: The *Trenton Times* runs an article regarding the "world premiere" of the *Bela Lugosi Horror and Magic Show*. This show and subsequent dates listed in this timeline reflect the revised tour schedule as it actually occurred.

Thursday 12/21: BL arrives in Trenton, NJ for rehearsals for the *Horror and Magic Stage Show*. Interviewed by the local press. Receives the "key to the city." BL is special guest at the annual "*Trenton Times* Newsboys Christmas Party" during the evening.

Friday 12/22: WJZ-TV Channel 7 in New York airs a repeat of BL's appearance on *Celebrity Time* at 10 p.m. (originally broadcast on January 22, 1950).

Sunday 12/24: The *Robert Q. Lewis Show* with BL is broadcast at 11PM EST on WCBS-TV, NYC.

Tuesday 12/26: BL stars in the premiere of the *Bela Lugosi Horror and Magic Stage Show*, RKO Capitol (1,878 seats), Trenton, NJ. Midnight show.

Thursday 12/28: Lillian Lugosi is the guest on *Okay Mother*, a radio show hosted by Dennis James on WABC-Radio, NYC.

Thursday 12/28: BL stars in the *Horror and Magic Stage Show* at RKO Proctor's Palace Theatre (2,060 seats), Yonkers, NY. Show at 8:30PM EST.

Friday 12/29: BL stars in the *Horror and Magic Stage Show* at RKO Proctor's Theatre (2,688 seats), New Rochelle, NY.

1951

Monday 1/1: BL stars in the *Horror and Magic Stage Show* at RKO Alden Theatre (1,888 seats), Jamaica, NY. Three shows.

Wednesday 1/3: BL scheduled for *Buddy Rogers Show* on WOR-Radio, NYC at 3PM EST. BL became ill and temporarily cancelled the spook show appearances the same day, so it is uncertain as to whether he appeared on Rogers' show.

Wednesday 1/3: BL scheduled for *The Bill Slater Show*, along with Richard Arlen and Arch Oboler, on WOR-TV, NYC at 7:30PM EST. With the announcement of BL's illness, it is uncertain if he was able to keep this television commitment.

Friday 1/5: The London-based theatrical agents for the proposed British *Dracula* tour starring BL suggest a March 1951 premiere. However, BL requests a June 1951 premiere. Ultimately, the tour debuted at the end of April 1951.

Saturday 1/27: BL's *Horror and Magic Stage Show* tour has resumed at least by this date with an appearance at RKO Dyker Theatre (2,142 seats), Brooklyn, NY.

Monday 1/29: BL guest stars on the *Betty Crocker Magazine of the Air* radio show, NYC.

Tuesday 1/30: BL's *Horror and Magic Stage Show* at RKO Keith's (2,929 seats), Flushing, NY. Show at 8:30PM EST.

Thursday 2/1: BL's *Horror and Magic Stage Show* at RKO Strand (1,750 seats), Far Rockaway, NY. Show at 8:30PM EST.

Saturday 2/3: BL's *Horror and Magic Stage Show* at RKO Richmond Hill (2,234 seats), Richmond Hill, NY. Midnight show.

Wednesday 2/7: BL guest stars on the *Johnny Olson Luncheon Club* radio show.

Thursday 2/8: BL's *Horror and Magic Stage Show* at RKO Regent Theatre (1,771 seats), Manhattan, NY. Midnight show.

Friday 2/9: BL's *Horror and Magic Stage Show* at Warner's Regent Theatre (1,949 seats), Paterson, NJ. Shows at 3:45PM, 7:30PM and 10:30PM EST.

Saturday 2/10: BL's *Horror and Magic Stage Show* at Warner's State Theatre (3,064 seats), Hartford, CT. Doors opened at 11:00AM EST, with continuous performances of the show into the evening hours.

Tuesday 2/13: BL *Horror and Magic Stage Show* at RKO Bushwick (2,004 seats), Brooklyn, NY. Show at 8:30PM EST.

Thursday 2/15: BL's *Horror and Magic Stage Show* at RKO Greenpoint (1,673 seats), Brooklyn, NY. Show at 8:30PM EST.

Saturday 2/17: BL in *Gasoline Cocktail* in a repeat broadcast of the *Crime Does Not Pay* radio show, NYC.

Tuesday 2/20: BL's *Horror and Magic Stage Show* at RKO Proctor's Palace Theatre (2,275 seats), Newark, NJ.

Thursday 2/22: BL makes live appearance at the National Photographic Show in NYC.

Friday 2/23: BL's *Horror and Magic Stage Show* at RKO Kenmore Theatre (3,017 seats), Brooklyn, NY. Midnight show.

Saturday 2/24: BL's *Horror and Magic Stage Show* in return engagement at RKO Greenpoint (1,673 seats), Brooklyn, NY. Midnight show.

Tuesday 2/27: BL's *Horror and Magic Stage Show* at RKO Madison (2,760 seats), Ridgewood, Brooklyn, NY. Show at 8:30PM EST.

Monday 3/5: BL's *Horror and Magic Stage Show* at Skouras Astoria Theatre (2,560 seats), Astoria, Long Island, NY.

Tuesday 3/6: BL's *Horror and Magic Stage Show* at Skouras Boulevard Theatre (1,821 seats), Jackson Heights, Long Island, NY. During this period, BL also brought the show to the Skouras Jamaica Theatre (1,620 seats), Jamaica, Queens, Long Island, NY where it was sandwiched between showings of *The Ape Man* (1943) and *The Devil Bat* (1940).

Thursday 3/17: BL's *Horror and Magic Stage Show* at RKO Stanley Theatre (2,213 seats), Camden, NJ. Midnight show. This was likely his final *Horror and Magic Stage Show*.

Tuesday 4/3: BL and Lillian board ship to go to England for the *Dracula* play revival. They will not return to NYC until December of 1951.

Lugosi as Jonathan Brewster in the Famous Artists Country Playhouse version of *Arsenic and Old Lace* in Fayetteville, New York in 1949.

Acknowledgments

The authors would like to offer their appreciation to the various archives, libraries, museums, and universities that kindly offered assistance during the research phase of this book project: the Albany Public Library of New York, the Allen County Museum of Ohio, the American Heritage Center at the University of Wyoming, the American Radio Archives at the Thousand Oaks Library in California, the American Museum of Vaudeville Collection at the University of Arizona Library, the Andover-Harvard Theological Library of Massachusetts, the Annenberg Rare Book and Manuscript Library at the University of Pennsylvania, the Ardmore Public Library of Oklahoma, the Atlantic City Free Public Library of New Jersey, the Bancroft Library at the University of California at Berkeley, the Beverly Historical Society of Massachusetts, the Billy Rose Theatre Division of the New York Public Library, the Boston Public Library of Massachusetts, the Brown County Historical Society of Wisconsin, the Burlington Public Library of Iowa, the Cambridge Historical Society of Massachusetts, the Cambridge Public Library of Massachusetts, the Chickasaw Regional Library System of Oklahoma, Cinegraph of Hamburg, the Cofrin Library at the University of Wisconsin-Green Bay, the Colorado Historical Society, the Community Library of the Shenango Valley in Pennsylvania, the Denver Public Library of Colorado, the Department of Special Collections at the University of California at Santa Barbara, the Des Moines County Historical Society of Iowa, the Detroit Public Library, the Duluth Public Library of Minnesota, the East Hampton Historical Society of New York, the Enoch Pratt Free Library of Maryland, the Fall River Public Library of Massachusetts, the Federal Bureau of Investigation, the Fergus Falls Public Library of Minnesota, the Free Library of Philadelphia, the Friends of the Lake Geneva Theatre of Wisconsin, the Geneva Public Library of New York, the Hamburg Area Historical Society of Pennsylvania, the Harry Ransom Center at the University of Texas at Austin, the Hartford History Center at the Hartford Public Library of Connecticut, the Hayden Library at Arizona State University, the Hennepin County Library of Minnesota, the Hillman Library at the University of Pittsburgh, Historic Denver Inc., the Historical Society of Pennsylvania, History Colorado, the Hoboken Public Library of New Jersey, the Holyoke Public Library of Massachusetts, the Howard Gottleib Archival Research Center at Boston University in Massachusetts, the Immigration and Naturalization Service, the John Drew Theatre of New York, the Kennebunk Free Library of Maine, the Kiplinger Research Library of Washington DC, the La Crosse Public Library of Wisconsin, the Lake Geneva Public Library of Wisconsin, the Lake Hopatcong Historical Museum of New Jersey, the Lake Hopatcong Historical Society of New Jersey, the Lake Region Public Library of North Dakota, the Library of Congress of Washington, DC, the Litchfield Historical Society of Connecticut, the Manitowoc Public Library of Wisconsin, the Margaret Herrick Library of the Academy of Motion Picture Arts and Sciences, the Mercer County Genealogy Society of Pennsylvania, the Millicent Library of Massachusetts, the Mount Vernon Public Library of New York, My.Movie.Memorabilia, the National Archives of the United States, the Negaunee Public Library of Wisconsin, the New Bedford Free Public Library in Massachusetts, the New Brunswick Public Library of New Jersey, the New Ulm Public Library of Minnesota, the New York State Historical Association, the

Newark Public Library of New Jersey, the New Hope Historical Society of Pennsylvania, the Norwich Historical Society of Connecticut, the Ohio County Public Library of West Virginia, the Orwigsburg Free Public Library of Pennsylvania, the Otter Tail County Historical Museum of Minnesota, the Paterson Free Public Library of New Jersey, the Pickering Educational Resources Library at Boston University, the Pottsville Free Public Library of Pennsylvania, the Public Library of New London of Connecticut, the Public Library of Youngstown and Mahoning County of Ohio, the Queens Public Library of New York, the Reading Public Library of Pennsylvania, the Red Wing Public Library of Minnesota, the Robert Beverly Hale Library of Rhode Island, the Rochester Public Library of New York, the *Rock River Times*, the Rockford Public Library of Illinois, St. Michael's College of Colchester, Vermont, the Salt Lake City Public Library of Utah, the Schuyler County Historical Society of New York, the Screen Actors Guild, the Sea Cliff Village Library of New York, the Sea Cliff Village Museum of New York, the *Seattle Times*, the Seattle Public Library in Washington, the Seattle Washington Museum of History and Industry in Washington, the Siouxland Libraries of North Dakota, the South Kingston Public Library of Rhode Island, the South St. Paul Public Library of Minnesota, the Special Collections Department at the University of Iowa, the Special Collections Division at the University of Washington Libraries, the Superior Public Library of Wisconsin, the Syracuse University Archives of New York, the Toronto Reference Library of Canada, the Trenton Free Public Library of New Jersey, the University of Central Oklahoma, the Warren-Trumball County Public Library of Ohio, the Watkins Glen Public Library of New York, the Wisconsin Center for Film and Theatre Research, the Yancy County Public Library of North Carolina, and the Yonkers Public Library of New York.

In addition, the authors would like to note their gratitude to the following individuals who have helped make this book possible: Dr. Henry Aldridge, Michael Ambrosino, Carolyn Edgington Anderson, Vicki Anderson, Jerry Armellino, Gyöngyi Balogh, Bruce R. Bardarik, Joan E. Barney, Brandon Barton, Marty Baumann, Dan Benedetti, Jeanette Berard, Scott Berman, Sophie Bieluczyk, H. C. Blaney III, the late Richard Bojarski, Bridget Bradley, Tom Brannan, Diane Briggs, Amanda Brouwer, Dianne Brown, Bart Bush, John Calhoun, Jennifer Callaway, Chrystal Carpenter, Mindy Carson, Janet D. Cate, Mario Chacon, Sarah Chester, Herbert Cheyette, James Clatterbaugh, Eileen Colletti, Dale Colston, Mary Ann Comstock, Michael Copner, James Crespinel, Richard Daub, Michael J. David, Randy Decker, Michael DuBasso, Frank J. Dello Stritto, Ronald Dupont Jr., the late David Durston, Robert Ray and Ruth Edgington, Robert Edgington Jr., Harriet Eisman, Jr., Scott Essman, Ken Etten, the late Philip R. Evans, the late William K. Everson, Tom Ewing, Arcadia Falcone, Ed Fields, Chris Finger, Lawrence Fultz, Jr., Diane Gallagher, Ellen K. Gamache, Cecile W. Gardner, Sean Giere, Sarah Gilmor, Wendy Gladston, Josh Gladstone, Raymond Glew, Stephanie Goodliffe, the late Richard Gordon, Julie Graham, Honora Greenwood, Claudia Gross, Gordon R. Guy, G. D. Hamann, Harry Haige, Agnes Hamberger, Faye Haskins, Shaun A. Hayes, Roger Hecht, Alexandra Henri, Candy Herbert, Linda M. Hocking, Emil Hoelter, David H. Hogan, Roger Hurlburt, Jane Huew, the late Alan Jefferys, Ellie Jordan, the late Steve Jochsberger, Marty Kane, Steve Kaplan, Amy Kastigar, Constance Kelly, Anthony Kerr, Nancy Kersey, Stephen Kiesow, Ginny Kilander, Eugene Kirschenbaum, Lorna Kirwan, Gavin Kleespies, Leanne Kubicz, Deborah Lang, Lee Lears, Maureen Lee, James Lewis, Zachary Liebhaber, Frank Liquori, Rosslyn Littman, Carolyn Longworth, Jean H. Lythgoe, Ada Lynn, Carolyn Marr, Jim Massery, Marcia Mattfield, Kimberly Matthews, Deborah Carder Mayes, Meredith Meier, Matt Metcalf, Peter Michaels, Mark A. Miller, Lynn Naron, Randy Nesseler, Jayne Altobell Newirth, Henry Nicolella, John Norris, Jim Nye, Mary O'Brien, Jackie Oshman, Alyssa K. Pacy, Albert A. Palacios, Dennis Payne, Bill Peterson, Victor Pierce, William Pirola, Pat Pitkin, Anne Ponticelli, Ted Post, Linda Rau, William V. Rauscher, Mike Ravnitzky, Robert Rees, Sara Reres, Jeffrey Roberts, George Robinson, Matthew Rodgers, Jacque L. Roethler, Pat Rothenberg, Tara Samul, Frank Schier, Bruce Scivally, Fred Scollay, Elizabeth B. Scott, Anna B. Selfridge, David Seubert, Toni Sheehan, Richard Sheffield, Don G. Smith, George R. Snell, Kathy Spalding, Melanie Stallings, John Storojev, Elaine Stritch, the late Dr. Andor Sziklay, Paul Szilard, Brian Taves, Maurice Terenzio, Mario Toland, Andrew Tompkins, John

Ulakovic, Dr. Steven Béla Várdy, Bill Vrandsitis, the late Stratton Walling, Jon Wang, Kay Weiss, Becki White, Jessica Wilson, Chuck Windley, the late Robert Wise, Clay Withrow, Amy S. Wong, Valerie Yaros, and Gregory Zatirka.

The authors would also like to extend their deepest thanks to a number of individuals who gave so much of their time and support that they proved crucial to this book's completion: Leonardo D'Aurizio, Buddy Barnett, Doug Bentin, Kevin Brownlow, Bob Burns, Bill Chase, George Chastain, Michael Copner, Darryl Cox, Robert Cremer, Kristin Dewey, Jack Dowler, Edward "Eric" Eaton, Phillip Fortune, Beau Foutz, Art Greenhaw, Lee Harris, Howard Jessor, Elena Kaffenberger, Dr. Michael Lee, Bela G. Lugosi, Constantine Nasr, Ben Ohmart, Dr. Desmond O'Rawe, Paul J. Phillips, Gerald Schnitzer, Samuel M. Sherman, Dr. Robert Singer, Lynne Lugosi Sparks, Billy Stagner, David Stenn, Alexander Webb, David Wentink, Glenn P. White, and Galen Wilkes.

Gregory William Mank and Tom Weaver deserve an extended round of applause for their assistance with proofreading, as does Michael Kronenberg, who has undertaken so much of his time to create a stunning layout design for this book.

Author Biographies

William M. (Bill) Kaffenberger currently works as a musician, freelance actor, writer, and Bela Lugosi researcher. He has appeared in such recent films as Spielberg's *Lincoln* (2012) and Colonial Williamsburg's *War of 1812* (2011). In addition, he served as co-producer of *Hi There Horror Movie Fans* (2011), a documentary about Virginia horror movie host The Bowman Body, and also provided original soundtrack music for the production. Kaffenberger has contributed Lugosi research to a number of books and magazine articles over the years. He is presently a member of Richmond, VA's folk-rock group The Totally Unrehearsed Band. Kaffenberger has also released a number of CDs of his original music, the latest of which is *Your Side of the Story* (2010).

Gary D. Rhodes, Ph.D., is a film historian and filmmaker. Currently he is Co-Director of Film Studies at The Queen's University of Belfast, Northern Ireland. His books include *The Perils of Moviegoing in America, 1896-1950* (Continuum, 2011) and *Emerald Illusions: The Irish in Early American Cinema* (Irish Academic Press, 2011). He has written for a range of different publications, including magazines like *Filmfax* and academic journals like *Film History: An International Journal*. Rhodes has also directed such films as *Banned in Oklahoma* (Criterion, 2005). In terms of his work on Bela Lugosi, Rhodes edited *The World of Bela Lugosi* newsletter (1987-1990), directed the documentary film *Lugosi: Hollywood's Dracula* (Spinning Our Wheels, 1999), wrote dozens of magazine articles on the actor, and authored the books *Lugosi* (McFarland, 1997), *White Zombie: Anatomy of a Horror Film* (McFarland, 2001), and *Bela Lugosi, Dreams and Nightmares* (Collectables, 2007).

Index

[Italics denote illustration]

Abbott and Costello Meet Frankenstein (1948) 9, 87, *112*, *115*, 117-126, 133, 155, 159, 195, 219, 227, 228, 231, 242, 259, 260, 292, 294, 296, 297, 320, 321, 322, 324
Abbott and Costello Meet the Killer, Boris Karloff (1949) 159
Abbott and Costello Show, The (radio) 219-220, 322
Abbott, Bud 112, *119*, 120, 122, *124*, 125, *126*, 219-220, 228
Abbott, John 15
Abbott, William *See Frank Orsino*
Abel, Walter 131
Ackerman, Forrest J 209, 212
Action Pictures 45
Adams, Marjorie 71, 73
Adams Theatre (Newark, NJ) 290
Adrian, Lou 54
Adventure of the Specialist in Cops (1947) 217
Adventures of Ellery Queen, The (radio) 217, 318
Aherne, Brian 268
Ainslee, Ann 22, *23*
Alda, Alan 195
Alda, Robert 194-195, 290, 321
Aldrich, Robert 268
Alexander the Great *See Campbell, Loring*
Allen, Ham 278
Altobell, Jayne *See Newirth, Jayne Altobell*
Altobell, Leonard 86, 87, 183, 184, 275
Ambrosino, Michael 278
Ames, Florenz 178
Andre, Jane 245-246
Ape Man, The (1943) 114, 236, 300, 304, 329
Arabesque (1925) 23, 227
Arch, Stephen 252
Arlen, Richard 99, 227
Arnold, Jack 66
Arsenic and Old Lace (1943) 80
Arsenic and Old Lace (1944, film) 80
Arsenic and Old Lace (1944, play) 80
Arsenic and Old Lace (1947, Deer Lake, PA) 79, 84-85, 320

Arsenic and Old Lace (1947, Fairhaven, MA) 85-86, 320
Arsenic and Old Lace (1947, New Hope, PA) 80-81, 84, 319
Arsenic and Old Lace (1947, Saratoga Springs, NY) *78*, 83-84, 319
Arsenic and Old Lace (1948, Sea Cliff, Long Island, NY) 147, 150, 322
Arsenic and Old Lace (1949, Atlantic City, NJ) 179, 183-184, 325
Arsenic and Old Lace (1949, Fayetteville, NY) *176*, 177-179, 324, 330
Arsenic and Old Lace (1949, Lake Hopatcong, NJ) *178*, 179, 180-181, 324
Arsenic and Old Lace (1949, Reading, PA) *182*, *183*, 184-187, 325
Art Linkletter's House Party (radio) 217, 325
Arthur, Robert 118
Artists Repertory Theatre (Denver, CO) 134, 150, 176
Atwater, Edith 93
Atwill, Lionel 39, *40*, 41, *42*, *43*
Aubert, Lenore 118, 121
Aubuchon, Jacques *140*, *144*
Avenging Conscience, The (1914) 91
Babbitt, Harry 195
Backstage at the Spa Summer Theatre (1947) 226, 319
Bailey, Jack 218, 317
Balderston, John L. 308
Ball, Lucille 79
Balogh, Reverend Steven E. 258
Bamberger, Theron 77-78, 80
Barber, Bobby 118, *119*, 120
Barnett, Buddy 214
Barry, Harold 228
Barton, Charles 115, 119, 124
Bat, The (1926) 42
Bat Whispers, The (1930) 42
Bates, Peg Leg 192
Bean, Reggie 229
Beast with Five Fingers, The (1946) 38
Bedlam (1946) 38, 39
Beebe, Ford 45
Bela Lugosi (song) 221
Bela Lugosi Horror and Magic Stage Show (1950-1951)

294, 295, 297-305, 309, 327, 328, 329
Bela Lugosi Meets a Brooklyn Gorilla (1952) 259
Bela Lugosi Show, The 231
Bellamy, Ralph 249
Bennett, Constance 79
Bennett, Lee 51
Bennett, Terry 202
Bergen, Edgar 228
Berle, Milton 7, *228, 229, 230*, 231, *325*
Bernthal, Murray 178-179
Berra, Yogi 75
Betty Crocker Magazine of the Air (radio) 217, 328
Beyer, Charles 162, 164, 176, 324
Bill and Fan Show (radio) 319
Bill Slater Show, The (TV) 227, 326, 328
Bird in the Head, A (1946) 38
Black Camel, The (1931) 57
Black Cat, The (1934) 52, 92, *93*
Black Cat, The (1941) 92, *100*, 102, 114
Black Dragons (1942) 7, 22, 114, 234, 250
Black Friday (1940) *100*, 102, 114
Black Sleep, The (1956) 259
Blaine, Viviane 180
Blair, Bob 264-265
Blair, Janet 194
Blake, Gladys *50, 55, 57, 58*
Blaney, H. C. 273, 274, 275, 277, 278
Blaney, H. C., Jr. 275, 277
Blaney, H. C., III 277, 284
Blankenship, John 179
Bluebeard (1944) 214
Bodge, Saralie 86, 87
Body Snatcher, The (1945) 15-19, 39, 41, *42*, 93, 114, 317
Borshy, Reverend George E. K. 258, 259
Boston Summer Theatre (Boston, MA) 78, 319
Bowery at Midnight (1942) 6, 7, 114
Bowery Boys, The 6, 7, 226
Brabin, Charles 91
Bracken, Eddie 228
Bradstreet, Charles 118
Bramson, Sam 288
Breen, Joseph I. 21
Brent, Romney 232, *233*, 234, 235
Bride of Frankenstein (1935) 114, 177
Bride of the Atom (1955) 311
Bride of the Monster (1955) *See Bride of the Atom*
Bridges, Harry 253
Bright, Jackie 191, 206
Broadway-Capitol Theatre (Detroit, MI) 195, *197*, 202, 322
Broder, Jack 259
Bromberg, J. Edward 175
Brown, Chamberlain 78, 155, 160, 161
Brown, Lyman 133, *137*, 155, *158, 159*, 160, *161*, 162,
177, 310
Brown, Wally 19, 22, 41, *42*, 43
Browning, Tod 23
Brute Man, The (1946) 38
Bucks County Playhouse (New Hope, PA) 77, 80, 319
Buddy Rogers Show, The (radio) 215, 328
Burg, Stephen 82
Burke, Billie 219, 220, 228, 230
Burns, Bob 294, 296, 300
Burrows, Abe 221
Cabanne, Christy 46, 50, 56
Cabinet of Dr. Caligari, The (1919) 38
Calamity Jane and Sam Bass (1949) 203
Cambridge Summer Theatre (Cambridge, MA) 78, 83, 319
Campbell, Loring 195-196
Candid Microphone (radio) 221
Cantor, Eddie 201
Capitol Theatre (Ottawa, Canada) 282, 327
Carlson, Dick 206
Carmen, Del 199
Carmichael, Rande *138, 140*
Carney, Alan *19*, 22, *39*, 41, *43*
Carpenter, Ken 214
Carradine, John 34, 80, 120, 132, 141, 214
Carson, Mindy 245-246
Carson, Helen 99
Carson, Mindy 215
Cashman, Ed 231
Casino, The (Boston) 71, 240
Cask of Amontillado, A (1949) 232-235, *325*
Cat and the Canary, The (1927) 57
Cat Creeps, The (1946) 38
Catman of Paris, The (1946) 38
Celebrity Time (1950) 227, 228, *325*, 328
Chandler, Helen 209
Chandu the Magician (1932) 288
Chaney, Lon, Jr. 34, *112*, 118, 120, 121, 125, 126, 260
Chaplin, Charlie 252
Chatterton, Ruth 85
Cheyette, Herbert 178
Chu Chang *See Yen Soo Kim*
Cinecolor 51, 53, 56
City of the Dead, The (1960) 58
Clark, Alexander 67
Clark, George 276
Coble, Harry 270
Coleman, Cy 229
Columbia Pictures 38, 155
Command Performance (radio) 218, 318
Commandos Strike at Dawn (1942) 201
Compton, Joyce 51, *57, 58*
Continental Varieties (1947) 250, 321
Cooper, Dulcie 85

Cooper, Jackie 131
Copa Club, The (Pittsburgh, PA) 239, *240*, 243-246, 326
Corman, Roger 91
Coronado Theatre (Rockford, IL) 100, 101, 321
Corpse Vanishes, The (1942) 7, 51, 114, 236
Cosgriff, Catherine 178
Costello, Lou 112, *118*, 120, 122, *124*, 125, *126*, 219-220, 228
Country Fair (radio) 218, 317
Court Square Theatre (Springfield, MA) 200-201, 323
Courtney, Robert S. 183
Crabtree, Paul 278
Cragen, William C. *See Cragin, William C.*
Cragin, William C. 139, *183*, *184*, 187
Creeper, The (1948) 125
Cremer, Robert 9
Crespinel, William 51, 56
Crime Does Not Pay (radio) 217-218, 325, 329
Criterion Theatre (New York, NY) *123*
Crosby, Bing 197
Cummings, Julia 200
Curran Theatre (San Francisco, CA) 26-27, 317
Curtis, Francis I. 81
Dade, Frances 209
Dale, Jack 33
Daly, John 228
Dane, Essex 241
Dark Eyes of London (1939) 114
David, William B. 50, 53
Deane, Hamilton 308
Death Kiss, The (1933) 236
Deer Lake Theatre (Deer Lake, PA) 79, 84-85, 320
Delevan Theatre (Lake Geneva, WI) 103
Denham, Reginald 274
Devil Also Dreams, The (1950) 9, 272, 273-285, 287, 326, 327
Devil Bat, The (1941) 114, 236, 304, 329
Devil Bat's Daughter (1946) 38
Dewey Sisters, The *201*, 202
Dienes, Laszlo 258
Dies, Martin 252
Dietrich, Marlene 252
Doak, Virginia 79, 95, 99, 155, 213, 321
Doctor Prescribed Death, The (1942) 212, 213
Douglas, Gordon 22
Douglas, Melvyn 250
Dracola (product) 287
Dracula–The Vampire Play (1927) 13, 33, 67, 79, 212-213, 227
Dracula (1931) 12, 13, 19, 23, 38, 87, 100, 102, 113, 114, 120, 122, 194, 209, 304, 311, 320
Dracula (1947, Boston, MA) 78, 82-83, 319
Dracula (1947, Cambridge, MA) 78, 83, 319
Dracula (1947, East Hampton, Long Island, NY) 77, 319

Dracula (1947, Litchfield, CT) *81*, *82*, *83*, *84*, *85*, 86-87, 177, 320
Dracula (1948, Denver, CO) *133*, 134-136, 150, 322
Dracula (1948, Norwich, CT) 9, 141, 143, 144-147, 150, 322
Dracula (1948, Reading, PA) 138-141, 322
Dracula (1950, St. Petersburg, FL) 263-265, 267-268, 326
Dracula (1950, Winsooki Park, VT) 211, 266-267, 269-273, 326
Dracula (1951, Great Britain/Northern Ireland) 9, 307-309, 310, 327, 328, 329
Dracula (1952, unproduced) 310
Dracula's Daughter (1936) 34, 86
Drake, Alfred 93
Drake, William A. 249
Durgin, Cyrus 69
Durston, David 85, 134-135
Duvey, Eliot 266, 270, 271-272
Dvorak, Ann 180
Dyrenforth, Harald *81*, 177
East Side Kids, The 7, 288
Ebsen, Buddy 78, 85
Eddington, Harry E. 39
Edgington, Carolyn 169, 170
Edgington, Robert "Bob" Jr. 169
Edgington, Robert Ray "Bob" 169-172
Eggerth, Marta 249
Elwell, Tom 105, 231, 320
Emperor Waltz, The (1948) 197, *200*
Evans, Hugh 65, 68, 69
Evans, Steve *203*, 204, 205
Everson, William K. 301
Exploring the Unknown (radio) 221
Faber, Robert 19
Face of Marble, The (1946) 38
Fairbanks, Henry G. 267, 269
Fairhaven Summer Theatre (Fairhaven, MA) 43, 44, 45, 320
Falk, Lee 82
Falkenburg, Jinx 241
Fall of the House of Usher, The (1928) 91
Famous Artists Country Playhouse (Fayetteville, NY) 176, 177-179, 279, 324, 327, *330*
Famous Artists Country Playhouse (East Rochester, NY) 277, 278, 327
Farrar, Anthony 85
Fay, Vivian 192
Faye, Joey 71, 72, 240
Federal Bureau of Investigation (FBI) 254, 257, 258, 259
Fejedelem, A (unproduced play) 164
Ferguson, Frank 121
Fidler, Jimmie 56
Fife, Bobby 244

Fletcher, Bramwell 175
Florey, Robert 91
Flying Serpent, The (1946) 38
Fog Island (1945) 15
Fontaine, Joan 197
Ford Television Hour (1949) 176
Foreman, Carl 6
Forrest, Helen 228
Fortner, Jayn 66, 69
Fortune Films Company 54
Fowley, Douglas 50, 51, 52, *53*, 58
Fox Theatre (St. Louis, MO) 203-204, 325
Frances, Kay 131
Francis, Arlene 228
Frankenstein (1931) 19, 21, 38, 113, *114*, 123
Frankenstein Meets the Wolf Man (1943) 80, 114, 153
Frechette, Marilyn 201, 323
Fredrik, Burry 179
Friedlander, Louis 92
Frisch, Erna *204*, 205
Frozen Ghost, The (1945) 15
Funt, Allen 221, 326
Gailmor, William S. 212
Garbo, Greta 250, 252
Garfield, John 240
Garrett, Patsy 200
Gasoline Cocktail (1949) 217-218, 329
Gates, Harvey 45
Geneva Theatre (Lake Geneva, WI) 103
Genius at Work (1946) 39-43, 99, 122, 317
George Jessel Show, The (radio) 213, 231
Gerard, Merwin 209
Ghost of Frankenstein (1942) 114, 117
Ghosts on the Loose (1943) 103, 114, 234, 250, 259, 321
Gibson, Hoot 239
Gilbert, Bert *204*, 205
Gilbert, Virginia 85
Gish, Lillian 268
Glen or Glenda (1953) 311
Glorious Adventure, The (1922) 51
Goddard, Paulette 218
Godwin, Frank 81
Goetz, William 115, 125
Golden Gate Pictures 45, 51, 52, 53, 54, 56, 318
Golly, Sidney 68-69
Gorcey, Leo 7
Gordon, Alex 147, *148*, 150, 307
Gordon, Paul 249
Gordon, Richard 147, *149*, 150, 307
Gorilla, The (1939) 22, 57, 231
Gourlay, Jack 52
Grade, Sir Lew 155
Grant, Barney 195, 200, 202
Gray Wolf Tavern, The (Masury, OH) 242-243, 323

Great Gatsby, The (1949) 202
Green Hills Theatre (Reading, PA) 138-141, *182*, *183*, 184-187, 322, 325
Haige, Harry 265
Hale, Monte 200
Hall, Huntz 7
Hamilton, George 228
Handsaker, Gene 52
Hanna, Phil 229
Harding, Ann 180
Harris, Jed 65, 66, 67
Harris, Lee 209, 210, 311
Harvey (unproduced play) 155, 158, 176, 184, 321
Harvey, Elwyn 181
Hemingway, Ernest 75
Herb Schriner Time, The (radio) 215, 323
Herrick, Jim 134, 136
Hersholt, Jean 249
Hill, Maury 140, *143*, *144*
Hippodrome Theatre (Baltimore, MD) 290, 321
His Majesty's Theatre (Montreal, Canada) 284, 327
Hitchcock, Alfred 38, 58
Hoberman, Oscar 134
Hoefle, Carl 54, 58
Holloway, Sterling 218, 220, 228
Hollywood Soundstage (radio) 319
Hope, Bob 103, 218
Hopper, Hedda 63, 133, 158
Hoover, J. Edgar 254, 257
Horner, Matt 270
Horthy, Miklós 251, 252, 253
Horton, Edward Everett 84, 85, 133, 175, 263
Houghton, Norris 133
House Committee on Un-American Activities (HUAC) 252
House of Dracula (1945) 34, 38, 80, 114, 123
House of Frankenstein (1944) 80, 120, 123
House of Horrors (1946) 38
Hoye, Gloria 145
Huber, John J. 257-258
Hughes, Elinor 82
Human Adventure (radio) 214
Human Monster, The See *Dark Eyes of London*
Hungarian-American Council for Democracy (HACD) 252-253, 255, 257, 258
Huntington, John 83
Huston, John 91
Hutton, Betty 197
Hyans, Eddie 181
I Love Trouble (1948) 194
I Walked with a Zombie (1943) 21, 169
I Want to Live! (1958) 141
Immigration and Naturalization Service 257, 258, 259
International House (1933) 226, 231
International Pictures 114

Invaders (1941) 201
Invisible Ghost (1941) 22, 114, 288
Isle of the Dead (1945) 15, 39
Jaeger, C. Peter 273, 274, 275, 278
James, Debbus 227
Jászi, Oscar 255
Jaynes, Betty 192
Jefferys, Alan 86-87
Jeffreys, Anne 41, *43*
Jessel, George 213, 220
Jessor, Howard 143-144, 145
Jevne, Jack 19
John Drew Theatre (East Hampton, Long Island, NY) 81, 319
Johnny Olson Luncheon Club (radio) 217, 329
Johnson, Blake 276
Johnson, Erskine 158, 214, 307
Jones, Darby 21
Jory, Victor 249
Jungle Captive, The (1945) 15
Jungle Death (1947) 221
Kapiera, Jan 249
Károlyi, Count Mihály (Michael) 251, 253, 255, 258
Karloff, Boris 15, 18, 19, 38, 45, 52, *64*, 65, 72, 75, 80, 81, 92, *93*, 100, 109, 114, *121*, 123, 126, 153, *156-157*, 159, 213, 227, 240, 252, 260, 273, 322, 323
Karr, Jack 282
Kattleman, Beth 287
Katzman, Sam 93
Kaye, Danny 231
Keats, Mickey 199
Kelemen, Victor 164
Kesselring, Joseph 80
Keith, Ian 22, 25, 27, 28-29, *31*, *32*, 33, 117
Kelly, Constance 263, 264, 267-268
Kelly, Helen 270
Key, Kim *See Campbell, Loring*
Kiley, Richard 141, 145
Kilgallen, Dorothy 158, 243, 246
Kim, Yen Soo 300-301
Kimble, Lawrence 21
King of the Gamblers (1948) 195
King Kong (1933) 21
King Sisters, The 218
Kirk, Lisa 228
Klausner, Bertha 275, 287, 307, 308, 309, 327
Klein, Charles 91
Kneeter, Herb 141
Knight, Evelyn 228
Kohn, Rose Simon 273
Krupa, Gene 202, 323
KTSL-TV Variety Show (1948) 227, 322
Kubrick, Stanley 57
Kuma the Magician *See* Yen Soo Kim

Kun, Béla 250, 251
Kutsch, Ralph 22
Ladd, Robin 270, 272
Lakeside Theatre (Lake Hopatcong, NJ) 178, 179, 180-181, 324
Lamont, Molly 50, *54*, *58*
Lancourt, Saul 276
Landess, Theodora *See Richman, Helen*
Landi, Elissa 79
Landis, Jesse Royce 67, 69, 71
Lang, Minda *203*, 204
Lansbury, Angela 274
Larson, John 178, 179
Laskin, Lillian 310-311
Laurel, Stan 97, 99
Lebow, Guy 227
Lederer, Francis 147
Lee, Don 227
Lee, Olga *160*, 161, 162
Lee, Pinky 228
Lee, Sandra 229
Lengyel, Melchior 252
Lennig, Arthur 9, 117
Lesser, Sol 249
Lester, Seeleg 209
Levene, Sam 66
Lewis, George 195
Lewis, Robert Q. 229
Lewton, Val 15, 21, 38, 39, 257
Linkletter, Art 217
Litchfield Summer Theatre (Litchfield, CT) 81, 82, 83, *84*, *85*, 86-87, 183, 275, 320, 324
Litman, Leonard "Lenny" 239, 243-244
Litman, Rosslyn 243-244, 246
Little Old New York (1950) 227, 326
Liveright, Horace 227
Lobero Theatre (Santa Barbara, CA) 23, 25, 317
Loder, John 180
Lombardi, Jo 194
LoMonaco, Martha Schmoyer 77
Longley, Ralph 145
Loosz, Bela 325
Lorre, Peter 159, 240, 257, 322, 323
Louis, Joe 105
Lowery, Harry 134, 136
Lubin, Arthur 249
Luce, Claire 274, 276, 277, 278, 279, 282, 284
Lugosi, Bela G. 30, 36, 39, 101, *116*, 136, 158, 169, 170, *174*, 175, 177, 180, *186*, 187, 270, 309, 310, *314*, 315, 324
Lugosi, Bela Jr. *See Lugosi, Bela G.*
Lugosi, Lillian 26, 27, 30, 33, 52, 68, 71, 81, 119, 134, 136, 137, 138, 141, 147, 153, 169, 170, 171, 175, 177, 185, 186, 187, 194, 227, 231-232, 263, 267,

270, 273, 282, 309, 310, 315, 317, 321, 322, 323, 324, 325, 326, 328, 329
Lugosi, Lajos 123
Lugosi: The Man Behind the Cape (1976) 9
Lukas, Paul *176*, 177, 278, 324
Lupino, Ida 131
Lynn, Ada 197-199, 200
Lyons, Gene 86
Lytell, Bert 241
Lytell, Marjorie 134
MacRae, Gordon 194, 195, 321
Madách, Imre 164
Magee, Joe 160
Magic (unproduced play) 161
Malek, Richard *140*, *144*
Man in the Shadows (1949) 217, 325
Man with Book and Pipe (radio) 210-211
Mank, Gregory William 117
Mantle, Mickey 75
Marion, Charles 6
Marlowe, Betty 100
Marlowe, Don 94, 95, 97, 99, 100, 101, 102, 103, 105, 117-118, 132, 133, 150, 155, 158, 159, 160, 161, 164, 192, 212, 231, 241, 263, 290, 320, 321, 322
Marshall, Oswald 274
Martha Deane Program (radio) 215, 322
Mask of Diijon, The (1946) 38
Massey, Ilona 131
Massey, Raymond 80
Mayan Theatre (Los Angeles, CA) 22, 317
Mayo, Virginia 205
McCrary, Tex 241
McGee, Gloria 66
McGuire, Dorothy 206
McGuire, George 56
McGuire, Paul 84
McLean, Robert *140*
McPhail, Douglas 192
Melvin, Edwin F. 69
Merrill, Robert 241
Metro-Goldwyn-Mayers Studios (MGM) 19, 113, 155, 158, 217, 250
Metropolitan Theatre (Seattle, WA) 33, 317
Meyers, Pete, Jr. 242
Miles, William 275
Miller, Gilbert 164
Mills Brothers, The 56
Milton Berle Show, The See *Texaco Star Theatre, The*
Missouri Theatre (St. Louis, MO) 18
Mitchell, Grant 241
Moholy-Nagy, László 252
Monogram Pictures Corporation 6, 22, 37, 38, 52, 93, 109, 114, 235, 304, 326
Monroe, Marilyn 75

Moore, Diane 288
Moore, Garry 228
Moorehead, Constance 82, 83
Mosier, Frank 134, 136
Mother Didn't Tell Me (1950) 206
Mother Riley Meets the Vampire (1951) 309
Moxey, John 58
Mummy, The (1932) 122, 175
Muni, Paul 201
Murder and Bela Lugosi (1950) *231*, 232, 327
Murder at the Vanities (1933) 191
Murder by Television (1935) 226
Murder on the Operating Table (1934) 46, 58
Murders in the Rue Morgue, The (1932) 8, 9, 91, 92, 114, 122, 213
Murray, Ken 214
Musicraft Records 209, 212, 221
My Dog Shep (1946) 45, 53
Mysterioso (unproduced record series) 209, 212, 221, 318
Mysterioso (unproduced TV show) 310
Mysterious Mr. Wong (1935) 236
Mystery House 214
Mystery of the Mary Celeste, The (1935) 114, 236
Mystery Writers of America 241, 326
Nagel, Conrad 85, 228
National Photographic Show (1951) 241, 329
Neff, Bill 287, 289-292, 293, 299, 321
New Hope Street Fair (1947) 81, 240
Newirth, Jayne Altobell 87, 183
Night of Stars (Madison Square Garden) 121, 323
Night of Terror (1933) 23
Nightmare of Horror, A (spook show) 288, 289, *293*, 294, 296, 297, 300, 318, 324
Ninotchka (1939) 250, 252
No Traveler Returns (1945) 9, 22-33, 192, 284, 317
Noble, Paul 304
Noel, Rafael 22
Norwich Summer Theatre (Norwich, CT) 141, 143-147, 322
Now Really, Peter (unproduced play) 154
Oakie, Jack 39
Oakland, Simon 141, 143, 145
Oboler, Arch 227
O'Brian, Jack 75, 87, 93, 209
O'Brien, Pat 240
Ocean Playhouse (Atlantic City, NJ) *179*, 183-184, 325
O'Day, Billie *214*, 215
Office of Strategic Services (OSS) 255
Okay Mother (1950) 227, 328
Olivier, Laurence 201
Olympia Theatre (Miami, FL) 197-200, 322
Old Dark House, The (1932) 57
Oliver Twist (1948) 274
One Body Too Many (1944) 22, 102, 320

One Night of Horror (1941) 286, 288-289
Oriental Theatre (Chicago, IL) 288
Orpheum Theatre (San Diego, CA) 288, 289, 293
Orpheum Theatre (Wichita, KS) 205, 325
Orsino, Frank 45-46, 50, 56, 58
Osterman, Bibi 229
Otchi Chornya (song) 231
Paige, Larry 195
Paleo, Ion 136
Pansy the Horse 101, 323
Panus, Frank 203, 204
Paramount 56, 113
Parker, Jean 85, 249, 268
Parrish, Helen 192
Paul Winchell Show, The (1950) 229-230, 327
Paul Winchell-Jerry Mahoney Show, The See *Paul Winchell Show, The*
Pauker, Dr. Edmond 92, 160, 164, 202
Peeples, Sam 99
Pembroke, George 22
Pendleton, Nat 50, 57, 58
Phantom Ship See *The Mystery of the Mary Celeste*
Philco Dealer's Dinner and Party 136, 322
Phillips, Paul J. 181
Phipps Auditorium (Denver, CO) 133, 134-136, 322
Pickens, Jane 241
Pillette, George 270
Pillow Death (1945) 15
Pinocchio (1940) 38
Pitts, Zasu 228
Plan 9 from Outer Space (1959) 311
Poe, Edgar Allan 91, 92, 93, 95, 105, 154, 209, 210, 211, 212, 232, 233
Portrait of Jennie (1948) 125
Post, Ted 141, 143, 146, 147
Postal Inspector (1936) 65
Potter, H. C. 66, 67
Powell, Jane 240
Pressburger, Arnold 51
Price, Roger 227, 326
Price, Vincent 91, 118, 257
Prisoners (1929) 199
Producers Releasing Corporation (PRC) 37, 38, 52, 109, 113, 236, 304
Production Code Administration (PCA) 21
Psycho (1960) 58, 141
Quick as a Flash 216, 217, 319
Raft, George 205
Rainey, Ford 83, 84
Rand, Ayn 56
Randolph, Jane 118, 120
Rank, J. Arthur 114, 115
Rathbone, Basil 217, 241, 325
Raven, The (1915) 91

Raven, The (1935) 92, 114, 214, 233
Raven, The (1948) 125
Raye, Martha 197
Realart Pictures, Inc. *110-111*, 114
Red Light (1949) 205
Red Skelton Show, The (1954) 259
Redpath Bureau 152, *154*, 155, 158
Reif, Harry 56
Reinhold, Del 187
Renegades (1930) 23
Republic Pictures 38
Return of Chandu, The (1934) 288
Return of Dracula, The (1958) 147
Return of the Ape Man (1944) 103, 114, 236, 321
Revolt of the Zombies (1936) 290
Rhapsody in Blue (1945) 194
Rice, Cathy 319
Rice, Vernon 131, 150
Richman, Helen *182, 184, 185*
Rinard, Florence 326
Ripley, Robert L. 240, 320
Ritz Brothers, The 22
RKO Pictures 15, 17, 19, 21, 38, 41, 42, 99, 113, 122, 317
Roache, Viola 81
Robert Q. Lewis Show, The (1950) 229, 327
Roberts, McCarl 289
Robinson, Bill "Bojangles" 230
Robinson, Jackie 230, 231
Rodgers, Greg *140, 142, 144*
Rogers, Buddy 215
Rohde, Les *190*, 197, 199
Rohn, Elissa 273, 274, 278, 281, 282
Rolling Home (1946) 53
Roosevelt, President Franklin D. 257
Rope of Sand (1949) 203
Rossitto, Angelo 47, 51, 52
Rotter, Fritz 273, 281, 282
Royal Alexandria Theatre (Toronto, Canada) 281, 327
Rudy Vallee Show, The (radio) 219, 318
Russell, Ann 194
Saint's Double Trouble, The (1940) 65
Sands, Dorothy 81
Sapera, Mollie 33
Sarecky, Barney 45
Scared to Death (1947) 44-59, 63, 100, 239, 273, 318, 319
Schallert, Edwin 34
Schatz, Thomas 37, 109
Schnitzer, Gerald 6-7, 226
Scholl, Henry 301
Schriner, Herb 215
Schutz, George 225
Scollay, Fred 254-255
Sconce, Jeffrey 212
Scott, Raymond 215

Screen Art Pictures 54
Screen Guild Productions 53, 54, 319
Sea Cliff Summer Theatre (Long Island, NY) 147, 150
Secret Life of Walter Mitty, The (1947) 45
Seger, Lucia 83
Seiderman, Maurice 19, 21
Seldes, Marian 269
Shadow of Chinatown (1936) 236
Shawn, Dick 206
Sheffield, Richard 209
Shining, The (1980) 57
Shop at Sly Corner, The (unproduced play) 161
Sidney, Sylvia 131
Simon, Mózes (Moses) 252, 253, 255, 257
Sinatra, Frank 75
Sinclair, Tiny 245
Siodmak, Curt 38, 125
Sir Lancelot 21
Slater, Bill 227
Slater, Milton 270-271
Slightly French (1949) 202
Smith, Alexis 274
Smith, Lester Al 275
Snell, George R. *135*, 138-139, 140, 141, 146, 164, *180*, *181*, 184, 185
Soanes, Wood 27, 260
Sokolsky, George E. 257
Somerset Summer Theatre (Fall River, MA) 275, 277, 327
Son of Dracula (1943) 34, 80
Son of Frankenstein (1939) 63, 100, 102, 114, 177
Sorry, Wrong Number (1948) 125
SOS Coast Guard (1937) 63, 65
Spa Summer Theatre (Saratoga Springs, NY) 78, 83, 319
Sparks, Sonny 201
Spellbound (1945) 38
Spengler, Thomas 65
Spider Woman Strikes Back, The (1946) 38
Spiral Staircase, The (1946) 38
Spitz, Leo 115, 125
Spook Busters (1946) 38
Spooks Run Wild (1941) 6, 7, 51, 103, 259, 288, 321
Squad Car (1960) 97
Squire, Katherine 67
Stanley, Charles 300, 309
Stardust Cavalcade (1940) 192
Starlit Time (1950) 229, 326
Steel Pier, The (Atlantic City, NJ) 183, 201, 323, 325
Steen, Sam 229
Steinbeck, John 274
Stevens, Onslow 93
Stevens, Richard 181
Stevens, Robert 232, 234
Stoker, Bram 91
Storm, Gale 67

Strange Case of Malcolm Craig, The (unproduced film) 156, 159
Strange Confession (1945) 15
Strange Deception (unproduced film) 154
Strange, Glenn *112*, 118, 294, 296, 324
Stritch, Elaine 67, 68, 69, 72, 82
Stromberg, Hunt, Jr. 63, 65-66. 67, 69, 72, 73, 105
Sullivan, Ed 192, 227, 326
Sullivan, Francis L. 273, 274, 276, 277, 278, 284
Sunset Blvd. (1950) 58
Super-Sleuth (1937) 39
Surprise Theatre (1949) 228, 324
Suspense (radio) 212, 213, 232
Suspense (TV) 232-235, 325
Svengali (1931) 175
Swanson, Gloria 85
Szep, Erno 164
Szmik, Lajos 123
Tabor, Thola Nett 281
Tales of Fatima (radio) 217, 325
Tell-Tale Heart, The (1928) 91
Tell-Tale Heart, The (1947) 93-95, 98, 99-103, *104*, 105, 241, 320-321
Tell-Tale Heart, The (undated recording) 209-212, 214
Texaco Star Theatre, The (TV) 228, 229, 230-231, 325
That We May Live (1946) 249, 259, 318
Thirsty Death, The 214
Thirteenth Chair, The (1929) 23
Thomas, Ann 67, 72, 105, 231
Thomas, Leslie 22
Three Indelicate Ladies (1947) 9, 63-72, 79, 82, 100, 105, 273, 284, 287, 289, 318, 319
Tone, Franchot 194
Tonge, Philip 134
Tony's Chi Chi Club (Salt Lake City) 241-242, 322
Tragedy of Man, The (unproduced play) 164
Train to Alcatraz (1948) 195
Tramor's Cafeteria (St. Petersburg, FL) 265, 326
Treacher, Arthur 192
True, Virginia 182, *184*
Truex, Ernest 141
Tuttle, Lurene 214
Twentieth-Century Fox 113, 159
Ulmer, Edgar G. 92
United Artists 259
Universal Studios 13, 34, 37, 38, 50, 80, 92, 109, 113, 114-115, 117, 119, 120, 122, 123, 158-159, 194, 213, 214, 229, 297
Urban, Charles 51
Valentino, Rudolph 158
Vallee, Rudy 219
Valley Arena Gardens (Holyoke, MA) 202
Valley of the Zombies (1946) 38
Vampire's Ghost, The (1945) 15

Vance, Bill 99
Vandeventer, Fred 227, 326
Varno, Roland 51, 53, 58
Vawter, Keith 158
Venetian Theatre (Racine, WI) 102
Venge, Karen 22, 30
Versatile Varieties (1950) 228-229, 325
Vickers, Martha 67
Vignoles, Mary 307, 308
Vitalis Program, The (radio) 213
Voice of Fighting Spain (1944) 253
Voodoo Man (1944) 114, 226, 289, 294
Walling, Stratton 68, 71
Walls Came Tumbling Down, The (1946) 38
Walsh, Thomas 66
Walston, Ray 67, 68, 71, 82, 232, 234
Walthall, Henry B. 91
Waring, Richard 274, 276, 184
Warner Bros. 38, 80, 113
Watson, James Sibley 91
Waycoff, Leon 9
Weaver, Marjorie 192
Webber, Melville 91
Welles, Halsted 233
Welles, Orson 75
Werewolf of London (1935) 85
West Side Story (1961) 141
Westmore, Bud 118
Which is Which? (radio) 214
Whispering Shadow, The (1933) 97
White, Hampton 153, 324
White Zombie (1932) 21, 236
Wilder, Billy 58
William Morris Agency 160, 164, 228, 259, 324, 325
Williams, Bill 229
Williams, John B. 227
Williams, Michael 308, 309
Williams and Woolley 307, 308
Wilson, Earl 287
Winchell, Walter 56
Windley, Charles 292
Wing, Grace 199
With Book and Pipe See *Man with Book and Pipe*
Wolf Man, The (1941) 38, 114
Wonder Man (1945) 231
Wynnekoop, Alice 45, 46, 50, 54
Wynnekoop, Gilbert 50
Yacovino, Nino 199
Yates, Irving 288, 289
Yellin, David 178
You'll Find Out (1940) 195
Youngman, Henny 239
Zombies on Broadway (1945) 19-22, 41, 42, 317
Zucco, George 48, 50, 58

Made in the USA
Middletown, DE
21 March 2022